THE EXPRESSIVE EYE

THE
EXPRESSIVE EYE

*Fiction and Perception in the Work of
Thomas Hardy*

J. B. BULLEN

CLARENDON PRESS · OXFORD

1986

Oxford University Press, Walton Street, Oxford OX2 6DP
Oxford New York Toronto
Delhi Bombay Calcutta Madras Karachi
Kuala Lumpur Singapore Hong Kong Tokyo
Nairobi Dar es Salaam Cape Town
Melbourne Auckland
and associated companies in
Beirut Berlin Ibadan Nicosia

Oxford is a trade mark of Oxford University Press

Published in the United States
by Oxford University Press, New York

© J. B. Bullen 1986

British Library Cataloguing in Publication Data
Bullen, J. B.
The expressive eye: fiction and perception in
the work of Thomas Hardy.
1. Hardy, Thomas, 1840–1928—Criticism and
interpretation
I. Title
823'.8 PR4754
ISBN 0-19-812858-4

Library of Congress Cataloging in Publication Data
Bullen, J. B.
The expressive eye.
Bibliography: p.
Includes index.
1. Hardy, Thomas, 1840–1928—Technique. 2. Visual
perception in literature. 3. Description (Rhetoric)
4. Landscape in literature. 5. Characters and
characteristics in literature. 6. Art and literature—
England. I. Title.
PR4757.T4B85 1986 823'.8 85-26946
ISBN 0-19-812858-4

Set by Downdell Ltd.
Printed in Great Britain
at the University Printing House, Oxford
by David Stanford
Printer to the University

For Martine

Preface

'Novel-writing as an art cannot go backward. Having reached the analytic stage it must transcend it by going still further in the same direction. Why not by rendering as visible essences, spectres, etc. the abstract thoughts of the analytic school?'[1]

The term 'visible essences' is one which Hardy used to describe the way in which sentiments, feelings, and even ideas could be rendered through images in literature. As all readers of his novels have known —from the very first reviewers right up to the youngest and most recent—Hardy had a highly developed visual imagination. It is his landscapes which probably stand out most in the memory —the vivid accounts of Egdon Heath in *The Return of the Native* or the valley of the Froom in *Tess of the d'Urbervilles*—but his novels also abound in detailed accounts of the appearances of the villages and towns of Wessex, and of the buildings with which he had been familiar since his boyhood. Hardy also 'sees' his characters with intense vividness. Tess's 'peony mouth', Alec d'Urberville's 'swaggering' moustache with its 'curled points', and Marty South's fine head of red hair all seem to bring the characters into sharper focus. Yet, closer inspection of Hardy's literary-visual effects does not necessarily confirm this first impression. The fact is that what may seem to be an objective record of a landscape, a building, or a character is frequently charged with feeling and ideas which are not, strictly speaking, visual at all.

Studies of this facet of Hardy's writing have concentrated mainly on two aspects—his literary pictorialism and his treatment of the West Country landscape—and there is no doubt that both painting and natural scenery were very important to him. Yet these approaches tend to overlook what Hardy actually made of the visual sources, and how he shaped and transformed images so that they became an appropriate vehicle for the drama of each particular narrative. What they rarely account for is the connection in Hardy's fiction between image and idea. Yet it is clear both from Hardy's own remarks about the art of novel-writing, and from his practice of literary visualization, that he regarded visual perception and meaning as intimately linked. For him, fiction did not involve the literal

[1] *EL*, p. 232.

transcription of scenes or characters, but was, instead, an expressive medium for communicating ideas and emotions through the selection and manipulation of the constituent elements of the physical world. In this book I have tried to point out some of the connections between observation and meaning in Hardy's fiction. I have attempted to demonstrate how, through his choice of subject, point of view, composition, and structure, Hardy endowed the visual properties of both man and the natural world with special significance—how, in other words, he employs visible essences in his writing.

J.B.B.

Acknowledgements

I am most grateful to the following who were kind enough to read sections of this typescript: Professor Lennart A. Björk, Dr David Gervais, Professor Ian Fletcher, Professor Donald L. Hill, Professor Ian Jack, Dr Patrick Parrinder, Professor Hugh Witemeyer, and Professor Carolyn Williams. I am especially grateful to Professor Björk, who allowed me to use the typescript of his edition of Hardy's *Literary Notebooks*. I am also indebted to the research board of Reading University, and to the following, whose advice and encouragement was invaluable in writing this book: Professors Rosa Maria Colombo Smith, Dale Kramer, Michael Millgate, and Drs Dinah Birch and Bernard Richards.

I also owe a debt of gratitude to many librarians in both the United Kingdom and North America, particularly at the Bodleian Library, Oxford, Cambridge University Library, Boston University Library, Reading University Library, the New York Public Library, and the Widener Library, Harvard. I am particularly grateful to Mr R. N. L. Peers and his staff at Dorset Country Museum, Dorchester, for their invaluable assistance, and to the many keepers and curators of art galleries and museums in the United Kingdom, on the Continent and in North America.

Contents

Illustrations   xiii

Abbreviations   xvii

Introduction   1

1. Hardy and the Visual Arts   13

2. Three Early Novels: Sketches in Form and Colour   31

3. *Far from the Madding Crowd*: Perception and
   Understanding   61

4. *The Return of the Native* and Literary
   Portraiture   88

5. *A Laodicean*: Architecture as Symbol   118

6. Visual Appearance and Psychological Reality
   in *The Mayor of Casterbridge*   139

7. *The Woodlanders*: Impressionism and Modernism   169

8. Patterns of Light and Dark in *Tess of the
   d'Urbervilles*   191

9. *The Well-Beloved*: The Renunciation of Art   223

10. *Jude the Obscure*: The Retreat from the Light   234

Conclusion   253

Appendix: Hardy and the Arctic   259

Select Bibliography   265

Index   271

Illustrations

. Figure I. Thomas Hardy: Diary page showing sketch of
Mangiarelli's painting *Near Porta Salara*   *facing page* 95
The Trustees of the Thomas Hardy Memorial Collection in the Dorset
County Museum, Dorchester, Dorset

PLATES

1. Giovanni Bellini: *The Agony in the Garden*   46
Reproduced by courtesy of the Trustees, the National Gallery, London

2. Carlo Crivelli: *Pietà*   46
Reproduced by courtesy of the Trustees, the National Gallery, London

3. Thomas Hardy: *From Blackheath Corner* (Hardy's first
attempt at sketching from nature)   47
The Trustees of the Thomas Hardy Memorial Collection in the Dorset
County Museum, Dorchester, Dorset

4. Thomas Hardy: *Higher Bockhampton, Hardy's Birthplace*   47
The Trustees of the Thomas Hardy Memorial Collection in the Dorset
County Museum, Dorchester, Dorset

5. Thomas Hardy: Illustration for 'Her Death and After'
from *Wessex Poems*   47
By courtesy of Birmingham Museums and Art Gallery

6. Thomas Hardy: Illustration for 'In a Eweleaze near
Wetherbury' from *Wessex Poems*   47
By courtesy of Birmingham Museums and Art Gallery

7. Antoine Wiertz: *La Belle Rosine*   78
Copyright ACL, Bruxelles

8. Antoine Wiertz: *The Spirit of the Civilization of the
Nineteenth Century*   78
Copyright ACL, Bruxelles

9. Spinello Aretino ['Giotto']: *Two Haloed Mourners*
(fragment from the Burial of St John the Baptist)   78
Reproduced by courtesy of the Trustees, the National Gallery, London

10. Thomas Webster: *A Village Choir*   79
By courtesy of the Board of Trustees of the Victoria and Albert
Museum, London

11. Follower of J. B. Greuze: *A Girl*   79
Reproduced by courtesy of the Trustees, the National Gallery, London

12. Giovanni Battista Moroni: *Portrait of a Man (The Tailor)*   79
Reproduced by courtesy of the Trustees, the National Gallery, London

13. Giovanni Boldini: *Ragazza in Bianco e Contadini (The Morning Stroll)*   108

14. Meindert Hobbema: *The Avenue, Middelharnis*   108
Reproduced by courtesy of the Trustees, the National Gallery, London

15. Thomas Hardy: *Rainbarrow and the Heath*   108
Copyright is held by the Trustees of the late Mrs J. M. Lock and the Dorset County Museum, Dorchester, Dorset

16. Dante Gabriel Rossetti: *Astarte Syriaca*   109
Manchester City Art Galleries

17. William Holman Hunt: *The Lady of Shalott*   109

18. Sir Joshua Reynolds: *Sarah Siddons as 'The Tragic Muse'*   140
The Henry E. Huntington Library and Art Gallery

19. Sir Joshua Reynolds: *Lady Anne Fermour, Wife of Thomas Dawson*   141

20. Sir Joshua Reynolds: *Elizabeth, Duchess of Manchester, and her son, George Viscount Mandeville*   141
The National Trust

21. Sir Joshua Reynolds: *Lady Charlotte Hill, Countess Talbot*   141
The Tate Gallery, London

22. Sir Joshua Reynolds: *Anabella, Lady Blake, as 'Juno Receiving the Cestus from Venus'*   141

23. Thomas Woolner: *Alfred Lord Tennyson*   172

24. Sebastiano del Piombo: *The Raising of Lazarus*   172
Reproduced by courtesy of the Trustees, the National Gallery, London

25. Augustus Welby Pugin: *St Pancras Chapel and Bishop Skirlaw's Chapel, Yorkshire*   173

26. Sir Hubert von Herkomer: *Hard Times*   173
Manchester City Art Galleries

27. Titian: *The Rape of Europa*   204
Isabella Stewart Gardner Museum, Boston, USA

28. Titian: *Diana and Acteon*   204
Duke of Sutherland Collection, on loan to the National Gallery of Scotland

29. James McNeill Whistler: *Harmony in Red Lamplight*
    (Mrs Beatrix Godwin)   205
    The Hunterian Art Gallery, the University, Glasgow

30. J. M. W. Turner: *The Angel Standing in the Sun*   236
    The Tate Gallery, London

31. J. M. W. Turner: *Stonehenge, Wiltshire*   237

32. J. M. W. Turner: *Salisbury, Wiltshire*   237

33. Jules Bastien-Lepage: *Poor Fauvette*   252
    Glasgow Art Gallery and Museum

34. George Clausen: *The Stonepickers*   252
    Tyne and Wear County Council

35. John Everett Millais: *The North-West Passage*   253
    The Tate Gallery, London

36. William Bradford: *The Steamer 'Panther' among the
    Icebergs and Field Ice in Melville Bay and the Light of the
    Midnight Sun*   253
    Reproduced by gracious permission of Her Majesty the Queen

Abbreviations

The Works of Thomas Hardy in Prose and Verse, Wessex Edition, 23 vols. (London: Macmillan, 1912–14), as follows:

DR	*Desperate Remedies (1871)*
UGT	*Under the Greenwood Tree* (1872)
PBE	*A Pair of Blue Eyes* (1873)
FMC	*Far from the Madding Crowd* (1874)
HE	*The Hand of Ethelberta* (1876)
RN	*The Return of the Native* (1878)
L	*A Laodicean* (1881)
MC	*The Mayor of Casterbridge* (1886)
W	*The Woodlanders* (1887)
TD	*Tess of the d'Urbervilles* (1891)
WB	*The Well-Beloved* (1897)
JO	*Jude the Obscure* (1895)

EL   Florence Emily Hardy, *The Early Life of Thomas Hardy: 1840–1891* (London: Macmillan, 1928)

LY   Florence Emily Hardy, *The Later Years of Thomas Hardy: 1892–1928* (London: Macmillan, 1930)

Letters   *The Collected Letters of Thomas Hardy*, ed. Richard Little Purdy and Michael Millgate (Oxford: Clarendon Press, 1978–)

LN   *The Literary Notebooks of Thomas Hardy*, ed. Lennart A. Björk, 2 vols. (London: Macmillan, 1985)

DCM   Dorset County Museum, Dorchester

Introduction

In his *Essay on Thomas Hardy* (1978) John Bayley explains the curious
mixture of poise and awkwardness, of moments of vision and patches
of dullness, in Hardy's novels by reference to two aspects of Hardy's
creative life. He says that the 'quality in the writing of both attention
and inattention, shifting between the language itself and what it
describes, is an aspect of what could be called Hardy conscious and
unconscious; and our feeling is for the alternation of the two'.[1] The
'conscious Hardy' is the Hardy of the learned allusion and the felicitous verbal effect, the stage manager of the theatrical device. The 'unconscious Hardy' is the author of the subtle and intuitive observation,
the creator of a structure of symbols at once refined, complex, and
delicate, which more closely resembles poetry than prose. Yet for
Bayley, who states the case very clearly, as well as for scores of other
readers whose response is less articulate, much of the power and fascination of Hardy's prose writing lies in the strange dualism of style
—the uncertainty as to whether Hardy is completely the master of his
own brilliant effects. This study is an attempt to describe one of the
points of contact between the two facets of his style—the point at
which the plain teller-of-tales becomes the more evasive, more ambiguous narrator—one who invests even his trivial incidents, his stray
observations, and his fragmentary sightings with meaning.

The point of contact which has been chosen is Hardy's literary
response to visual effects, or more accurately, his translation of
observed phenomena into verbal 'visible essences'. It is here that the
two aspects of his creative personality can be seen very clearly,
sometimes operating in unison, sometimes far apart. It is here that he
is sometimes at his most self-conscious, his most 'aesthetic', and
where he writes in what one nineteenth-century critic called his
'Grosvenor Gallery style'. But it is also here that Hardy is at his most
intuitive and his most perceptive, and it is in his verbal-visual effects
that he often draws from the deepest springs of his creative powers.
'Those who remember Greuze's "Head of a Girl" have an idea of
Cytherea's look askance at the turning' (*DR* 61): This observation
from *Desperate Remedies* might well provoke the response, 'Who *does*
remember Greuze's "Head of a Girl"?' And what are we to make of a

[1] John Bayley, *An Essay on Hardy*, p. 31.

field 'speckled as thickly' with cattle 'as a canvas by Van Alsloot or Sallaert with burghers' (*TD* 133), as Hardy describes it in *Tess of the d'Urbervilles?* Robert Gittings and Norman Page are not the only critics who argue that this is Hardy parading his newly acquired knowledge.[2] Though this is neither the most interesting nor the most valuable explanation, what we do see in these references is the 'conscious Hardy' at work. When Tess on her marriage day, however, is possessed of that 'condition of mind, wherein she felt glorified by an irradiation not her own, like the angel whom St. John saw in the sun' (*TD* 272), the writing is of quite a different order, and the pictorialism runs too deep for the eye of a casual observer. On the face of it this is not a visual effect at all; but the presence of the sun in the simile communicates a symbolic significance to the figure of speech, whose roots can be traced to visual perception. First, the simile derives much of its potency from its association with the multiplicity of sunlit scenes in the novel—the literal light of the sun which illuminates the landscape —but it also relates to the mythos of solar legend which Hardy employs throughout the novel—the sun as a divinity or a fertility god. Yet there is also a pictorial allusion here: Tess's state of mind stands in an analogical relationship to the paintings of Turner, and to his picture *The Angel Standing in the Sun* in particular. In this example it is the 'unconscious Hardy' who weaves the pattern of imagery, who evolves firmly, but unobtrusively, the structure of visual symbolism, half-hidden beneath the narrative surface, in which the individual elements (of which this is one) relate to the meaning of the whole.

The reason for choosing the visual elements in Hardy's fiction derives from elements within Hardy's own temperament. He was a writer for whom images, in the form of mental 'pictures', actually preceded the formulation of ideas in language. He confessed to at least two of his biographers that ideas which were later clothed in verse or prose frequently presented themselves to him at first as pictures, and were first set down as pen-and-ink or pencil drawings.[3] Some of those impressions remain to this day, and are collected together in Dorchester County Museum; but even without their testi-

[2] Robert Gittings, *Young Thomas Hardy*, p. 141, and Norman Page, *Thomas Hardy*, p. 66. J. Hillis Miller claims that 'Hardy's pictorial symbolism is usually so blunt and unsubtle . . . that one hesitates to read anything into [it]'. Introduction to the New Wessex edition of *The Well-Beloved*, p. 211, n. 106.

[3] Ernest Brennecke Jr., *The Life of Thomas Hardy*, pp. 113–14, and Clive Holland, *Thomas Hardy OM*, p. 60. Both these sources must be treated with caution, but there seems no reason to doubt their authority in this instance.

mony, it would be easy to see the importance to Hardy of the objectification of scenes, characters, and even ideas in the form of pictures.
The word 'impression', for example, crops up again and again in his
critical remarks and in his fiction. His poems, he said, were 'mere impressions of the moment, and not convictions or arguments'; and in
his preface to *Poems of Past and Present* he spoke of the way in which
'unadjusted impressions have their value'.[4] Tom Paulin stresses the
connection in Hardy's mind between the 'impression' and the work-
ings of memory,[5] and in the way in which Hardy uses the word, the
visual connotations are never insignificant. 'A writer', Hardy once
said, 'looks upon the world with his personal eyes, and in his peculiar
moods'; and he called 'erroneous . . . the assumption that a novel is
the thing and not a view of the thing'.[6] As Judith Wittenberg points
out:

The terms 'eyes' and 'view', as Hardy uses them here, refer both to physical
vision and idiosyncratic opinion—which cannot, in actuality, as E. H. Gombrich tells us, be separated—or sight and in-sight, which are at the deepest
level the same. It is this viewing, with all its implications, that constitutes the
voyeuristic moment so fundamental both technically and thematically, to
Hardy's fiction.[7]

Hardy's understanding of his own work was intimately bound up
with modes of visual perception. He said that he hated '*word-
painting*', and added, 'I never try to do it; all I endeavour is to give
an *impression* of a scene as it strikes me.'[8] Here again is that word
'impression'—a word which features prominently in the novels themselves. 'Every woman who makes a permanent impression on a man
is usually recalled to his mind's eye as she appeared in one particular
scene' (*PBE* 18), he wrote in *A Pair of Blue Eyes*. This was in 1873,
long before French Impressionism had made any impact in England.
When it did, however, the visual associations of the world were further strengthened for Hardy. Barber Percombe's sight of Marty
South's hair formed an 'impression-picture of extremest type' (*W* 9)
in his mind; and here the word refers explicitly to a subjective mode
of perception. Consequently, when in 1892 he wrote in the preface to

---

[4] *Wessex Poems and Poems of Past and Present*, p. ix.
[5] Tom Paulin, *Thomas Hardy: The Poetry of Perception*, p. 43 and 52-3.
[6] 'The Profitable Reading of Fiction' (1888), in *Thomas Hardy's Personal Writings*,
ed. Harold Orel, pp. 122 and 124.
[7] Judith Bryant Wittenberg, 'Early Hardy Novels and the Fictional Eye', p. 152.
[8] *The Bookman*, 2 (Apr. 1892), p. 6; Hardy's emphasis.

Tess of the d'Urbervilles that a novel is 'an impression not an argument', or later that 'the mission of poetry is to record impressions, not convictions' (*LY* 178), seeing and understanding are closely linked by a common visual frame of reference.

The 'conscious' Hardy is the polemicist, the man who once knew John Stuart Mill's *On Liberty* by heart, the Darwinian, the writer with cynical views about marriage. The 'unconscious' Hardy is the watcher, the observer, the recorder of impressions. In this he somewhat resembles Ruskin, who was for ever attempting to reconcile reason and visual imagination, and whose influence over him is far greater than is generally believed. Like Ruskin's too, Hardy's was a lonely temperament, and in common with many of his own most sensitive and observant watchers—Gabriel Oak, Diggory Venn, Marty South, and, most of all, Elizabeth-Jane—Hardy is 'out of the group' observing 'all from afar' (*MC* 208). Life is lived inwardly through the intensity of sensuous experience—in the ear (sounds are important to him), in the sense of touch, but above all in the eye. Even as a child he derived a lonely, but intense, pleasure from the sunlight illuminating a red wall at the same time each day. He tells us that he 'used to wait for this chromatic effect, and, sitting alone there, would recite to himself "And now another day is gone" from Dr. Watts's Hymns' (*EL* 19). As for Ruskin before him, visual effects were imbued with a life independent of specific meaning, and his notebooks and diaries are filled with observations of such effects. Sunsets had a peculiar power over his mind, and he records dozens of them, sometimes in notebooks, sometimes in fiction: 'A sunset: a brazen sun, bristling with a thousand spines which struck into and tormented my eyes'; 'A sunset. The sun a vast bulb of crimson pulp'; 'A rainy sunset. The sun streaming his yellow rays through the wet atmosphere like straying hair'.[9] The retinal image acquires meaning as it is translated into language by a process of mental association. Hardy explains this process in an episode in *Desperate Remedies*, in which the heroine, Cytherea Graye, for ever connects the light of the setting sun with the death of her father.[10] Thereafter, each novel contains at least one important

[9] *Thomas Hardy's Notebooks*, ed. Evelyn Hardy (London: Hogarth Press, 1965), pp. 43 and 52–3.

[10] 'Emotions', says the narrator, 'will attach themselves to scenes that are simultaneous—however foreign in essence these scenes may be—as chemical waters will crystallise on twigs and wires. Even after that time any mental agony brought less vividly to Cytherea's mind the scene from the Town Hall windows than sunlight streaming in shaft-like lines'. (*DR* 11).

sunset, strongly visual in itself, whose emotional or conceptual significance is determined by the context. In *Far From the Madding Crowd* the light of the sunset is charged with a sexual potency as it lights up the 'hollow among the ferns', providing the illumination for Frank Troy's sword exercises. In *The Return of the Native* it is suggestive of a certain paralysis of will, as it accompanies Clym Yeobright's reluctant decision to marry Eustacia Vye. The sunset which opens *A Laodicean* possesses melancholy associations of a general kind connected with the passing of old ways of life; but the sunset which greets the entry of Elizabeth-Jane and her mother into Casterbridge is part of a personal myth, and announces the end of Henchard's triumphant days in the provincial town. The emotional exaltation which Grace Melbury experiences in the love of Giles Winterborne is expressed through their mutual pleasure in a fine sunset seen from High Stoy Hill. But the realization of that love has come too late for both of them; the sunset is an autumn one, and winter is not far away. The sunsets of *Tess of the d'Urbervilles* are among Hardy's finest, and are perfectly integrated into the solar symbolism of the novel. The sun sets over Chaseborough in Turner-like splendour, and before it rises again, Tess has lost her virginity. When it sets on the day of the marriage of Tess and Angel, it brings to a close not only the day and the year, it also signals the end of a whole way of life—a terrestrial paradise—to which the couple can never return. In *Jude the Obscure* the sunset has almost lost its visual energy. The rays of the dying sun serve merely to generate for Jude a romantic mirage, a mental will-o'-the-wisp, as their light touches the slates and the spires of the distant Christminster.

Hardy was encouraged to exploit his natural visual propensity by the importance which Victorian audiences—reviewers and common readers alike—attached to the power of a novelist to vivify and particularize his characters and events. In his book *George Eliot and the Visual Arts* Hugh Witemeyer writes:

We know from the popularity of literary illustration that the Victorian audience liked to 'see' its fiction, and novelists catered to the same taste by providing abundant visual description. Conrad was only reiterating a commonplace of Victorian aesthetics when he said that the 'task which I am trying to achieve is, by the power of the written word, to make you hear, to make you feel—it is, before all, to make you *see*'.[11]

---

[11] Hugh Witemeyer, *George Eliot and the Visual Arts*, pp. 1–2.

Visualization in fiction was endorsed by the findings of contemporary psychology and supported by literary criticism. The philosophy of John Stuart Mill, the experimentation of Alexander Bain, and the scientific theories of a popular writer like Helmholtz all stressed the supremacy of the sense of sight over and above the other senses in 'discriminating and . . . identifying natural things',[12] and their ideas were taken up by the critics. G. H. Lewes, in praising Ruskin for his literary, visual power, said that 'it is because the eye is the most valued and intellectual of our senses that the majority of metaphors are borrowed from its sensations'[13] Inevitably, the single most highly organized and the most carefully structured visual effect open to the novelist was pictorialism, and Hardy, who was well versed in the ways of both the draughtsman and painter, frequently adopts pictorialist techniques. Ralph Elliott, in his study of Hardy's use of the English language, endorses the view that Hardy's vision was a 'strongly pictorial one'.

We may remember the gist of some of Ethelberta's arguments or the often stilted dialogue between Sue and Jude, but the unforgettable moments in Hardy's fiction are those in which—whatever their symbolism—the pictorial details of a scene, a landscape, or a person's appearance are imprinted on the reader's mind and memory.[14]

Pictorialism is not, however, a simple category, and, though it is one of the principal means of verbal-visual effects in fiction, it has many different modes. In Hardy's writing it ranges from the self-conscious arrangement of form and colour in the manner of some particular painterly style to subtler organization of illumination, space, or symbolism analogous to the light, perspective, or emblems in works of visual art. Mr Penny in his workshop resembles a study by 'some modern Moroni'; Fitzpiers on the back of the horse Darling looks like 'a Wouvermans eccentricity'; and Clym Yeobright's face appears before Eustacia Vye as a Rembrandt portrait. The precise function of the reference varies from novel to novel, but each time it operates as an anti-naturalistic device. For Hardy, the literal transcription of the physical world was uninteresting; 'realism', he said, 'is not Art' (*EL* 299), and the presence of the pictorial simile is a reminder to the reader that, like the painted picture, the verbal text is an artefact. The

[12] Alexander Bain, *The Senses and the Intellect* (1855), 3rd edn. (1868), p. 238.
[13] G. H. Lewes, 'The Principles of Success in Literature', pp. 583.
[14] Ralph W. V. Elliot, *Thomas Hardy's English*, p. 234.

picture serves to create and preserve the distance between the reader and the events of the narrative. Mr Penny would never have heard of Moroni, and Eustacia Vye would never have seen a Rembrandt: but what Moroni did for his tailor, and what Rembrandt did for the humble figures of Haarlem, Hardy does for his provincial and rustic characters: he transforms them into works of art. More persuasive, however, is that kind of pictorialism in which names are not mentioned. The influence of Turner's use of light and colour on the style of *Tess of the d'Urbervilles* is more powerful for being unobtrusive, and for being part of a private source of inspiration which Hardy does not care to parade in the text. Similarly, in the genre studies of *Far From the Madding Crowd* and the multiplicity of 'portraits' in *The Return of the Native*, Hardy has employed the devices of the painter—the organization of colour or space—to structure reality in a pictorial manner, but without feeling the necessity to confess his sources.

In certain important respects Hardy's pictorialism is markedly different from that of novelists who were his contemporaries. Unlike Henry James, for example, he rarely introduces tangible works of art into the text. A large number of James's stories, from an early one like 'The Story of a Masterpiece', with its portrait of Marian Everett, to *The Ambassadors*, with its more allusive picture by Lambinet, use the presence of the canvas itself to create suggestive connections between art and life. In Hardy's hands the device is wooden and lifeless. The de Stancy portraits in *A Laodicean* and the d'Urberville portraits in *Tess of the d'Urbervilles* are merely illustrations of aristocratic lineage, and add little to the visual elements of their respective narratives. To some extent Hardy's pictorialism is closer to that of George Eliot. Like her, he delighted in 'rural painting of the Dutch School', and when he gave *Under the Greenwood Tree* this subtitle, he did so in full knowledge of the famous seventeenth chapter of *Adam Bede*. Yet his use of the genre subject and the conversation piece is markedly different from George Eliot's. She is essentially a conceptualist, whereas he is what he called a 'technist'. George Eliot draws heavily on the associations which these pictures create in the mind of the reader. For her the humble Dutch study represents the apotheosis of the commonplace, and the Raphael Madonna presents an image of perfect maternity. Hardy, however, is more engaged with the technical means by which images are created. He persistently employs the terminology of painting and art criticism—'line', 'perspective', 'profile', 'foreground', 'background', and so on—and his vocabulary of over two hundred colour words[15] is evidence of his precise, keen, and discriminating verbal palette. It is the image itself with which he is preoccupied, so he reduces the appearance of the Mellstock choir to a series of flat, two-dimensional shapes for comic effect; and the 'impression-picture' which forms in the mind of Barber Percombe as he contemplates Marty South's hair derives precisely and explicitly from a viewpoint peculiar to Impressionist painting.

Perhaps more than any other Victorian novelist, Hardy employed the visual image to communicate meaning and feeling. The more clearly something is seen in his work, the more clearly it is understood, and he used every device at his disposal to make the image as vivid and as sharply focused as possible. Consequently, the 'picture' in his writing is not an illustration, a way of elaborating or expanding a preconceived idea or sentiment; it is the primary vehicle for the expression of ideas and sentiments. A good example of his spontaneous tendency to think and feel in images is conveyed in a letter which he wrote in 1906.

It concerns John Stuart Mill, the centenary of whose birth fell in that year. It was addressed to the readers of *The Times*, and in it Hardy told of once having heard Mill lecture in public. 'It was a day in 1865,' Hardy wrote, 'about three in the afternoon, during Mill's candidature for Westminster. The hustings had been erected in Covent Garden, near the front of St. Paul's Church; and when I—a young man living in London—drew near to the spot, Mill was speaking.' (*EL* 118). The influence of Mill on Hardy was exclusively intellectual, and one might expect some account of what Mill said on this occasion. But in fact there is nothing in the description which follows about Mill's ideas, attitudes, or philosophy. Instead, Hardy provides his readers with a series of images—a series which strongly resembles his fictional procedures, in which the visual, the metaphorical, and the pictorial are rapidly and deftly intertwined.

He stood bareheaded, and his vast pale brow, so thin-skinned as to show the blue veins, sloped back like a stretching upland, and conveyed to the observer a curious sense of perilous exposure. The picture of him as personified earnestness surrounded for the most part by careless curiosity derived an added piquancy—if it can be called such—from the fact that the cameo clearness of his face chanced to be in relief against the blue shadow of a church which, on its transcendental side, his doctrines antagonized. (*LY* 119.)

---

[15] Ibid., p. 249.

This is one of those Hardy 'impressions', highly personal, highly selective, in which visual activity is matched by verbal ingenuity. The delicate and sensitive detail with which the description opens instantly shifts into a strange and curious simile. Of all the aspects of Mill's appearance which Hardy might have mentioned, it is the 'vast pale brow, so thin-skinned as to show the blue veins' which draws his attention. Mill's great mind is scarcely protected by its covering membrane, and the intellectual power of that mind is conveyed by the monumentality of its physical shape and form. At this point the visual strategy changes. The perspective lengthens, the 'observer' withdraws slightly, and the closely rendered detail of one aspect of Mill's physiognomy gives way to the full-length figure surrounded by his audience. The mental perspective also shifts. What started out as a transcription of naturalistic detail now becomes pictorial. The 'picture' is an allegorical one, in which Mill plays the part of 'personified earnestness', and the crowd acts out the role of 'careless curiosity'. The picture is a commentary on Mill's intellectual relations with the ordinary man—with those on the hustings, as Hardy put it elsewhere in the letter, 'who, with few exceptions, did not care to understand him fully, and a crowd below who could not.' (LY 119). But this picture almost instantly dissolves, and gives way to yet another, in which the visual and intellectual perspectives are lengthened still further. A background is introduced, the audience in the foreground disappears, and allegory gives way to symbol. Throughout the first half of the nineteenth century, Mill's ideas met, not only with the incomprehension of the common man, but with the hostility of the Church; and Hardy's view of Mill on this afternoon in 1865 provided him with a perfect emblem of this second idea. The 'cameo clearness' of the face suggests something of the clarity and reasonableness of the arguments of *On Liberty* which Hardy and his contemporaries 'knew almost by heart', while the blue shadow of St Paul's provides a visual motif for the religious orthodoxy which Mill's doctrines 'antagonized'.

On the previous day in *The Times*, John Morley had given a more conventional account of Mill's contribution to nineteenth-century intellectual life. Hardy's is characteristic of a mind which thinks in images rather than concepts. Those images pass with such rapidity that they create an almost cinematographic effect; but in fact they are not moving pictures, but a series of 'stills'; and the way in which Hardy communicates his impression of Mill represents on a small scale what he does in a larger and more extended way in the novels.

Tess of the d'Urbervilles provides a whole panoply of such effects, from the techniques of artists in general, where 'the atmosphere . . . is so tinged with azure that what artists call the middle distance partakes also of that hue' (*TD* 10), to the use of pictorial allegory, where the Durbeyfield family bidding farewell to Tess forms 'a picture of honest beauty flanked by innocence, and backed by simple-souled vanity' (*TD* 591); from a personal and private allusion to the style of individual artists, where 'humanity stood before' Angel 'no longer in the pensive sweetness of Italian art, but in the staring and ghastly attitudes of a Wiertz Museum, and with the leer of a study by Van Beers' (*TD* 331), to a specific reference to an actual work of art. When Angel returned from South America, 'you could see the skeleton behind the man, and almost the ghost behind the skeleton. He matched Crivelli's dead *Christus*. His sunken eye-pits were of morbid hue, and the light in his eyes had waned.' (*TD* 470).

Of course, this is an aspect of Hardy's writing which has not been neglected by criticism. Writers like Alastair Smart, Norman Page, and Joan Grundy[16] have all drawn attention to the widespread pictorialism of the fiction, and, collectively, they have identified allusions to a large number of specific painters and works of art. The limitation of their work is that it tends to become piecemeal parallelism—a concordance of passages and their sources or analogues in works of visual art. They tend to treat pictorialism in isolation from Hardy's other visual techniques, and in isolation, too, from his more general concerns with the nature of visual perception. These critics have largely neglected the way in which Hardy's 'picturing' is but one aspect of a wider concern with the relations between eye, mind, and word.

Hardy himself was fully conscious of his visual propensities: he realized that not only did characters and scenes present themselves to his mind as pictures, but that even abstract ideas, concepts, and mental propositions came to him most readily in the form of images. Both his novels and poetry make it clear that he was much concerned with the precise nature of these mental pictures—with retinal images, and

[16] Alastair Smart, 'Pictorial Imagery in the Novels of Thomas Hardy', pp. 262–80, and Joan Grundy, *Hardy and the Sister Arts*. Carl J. Weber, in *Hardy of Wessex*; Richard C. Carpenter, in 'Hardy and the Old Masters', pp. 18–28; Arlene M. Jackson, in *Illustration and the Novels of Thomas Hardy*; Lloyd Fernando, in 'Thomas Hardy's Rhetoric of Painting', pp. 62–73; and Norman Page, in *Thomas Hardy* (see n. 2), 'Hardy's Dutch Painting: *Under the Greenwood Tree*', pp. 39–42; 'Hardy's Pictorial Art in *The Mayor of Casterbridge*', and 'Visual Techniques in Hardy's *Desperate Remedies*', all deal with aspects of Hardy's pictorialist techniques.

with their significance for the mind. But for someone with such a
highly developed visual sensibility, the life of the eye raised a number
of important questions. To what extent is human consciousness
moulded by the pictures which are fed to it by the eye? What is the
connection between what the eye sees and those aspects of reality
which lie beyond its range? And, perhaps above all, what part does
the mind itself play in interpreting those images and in creating its
own version of 'reality'? In the same year that he first saw John Stuart
Mill, he was pondering these questions. In 1865 he wrote: 'The
poetry of a scene lies in the minds of the perceivers. Indeed, it does
not lie in the scene at all.' (*EL* 66). Nearly forty years later he was
contemplating similar questions: 'We don't always remember as we
should that in getting at the truth, we get only at the true nature of the
impression that an object, etc., produces on us, the true thing in itself
being still, as Kant shows, beyond our knowledge.' (*LY* 9). The
notion that the world is 'only a psychological phenomenon', as he
put it in *Tess of the d'Urbervilles* (*TD* 108), may well have come to him
from Kant; or it may have come, as Tom Paulin suggests, from
Fichte.[17] What is more likely is that Hardy borrowed it from Shelley,
a poet whom he admired deeply, and who, in a poem like 'The Sensitive Plant', makes a strong case for the intensely subjective nature of
experience.[18] Hardy articulates the dilemma in more specifically
visual terms than does Shelley, however, and in this he was probably
encouraged by his reading of Ruskin and Pater. It would not be difficult to interpret the early volumes of *Modern Painters* as an extended
account of the way in which the mind—especially the mind of Turner
—shapes the world in accordance with moral principles, and how
visual perception is the active agent of the 'imagination penetrative'.
Pater's view is more extreme, and in his conclusion to *The Renaissance*
he paints a graphic picture of the disjunction between reality and the
'impression'—a word which runs through the book like a leitmotif—between the material world and the mind which perceives it at
a distance. With the exceptions of George Somerset in *A Laodicean*
and Elizabeth-Jane in *The Mayor of Casterbridge*, few of Hardy's

---

[17] See Paulin, *Thomas Hardy: The Poetry of Perception*, pp. 51–61. The phrasing is very
similar to F. A. Aulard's 'Le monde n'est qu'un phénomène cérébral', in his 'Essai
sur les idées philosophiques et l'inspiration poétique de Leopardi', in *Poésies et œuvres de
Leopardi*, trans. F. A. Aulard (Paris, 1880), p. 48—a phrase which Hardy translated as
'The world is only a cerebral phenomenon'. See *LN*, '1876' Notebook, entry 175.

[18] As F. B. Pinion points out, Hardy half-quotes from Shelley's 'The Sensitive
Plant' in *Desperate Remedies*. p. 141. See *A Hardy Companion*, p. 165.

characters are sufficiently sophisticated to address these problems directly; but frequently the narrator will draw attention to the fact that the eye is fallible, that it distorts what it sees, and that it tends to observe parts rather than wholes. 'In making even horizontal and clear inspections', says the narrator in the opening pages of *Far From the Madding Crowd*, 'we colour and mould according to the wants within us whatever our eyes bring in' (*FMC* 16), and within the texts themselves Hardy will frequently employ the presence or absence of illumination to suggest clear-sightedness or partial-sightedness. Unlike James or Virginia Woolf, Hardy rarely permits us to see *through* the eyes of a character; instead, he uses sunlight, darkness, firelight, or lamplight as emblems of states of consciousness or moral enlightenment. Here the pictorial, the perceptual, and the moral impinge closely upon each other. The darkness of Bathsheba Everdene's fir plantation, the obscurity of Egdon Heath, the impenetrable blackness of Cranborne Chase in *Tess of the d'Urbervilles*, and the dark nights of *Jude the Obscure* are all visually memorable, but they are also suggestive of mental and moral perspectives.

Again, this is an aspect of Hardy's writing which has not been completely overlooked. The symbolism of light and colour, of darkness and light, has been touched upon by Tony Tanner and Penelope Vigar, and in his book *Thomas Hardy: Distance and Desire* Hillis Miller has dealt extensively with Hardy's manipulation of viewpoint.[19] But, once again, their view is a partial one. Each of them has subjected Hardy's text to close scrutiny; and each has discovered patterns in the writing of considerable complexity and interest. But they have tended to ignore the milieu in which Hardy was writing. The visual symbolism of Hardy's fiction can only be clearly understood in conjunction with his taste in painting, his reading of Ruskin, his attitude to the psychology of perception, and his reinterpretations of other literary forms such as Nordic and Greek myths.

This study, then, is neither a comprehensive account of Hardy's pictorialist techniques, nor an attempt at a complete reading of each of the major novels. What it tries to do is to offer insight into one of the mainsprings of Hardy's creative process, to show how Hardy drew on his temperamental predisposition to structure his novels as a series of images, and to demonstrate something of the reciprocal relations between the conscious and the unconscious Hardy within the fiction.

[19] Tony Tanner, 'Colour and Movement in Hardy's *Tess of the d'Ubervilles*', pp. 219–39, and Penelope Vigar, *The Novels of Thomas Hardy: Illusion and Reality*.

1

Hardy and the Visual Arts

Though Hardy never elaborated a formal theory of *ut pictura poesis*, a very high proportion of his remarks about the nature of artistic production assume a close analogy between literary and visual art. For him the artist is a 'seer', not only in the conventional sense that he is gifted with spiritual and moral insight, but also in the sense that a seer is one who watches and observes the life around him. In 1882 Hardy wrote: 'As, in looking at a carpet, by following one colour a certain pattern is suggested, by following another colour, another; so in life the seer should watch that pattern among general things which his idiosyncrasy moves him to observe, and describe that alone.' (*EL* 198). 'This is,' he added, using a visual metaphor in a literary context, 'quite accurately, a going to Nature: yet the result is no mere photograph, but purely the product of the writer's own mind.' (*EL* 198). Here, as so often in Hardy's observations on aesthetic matters, he speaks of art as a form of self-expression; and his language, terminology, and frame of reference are visual. Art, he wrote in 1890, 'is a changing of the actual proportions and order of things, so as to bring out more forcibly than might otherwise be done that feature in them which appeals most strongly to the idiosyncrasy of the artist.' (*EL* 299).

Hardy's tendency to draw parallels between the activities of writing and painting was the product of a highly developed visual sensibility, but it was encouraged by two important theoretical influences. In his early years as a novelist he read Ruskin, who conceived of both literature and painting in terms of accurate or inaccurate perception; and in his later years he followed the debate in the French press between the advocates of realism and symbolism in art—a debate which frequently crossed the boundaries of the verbal and the visual. The problem of mimesis was central to both Ruskin and the French, and in his support of the view that true art eschews literal transcription or copying, Hardy came very close to the symbolist position taken up by Frédérique Brunetière in the *Revue des deux mondes*.[1] Art, Hardy argued, involves

[1] In 1886 and 1887 Hardy transcribed and translated large extracts from the *Revue des deux mondes*. See *LN*, entries 1435, 1436, 1438, 1439, 1440, 1441, 1558, 1561–7.

a disproportioning—(i.e. distorting, throwing out of proportion)—of realities, to show more clearly the features that matter in those realities, which, if merely copied or reported inventorially, might possibly be observed, but would more probably be overlooked. Hence 'realism' is not Art. (*EL* 299.)

True realism, for Hardy, resembles a mode of visual perception—of seeing beyond the superficial nature of things, and penetrating to their inner essence. He might have quoted Ruskin as his source for this idea, but in fact he turns to Wordsworth. 'Consider', he says,

the Wordsworthian dictum (the more perfectly the natural object is reproduced, the more truly poetic the picture). This reproduction is achieved by seeing into the *heart of a thing* (as rain, wind, for instance), and is realism, in fact, though through being pursued by means of the imagination it is confounded with invention. (*EL* 190; Hardy's emphasis.)

Wordsworth's poem 'Elegiac Stanzas suggested by a Picture of Peele Castle' supplied Hardy with yet another visual metaphor for literary art. The 'art' of 'poetry and novel writing', he said, lay in making the 'defects [of nature] the basis of a hitherto unperceived beauty, by irradiating them with "the light that never was" on their surface, but is seen to be latent in them by the spiritual eye' (*EL* 151). In his poem, Wordsworth envies the capacity of the painter to fix for ever what, in the poet, is merely a 'dream', a longing, or an aspiration. Having observed Peele Castle in a mood of tranquil beauty many years previously, Wordsworth exclaims:

> Ah! THEN, if mine had been the Painter's hand,
> To express what then I saw; and add the gleam,
> The light that never was, on sea or land,
> The consecration, and the Poet's dream,
>
> (11. 13–16)

Sir George Beaumont's work was Wordsworth's source of inspiration; but for Hardy it was more especially Turner who irradiated landscape with the imaginative 'light that never was'; and it was Turner who, gifted with what Ruskin called the 'imagination penetrative', was able to see into 'the heart of a thing'. When Hardy came to make direct comparisons between his work and the art of the painter, however, it was not Turner he chose, but two artists of quite a different caste. 'My art', he wrote in 1887, 'is to intensify the expression of things, as is done by Crivelli, Bellini, etc., so that the heart and inner meaning is made vividly visible.' (*EL* 231–2). When Hardy wrote this, he had not yet seen the work of Crivelli and Bellini in their native Venice; but since his arrival in London in 1862 he had been familiar with Bellini's *Agony in the Garden* (Plate 1) and Crivelli's *Pietà* (Plate 2), both of which are in the National Gallery. In style, subject matter, and technique, nothing could be further removed from the work of Turner, yet for Hardy and his contemporaries there was one factor which the paintings shared. These painters used form expressively. Crivelli and Bellini in the Venetian Renaissance, and Turner in the modern period, endowed the objective world with imaginative meaning by altering and changing appearances to suit their own purposes. The work of all three involved a form of self-expression, 'a disproportioning . . . of realities.' (*EL* 299). When T. S. Eliot, who was not an admirer of Hardy's work, said that he seemed to him 'to have written as nearly for the sake of "self expression" as a man well can',[2] the comment was meant to be derogatory. In fact, it conformed with one of Hardy's most dearly held literary ideals, and the painting which he most admired involved for him a high degree of self-expression.

If the prominence which Hardy gave to the analogy between the arts derived from his tendency to think in images—on account of the way in which 'ideas presented themselves to his mind in the first instance more in the guise of mental pictures than as subjects for writing down'[3]—then the images themselves came to him as the result of his passionate interest in the art of painting, and his lifelong habit of drawing and sketching out of doors. Some of his earliest and happiest memories were bound up with what for him was an enormously pleasurable activity. The benign figure of Henry Moule, for example, emerges from the past as his first tutor in water-colour painting:

My first distinct recollection of Henry Moule carries me back, through a long avenue of years, towards the middle of the last century. His figure emerges from the obscurity of forgotten and half-forgotten things somewhere between 1856 and 1860, when I recall him as he stood beside me while I was attempting a sketch from nature in water colours. He must have been about thirty, and had already become an adept in out-door painting. As I was but a youth, and by no means practised in that art, he criticized my performance freely.[4]

[2] T. S. Eliot, *After Strange Gods*, p. 54.
[3] See Introduction, n. 3.
[4] Hardy's preface to H. J. Moule's *Dorchester Antiquities* (1906), in *Personal Writings*, ed. Harold Orel, p. 66.

A few of Hardy's paintings from this period are collected in Dorchester County Museum. Some of them are animal studies—a rabbit and a kingfisher, for example—but most of them are topographical sketches, like the one he refers to here (Plate 3). The area around the cottage at Bockhampton continued to feed Hardy's imagination for the rest of his life, and much of the conviction and authenticity which he brought to his literary settings derives from hours of careful drawing in his youth. An accomplished study of the Old Manor House, Kingston Maurward, painted in 1859 provided him with an image which he transformed into Knapwater House of *Desperate Remedies*, and his drawings of the streets and cottages of Bockhampton and Stinsford found literary expression in the architectural details of Mellstock in *Under the Greenwood Tree*. The close identification in Hardy's mind between fiction and reality, between visual image and verbal equivalent, is illustrated by a sketch of his parents' cottage and neighbouring Puddletown Heath, where a note on the back of the drawing conflates fiction and reality. It reads 'Bockhampton Cottage and Egdon Heath'. The central importance to Hardy of the visual image of Bockhampton, however, is nowhere better illustrated than in the opening pages of his disguised autobiography. The *Early Life* starts with a loving, almost passionate, verbal recreation of his birthplace, 'quaint, brass-knockered, and green-shuttered', and is illustrated with a detailed and meticulous drawing by Hardy of that same cottage nestling in the foliage, protected by trees, and with Puddletown Heath just discernible behind the roof (Plate 4). When Hardy went to London in 1862 and joined the thriving architectural practice of Arthur Blomfield, his energies as a draughtsman seem to have been largely absorbed by technical drawing of the kind recorded in his architectural notebook, now in Dorchester County Museum. Apart from a small sketch of St James's Park and a view from his lodgings at Westbourne Park Villas, London seems to have held no special visual interest for him, and all the topographical drawings in this decade were done away from the capital. A view over Windsor Castle and a picture of the sun setting over the Channel at Dover date from 1862; in September 1863 he drew Warbarrow Bay, near Lulworth, and Gad Cliff; a visit to his home in 1863 resulted in a drawing of Dorchester from Stinsford Hill and a view of Dogberry Down from the Devil's Kitchen. Later in the same decade he made a study of Denchworth, near Wantage, the country of *Jude the Obscure*, and one of Lulworth Cove, which became Lulwind Cove in *Desperate Remedies*.

His meeting with Emma Lavinia Gifford—his future wife—in 1870
acted as a stimulus to his efforts in drawing and painting. She was an
enthusiastic water-colourist—drawings and sketches appear everywhere in her diaries—and she and Hardy frequently went out on
painting expeditions. Hardy's drawings done in the Vallency valley,
near Emma's Cornish home, in 1870–2 are reproduced in *The Early
Life*, and this same valley provided many of the settings for *A Pair of
Blue Eyes*. Hardy actually supplied the editor of *Tinsley's Magazine*
with a number of drawings to aid the artist in his illustrations,[5] and
the text itself often replicates the configurations of a landscape study.
For example, the account of 'two bold escarpments sloping down
together like the letter V', towards 'the bottom, [of which] like liquid
in a funnel, appeared the sea, grey and small' (*PB* 21) reproduces
something of the visual pattern of one of Hardy's drawings from this
spot in North Cornwall.

The Vallency valley appears again in a drawing Hardy made of
Emma as she tried to retrieve a glass which had fallen into a pool by a
waterfall. In 'Under the Waterfall' Hardy recalls how he and Emma
went to the valley 'to paint the scene', and the drawing shows Emma
reaching into the pool, in the words of the poem, 'with long bared
arms'. Several days later, on August 22nd, Emma appears again in
one of Hardy's drawings, this time on Beeny Cliff. The image continued to haunt Hardy, and in 'The Figure in the Scene' from *Moments
of Vision* (1917) he remembers how

> It pleased her to step in front and sit
> Where the cragged slope was green,
> While I stood back that I might pencil it
> With her amid the scene.
>
> (ll. 1–4)

Emma appears again as an image in 'Why did I Sketch', in which the
'silhouette' on 'down or cliff' resembles an unfinished drawing of
1875 in which Emma is depicted sitting under a cliff at Swanage.

Some of Hardy's extant drawings were done specifically in preparation for the writing of the novels. In 1873 he sketched 'smockfrocks,
gaiters, sheep-crooks, rick, "staddles", a sheep-washing pool, one of
the old-fashioned malt-houses, and some out-of-the way things' (*EL*
128) as a preliminary exercise for *Far from the Madding Crowd*. His
study of an old Wessex milking-pail, now in Dorchester County

---

[5] *Letters* i. 17–18. Letters dated 27 July and 30 Aug. 1872.

Museum, may well be one of these. More drawings were done for *The Return of the Native*, and in 1878 he sent studies of mummers' clothing and stage properties to Arthur Hopkins, who was illustrating the novel in *Harper's New Monthly Magazine*.[6] Later, Hardy climbed the downs near Sutton Pointz to sketch the scene for *The Trumpet Major*. In the 1880s he made drawings and extensive notes on the portraits of Julia and Francis Turberville at Woolbridge Manor House, and on a pencil study of 'Old Groves Place' in Shaftesbury, he wrote that it was 'sketched on the spot for a novel called "Jude the Obscure"'.[7]

Hardy's drawings are certainly not outstanding in terms of artistic merit, but they demonstrate very clearly the importance that he attached to the visual image in a literary context. Throughout his life he used drawing as a way of reifying his mental images and of focusing his mind on the details of a scene, a building, or a place, by transcribing it first in graphic terms. Some of his most accomplished graphic work, however, is to be found in the vignettes attached to the *Wessex Poems*.[8] He did these in the late 1890s with a view to publication, and as such they are very different from the drawing which he made for his own, private purposes. They do not serve to clarify the visual images of the verse, nor are they illustrations of the incidents in the poems. Instead, they act as enigmatic, economical commentaries on the poetic themes. Many of them are architectural fragments, buildings, street scenes, and townscapes, and a very large number employ one of Hardy's favourite motifs—the road which winds across a landscape disappearing at the horizon into infinity. Most of them are highly symbolic—the vase of dead flowers for the poem 'To Outer Nature', the highly stylized conjunction of townscape, earthworks, and graveyard for 'Her Death and After' (Plate 5) and, most famous of all, the enormous pair of spectacles that appears to be resting in a field for the poem 'In a Eweleaze near Weatherbury' (Plate 6). This last example is splendidly ambiguous. On closer inspection it can be seen that the spectacles do not lie on the landscape at all. Instead, they are poised in mid-air between the eweleaze and the observer, permitting a bifocal view of the field. Like the reader, the spectator of the vignette perceives the romantic spot both as it is in itself, and through the spectacles of old age, so that both the poem and the picture are

---

6 *Letters* i. 54–5. Letter dated 20 Feb. 1878.
7 These and all the pictures mentioned above are in DCM.
8 These are all reproduced in *The Complete Poetical Works of Thomas Hardy*, ed. Samuel Hynes, i. 1–106.

studies in simultaneous 'vision'. In the poem the double perspective is created by the passage of time; in the picture it is rendered literally, as two views of the same image.

If the vignettes to the *Wessex Poems* represent both the strengths and the limitations of Hardy's technical ability, his talents as a draughts-man were sufficient for him to admire the genius of others, and from an early age he possesed a keen interest in all kinds of painting, ancient and modern. Before going to London in 1862, it was the art journals, particularly *The Illustrated Magazine of Art*, which formed the basis of his art education, and later in life he recommended these same jour-nals as a way of introducing children to the pleasures of painting. But it was London which opened his eyes to the real power and vitality of visual art. In *The Early Life* he says that he was influenced in his de-cision to 'migrate' to the capital by the opening of the International Ex-hibition (*EL* 46), and the centre-piece of this show was a huge gallery of pictures borrowed from many countries around the world. The British section alone comprised 790 oil paintings, 600 water-colours, and 500 engravings, and there were thousands of pictures from else-where. Hardy clearly revelled in this new visual experience. He was constantly travelling to South Kensington and visiting 'the Exhibition for an hour in the evening two or three times a week (*EL* 50). Sometimes he went alone, but sometimes he took his sister Mary, his cousin Martha Sparks, and on at least one occasion went with his friend Horace Moule, whose poem on Gérôme's *Roman Gladiators* was published in *Once a Week*.[9]

During this period he began to stock his mind with images which were later to influence his writing, and it was here that he saw for the first time the work of artists whose acquaintance he would make later in life. The British section was the largest, but the greatest revelation of the show for English audiences was the painting that came from France. Ingres's *La Source* and Delacroix's *The Murder of the Bishop of Liège* dominated the French entry, but the 'modern' French school was well represented by Meissonier—described as 'the idol of the Paris salons'[10]—and by the work of the French landscape artists whose techniques Hardy later mentioned in *Desperate Remedies*— Théodore Rousseau, Charles Daubigny, Paul Baudry, and most especially Constant Troyon and Rosa Bonheur. In the English

---

[9] Horace Moule, 'Ave, Caesar!' *Once A Week*, 7 (1862), p. 294.
[10] *What do you think of the International Exhibition? A collection of the best descriptive criticisms*, ed. Robert Kemp (1862), p. 162.

section, Pre-Raphaelitism was strong, with, among other works, Holman Hunt's *Light of the World, Lantern Maker's Courtship*, and *Valentine and Sylvia*, Millais's melancholy but lyrical *Autumn Leaves* and *Vale of Rest*, William Dyce's mysterious *Pegwell Bay* and *The Meeting of Jacob and Rachael*, and John Brett's famous study of the Aosta Valley. From the earlier English school were Turner's *Falls at Schaffhausen* and *Seventh Plague of Egypt*, Danby's *The Passage of the Red Sea*, and Constable's *Hay Wain*—though, according to at least one authority, this was thought to lack 'penetrative imagination'.[11] Leighton's *Cimabue's Madonna* and the paintings of Watts and Sir Charles Eastlake were more academic in their bias, whereas the narrative tradition was represented by William Augustus Egg's *Past and Present* (then more graphically entitled *The Adultress and her Fate*) and by W. P. Frith's huge and bustling *Ramsgate Sands*. Sculpture was not overlooked, and it was here that Hardy had his first opportunity to see the work of Thomas Woolner, an artist whose images were to significantly influence the writing of *The Return of the Native*. But the most prominent artist in the British section was not a modern at all. It was Sir Joshua Reynolds, and the very large number of Reynolds portraits—thirty in all—were widely admired and much praised for their technical skill and psychological insight. The most dramatic was undoubtedly his study of Sarah Siddons as 'The Tragic Muse' (see Plate 18)—a picture which Hardy saw on a number of occasions later in life, and which contributed materially to his creation of Eustacia Vye.

The immediate effect upon Hardy of so much fine painting was that he rapidly and systematically began to make up for his lack of formal art education. The National Gallery was the obvious place to start, so on every day that the gallery was open he devoted 'twenty minutes after lunch to an inspection of the masters hung there, confining his attention to a single master on each visit, and forbidding his eyes to stray to any other.' (*EL* 69). Anticipating the charge of too earnest autodidacticism, Hardy adds that 'he went there from sheer liking, and not with any practical object', and went on to recommend the plan to the young, telling them 'that they would insensibly acquire a greater insight into schools and styles by this means than from any guide-books to the painters' works and manners.' (*EL* 69). This admirable piece of advice is all the more appropriate when seen in the context of the guidebook which Hardy consulted in these early years.

---

[11] Ibid., p. 175.

In 1863 he began to keep a notebook entitled 'Schools of Painting', containing entries about painters and their works copied from some unidentified source. The comments are cryptic, misleading, often inaccurate, and hopelessly out of date by the standards of 1863. Both the chronological range and the neoclassical taste suggest that they come from an early nineteenth-century encyclopaedia, from which Hardy learnt that Cimabue represented 'bold sublimity', Constable 'truth', and Bonington 'elegance'. Raphael Mengs, a stauch upholder of eighteenth-century academicism, is quoted on one of the painters Hardy often mentions in the novels—Correggio. His works, according to this source, represent 'an ideal beauty, with not so much of heaven as Raph[ae]l, yet surpassing that of nature, but not too lofty for our love'.[12]

In spite of such misdirected information, Hardy's visits to the National Gallery familiarized him with the work of a wide range of Old Master painters. It was here that he first saw the work of 'Giotto',[13] of Crivelli and Bellini, of Sebastiano del Piombo, of Moroni and Greuze, allusions to whose paintings appear in the novels. It was here, too, that he saw what the subtitle to *Under the Greenwood Tree* calls 'rural painting of the Dutch school', when, in 1871, the gallery was augmented by a very large number of Dutch paintings from the Peel collection. The National Gallery also possessed a fine collection of paintings by Turner, an artist whose work came to mean a great deal to Hardy when he was writing *Tess of the d'Urbervilles*, and there were more Turner canvases in another collection which Hardy frequently visited, at South Kensington. The iron sheds, jokingly known as 'The Brompton Boilers', were the temporary home of the paintings collected by the Regency connoisseurs Vernon and Sheepshanks. These two had left their pictures to the nation, and in 1857 they were made available to the public.[14] The habitués of this gallery were London art and architectural students— of whom Hardy was one—who also came to South Kensington to use the newly established collection of art reference books. There was no

[12] *The Personal Notebooks of Thomas Hardy*, ed. Richard H. Taylor, pp. 105, 114, and 108–9. Taylor does not identify the source of these notes.

[13] The Giotto painting which Hardy mentions in *Tess of the d'Urbervilles* (*TD* 507) is now thought to be the Two Haloed Mourners from the *Burial of St John the Baptist* by Spinello Aretino. See Martin Davis, *National Gallery Pictures: the Early Italian Schools*, p. 498.

[14] The paintings later became part of the collection of the Victoria and Albert Museum.

finer collection of English paintings of the early nineteenth century than this one, and though there were some works by other masters, the bulk of the collection was made up of genre and narrative painting. Here Hardy has access to works by Mulready, Wilkie, and Webster —works whose lively conjunction of narrative and image made them very popular with English audiences. The master of this style of painting, however, was very much alive and flourishing; and in 1862 Hardy was almost certainly one of the 83,000 people who crowded into a small gallery in the Haymarket between April and September to marvel at W. P. Frith's *The Railway Station*.[15]

If the National Gallery introduced Hardy to the works of the Old Masters, and the South Kensington collection provided him with his first experience of narrative painting, his art education was further extended by the exhibitions at the Royal Academy. For Hardy, however, the Academy was much more than just an exhibition space. He loved it as an institution, and not only did he regularly attend the annual exhibitions, but, as his fame as a novelist grew, he was invited to the private viewings and to the dinners held there. Something of the importance of the Royal Academy to Hardy is expressed in *The Hand of Ethelberta*. Ethelberta, like Hardy himself, is 'a firm believer in the kindly effects of artistic education' (*HE* 191), so she takes her two humble brothers on a didactic trip to the annual exhibition. With their untutored taste they tend to indulge in 'curious speculations on the intrinsic nature of the delineated subject', but Ethelberta knows better. 'Catalogue in hand', she encourages her brothers to see beyond the anecdotal and the curious and to appreciate the pictures 'as art'—to appreciate them in terms of style and technique rather than simply as illustrations (*HE* 191–2).

In this episode it is the summer exhibition of modern painting which Ethelberta is attending, but the winter exhibitions were equally impor-

[15] Aubrey Noakes, *William Frith: Extraordinary Victorian Painter*, p. 74. In 1888 Hardy wrote to W. P. Frith to thank him 'for the handsome way' he had mentioned Hardy in his reminiscences. (See *My Autobiography and Reminiscences* iii. 432.) In the same letter Hardy remembered 'the time when I first heard your name: one fine afternoon in May, many years ago now (terribly many, indeed!) on an occasion when I strolled into the old Academy rooms in Trafalgar Square and saw a crowd round a picture, which crowd I naturally joined—and learnt from a friend who had accompanied me all that he could tell me of this renowned painter of the Derby Day.' (*Letters* i. 183.)
Hardy may have been confused about which of Frith's pictures he first saw. Frith usually exhibited his pictures at the Academy, and indeed *Derby Day* was shown there, and drew large crowds. That, however, was in 1858, and before Hardy visited London. It seems more likely that Hardy saw *The Railway Station* in the same year that he went to London. This picture is now at Royal Holloway College, London.

tant in Hardy's calendar. These were started in 1870, and the pictures were drawn largely from private collections usually closed to the public. In the early years the paintings of Sir Joshua Reynolds featured prominently, and for the first time people began to appreciate the diversity and subtlety of his portraits. In the mid-1880s it was the turn of J. M. W. Turner, and Hardy was deeply impressed by the painter's substantial imaginative range.

In his early years in London, Hardy's knowledge of art was enlarged by two other sources. During his student days he began to frequent the smaller, private galleries which tended to show paintings of a more ambitious or avant-garde nature. The French Gallery, for example, put on an annual show of works selected from the official Salon of the previous year, and when the Grosvenor Gallery opened in 1877 to show works which would not be acceptable at the Academy, Hardy made a point of attending.[16] It was in these smaller galleries that he was introduced to the work of the Impressionists, the New English Art Club, and the school of French realist painting led by Bastien-Lepage. Finally there were the critics. As early as 1862 Hardy had told his sister that he was reading Ruskin's *Modern Painters*, and as a young architect he could not have failed to have read *The Seven Lamps of Architecture* and *The Stones of Venice*. Hardy rarely mentions Ruskin by name, but his literary notes show that, during his life, he frequently turned to Ruskin's views on the nature of perception, or his ideas about verisimilitude in painting and literature. He also read the histories of Renaissance painting by Quatremère de Quincy and Richard Duppa, and was a keen student of the works of John Addington Symonds. He made notes from the writings of Francis Palgrave, and the influence of Walter Pater, whom he met in 1886, can often be detected in his writing.

Hardy's knowledge of painting and his feeling for the principles of art criticism were gained in the first place from his visits to galleries in England and his reading in the English press, but his understanding of the visual arts was considerably broadened by his numerous Continental journeys. Part of his honeymoon, in 1874, was spent looking at the pictures in the Louvre, and when he and Emma went to Versailles, Hardy bought two reproductions of Napoleonic subjects, one by Vernet, the other by Philippoteaux.[17] In the autumn of 1882 he was

[16] For the founding of the Grosvenor Gallery, see J. B. Bullen, 'The Palace of Art. Sir Coutts Lindsay and the Grosvenor Gallery', pp. 352–7.

[17] These are in DCM. Henri Philippoteaux (1815–84) painted battle scenes of which many hang in Versailles; Antoine Vernet (1758–1836) also specialized in Napoleonic scenes.

once again 'studying the pictures at the Louvre and the Luxembourg' (*EL* 201), and in 1887 he and his wife passed through Paris yet again. In 1888 they returned to the French capital, and this time went to see the June exhibition of the offical Salon and visited an exhibition of the drawings and manuscripts of Victor Hugo (*EL* 273–4).

Another Continental journey—this time taking in Holland, Germany, and Belgium—seems to have been especially important to Hardy, since he makes a number of half-hidden references to it in the novels. It took place in 1876. Hardy's diaries for this period were destroyed, but his wife's have been preserved, and she records many of the towns they visited and the pictures they saw. At the Hague she made a slight sketch of a painting by Paul Potter; in Antwerp she remarks that they saw several pictures by Rubens; but when they reached Brussels, she began to tire. Consequently Hardy went alone 'to see the picture gallery which', Emma said, 'was closed yesterday'. One of his visits was almost certianly to the Wiertz Museum, which Cook's *Handbook* described as 'one place that no one must fail to visit'.[18] The pictures of Antoine Wiertz (1806–65) were profoundly macabre, intensely violent, and highly melodramatic, but they were calculated to appeal to Hardy's temperament, with its penchant for the grotesque. Wiertz's best-known picture, *Deux Jeunes Filles*, or *La Belle Rosine* (1847) (Plate 7), has a curious affinity with a note Hardy made several years later, and which it may have unconsciously prompted. The juxtaposition of a girl's youthful body and a skeleton in the picture carries with it emotions and sentiments resembling Hardy's strange view of Montmartre cemetery through a window. In front of the window, and with the cemetery as a background, Hardy observed 'young women dancing the *cancan*' (*EL* 300).

Wiertz's painting was often compared with that of his fellow countryman Jan Van Beers (1825–1927), and in March and April of 1887 an exhibition of 'one or two new horrors'[19] from Van Beers was held in Bond Street in London. Hardy and his wife stayed in London between April and July of 1887 on their way back from Italy, and, since Hardy made a special point of visiting London exhibitions whenever the opportunity arose, he almost certainly saw this one. The evidence that he did so is contained in *Tess of the d'Urbervilles*. In one brief, but suggestive, sentence, Hardy's memory of the Wiertz Museum,

---

18 *Cook's Tourist's Handbook for Holland, Belgium and the Rhine* (1874), p. 56.

19 *Art Journal*, NS 50 (1887), p. 94. See also anon., *Antoine Joseph Wiertz* (Paris 1869), and H. T. Sherman, 'Belgium's Eccentric Painter, Antoine Wiertz', pp. 21–8.

6 the appearance of female field-er,6667777777777777777777777777777777777777777777777777777777777777777777777777777777777777777777777777

stimulated by his visit to the Van Beers show, is set against his recent experience of Italian art in the galleries and churches of Florence and Venice. Angel and Tess have just separated, and this separation forces Angel to take a new and different view of humanity. It now 'stood before him,' Hardy wrote, 'no longer in the pensive sweetness of Italian art, but in the staring and ghastly attitudes of a Wiertz Museum, and with the leer of a study by Van Beers.' (*TD* 331). The Wiertz picture Hardy had in mind may well have been his *Civilization of the Nineteenth Century* (Plate 8), which was both a profoundly cynical commentary on nineteenth century values and a highly appropriate image for *Tess of the d'Urbervilles*. In 1869 the *Art Journal* described the way in which the soldiers with 'cruel, jeering faces' chase, 'like some terrified gentle animal, a beautiful, young frantic mother, . . . her new-born infant in her arms'. She is driven 'to the window, and is on the point of hurling herself and her child downwards to destruction. . . . Into the arms of death she rushes now, as into her sole city of refuge.'[20]

The appearance in a fictional context of the names of Wiertz and Van Beers is curious, because their significance for Hardy was so personal, but the general meaning is clear. Hardy is making a contrast between the stark realities, the cruelty and the violence of the present, and the gentleness, the dignity and the humanity of a mythical past. Elsewhere in the same novel Hardy discovers affinities between Italian art with its 'pensive sweetness' and the appearance of female field-workers in whom 'the pensive character which the curtained hood lent to their bent heads would have reminded the observer of some early Italian conception of the two Marys.' (*TD* 364). He also finds it in the bent heads of Angel and 'Liza-Lu; on leaving Wintoncester gaol, the 'drooping of their heads' resembled 'that of Giotto's "Two Apostles".' (*TD* 507) (Plate 9).

The contrast between modern Belgian art and early Italian art presented itself most forcibly to Hardy's mind when he returned home from Italy in 1877. Genoa impressed Hardy and his wife sufficiently for Hardy to make a comparison between the famous *palazzi* and the appearance of the buildings in 'Chief Street', Christminster in *Jude the Obscure*. From Genoa they went to Pisa, visiting the Baptistry and the famous Campo Santo, and in Florence they spent some time going 'through the galleries and churches' (*EL* 246), including a visit to the

[20] *Art Journal*, NS 8 (1869), p. 365.

'Assisi frescoes' in Santa Croce where she recollected that Ruskin had admired two *basso relievos* near the door. From there they went to Rome, where they spent a large part of the month of March. Hardy confesses that he was rather oppressed by the overwhelming sense of history everywhere in Rome, and was disappointed with the state of preservation and the restoration of much early Italian work. His account of the Italian trip in *The Early Life* is very brief, but Emma's diary is more explicit about what they saw. They visited the Pinacotecà in the Vatican several times but classical sculpture seems to have featured more prominently in this part of their journey, and they returned to the Vatican on April 1st to see the collection of marbles. They also spent some time in the Capitoline Museum, where Emma remarked that a figure of Venus had 'both little toes crumpled under as if she had worn boots',[21] and Hardy bought five photographs of sculptural subjects, including the Belvedere Apollo, a Faustina, and a Juno. No doubt these served as *aides-mémoire* for the form of Car Darch, the rustic girl at Chaseborough, 'beautiful as some Praxitelean creation' (*TD* 82). He may also have bought in Rome the two busts—one of Caesar, the other of Venus de Milo—which stood for many years in his study at Max Gate. We know for certain that he purchased two pictures in Rome. They were a *St Bonaventura* and a *Head of a Monk*, and they remained at Max Gate until his death.[22]

By April 3rd they were back in Florence, where Emma noticed 'the bridge where Dante first see [sic] Biatrice [sic] (the etching we have at home)',[23] but she had very mixed feelings about the frescoes which they revisited in San Marco, Santa Croce, and San Giovanni. 'Old frescoes are *horrid* entre-nous,'[24] she confided to her diary. The nudity of Michelangelo's *David* shocked her slightly,[25] and the numerous visits to the Uffizi tired her, so when Hardy proposed a visit to Siena, where, presumably, he saw Duccio's *Maestà*, he rose at five in the morning and went alone.[26]

21 *Emma Hardy's Diaries*, ed. Richard H. Taylor, p. 149.
22 *Catalogue of Furniture and Paintings and Prints . . . from Max Gate*, entries 131–2. The *St Bonaventura* is described as being 'in old carved gilt frame, written on back "bought in Rome by T. H." 16" × 13"', and the *Head of a Monk* is said to have 'written on back "purchased in Rome in 1887 by T. Hardy, Max Gate".'
23 *Emma Hardy's Diaries*, p. 127.
24 Ibid., p. 161.
25 Ibid., p. 162.
26 Ibid., p. 164.

On April 12th they left Florence, arriving on the 15th in Venice, where they immediately began visiting churches and galleries. According to Hardy himself, he 'found more pleasure in Venice than in any other Italian city' (*EL* 252), even though the weather was not the best for sightseeing. He thought that San Marco was squat as it stood on 'the glassy marble pavement of the Grand Piazza', and remembered Ruskin's description of the church in *The Stones of Venice* as 'conventional' in its ecstasy (*EL* 253). Nevertheless, the interior impressed him with its 'mosaics, mosaics, mosaics, gilding, gilding, gilding, everywhere inside and out'. He noticed the domes 'like inverted china bowls within—much gilt also.' (*EL* 253). Emma's diary suggests, as one might expect, that the highlight of this part of the journey was the painting of Giovanni Bellini. 'My art', Hardy had written in the previous year, 'is to intensify the expression of things, as is done by . . . Bellini' (*EL* 232), and Emma records detailed descriptions of the Bellinis in the Accademia and in the sacristy of the Salute.

When Hardy was in Florence, he struck up an acquaintance with the American sculptor Richard Henry Park, and went to his studio, presumably to discuss his work. This was very characteristic of Hardy, because, although he was not an eminently sociable man, he seems to have been very much at ease in the company of artists. Back in England he was welcome in the homes of W. P. Frith and Laurence Alma-Tadema. He certainly knew Helen Paterson, Arthur Hopkins, and George du Maurier, and he struck up acquaintances with some of the illustrators of the later books. In 1884 he met Edward Burne-Jones (*EL* 217), in 1886 he met Whistler (*EL* 237), and in 1891 he was impressed by the studio of G. F. Watts (*EL* 311). Hardy also made friends with two sculptors. In 1880 he met Thomas Woolner, and gave him a copy of *The Return of the Native*; in return, Woolner sent Hardy some of his verse, and gave Emma a picture attributed to Richard Parkes Bonington. Hardy was much closer to Hamo Thornycroft, however, and when the latter died in 1925, Hardy recalled all the 'pleasant hours' he had spend in Thornycroft's studio. Thornycroft was one of the many artists whom Hardy invited to his home at Max Gate. Feeling that the Wessex countryside had been neglected by landscape painters 'though within a four hours' journey from London' (*TD* 9), as he wrote in *Tess of the d'Urbervilles*, Hardy asked two artists—Alfred Parsons and Rosamund Thomson—to rectify the oversight. Parsons, whom Hardy called 'one of the most promising painters of the English landscape school',[27] agreed to come, and the two men spent much time searching the countryside for suitable subjects. In 1881 Hardy considered writing the text for a series of Dorset landscape illustrations by his first mentor in the art of water-colour, Henry Moule, and in 1905 he attended an exhibition of land-scapes by Walter Tyndale, for some of whose pictures Hardy claimed to have offered subjects (*LY* 112).

As for Hardy's own taste in art, the interior of Max Gate suggested a preference for visual objects with personal associations. In 1886 Helen Paterson's drawings for the illustrations to *Far from the Madding Crowd* were placed above one of the principal doors of the house, together with several water-colour paintings by Emma Hardy repre-senting 'actual spots that are described under fictitious names'[28] in the novels. In his study Hardy had life-size profiles of his family 'por-trayed by himself on the principle of the silhouette reversed'.[29] The sitting-room was decorated with various trophies of Continental visits, including the two portrait heads which the Hardys had bought in Rome.[30] Hardy's most prized possessions, however, were several pictures of the Dutch school. An early seventeenth-century canvas portrayed a wooded landscape with figures engaged in an archery contest, and there were two Dutch merry-making scenes showing peasant figures dancing and feasting.[31] He also owned a picture attri-buted to the Dutch painter Godfried Schalken (1643–1703)—a candle-lit interior with a group of figures.[32] Two other paintings had

[27] *Letters* i. 187. Letter to Robert Pierce Edgcumbe dated 25 Jan. 1889. Edgcumbe, who was a descendant of Sir Joshua Reynolds, owned, among other pictures, several by Reynolds.

[28] 'Celebrities at Home, no. 440: Mr Thomas Hardy at Max Gate', *The World*, 17 Feb. 1886. The anonymous writer also noticed portraits of Teniers, Mozart, Balzac, and a 'fine engraving of Sand in her prime'. Hardy's study was decorated with por-traits of Burns, George Eliot, and Admiral Sir Thomas Hardy (now in DCM), together with a number of prints, including a lively but crude 'Death of Nelson' published in 1805 by Ackerman, and a Boydell engraving of William Penn's treaty with the Indians.

[29] Ibid.

[30] These are in DCM.

[31] *Catalogue of Furniture and Paintings*, entry 124: 'A Wooded Landscape with Figures', in the foreground The Holy Family journeying, to the right an Archery con-test, and other 16th Century figures among trees, the spires, stepped gables and roofs of a City in the background. 38″ × 48″ (This picture was highly prized by Thomas Hardy and had been in his possession for many years.)' And entry 125: 'A Dutch Merrymaking'—numerous peasant figures, dancing and feasting, watched by a Group of Cavalier, Lady and Children—summer evening effect. 18″ × 25″.

[32] Ibid., entry 127: 'Interior with group of figures by candlelight by or attributed to Schalken. 9.5″ × 7″.'

personal associations for Hardy. Thomas Woolner's present to Emma—the painting ascribed to Bonington—which he kept until his death,[33] and a study of the 'Three Marys', bought from the sale of the estate of his friend William Barnes, the Dorsetshire poet,[34] which he also kept.

During his career as a novelist Hardy's taste in pictures underwent considerable change. In his early years, up to *Far from the Madding Crowd*, he was much influenced by the genre study, the narrative painting, and works which had very clear implications for literary texts. Towards the end of the 1870s he was drawn to portraiture and to certain kinds of landscape painting which integrated human figures and natural settings. When Impressionism made its mark on the London exhibitions, he was very struck by its literary potential, and a little later he seems to have made connections between this new French technique and the late works of Turner. There is some evidence that his last works, particularly *Jude the Obscure*, were influenced by another French style—the rather melancholy realism of Bastien-Lepage—which also had a profound effect on contemporary English painting. The Old Masters exerted a permanent power over his imagination, but one factor underlies his attitude to all these pictures. For Hardy, the visual image, whether a slight sketch of his own or a canvas by Rembrandt, acted as a kind of reservoir of ideas and feelings. Gérôme's *Death Upon the Cross*, which he saw at the Royal Academy in 1870, was, he said, 'a fine conception' (*EL* 100), and Gabriel Guays's *Death of Jezebel*, which he saw at the Paris Salon in 1888,[35] was also important to him, because each told its story 'in a flash.' (*EL* 273). These pictures were vivid and economical, and they stored their energy in a single image.

Hardy is neither an art-dilettante, as Norman Page would have us believe, nor the 'painter manqué' of Joan Grundy's conception;[36] his attitude to visual art is more complex than either of these two critics suggest. His taste was passionate, eclectic, and highly personal, and it grew out of a faith in the expressive power of the image. In the paintings of Crivelli and Bellini he detected the presence of the artist's

[33] Ibid., entry 130: '"Landscape of Down and Stream", inscribed on back in pencil R. Bonnington [sic] from T. Woolmer [sic] R. A. 6″ × 9″.'

[34] Ibid., entry 129: '"The Three Marys", inscribed by Hardy, "bought at Sale of Wm. Barnes, Dorset Poet, by Tho. Hardy". 7.5″ × 11″.'

[35] *The Times*, 30 Ap. 1870 and 26 May 1888, printed detailed accounts of the pictures by Gérôme and Guays respectively.

[36] Page, *Thomas Hardy*, p. 66, and Grundy, *Hardy and the Sister Arts*, p. 23.

sensibility operating on, and transforming, the objects of visual perception as a vehicle for that sensibility. He tired of pictures by Bonington because he felt that Bonington reproduced the 'simply natural', and turned, instead, to the unfashionable late Turners because they went beyond mere appearances to the 'heart and inner meaning' of visual phenomena. For Hardy, these pictures were the quintessence of expressiveness; they were 'landscape *plus* a man's soul.' (*EL* 283). Every line and every brush-stroke was permeated with human consciousness in such a way that for Hardy—to modify T. S. Eliot's remark[37]—Turner was a man who seemed to paint as nearly for the sake of self-expression as a man well can.

[37] See n. 2.

2

Three Early Novels:
Sketches in Form and Colour

'It is the artist's duty to perpetuate . . . fugitive perfections.'[1]

Though Hardy's first three published novels, *Desperate Remedies* (1871), *Under the Greenwood Tree* (1872), and *A Pair of Blue Eyes* (published serially between 1872 and 1873), are interesting intrinsically, in terms of their visual techniques, they can be regarded as a series of experiments for his later, more complete performances. Of the three, *Desperate Remedies* is the most uneven; but in some ways it is also the most ambitious. It contains a number of powerfully realized moments of great visual power, but the twists and turns of the complicated narrative inhibit the development of the visual techniques in such a way that they never manage to form a coherent pattern. *Under the Greenwood Tree* is more controlled, but also more limited. As its subtitle—'A Rural Picture of the Dutch School'—suggests, its visual mode is highly pictorial: through a series of vignettes of country life, Hardy explores some of the potential of graphic images in a verbal context. Finally, in *A Pair of Blue Eyes*, Hardy approaches the relationship between image and word in quite a different way. In this novel he tries to develop simultaneously a verbal and a visual pattern: through a number of highly stylized and graphic tableaux, he creates a visual means of expression for a plot which is equally stylized and 'unnatural' in its form.

Desperate Remedies

Desperate Remedies is in part the fruit of rejection. It was written in 1869, when, on the advice of George Meredith, Chapman's rejected *The Poor Man and the Lady*. Much of the intrigue, mystery, and suspense of the plot are Hardy's attempt to comply with Meredith's suggestion that he write a story which would capture the public

---

[1] John Addington Symonds, *Essays Speculative and Suggestive* i. 223, in *LN*, entry 1834.

imagination; but within the fast-moving narrative there are many moments which seem quite out of place in a 'sensation' novel— moments which have a hallucinatory, almost visionary power. In them the pace of the narrative is slowed down or arrested, and outward events seem to take on an inner meaning unrelated to the more mechanical cause-and-effect of the murder mystery. These moments are eminently characteristic of Hardy's later writing, and they are all strongly visual in their tone. Take, for example, the death of Mr Graye the architect, early in the story. Cytherea, his daughter, is attending a function in Hockbridge Town Hall, while her father is supervising some work on a nearby church-spire. She catches sight of him through the window, and, as she watches, he slips and falls to his death. Such a dramatic incident might have been handled violently or sensationally, but Hardy chooses instead to distance the event, using a highly pictorial technique. It takes place as if in slow motion, through a series of vignettes—vignettes which Cytherea, paralysed and powerless, observes through the window of the town hall. In the first of these she catches sight of her father framed in a little picture which depends for its effect on chiaroscuro—light against dark, dark against light.

Round the conical stonework rose a cage of scaffolding against the blue sky, and upon this stood five men—four in clothes as white as the new erection close beneath their hands, the fifth in the ordinary dark suit of a gentleman. (*DR* 9.)

The unusual pattern of light and dark derives from an incident which Hardy himself witnessed in his youth, and which also involved the death of a man. When Hardy was seventeen, he saw a hanging in Dorchester gaol; but he watched it not close up, as an event in life, but from three miles away, as a series of small images in a telescope. In the third-person manner of his autobiography Hardy recalled the event vividly in later life:

The sun behind his back shone on the white stone façade of the gaol, the gallows upon it, and the form of the murderer in white fustian, the executioner and officials in dark clothing and the crowd below being invisible at this distance. . . . At the moment of his placing the glass to his eye the white figure dropped downwards, and the faint note of the town clock struck eight. (*EL* 37.)

In his re-creation of the event in *Desperate Remedies*, Hardy reverses the colour contrast of the clothing, but he preserves from his experience outside Dorchester the feeling of height, the whiteness of the masonry, and the presence of a scaffold. In the novel the eyepiece of the telescope becomes the frame of the town hall window, but both the real incident and its fictional counterpart present the image in miniature. This 'picture', as Hardy calls it in the novel, 'thus presented to the spectator in the Town Hall was curious and striking', and he goes on to describe it as though it were a precise, but tiny, work of art. 'It was', he says, 'an illuminated miniature, framed in by the dark margin of the window, the keen-edged shadiness of which emphasized by contrast the softness of the objects enclosed' (*DR* 9). Like the hanged man at Dorchester, Mr Graye 'suddenly [disappeared] downwards' to his death. Hardy's reaction to this event was dramatic; 'the glass nearly fell' from his hands. But Cytherea's response to the 'sky-backed picture' is even more dramatic: she falls to the floor in a dead faint.

As Norman Page and Joan Grundy both point out,[2] Hardy employs the 'framing' device throughout his novels and short stories; but in this, the first of such pictorial incidents, Hardy's intentions seem purely experimental. He appears to be testing in literary form an effect which had great potency in life, and its success encouraged him to adopt it extensively in his later work. In the case of the death of Mr Graye, however, Hardy fails to exploit the device, and the fall from the church-spire is important only for the development of the narrative. Yet there are visual techniques in this novel the emotional and thematic power of which Hardy does begin to realize to the full. One of the most fruitful is used in the first meeting between the heroine, Cytherea Graye, and her future employer, Miss Aldclyffe. The meeting takes place in a Budmouth inn, and it is notable for Hardy's manipulation of setting, colour, and mood, and for the way in which pictorialism is introduced as an integral part of the narrative strategy.

Cytherea is shown into an ante-room of the inn to wait for Miss Aldclyffe. It is 'a nondescript chamber, on the shady side of the building', and its situation and colouring form a correlative to the young woman's state of mind.

The prevailing colour of the walls, curtains, carpet, and coverings of furniture, was more or less blue, to which the cold light coming from the north-easterly sky, and falling on a wide roof of new slates—the only object the small window commanded—imparted a more striking paleness. (*DR* 57.)

---

[2] Page, *Thomas Hardy*, pp. 79–80, and Grundy, *Thomas Hardy and The Sister Arts*, p. 41.

Cytherea feels unwanted, unemployable, and insignificant—emotions for which the lowliness of the waiting-room, together with its coldness and paleness, are an admirable vehicle. Her one hope of escape from this condition lies with Miss Aldclyffe, whom she will meet in the adjoining apartment. Once again, Hardy uses light as the vehicle for the expression of Cytherea's agitated state of mind. Underneath the door shone 'an infinitesimally small, yet very powerful, fraction of contrast—a very thin line of ruddy light, showing that the sun beamed strongly into this room adjoining' (*DR* 57).

At first Cytherea begins 'picturing a wonderful paradise on the other side as the source of such a beam'—a paradise which forms a great contrast with her present state. But when the door opens to reveal Miss Aldclyffe herself, she stands not in paradise but in a fiery furnace:

The direct blaze of the afternoon sun, partly refracted through the crimson curtains of the window, and heightened by reflections from the crimson-flock paper which covered the walls, and a carpet on the floor of the same tint, shone with a burning glow round the form of a lady standing close to Cytherea's front with the door in her hand. The stranger appeared to the maiden's eyes—fresh from the blue gloom, and assisted by an imagination fresh from nature—like a tall figure in the midst of fire. (*DR* 58–9.)

Momentarily, Cytherea's senses are overwhelmed by the sight of Miss Aldclyffe, much as they are overwhelmed later in the book by Edward Springrove and by Aeneas Manston; but a shift of authorial perspective immediately serves to change the psychological balance between the two women. They move into the sunlit room, and as they sit by the window, they are perceived objectively side by side.

Both the women showed off themselves to advantage as they walked forward in the orange light; and each showed too in her face that she had been struck with her companion's appearance. The warm tint added to Cytherea's face a voluptuousness which youth and a simple life had not yet allowed to express itself there ordinarily. (*DR* 59.)

Visually, the emphasis shifts from colour to form, and an allusion to the fine arts gives Cytherea precedence over the older woman. Miss Aldclyffe is likened to classical statuary: she has 'clear steady eyes, a Roman nose in its purest form, and . . . the round prominent chin with which the Caesars are represented in ancient marbles.' (*DR* 59). Cytherea, on the other hand, resembles an image from the romantic art of painting, and the stasis of sculpture is contrasted with the grace and subtlety of painted movement. As Cytherea 'turned away towards the door',

the movement chanced to be one of her masterpieces. It was precise: it had as much beauty as was compatible with precision, and as little coquettishness as was compatible with beauty. (*DR* 61.)

The 'masterpiece' is not only Cytherea's, it is also that of Greuze, for,

those who remember Greuze's 'Head of a Girl', have an idea of Cytherea's look askance at the turning. . . . The action that tugs the hardest of all at an emotional beholder is this sweet method of turning which steals the bosom away and leaves the eyes behind. (*DR* 61.)

Though the picture in the National Gallery to which Hardy refers [Plate 11] is no longer thought to be by Greuze, its mention in the text not only helps to objectify Cytherea's movement, it momentarily fixes that attitude, and holds it steady against the strong forward momentum of the narrative. Norman Page, in an article on *Desperate Remedies*, makes a similar point when he says that

part of the novelist's strategy is to detain the reader's progress through his story, briefly but perceptibly, compelling him to bestow upon such moments a closer attention than usual and demanding from him a more definite imaginative reconstruction of the scene as originally visualized.[3]

Page goes on to stress the importance of pictorialism in the novel, and undoubtedly, pictorial elements do play an integral part in the visual techniques of *Desperate Remedies*. But it could be argued that the most innovative and successful effects in the book are not actually pictorial at all. Instead, they involve the eploitation of the emotional associations of light and colour. In the course of the narrative we can observe the way in which, cautiously and tentatively, Hardy has begun to experiment with links between mood and setting, between subjectively experienced emotions and illumination, and between the life of the eye and the life of the mind.

The theme is announced early in the book, when Cytherea and her brother are travelling by train to take up a new life in Budmouth after the death of their father. The scene outside the carriage window is animated with light and colour:

The wide expanse of landscape quivered up and down like the flame of a taper, as they steamed along through the midst of it. Placid flocks of sheep

[3] Page, 'Visual Techniques in Hardy's *Desperate Remedies*', p. 70.

reclining under trees a little way off appeared of a pale blue colour. Clover fields were livid with the brightness of the sun upon their deep red flowers. (*DR* 18.)

The importance of this scene is that it is perceived only by Cytherea and her brother: they alone are gifted with the power of the innocent eye. Rather in the manner of Ruskin, Hardy moralizes about this capacity for active, visual perception:

To see persons looking with children's eyes at any ordinary scenery is a proof that they possess the charming faculty of drawing new sensations from an old experience. . . . [It is] the mark of an imperishable brightness of nature. Both brother and sister could do this; Cytherea more noticeably. They watched the undulating cornlands, monotonous to all their companions. (*DR* 18.)

Cytherea's exceptional visual sensitivity has one important implication in the text that follows: she is always present at the moments of greatest visual intensity, and she is at the centre of the field of vision where, for the first time in his writing career, Hardy attempts to establish connections between the perceived world and the mental state of his protagonist.

We have already seen how, in the meeting between Cytherea and Miss Aldclyffe, Hardy employs colour, lighting, and setting in the context of mood and feeling, and how the physical appearances of the two interiors reflect the gloom and anticipation in Cytherea's mind. Thereafter, the narrative is punctuated by similar moments—moments in which the visible is brought into great prominence, not so much for its own sake, but rather as a commentary on a deeper psychological theme.

One of these occurs soon after Cytherea's arrival in Budmouth. She and her brother visit Lulwind Cove; Owen goes off by himself to explore some local ruins, and Cytherea waits on the coast for his return. She is met not by her brother, who has accidentally twisted his ankle, however, but by Edward Springrove, Owen's architect colleague, in whom she already has a romantic interest. The emotional importance of this episode is signalled by the intensity of light and colour in the landscape, which assume a significance out of strict keeping with the development of the narrative. Where Cytherea awaited her brother,

nothing was visible save the strikingly brilliant, still landscape. The wide concave which lay at the back of the hill in this direction was blazing with the western light, adding an orange tint to the vivid purple of the heather, now at the very climax of bloom, and free from the slightest touch of the invidious brown that so soon creeps into its shade. The light so intensified the colours that they seemed to stand above the surface of the earth and float in mid-air like an exhaltation of red. (*DR* 27.)

Like the heather itself, Cytherea is 'at the very climax of bloom': she is ripe for an amorous encounter, and, with the advent of Edward Springrove, even night cannot extinguish the glow of colour from the scene in which their intimacy develops. As the couple return to Budmouth Bay on the ferry-boat, the bay is transformed into a nocturne of white, red, green, and gold.

Night had quite closed in by the time they reached Budmouth harbour, sparkling with its white, red, and green lights in opposition to the shimmering path of the moon's reflection on the other side, which reached away to the horizon till the flecked ripples reduced themselves to sparkles as fine as gold dust. (*DR* 32.)

Cytherea's second meeting alone with Edward Springrove perpetuates the conjunction of emotional arousal and heightened sensuous response. On this occasion, the occasion of their first kiss, they exchange the sturdy Lulwind ferry for a vessel of frailer proportions, and in it they sail into the deep waters of emotional entanglement. The moment of their kiss is charged with uncertainty, suspense and longing; it is emotionally important, and, like the previous aquatic scene, its uniqueness finds expression in the visual appearance of the setting.

The breeze had entirely died away, leaving the water of that rare glassy smoothness which is unmarked even by the small dimples of the least aërial movement. Purples and blues of divers shades were reflected from this mirror accordingly as each undulation sloped east or west. They could see the rocky bottom some twenty feet beneath them, luxuriant with weeds of various growths, and dotted with pulpy creatures reflecting a silvery and spangled radiance upwards to their eyes. (*DR* 50.)

The couple seem to hang in space suspended from all the gross, material constituents of life, and remote, too, from society. In the little world created by their mutual attraction, colour plays an integral part in generating 'the supremely happy moment of their existence'. At this moment 'the "bloom" and the "purple light" were strong on the lineaments of both. Their hearts could hardly believe the evidence of their lips.' (*DR* 51).

The colours in this episode suggest an interesting conjunction of art and life. As C. J. P. Beatty indicates,[4] the quotation marks hint at an allusion to the 'bloom of young desire, and purple light of Love' from Gray's 'The Progress of Poetry'. But, as Donald Davie points out, Hardy often connects the colour purple with strong sexual feeling.[5] One of the examples that he gives is the poem 'Beeny Cliff' from *Satires of Circumstance*, where the poet and his new love watched as 'purples prinked the main' (1.9). Though this poem was written in 1913, it is a reminiscence of an event which took place in March 1870, when Hardy 'went with E[mma] L[avinia] G[ifford] to Beeny Cliff. She on horseback. . . . On the cliff.' (*EL* 99). Like the two lovers in *Desperate Remedies*, the two characters in 'Beeny Cliff' are set apart, alone in a world of their own. The waves 'seemed far away' (1.4), and they were 'cloaked' in a 'little cloud' (1.7). By the time Hardy met Emma, he had already sent the manuscript of *Desperate Remedies* to Macmillan's for publication; but less than a month after the Beeny Cliff incident Macmillan returned it to him 'on the ground (it is conjectured) of their disapproval of the incidents.' (*EL* 100). In the absence of the original manuscript, it is tempting to suggest that the boating episode, with its highly charged sexual overtones and its ' "purple light" ', was either inserted or worked up in the text before it was sent off to Tinsley later in the month.

In the context of the story, however, the moment is brief and intensely fragile: Edward confesses that he is engaged to another woman, Cytherea is plunged into gloom, and the visual beauty of Budmouth Bay is shattered. Night engulfs the couple, and the lights in the harbour—the same lights which had painted such a beautiful nocturne on their return from Lulwind Cove—take on a sinister appearance, sending 'long tap-roots of fire quivering down deep into the sea.' (*DR* 53).

Thereafter, the sun never shines quite so brightly for Cytherea, and the colours of the novel modulate into deeper and more sombre tones as she makes her journey inland to Knapwater House, the employee of Miss Aldclyffe. The meeting between Cytherea and Edward Springrove is played out to the accompaniment of strong and vibrant colour, but in the second part of the book, there is another important meeting—this time between Cytherea and Aeneas

---

[4] C. J. P. Beatty, Introduction to the New Wessex Edition of *Desperate Remedies*, p. 15.

[5] Donald Davie, 'Hardy's Virgilian Purples', pp. 221–35.

Manston—which is conducted in colours of a very different hue. The encounter takes place one afternoon when Cytherea has been collecting money for a missionary enterprise. A local farmer had warned her about the possibility of inclement weather, but she had set out regardless. Soon,

the clouds rose more rapidly than the farmer had anticipated: the sheep moved in a trail, and complained incoherently. Livid grey shades, like those of the modern French painters, made a mystery of the remote and dark parts of the vista, and seemed to insist upon a suspension of breath. (*DR* 147–8.)

The suspended animation and the sense of expectancy in Budmouth Bay are accompanied by a heightening of visual awareness. The 'suspension of breath' which Cytherea experiences in the grounds of Knapwater House is more closely related to torpor and inertia—a feeling which is substantiated by the reference to French art. This is not, as has been suggested, an allusion to the work of Manet and Courbet,[6] which was little known in England in 1869.[7] Instead, Hardy is much more likely to have had in mind the work of Théodore Rousseau, Charles Daubigny, Constant Troyon, Rosa Bonheur, and Jules Breton, which he had seen for the first time at the 1862 International Exhibition. The English found the tonal range of these pictures extremely puzzling. 'Frenchmen', said one contemporary reviewer, 'are addicted to looking at nature through a glass darkly; they paint in a low key, [and] they show their preference for sombre colours.' Furthermore, a remark in the *Art Journal* of 1868 throws light on Hardy's allusion by suggesting the kind of emotion which these French paintings stirred in the British. 'The French', he wrote, 'talk in ridicule of the weather when Englishmen hang themselves; such are the dreary days on which Daubigny goes sketching. His pictures are not so much solemn and grand as dim and dirty.'[8]

The subdued colours of modern French landscape paintings set the emotional key for Cytherea's meeting with Manston, and the effect is backed up by Hardy's manipulation of composition and scale. As Cytherea drew near to the Old House in which he lived it 'rose before

[6] It is Alastair Smart who suggests this in his 'Pictorial Imagery in the Novels of Thomas Hardy', p. 278.

[7] It is true that there *was* a picture by Courbet at the International Exhibition, but, as Kenneth McConkey points out, his *Fighting Stags* 'would, in English eyes, have prompted comparison with Landseer'. See McConkey, 'Rustic Naturalism in Britain', p. 218.

[8] *Art Journal*, NS 8 (1868), p. 129.

her against the dark foliage and sky in tones of strange whiteness', and Manston's appearance has a pronounced Gothic quality.

> On the flight of steps, which descended from a terrace in front to the level of the park, stood a man. He appeared, partly from the relief the position gave to his figure, and partly from fact, to be of towering height. He was dark in outline, and was looking at the sky, with his hands behind him. (*DR* 148.)

The synaesthesia of Cytherea's encounter with Springrove in Budmouth Bay has obvious parallels in this encounter with Manston. In the earlier episode, aural, tactile, and, above all, visual sensations united to create a sense of harmony and unity; here, the same sensations conspire to mesmerize her. The touch of Manston's clothing, the sound of his organ playing, the rumble of thunder, and the unnatural light in which 'everything' was pervaded by 'a general unearthly weirdness' (*DR* 154) have a paralysing and confusing effect on her mind. It is her sense of sight, however, which is most affected, and the light of the setting sun fills her mind with a stream of conflicting images.

> The wet shining road threw the western glare into her eyes with an invidious lustre which rendered the restlessness of her mood more wearying. Her thoughts flew from idea to idea without asking for the slightest link of connection between one and another. One moment was full of the wild music and stirring scene with Manston—the next, Edward's image rose before her like a shadowy ghost. (*DR* 157.)

The light of the setting sun is especially important here, because Hardy almost manages to create a symbol for the unconscious movement of the mind. Sunsets had a powerful effect on Hardy as we have already seen, and in *Desperate Remedies* sunsets usually involve extreme mental states. When Cytherea recovers from witnessing the death of her father, for example, the first sight which greets her eyes is 'the southwestern sky', and 'without heeding', or as we might say unconsciously, she perceived 'white sunlight shining in shaft-like lines from a rift in a slaty cloud.' (*DR* 11). Hardy, in an authorial aside, explains the significance of this event. 'Emotions,' he says,

> will attach themselves to scenes that are simultaneous—however foreign in essence these scenes may be—as chemical waters will crystallize on twigs and wires. Ever after that time any mental agony brought less vividly to Cytherea's mind the scene from the Town Hall windows than sunlight streaming in shaft-like lines. (*DR* 11.)

'There are few', says the narrator in *A Laodicean*, 'in whom the sight of a sunset does not beget as much meditative melancholy as contemplative pleasure' (*L* 3–4), and in Hardy's mind sunsets seemed to be especially associated with the melancholy of unhappy marital relations. In *The Mayor of Casterbridge* the sale of Susan Henchard is accompanied by a brilliant sunset; in *The Woodlanders* Grace watches Fitzpiers ride eastwards to his rendezvous with Felice Charmond as the sun sinks in an even more colourful display in the west; in *Tess of the d'Urbervilles*, Angel and Tess become engaged in the 'almost horizontal' shadows of the sun setting over Talbothays; and in Hardy's own life the sun seems to have co-operated to produce an extraordinary effect at the point when marital difficulties were raising themselves between him and Emma. Emma's diary makes it clear that she and Hardy were out of sympathy on their journey up the Rhine in 1876. Against her will he insisted that they climb to the top of the tower on the Königsstuhl, where the setting sun produced 'an optical effect that was almost tragic.' (*EL* 145). But it is in *Desperate Remedies* that he makes the first link between the 'melancholy' light of the sun's decline and the pains of marriage. Manston is about to propose to Cytherea once again, and she knows that she will not have the power to resist him. The episode takes place in a setting filled with images of dissolution—a ruin in the foreground and an overgrown garden in the background—and the whole landscape is coloured by the light of the setting sun.

They were standing by the ruinous foundations of an old mill in the midst of a meadow. Between grey and half-overgrown stonework—the only signs of masonry remaining—the water gurgled down from the old mill-pond to a lower level, under the cloak of rank broad leaves—the sensuous natures of the vegetable world. On the right hand the sun, resting on the horizon-line, streamed across the ground from below copper-coloured and lilac clouds, stretched out in flats beneath a sky of pale soft green. All dark objects on the earth that lay towards the sun were overspread by a purple haze, against which a swarm of wailing gnats shone forth luminously, rising upward and floating away like sparks of fire. (*DR* 254.)

This sunset proposal stands in strong contrast to Springrove's sunset kiss. What was brilliant in the earlier episode has become cloying—copper, lilac, green, purple, and gold—in the later one, and what was suspended animation has become stagnancy and paralysis. In Budmouth Bay the two lovers had been the focus of natural, pleasurable sensations; in the water-meadows all is ruinous and rank, and, says the narrator, 'the helpless flatness of the landscape gave [Cytherea] . . . as it gives all such temperaments, a sense of bare equality with, and no superiority to, a single entity under the sky.' (*DR* 254). Hardy even evokes the idea of an aquatic journey to stress the contrast between the earlier and the later episode. It was in a rowing boat, and with eyes open, that Cytherea had experienced 'the supremely happy moment of [her] existence'; now, with Manston about to renew his offer of marriage, she felt 'as one in a boat without oars, drifting with closed eyes down a river—she knew not whither.' (*DR* 255).

The visual patterns of *Desperate Remedies* remain incomplete however; they are never fully developed, and are finally destroyed by the exigencies of the plot. Nevertheless, even in this early work, Hardy exploits something of the symbolic power of the visual image, and he begins to manipulate light and colour to produce scenes of great strength and vividness. In the next two novels—*Under the Greenwood Tree* and *A Pair of Blue Eyes*—he abandoned this particular line of exploration, and it was not until he came to write *Far from the Madding Crowd* in 1873 that he once again utilized the associative potential of illumination and the emotional significance of colour contrasts.

Under the Greenwood Tree

Under the Greenwood Tree is a much more unified narrative than *Desperate Remedies*, and that unity is achieved, at least in part, through simplification. The complex plot of the earlier novel is replaced by the simple story of Mellstock choir and the courting of Fancy Day by Dick Dewy. The setting of the story is confined to a corner of the Wessex countryside, and the social spectrum of the narrative is limited to Parson Maybold at one end and the cottagers at the other. All the vistas, the panoramas, the light and the colour of *Desperate Remedies* have gone, and instead, Hardy's eye is focused on cottage interiors, small sections of Mellstock village, vignettes of roadway and garden. To put it more abstractly, the action of *Under the Greenwood Tree*, unlike that of *Desperate Remedies*, takes place in the foreground and middle-ground. Long perspectives rarely open before the reader; he never catches a glimpse of the horizon; and the novel contains none of those moments of almost supernatural, heightened visual awareness which were so effective in the previous book.

The change in Hardy's style can be attributed, in part, to his response to criticism. We know that at this early stage of his career he was extremely sensitive to the comments of reviewers, and that he reacted bitterly to the slightest hint of faultfinding. He was probably equally sensitive to praise, and the one thing about *Desperate Remedies* that the critics agreed on was Hardy's masterly depiction of rural life. The rustic scenes, said the reviewer in the *Spectator*, reminded him of 'the paintings of Wilkie and still more perhaps of those by Teniers',[9] and he went on to suggest that Hardy possessed 'powers that might and ought to be extended largely in this direction'. Writing in the *Saturday Review*, Hardy's friend Horace Moule expressed similar views. The cider-making episode around Mr Springrove's cottage, he said, was 'the same sort of thing in written sentences that a clear fresh country piece of Hobbema's is in art'.[10] With the names of Wilkie, Teniers, and Hobbema before him, Hardy seems to have made up his mind that his next novel would indeed be a 'clear, fresh, country piece', and to make sure that the critics were in no doubt about this he gave it the subtitle 'A Rural Painting of the Dutch School'.

Hardy's choice of Dutch art for his subtitle was determined by a number of factors. One of these must have been George Eliot's praise of Dutch art in her second novel, *Adam Bede*, for its 'rare, precious quality of truthfulness . . . which lofty-minded people despise'.[11] She was, of course, quite right about the status of Dutch art amongst connoisseurs. Earlier in the century it had enjoyed considerable vogue, but by 1859 collectors, influenced by Ruskin, Lord Lindsay and other critics had turned their attention to early Italian art. Just at the moment when Hardy was writing *Under the Greenwood Tree*, however, an event took place which temporarily reversed this trend. In June 1871 a large collection of Dutch paintings was put on show at the National Gallery. It comprised seventy pictures from the collection of Sir Robert Peel, and was the largest single addition to the National Gallery since its foundation in 1824. Now, in one gallery, Hardy was able to see several examples of the works of those painters with which his own rustic scenes in *Desperate Remedies* had been compared. There were eight pictures by Teniers and four by Hobbema, including his *Avenue at Middelharnis* [see Plate 14] which was later to play such an important part in Hardy's attitude to landscape.[12] The Peel Collec-

---

[9] The *Spectator*, 22 Apr. 1871, pp. 481–83, in *Thomas Hardy: The Critical Heritage*, ed. R. G. Cox, p. 4.   [10] *Saturday Review*, 30 Sep. 1871, in *ibid.*, p. 8.
[11] *The Works of George Eliot*, Cabinet Edition, *Adam Bede* (1859) i. 268.
[12] See Ch. 4 below.

tion also contained paintings by English artists who had succeeded to the Dutch tradition. David Wilkie, for example, was represented by his *John Knox Preaching Before the Lords of the Congregation*. But Hardy was already familiar with Wilkie's painting from his visits to the 'Brompton Boilers', and in certain important ways the spirit of English rustic genre painting is closer than the works of the Dutch painters to the scenes of *Under the Greenwood Tree*. Pictures like Thomas Webster's *A Village Choir* (1847) [Plate 10] or William Collins's *Rustic Civility* (1837) are often associated with Hardy's novel,[13] and were, in their own day, enormously popular. Their appeal lay in the Englishness of their settings, and the fact that they excluded all boorishness, bawdiness, and vulgarity, which, in the eyes of the Victorian public, frequently marred scenes of Dutch merry-making. It is these sentiments which underlie Richard Redgrave's praise of English genre painting in the South Kensington catalogue where he wrote that these pictures are 'illustrations of everyday life and manners among us, appealing to every man's observations of nature and to our best feelings and affections'.[14] The drunkenness and lechery of Dutch low life were carefully excluded from the English version of the pastoral.

In his book *George Eliot and the Visual Arts*, Hugh Witemeyer points out how extensively George Eliot draws upon genre paintings. He gives many examples of scenes whose subjects resemble not only Dutch genre painting, but also English narrative painting, 'conversation pieces', group and portrait studies. Witemeyer explains that the attraction for George Eliot lay in the sanctification of domesticity. 'Often', he writes,

the painter appears to value quotidian existence so much that he invests profane subjects with a numinous, radiant, almost sacred aura that evokes memories of the religious art from which secular painting originally derived.[15]

Undoubtedly Hardy shared with George Eliot the desire to celebrate the quiet dignity of rural life, and that notion of dignity had been implanted in the public imagination by the experience of genre painting. Furthermore, he must have been strongly influenced by George Eliot's success in exploiting the pictorial image in a literary text;

---

[13] As, for example, by Page, 'Hardy's Dutch Painting', p. 40.
[14] Richard Redgrave, *A Catalogue of the British Fine Art Collections at South Kensington*, p. 10.
[15] Witemeyer, *George Eliot and the Visual Arts*, p. 106.

indeed, many of the genre studies which both Joan Grundy and Norman Page identify in Hardy's work owe something to George Eliot's example.[16] Yet there is an important difference between the way in which George Eliot employs images from paintings and Hardy's use of similar images. This is well illustrated by her account of the dairy at Hall Farm in *Adam Bede*, which, as Witemeyer points out, is unmistakably a Dutch scene.[17]

The dairy was certainly worth looking at: it was a scene to sicken for with a sort of calenture in hot dusty streets—such coolness, such purity, such fresh fragrance of new-pressed cheese, of firm butter, of wooden vessels perpetually bathed in pure water; such soft colouring of red earthenware and creamy surfaces, brown wood and polished tin, grey limestone and rich orange-red rust on the iron weights and hooks and hinges. But one gets only a confused notion of these details when they surround a distractingly pretty girl of seventeen, standing on little pattens and rounding her dimpled arm to lift a pound of butter out of the scale.[18]

The colours—red, cream, brown, grey, and orange—in George Eliot's prose, convey a strong sense of the pictorial, a sense which is increased by the presence of the anonymous girl of seventeen framed by the objects of butter and cheese-making. The pictorialism of the scene holds the image of the dairy in the mind, and enhances its power as an emblem of purity, coolness, and rural wholesomeness. Yet George Eliot's response to her self-created artefact is not exclusively visual. Tactile and olfactory words—the 'firmness' of the butter and the 'fragrance' of the new-pressed cheese—serve to enhance the qualities with which she wishes to endow the dairy. So what she is communicating to her reader through her use of the English or Dutch genre picture is not just a number of formal qualities. She is interpreting what she sees by selecting those things which impress her most, and not all of them impress just her eyes. If this description of the Hall Farm dairy is compared with the appearance of the Mellstock choir when it arrives as a group in Parson Maybold's study, the difference between George Eliot's treatment of pictorial forms and Hardy's becomes immediately apparent.

The choir, led by Mr Dewy, has come to Parson Maybold in the form of a deputation, to enquire about the new arrangements for church services. Dewy is already in the room, the parson drops his

[16] Grundy, *Hardy and the Sister Arts*, p. 31; Page, *Thomas Hardy*, p. 68.
[17] Witemeyer, *George Eliot and the Visual Arts*, p. 108.
[18] *Adam Bede* i. 120.

pen, and, anticipating a fight between the two men, the remainder of the choir push into the doorway.

Thus, when Mr Maybold raised his eyes after the stooping he beheld glaring through the door Mr Penny in full-length portraiture, Mail's face and shoulders above Mr Penny's head, Spinks's forehead and eyes over Mail's crown, and a fractional part of Bowman's countenance under Spinks's arm—crescent-shaped portions of other heads and faces being visible behind these—the whole dozen and odd eyes bristling with eager inquiry. (*UGT* 88.)

Hardy's account of the choir has often been compared with Thomas Webster's painting *A Village Choir* (1847) [see Plate 10], which he must have seen in the collection at South Kensington. Certainly, Hardy's arrangement of the figures in Mr Maybold's doorway is similar to that in Webster's composition, each figure partly obscured by the one in front, and the whole group exuding rustic joviality. In verbal terms, however, Hardy's rendition of the pictorial image is decidedly more technical than George Eliot's account of the Hall Farm dairy. Hardy focuses exclusively on the visual image as it might appear in a picture; appeal is made only to the sense of sight, and associations of a non-visual kind are excluded. Whereas George Eliot's prose represents a meditation before a picture—a meditation which sets in train a number of extra-visual associations—Hardy is concerned with his 'picture' simply as an amusing image. For George Eliot the picture is a powerful source of sentiment. Hardy's view is more professional, and, like his own heroine in *The Hand of Ethelberta*, he prefers to view his pictures 'as art', rather than 'to indulge in curious speculations on the intrinsic nature of the delineated subject' (*HE* 192).

　　It would, of course, be absurd to suggest that Hardy employs pictorialism solely for formal reasons, or that he responds exclusively to line, shape, and colour. In *Under the Greenwood Tree*, and elsewhere in his work, he is as sensitive to sentiment and emotions generated by pictures as any of his contemporary novelists. Nevertheless, both in art and in life, he has a greater propensity to respond to visual configurations for their formal properties first and their sentimental characteristics second. The amusement which he extracts from the account of the Mellstock choir depends to a much greater extent than George Eliot's view of the Hall Farm dairy upon its intrinsically pictorial nature, and upon the way in which human beings appear when they are painted as a group on canvas. *Under the Greenwood Tree* is filled

1. Giovanni Bellini: *The Agony in the Garden*. 1465? National Gallery, London (81×127 cm)

2. Carlo Crivelli: *Pietà*. National Gallery, London (72.4×55.2 cm)

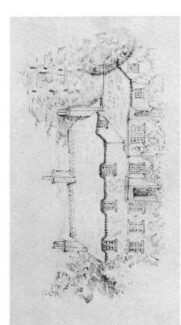

3. Thomas Hardy: *From Blackheath Corner* (Hardy's first attempt at sketching from nature). 1850? Dorset County Museum, Dorchester

4. Thomas Hardy: *Higher Bockhampton, Hardy's Birthplace.* n.d. Dorset County Museum, Dorchester

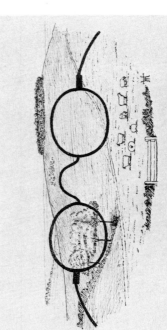

5. Thomas Hardy: Illustration for 'Her Death and After', from *Wessex Poems.* 1898. City of Birmingham Museum and Art Gallery

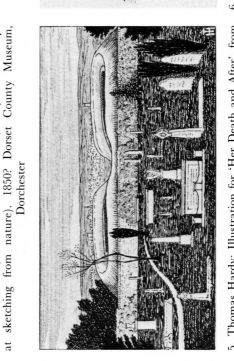

6. Thomas Hardy: Illustration for 'In a Eweleaze near Wetherbury', from *Wessex Poems.* City of Birmingham Museum and Art Gallery

with glimpses of Mellstock society, seen not as it might be in life, but as it would be if painted on canvas. When, for example, Dick Dewy visits Fancy Day to return her handkerchief, Hardy employs the motif of the girl at the cottage door familiar in both Dutch and English painting:

The door opened, and three-quarters of the blooming young school mistress's face and figure stood revealed before him; a slice on her left-hand side being cut off by the edge of the door. (*UGT* 63.)

In describing a similar scene George Eliot would have undoubtedly used the form 'her face and figure hidden by the edge of the door' to describe Fancy Day.' Hardy's word 'slice' represents what Roger Fry much later called 'the artist's vision'.[19] It is an observation made by a trained draughtsman familiar with the foreshortening and truncation of the retinal, stereoscopic image when it appears on canvas. In *Under the Greenwood Tree* Hardy's images are frequently pictorial in this special sense. Whereas George Eliot's pictorialism involves responses analagous to those which the general art-lover might experience before a picture, Hardy's often develops the comic potential latent in the difference between a scene in nature and its two-dimensional representation on a flat surface.

This self-conscious stylization of the image extends to the many individuals and groups of figures found in this novel. In *Desperate Remedies* we saw how the framing of Mr Graye's death imparted a peculiar hypnotic power to the event; in *Under the Greenwood Tree* incidents or characters are often contained in 'frames', but the device does not endow them with any sense of mystery. On the contrary, it tends to focus attention on them as characteristic and thoroughly delightful examples of the humble and the homely. When, for example, the Mellstock choir sings outside Fancy Day's cottage, the blind in her window is pushed up, 'revealing to thirty concentrated eyes a young girl framed as a picture by the window architrave' (*UGT* 29). Her beauty is illuminated 'to a vivid brightness by a candle she held in her left hand close to her face'.

Her appearance, which is familiar in Dutch art, but which Norman Page ingeniously likens to Rossetti's poem and painting *The Blessed Damozel*,[20] provides a foil to a more abstract and comic rendering of

---

[19] Roger Fry, 'The Artist's Vision', in *Vision and Design*, ed. J. B. Bullen (Oxford: Oxford Univ. Press, 1981), pp. 33–8.
· [20] Page, *Thomas Hardy*, p. 69.

the same situation. Farmer Shiner appears in his window when he, too, hears the choir. Unlike Fancy Day, he does not welcome the interlude, and can be seen 'wildly flinging his arms and body about in the forms of capital X's and Y's' (*UGT* 31).

Joan Grundy suggests that Hardy uses the devices of pictorialism to endow his scenes with a special kind of clarity. 'Most of the time in reading [Hardy's] work', she says,

we know though with varying degrees of awareness, that we are looking at pictures. But the effect, after that first sense of alienation . . . has worn off, is to heighten rather than to diminish our sense of reality. The pictures are so vivid that they have life, as actual pictures . . . have it. Their effect is simultaneously to idealise and to reify. The pictures have such finish and perfection *as* pictures that we seem to see the scenes and objects depicted with an almost hallucinatory clarity.[21]

Though one might agree that sometimes the function of the pictorialism in Hardy's writing is to idealize life, does his use of the pictorial image really increase our sense of 'reality', as Joan Grundy would have us believe? Surely it is the reverse. The consciousness of the picture within the text creates the effect of observing life at one remove, and as such, it is surely a deliberate and anti-naturalistic device. Hardy's own remarks about the art of novel-writing suggest that he had no interest in 'mere photography'—producing a transcript of observed phenomena. Instead, pictorialism is a subtle reminder to the reader that the text, like the pictures which are used as models, is in fact a work of art; the very presence of 'pictures' in the text draws attention to the fact that the scenes are not fragments of life but are essentially verbal transcriptions of visual effects.

One of the most famous vignettes in *Under the Greenwood Tree* brings this out very clearly. In it, the Mellstock choir is 'discovered' in a group outside Mr Penny's workshop. Visualization in this scene is stressed by Hardy's careful arrangement of the source of light. 'It was', he says, 'the evening of a fine spring day. The descending sun appeared as a nebulous blaze of amber light, its outline being lost in cloudy masses hanging round it like wild locks of hair.' (*UGT* 68).

The choir is then grouped in this light as it stands near Mr Penny's workshop.

The chief members of Mellstock parish choir were standing in a group in front of Mr Penny's workshop in the lower village. They were all brightly il-

---

21 Grundy, *Hardy and the Sister Arts*, p. 23.

luminated, and each was backed by a shadow as long as a steeple; the lowness of the source of light rendered the brims of their hats no use at all as a protection to their eyes. (*UGT* 68.)

Mr Penny forms a picture within this picture. He is placed in his shop which was 'low and wide, and was open from morning till evening, Mr Penny himself being invariably seen working inside like a framed portrait of a shoemaker by some modern Moroni.' (*UGT* 68). Finally, Hardy adds the multiple details of the full genre study:

He sat facing the road, with a boot on his knees and the awl in his hands. . . . Rows of lasts, small and large, stout and slender, covered the wall which formed the background in the extreme shadow of which a kind of dummy was seen sitting. (*UGT* 68.)

Like the famous Moroni *Portrait of a Man (The Tailor)*, in which the tailor is standing in 'flannel jacket, red breaches . . . at his board with shears in his hand, about to cut a piece of black cloth',[22] [Plate 12] Mr Penny is depicted in the act of practising his trade. Hardy's choice of Moroni might well have been influenced by the sight of three of his portraits at the exhibition of Old Masters at the Royal Academy in 1870. Moroni's work, said the critic of *The Times*,

excels both in the power of seizing the subtlest elements of his sitter's personality, and of so setting them before us that, no matter how tame, homely, or commonplace the man, they not only live for us, no more to be forgotten, but interest us as the living personage never could have done.[23]

Hence, Moroni not only imparts interest to the commonplace, he actually manages to make it more intriguing than it would be in reality. This is important in the context of *Under the Greenwood Tree* because it provides a useful clue to Hardy's use of pictorialism in this novel. Like Moroni in his portraits, Hardy constantly strives to keep some kind of aesthetic distance between the reader and the events depicted. The placing of the events at some unspecified period between 1820 and 1830 and the choice of a remote location in Wessex both contribute to the impression of a 'clear, fresh, country piece'—an impression which the substitution of the name of a contemporary realist like Courbet[24] for Moroni would instantly destroy. The view in

[22] R. N. Wornum, *The Abridged Catalogue of the Pictures in the National Gallery: Foreign Schools*, pp. 67–8.

[23] *The Times*, 17 June 1870, p. 4.

[24] Philip Gilbert Hamerton wrote extensively about Courbet in his *Painting in France After the Decline of Classicism*, p. 13.

Under the Greenwood Tree is lent further enchantment by Hardy's visual techniques: all the harshness of agrarian life is excluded (which is not the case in some of the later novels), and the scenes around Mellstock are literally 'picturesque'.

There are, of course, many pictures in the narrative of *Under the Greenwood Tree*, but what they share with one another is not so much their effects of colour and lighting as their close attention to form—to arrangement in space, to composition, and to grouping. Many of them are comic, and frequently they depend for their humour on the simple observation of formal properties. The interior of Mr Day's cottage, for example, resembles a Victorian puzzle picture:

The most striking point about the room was the furniture. This was a repetition upon inanimate objects of the old principle introduced by Noah, consisting for the most part of two articles of every sort. (*UGT* 97.)

In addition to the two clocks made by the Casterbridge clock-makers, 'whose desperate rivalry throughout their lives was nowhere more emphatically perpetuated than here at Geoffrey's', there were, the narrator tells us,

a couple of kitchen dressers, each fitted complete with their cups, dishes, and plates, in their turn followed by two dumb-waiters, two family Bibles, two warming pans, and two intermixed sets of chairs. (*UGT* 97.)

This comic stylization runs like a thread through the book, particularly in the treatment of human figures. The boot-maker, for example, as he drinks from his mug, has 'all but the extremes of . . . [his] face . . . eclipsed by the circular brim of the vessel' (*UGT* 18). Hardy uses geometric shorthand to describe Mrs Penny's eyes as 'little straight lines like hyphens' (*UGT* 49), or the eyes of the innkeeper who serves Dick and Fancy as drawn 'into circles.' (*UGT* 132).

The simplest manner of reducing the human shape to pictorial form is by means of the silhouette, and *Under the Greenwood Tree* is filled with silhouettes. The anonymous observer of the first scene sees the approaching choir led by Dick Dewy: 'Having come more into the open he could now be seen rising against the sky, his profile . . . like a portrait of a gentleman in black cardboard.' (*UGT* 4). We know that Hardy had a personal interest in portrait silhouettes, because in his youth he drew a number of the members of his family in this way.[25] In 1886 he had them displayed in his study, giving to the room,

25 Now in DCM.

according to the writer in *The World*, 'a weird and sombre effect'. The silhouettes stood like

a procession of Acherontic ghosts, pallidly emerging from black fog, but really life-sized profiles of various members of Mr Hardy's family, portrayed by himself on the principle of the silhouette reversed and somewhat suggestive of the groups of family portraits by Ambrogio Borgonone in the National Gallery.[26]

Hugh Witemeyer points out the connection between the silhouette and its use in the study of phrenology. The standard form of illustration in Lavater's writings on the subject was the silhouette, and Witemeyer suggests that the first portrait of Amos Barton in George Eliot's *Scenes of Clerical Life* bears the impress of George Eliot's own interest in phrenology.[27] Since Hardy visited a phrenologist in 1864, and thought it worthwhile to keep the report for the rest of his life,[28] it must be presumed that he, too, attached importance to the evidence of physiognomy as a guide to character. Certainly the introduction of Dick Dewy and the Mellstock choir into *Under the Greenwood Tree* bears a very close resemblance to George Eliot's treatment of Amos Barton. As Dick is seen as a silhouette against the sky, he 'assumed the form of a low-crowned hat, an ordinary-shaped nose, an ordinary chin, an ordinary neck, and ordinary shoulders. What he consisted of further down was invisible from lack of sky low enough to picture him on.' (*UGT* 4–5). In *Scenes of Clerical Life*, 'as Mr Barton hangs up his hat in the passage, you see that a narrow face of no particular complexion . . . with features of no particular shape, and an eye of no particular expression, is surmounted by a slope of baldness gently rising from brow to crown'.[29] Both Dick Dewy and Amos Barton are humble, commonplace characters, and their appearance as silhouettes confirms this fact. Hardy's use of the silhouette, however, unlike George Eliot's is exclusively visual. Its effect is comic, and the comedy lies, once again, in the reduction of human forms to flat two-dimensional images. Hardy often uses the silhouette in this way. For example, towards the end of the novel Fancy and Dick see in front of them a farmer, his wife, and another man as they all ride out of Budmouth. Fancy and Dick 'both contemplated the picture presented in front, and noticed how the

[26] *The World*, 17 Feb. 1886. The reference to Borgonone, or Bergonone, is to his *Members of a Confraternity*, a series of heads or busts formerly entitled *Family Portraits*.
[27] Witemeyer, *George Eliot and the Visual Arts*, p. 46.
[28] The report is in DCM.
[29] *Scenes of Clerical Life* i. 23.

farmer's wife sat flattened between the two men, who bulged over each end of the seat to give her room till they almost sat upon their respective wheels' (*UGT* 124). Only once in the novel does he use the effect in a situation which is not comic, and its sudden appearance towards the end of the story provides an interesting insight into the precise visual limitations which Hardy imposed upon himself while writing *Under the Greenwood Tree*.

> The scene was the corner of Mary Street in Budmouth-Regis, near the King's statute, at which point the white angle of the last house in the row cut perpendicularly an embayed and nearly motionless expanse of salt water projected from the outer ocean—to-day lit in bright tones of green and opal. Dick and Smart had just emerged from the street, and there on the right, against the brilliant sheet of liquid colour, stood Fancy Day. (*UGT* 121.)

The stress on shape—foreshortening and profile—is quite consistent with the pictorialism of this novel. What is unusual, however, is the intense burst of light and colour. Hardy had exploited the connection between strong colour and strong feeling in *Desperate Remedies*, but in *Under the Greenwood Tree* he largely excluded it. Only on this one occasion does he allow it to intrude, and here, when it does, we can see that the 'green and opal' and the 'liquid colour' of the scene derive as much from Dick Dewy's feelings for Fancy Day as from the sunlight falling on the water.

In spite of the slight hints of tragedy at the close of *Under the Greenwood Tree*, the main emphasis in the story is on the sociability and continuity of rustic life. In this respect Hardy comes close to George Eliot and her sense of the dignity of rural life, and, like her, he has chosen points of view and visual perspectives which foster this idea. The cottage and tavern interiors, which draw their inspiration from genre painting, serve to enhance the feeling of social unity, while the domestic details and the intimate grouping of the figures suggest mutual interdependence and affection. Even in outdoor scenes, figures are observed in close proximity. Nature never threatens man's existence, and hedges and streams are employed by Hardy quite specifically to prevent the mental eye from wandering beyond the events in the literary foreground. The carefully composed scenes of rustic life, with their bee-keeping, 'tranting', cobbling, and so on, all stress the value of the commonplace, while the greenwood tree itself, although it appears only at the end of the novel, provides an emblem of gentle confinement and social harmony.

The point in Yarlbury Wood which abutted on the end of Geoffrey Day's premises was closed with an ancient tree, horizontally of enormous extent though having no great pretensions to height. Many hundreds of birds had been born amidst the boughs of this single tree; tribes of rabbits and hares had nibbled at its bark from year to year; quaint tufts of fungi had sprung from the cavities of its forks; and countless families of moles and earthworms had crept about its roots. (*UGT* 206.)

The tree as a symbol of the continuity and the fruitfulness of social life is a prominent feature of the eighteenth-century conversation piece,[30] and Hardy had probably been impressed by George Eliot's picture of the Garth family grouped around a large tree in Chapter 57 of *Middlemarch*. In *Under the Greenwood Tree* it forms the centre-piece of the last vignette of the novel. It is shut in and protective, substantial but not threatening; it is broad enough to sustain much life; it is ancient, dependable, and solid. It is around this tree that Hardy gathers his little community in a final image of personal and social stability. Such an image was rarely to occur in his work again.

A Pair of Blue Eyes

For the setting of his third novel, Hardy moved from Mellstock—based upon Bockhampton of his birth—to what he called 'Outer Wessex', or North Cornwall. The cosy village scenes, the engaging but diminutive characters, all the panoply of the 'portfolio of pictures', with its amusing anecdotes and illustrative scenes, are put aside in favour of something much grander and more rugged. The difference between the sheltered environment of Mellstock and the open spaces of the cliffs of North Cornwall is pointed up by an early view from Endelstow Church. Beyond the church,

the serene and impassive sea, [was] visible to a width of half the horizon, and meeting the eye with the effect of a vast concave, like the interior of a blue vessel. Detached rocks stood upright afar, a collar of foam girding their bases, and repeating in its whiteness the plumage of a countless multitude of gulls that restlessly hovered about. (*PBE* 26.)

The expansive, almost panoramic quality of the writing is not just a consequence of the new setting. Hardy's articulation of space, size,

[30] Ronald Paulson, in his *Emblem and Expression: Meaning in English Art of the Eighteenth Century*, points out that Zoffany liked to 'arrange children . . . divided according to sex—playing around the base of an enormous old tree, signifying the continuity of generations' (pp. 154–5).

and scale is all part of a fresh approach to the relationship between character and setting and between the narrative and the visual terms in which that narrative is conceived.

In *Desperate Remedies* the visual effects and the narrative tend to work against each other until eventually the subtler patterns of light and colour are swallowed up by the plot mechanism. In *Under the Greenwood Tree* the narrative is relatively slight, but so are the comic miniatures, and the relationship between story and visual effect resembles that between text and illustration. The tavern scenes, the cottage interiors, and the activities of the choir provide material for a number of incisive and delicate rural studies, but they have little bearing on the narrative structure. In this respect *A Pair of Blue Eyes* represents a new departure for Hardy, and the command of a new skill. If *Desperate Remedies* can be seen as an experiment in visual symbolism, and *Under the Greenwood Tree* as an essay in literary pictorialism, then *A Pair of Blue Eyes* is the point in Hardy's career at which he began to develop an organic connection between the features of a plot and the visual components through which that plot is expressed. That connection is based upon a particular kind of stylization, in which Hardy punctuates a narrative filled with unlikely coincidences, strange repetitions, and echoes of past events with a number of unusual tableaux whose visual characteristics sum up or emphasize the geometric structure of the story. Displacement is one of the novel's principal themes. At the narrative level, social displacement is most graphically illustrated by Elfride's use of her lovers as stepping-stones as she moves from vicar's daughter to Lady of the Manor, but displacement also plays an important part in the visual symbolism. Many of the most memorable scenes depend for their effect upon peculiar and arresting conjunctions. The interview between Elfride and Henry Knight in a moonlit church from which one whole wall has been removed, and Elfride with her new lover and her displaced lover in a macabre little group around the coffin of Lady Luxellian, both make use of unusual physical arrangements, and in the scene in which Knight hangs dangerously from the 'Cliff Without a Name', suspended only by Elfride's underwear, the sense of displacement and incongruity verges on the absurd.

The difference between the illustrative techniques of *Under the Greenwood Tree* and the expressive ones of *A Pair of Blue Eyes* is nowhere better seen than in the way in which Hardy uses silhouette in the two novels. In *Under the Greenwood Tree* the reduction of the human form to two dimensions had a simple comic effect. In *A Pair of Blue Eyes* the silhouette is employed to suggest loneliness, isolation, even tragedy. In both novels the central figures appear for the first time as silhouettes against the sky, but Stephen Smith's journey to Endelstow Rectory has none of the sociable familiarity of the entry of the Mellstock choir. It is evening, when

> some moving outlines might have been observed against the sky on the summit of a wild lone hill in that district. They circumscribed two men, having at present the aspect of silhouettes sitting in a dog-cart and pushing along in the teeth of the wind. Scarcely a solitary house or man had been visible along the whole dreary distance of open country they were traversing. (*PBE* 5.)

The wide and bleak landscape in which individuals are reduced to mere outline suggests an environment which is vast, threatening, and inimical to man. This sense of foreboding is taken up much later in the novel by another silhouetted figure. It is that of Elfride herself, standing against the sky as she and Henry Knight take their leave for the last time. Knight descends into the valley, looks up and sees 'the stubble-field, and a slight girlish figure in the midst of it—up against the sky. Elfride, docile as ever, had hardly moved a step, for he had said Remain.' (*PBE* 384).

The image of Elfride has vested in it a power far greater than any image of Fancy Day or even Cytherea Graye. The sight of Elfride in the stubble-field remained with Henry Knight for 'weeks and months'. The picture was so vivid that it was 'engraved for years on the retina of Knight's eye: the dead and brown stubble, the weeds among it, the distinct belt of beeches shutting out the view of the house, the leaves of which were now red and sick to death.' (*PBE* 383). In an important sense Elfride is an image before she is a character; throughout the novel she is remembered by her lovers as an image carried on the mental retina—she is almost the projection of something within their own minds. Hardy is fully conscious of this notion, for he introduces his heroine into the novel as the bewitching, eponymous pair of blue eyes.

> These eyes were blue; blue as autumn distance—blue as the blue we see between the retreating mouldings of hills and woody slopes on a sunny September morning. A misty shady blue, that had no beginning or surface, and was looked *into* rather than *at*. (*PBE* 1–2.)

This extraordinary passage avoids all human associations. Elfride has no existence in her own right: she is the reflection of the image already in the eye of the beholder. The evasiveness of the analysis is extended to Elfride's temperament, which is also a series of reflections, but this time reflections from famous works of art.

Elfride had as her own the thoughtfulness which appears in the face of the Madonna della Sedia, without its rapture: the warmth and spirit of the type of woman's feature most common to the beauties—mortal and immortal—of Rubens, without their insistent fleshiness. The characteristic expression of the female faces of Correggio—that of the yearning human thoughts that lie too deep for tears. (*PBE* 2.)

Elfride's subsequent relationships with men tend to bear out this view of her as a composite of well-known master-works. Knight, who is old enough to know better, but is inexperienced in the ways of women, tends to idealize her, and is unable to see beyond the image which he has created. Stephen Smith's image of Elfride is fixed soon after his arrival at Endelstow Rectory, when, on the first evening, he asks her to sing to him. She does so, and in the ensuing tableau he is deeply moved by her appearance. While she sang, Elfride's image (the word is Hardy's) 'chose the form . . . for her permanent attitude of visitation to Stephen's eyes during his sleep and waking hours in after days' (*PBE* 18). In this highly pictorial scene, the reader is invited to examine this image:

The profile is seen of a young woman in a pale grey silk dress with trimmings of swan's-down, and opening up from a point in front, like a waistcoat without a shirt; the cool colour contrasting admirably with the warm bloom of her neck and face. (*PBE* 18.)

The colour in this passage, together with the sensuous 'bloom' on Elfrides' skin, is suggestive, as strong colour often is in Hardy's work, of sexual arousal, and the lighting contributes further to create a pictorial image:

The furthermost candle on the piano comes immediately in a line with her head, and half invisible itself, forms the accidentally frizzled hair into a nebulous haze of light surrounding her crown like an aureola. (*PBE* 18.)

Out of the first picture—a portrait study of a young girl at the piano—Hardy develops a second, more stylized image. The aureole around Elfride's head becomes the halo of a saint, and for a moment she is transformed into a medieval patroness of love.

Every woman who makes a permanent impression on a man is usually recalled to his mind's eye as she appeared in one particular scene, which seems ordained to be her special form of manifestation throughout the pages of his memory. As the patron Saint has her attitudes and accessories in medieval illumination, so the sweetheart may be said to have hers upon the table of her true Love's fancy. (*PBE* 18.)

The impression which Elfride makes on the 'table' of Stephen Smith's fancy is indeed a permanent one, and it recurs frequently in the course of the story. At the end of the novel Henry Knight finds some drawings on Smith's desk in a London hotel. Among the sketches of architectural details he sees 'rough delineations of medieval subjects for carving or illumination—heads of Virgins, Saints, and Prophets.' (*PBE* 407). Of these, 'all the feminine saints had one type of feature,' and each of them resembled Elfride as she sang to Stephen Smith at Endelstow Rectory: 'There were large nimbi and small nimbi about their drooping heads, but the face was always the same. That profile—how well Knight knew that profile.' (*PBE* 407). The modulation of an image in life into an image in portraiture in this early musical interlude is a device which Hardy frequently employs in the later novels.

Portraiture seems to have held a special fascination for him, since it represents a fine balance between naturalism and stylization, between the fleeting moment and the pose which is held in perpetuity. The portrait can be both psychologically penetrating yet simultaneously filled with symbolic adjuncts, and in *The Return of the Native* Hardy exploits to the full the power of painted portraits, portrait busts, sketches, and profiles. Even in the two novels written before *A Pair of Blue Eyes* several of the characters are transformed into portrait studies. Cytherea's 'masterpiece' of expressive movement is likened to the work of Greuze, and the individualistic features of Mr Penny resemble those in a painting by 'some modern Moroni'. In *A Pair of Blue Eyes* portraiture is everywhere. The servant who opens the gate of Endelstow House, for example, has 'a double chin and thick neck, like the Queen Anne portrait by Dahl' (*PBE* 37), and at one point Stephen Smith has the 'piquantly pursed-up mouth of William Pitt, as represented in the . . . bust by Nollekens' (*PBE* 22).[31] It is Elfride, however, who is most often portrayed as a painted image. Life is fleetingly transformed into art as she appears seductively 'with her head thrown sideways in the Greuze attitude' (*PBE* 88), while on another occasion she resembles a study by the seventeenth-century

---

[31] This bust is in the National Portrait Gallery.

Roman painter Guido Reni. She emerges from the Luxellian vault with 'the conscience-stricken look of Guido's Magdalen, rendered upon a more childlike form.' (*PBE* 298).

The most successful visual effect in *A Pair of Blue Eyes*, however, and the one which most consistently develops the connection between image and narrative, is the tableau. Marcel Proust was one of the first to point out the link between the visual symmetry of these strange set pieces and the symmetrical structure of the narrative. In a late section of *A la recherche du temps perdu* entitled 'La prisonnière', Marcel reminds Albertine of how in *A Pair of Blue Eyes*, 'the parallelism of the tombs, and also the parallel line of the boat, and the contiguous railway carriages containing the two lovers and the corpse' relate to a story where 'the woman loves three men'.[32] In fact the elements which go to make up the plot of *A Pair of Blue Eyes* are composed of many more parallels and repetitions than Proust suggests. Each of Elfride's relationships with her lovers, for example, resembles and grows out of the previous one. Her affair with the youth Simon Jethway is superseded by her love for Stephen Smith—a young man—which, in turn, is transferred to the older man Henry Knight. Finally she marries the oldest and most experienced of the group— Lord Luxellian—and dies almost immediately. There is something symmetrical, almost geometrical, about the way in which she progresses through the lives of these men. Elfride, the narrator tells us, 'looked up at and adored her new lover [Henry Knight] from below his pedestal,' just as she had 'smiled down upon Stephen from a height above him' (*PBE* 276), and this pattern of repetition extends even backwards in time to Elfride's ancestors. At one point in the story we learn that Elfride's grandmother, a Luxellian also called Elfride, eloped with a singer. The child of this union—Elfride's mother—ran away from home with Parson Swancourt, whom she later married. In the course of the novel, Elfride, like her mother and her grandmother before her, also runs away: she elopes to London with Stephen Smith. Elfride's history comes full circle when she finally marries Lord Luxellian and regains her grandmother's title. In this history physical resemblance, too, plays an important role. Elfride and her grandmother were, we are told, 'as like as peas.' (*PBE* 286).

---

32 Marcel Proust, *A la recherche du temps perdu*, (Paris: Bibliotheque de la Pléiade, 1954), iii. 376–7. My translation. J. Hillis Miller points this out in *Fiction and Repetition*, p. 152.

Furthermore, Elfride also bears a resemblance to the Lady Luxellian into whose place she marries (*PBE* 40).

At certain points in the novel, this strangely symmetrical plot receives explicit visual expression; in a number of scenes, the intangible narrative components momentarily crystallize into physical relations. The most memorable of these, and one which Proust mentions, occurs immediately after the death of Lady Luxellian, and it takes place in the Luxellian vault. It is the only scene in the book where all the major protagonists appear together, and it is the moment when Elfride's involvement with Stephen Smith briefly overlaps that with Henry Knight. Stephen Smith is already in the family vault when Knight enters, closely followed by Elfride. The scene then composes itself:

> The blackened coffins were now revealed more clearly than at first, the whitened walls and arches throwing them forward in strong relief. It was a scene which was remembered by all three as an indelible mark in their history. Knight, with an abstracted face, was standing between his companions, though a little in advance of them, Elfride being on his right hand and Stephen Smith on his left. The white daylight on his right side gleamed faintly in, and was toned to a blueness by contrast with the yellow rays from the candle against the wall. Elfride, timidly shrinking back, and nearest the entrance, received most of the light therefrom, whilst Stephen was entirely in candle-light, and to him the spot of outer sky visible above the steps was as a steely blue patch, and nothing more. (*PBE* 297.)

The strange regular patterning of the figures left and right, and the equally strong pattern of light against dark, dark against light, resembles in its formality the construction of the novel itself; and the ironic significance of the scene is increased when we know that neither of these men will marry Elfride, and that she will be the next person to be placed in a coffin in that same vault.

When Hardy completed *A Pair of Blue Eyes*, he realized that, unlike either *Desperate Remedies* or *Under the Greenwood Tree*, it was 'visionary [in] nature' (*EL* 96). Something of the kind must have been in the mind of the writer in the *Saturday Review* when he described the book as 'the most artistically constructed of the novels of its time' (*EL* 126). Moreover, Hardy noticed with approval Coventry Patmore's idea that poetry, rather than prose, might have been a more suitable medium for such a tale (*EL* 138). Patmore may have been responding to the imagery of the novel, for so many of the images in *A Pair of Blue Eyes* are unusual and highly memorable. Not least of these is the image of Elfride herself—or the multiplicity of images which go to make up her character. Unlike the roles of either Cytherea Graye or Fancy Day, Elfride's role is intimately bound up with how others see her, and even the way in which the narrator presents her suggests that his is no more than another interpretation of a number of images. This rather enigmatic portrayal of a central character raises the question as to whether she has an existence in her own right, or whether she is merely the sum of the ways in which others perceive her. In his next novel, *Far from the Madding Crowd*, Hardy pursues a similar theme, but from a different standpoint. His images, scenes, and setting are not visionary in the way in which they are in *A Pair of Blue Eyes*. The location is closer to his own home, but the question as to the trustworthiness of images becomes of overwhelming importance.

3

Far from the Madding Crowd:
Perception and Understanding

'It is a man's sincerity and *depth of vision* that make him a poet.'
'The gifted man is he who *sees* the essential point, and leaves all the
rest aside as surplusage.'[1]

Far from the Madding Crowd owes something to each of Hardy's previous
novels. In it Hardy manages to combine the brilliance of some of the
writing in *Desperate Remedies* with the control over form which he had
developed in *A Pair of Blue Eyes* in a context which is exclusively rural
like the Mellstock of *Under the Greenwood Tree*. In fact, it was written in
the hamlet of Bockhampton—the model for Mellstock—when Hardy
was staying in his parents' cottage between July 1873 and July 1874.[2]
Yet its treatment of rural life is significantly different from that in
Under the Greenwood Tree. The activities of country life are observed
with clarity and precision (as in Hardy's earlier novel) but they now
have a freshness and an immediacy which was lacking before. In the
scenes of sheep-washing, sheep-shearing, the harvest supper, and so
on, one can still detect something of the genre mode; but it is as if
Hardy had revised his response to genre-painting in the light of his
own direct experience of country life. A letter to Leslie Stephen bears
this out. Hardy wrote to Stephen, who was about to publish the novel
in the *Cornhill Magazine*: 'I have sketched in my note-book during the
past summer a few correct outlines of smockfrocks, gaiters, sheep-
crooks, rick-"staddles", a sheep-washing pool, one of the old-fashioned
malt-houses, and some out-of-the-way things.' (*EL* 128). The practice
of drawing details of scenes from his novels was one which Hardy
continued throughout his novel-writing career. He would frequently
offer them as *aides-mémoire* to the magazine illustrators (just as

---

[1] Thomas Carlyle, 'The Hero as Poet', in *Heroes and Hero Worship*; Hardy's emphasis in *LN*, entries 1404 and 1405.

[2] In January 1874 Hardy wrote to Leslie Stephen: 'I have decided to finish it [i.e.
Far from the Madding Crowd] here, which is within a walk of the district in which the
incidents are supposed to occur. I find it a great advantage to be actually among the
people described at the time of describing them. (*Letters* i. 27).

these were offered to Helen Paterson), but in this case they were done principally for his own use. The 'correct outlines' of country objects, Hardy says, were drawn 'last summer'; in other words, they were not recent sketches to aid the illustrator, but visual notes for Hardy's own benefit—a way of bringing the scenes in and around Weatherbury Farm into sharper focus. Even the actual writing of the novel—its composition and development—was done amidst the scenes which Hardy was describing. It was written, he says, 'sometimes indoors, sometimes out', and ideas were often jotted down on 'large dead leaves, white chips left by the wood-cutters, or pieces of stone or slate that came to hand.' (*EL* 127).

Hardy's drawing of the sheep-dip at Lower Waterston Farm, for example, is now lost, but in *Far from the Madding Crowd* the verbal rendition remains. The sheep-washing pool was, says Hardy,

a perfectly circular basin of brickwork in the meadows, full of the clearest water. To birds on the wing its glassy surface, reflecting the light sky, must have been visible for miles around as a glistening Cyclops' eye in a green face. The grass about the margin at this season was a sight to remember. . . . Its activity in sucking up the moisture from the rich damp sod was almost a process observable by the eye. . . . To the north of the mead were trees, the leaves of which were new, soft, and moist, not yet having stiffened and darkened under the summer sun and drought, their colour being yellow beside a green—green beside a yellow. (*FMC* 142.)

What distinguishes such a description from descriptions of similar scenes in *Under the Greenwood Tree* is the curious angle of vision. The bird's-eye view, unusual in itself, is made even more startling when the perspective is suddenly and radically changed. The panoramic is displaced by the microscopic, and from the aerial view of the pool and surrounding landscape, the narrator's eye moves rapidly to the pollen on farmer Boldwood's boots. 'Boldwood went meditating down the slopes with his eyes on his boots, which the yellow pollen from the buttercups had bronzed in artistic gradations.' (*FMC* 142). The view point finally settles at human eye-level. We see the farm hands 'dripping wet to the very roots of their hair', and it is from this vantage point that we witness the interview between Boldwood and his new neighbour, Bathsheba Everdene.

In the previous novels Hardy's techniques of visualization had been largely static in character. The set pieces of *Desperate Remedies*, the vignettes of *Under the Greenwood Tree*, and the tableaux of *A Pair of*

Blue Eyes tended to use a single point of view. In *Far from the Madding Crowd* the eye is far more agile, and in his use of close-ups, distant views, aerial views, and multiple perspectives. Hardy, as David Lodge points out, anticipates some of the effects of cinema.[3] Hardy also resembles Ruskin in this respect, for of all Hardy's contemporaries Ruskin was the master of the articulate eye. In 1874 Ruskin's *Stones of Venice* was reissued, and in one of the most famous passages Ruskin illustrates the geographical roots of Gothic style by taking his reader on a mental journey across Europe. The way in which Ruskin makes the reader see the climatic bands running northwards from the Mediterranean is very similar to the way in which Hardy, on a much smaller scale, describes the sheep-washing pool. 'We know', says Ruskin, 'that gentians grow on the Alps . . . [but] we do not enough conceive for ourselves that variegated mosaic of the world's surface which a bird sees in its migration.'[4] As Hardy had observed the forms and colours above Weatherbury Farm, so Ruskin takes his reader aloft and imagines 'the Mediterranean lying beneath like an irregular lake and all its ancient promontories sleeping in the sun'. Ruskin, like Hardy, moves dramatically from the aerial perspective to the terrestrial view. 'Let us go down nearer', he says, 'and watch the . . . change in the belt of animal life . . . striped zebras and spotted leopards, glistening serpents, and birds arrayed in purple and scarlet'. But Ruskin's principal subject, like Hardy's, is a human one, and his journey ends at human eye-level. 'Let us watch [man] . . . with reverence. . . . Let us stand by him, when . . . he smites an uncouth animation out of the rocks.'

Hardy may also have learned from Ruskin a more satisfactory way of activating the pictorial image for literary ends. *Modern Painters*, which Hardy first read in the early 1860s, and to which he continued to refer throughout his life,[5] contains many animated accounts of individual pictures or details from pictures. In the second volume, for example, Ruskin gives his reader an account of Tintoretto's *Massacre of the Innocents*. 'The scene', he says,

is the outer vestibule of a palace, the slippery marble floor is fearfully barred across by sanguine shadows, so that our eyes seem to become bloodshot and strained with strange horror and deadly vision. . . . A huge flight of stairs,

[3] David Lodge, 'Thomas Hardy and Cinematographic Form', pp. 246–54.
[4] John Ruskin, *The Works* x. 186–7.
[5] See *LN*, entries 1376, 1377, 1381, 1382, and 2199; also *EL* 50 and 253.

without parapet, descends on the left; down this rush a crowd of women mixed with the murderers; the child in the arms of one has been seized by the limbs, *she hurls herself over the edge, and falls head downmost, dragging the child out of the grasp by her weight;*—she will be dashed dead in a second.[6]

Animating the static image through a multiplicity of verbs, Ruskin turns the process of observation from a passive act into an active one. The verbal rendition of the picture preserves the visionary quality of the original, but it also acts as a commentary on the episode. In *Far from the Madding Crowd* Hardy frequently employs similar devices. In the famous sheep-shearing scene, for example, he holds his figures pictorially by setting up 'a picture of today in its frame of four hundred years ago' (*FMC* 166). But that picture is not some frozen likeness,— 'a mere photograph'; instead, Hardy animates it, as Ruskin animated the Tintoretto, linking presentation and commentary.

To-day the large side doors [of the barn] were thrown open towards the sun to admit a bountiful light to the immediate spot of the shearers' operations, which was the wood-threshing floor in the centre, formed of thick oak, black with age and polished by the beating of flails for many generations, till it had grown as slippery and as rich in hue as the state-room floors of a Elizabethan mansion. Here the shearers knelt, the sun slanting in upon their bleached shirts, tanned arms, and the polished shears they flourished, causing these to bristle with a thousand rays strong enough to blind a weak-eyed man. (*FMC* 165.)

The development in Hardy's style can be measured by comparing this scene with the account of Mr Penny's workshop in *Under the Greenwood Tree*. Both are highly pictorial: both are carefully lit, and the figures consciously grouped, but where as Mr Penny's shop provides a general illustration of village gregariousness, the scene at Weatherbury is a much richer emblem of social interdependence. Hardy invites the reader to look at the vignette of Mr Penny and the Mellstock choir; but he invites the reader to look *into* his 'picture of today' because all its details are charged with meaning. The building, for example, gains its dignity in part from association with the Elizabethan mansion, in part from the church whose shape it resembles. But the worshippers do not kneel to a God who is dead; they bow before the active principle of sunlight itself, which floods the whole episode with beneficence. Mr Penny's shop provided a static image; here the building is alive with the bustle of activity. But the activity of sheep-

6 Ruskin, *Works* iv. 272-3.

shearing is carefully structured in social terms: there are groups within groups. The six shearers form one group, the women another, while Gabriel and Bathsheba create a third group 'exclusively their own' containing 'no others in the world' (*FMC* 167). The underlying principle is still a pictorial one, but the structures of pictorial representation are now loaded with meaning, and all speak of social harmony, mutual respect, and serve to depict an integrated organic community in which each has his allotted place. All the picturesque details of a country activity help to reinforce this view, but they do so only through the manner in which, and by which, they are presented to the reader. Hardy has effectively animated his eyes, and what Ruskin said about Tintoretto might justifiably be applied to Hardy himself. 'There is not the commonest subject', said Ruskin, 'to which he will not attach a range of suggestiveness almost limitless; nor a stone, leaf, or shadow, nor anything so small, but he will give it meaning and oracular voice.'[7]

The development in Hardy's style has a parallel in his views on literary theory. While he was writing *Far from the Madding Crowd*, he was beginning to formulate a theory of writing which involved an active, penetrative attitude to the perception of natural effects. In 1877 he was pondering the nature of realism in literature. 'If Nature's defects', he wrote, 'must be looked in the face and transcribed, whence arises the *art* in poetry and novel writing? which must certainly show art, or it becomes merely mechanical reporting.' (*EL* 150-1). His own answer was that the inner eye is able to animate the surface of things, to reveal them, and to lay them bare: 'I think the art lies in making these defects the basis of a hitherto unperceived beauty, by irradiating them with 'the light that never was' on their surface, but is seen to be latent in them by the spiritual eye.' (*EL* 151). Though the words Hardy quotes are those of Wordsworth, the views are very similar to those of Ruskin. In *Modern Painters* Ruskin is careful to distinguish between two responses to the natural world— literal transcription (what Hardy calls 'mechanical reporting') and the vivid presentation of the physical world through what he calls the 'imagination penetrative'. For Ruskin it was not enough that either literature or painting should set before its audience the object or scene in a purely objective sense. The 'imagination penetrative', said Ruskin, 'never stops at crusts or ashes, or outward images . . . it

[7] Ibid. iv. 262.

describes not by outward features.'[8] Or, in a phrase which Hardy carefully copied into his notebook, 'the imaginative faculty seizes outward things from within.'[9] 'The virtue of the Imagination', Ruskin added, using an idea very similar to Hardy's notion of the 'spiritual eye', is 'its reaching, by intuition and intensity of gaze . . . a more essential truth than is seen on the surface of things'.[10] The measure of correspondence between Ruskin's views, as he set them out in *Modern Painters*, and Hardy's, as they occur in *The Early Life*, is impressive. For both, art is not mere reproduction; it involves active perception by the imagination. True art reveals to the beholder that which lies hidden beneath the surface of things. 'The power of every picture', said Ruskin, 'depends on the penetration of the imagination into the TRUE nature of the thing represented, and on the utter scorn of the imagination for all shackles and fetters of mere external fact that stand in the way of its suggestiveness.'[11] The true poetry of literary work, said Hardy, 'is achieved by seeing into the *heart of a thing* . . . and is realism, in fact, though being pursued by means of the imagination it is confounded with invention' (*EL* 190).

The primacy of the eye—whether it is the literal observing organ or the metaphorical image-making 'inner eye'—in the working of the artistic imagination is an idea shared by Hardy and Ruskin. It goes back of course to Cicero and Horace,[12] but the most recent and influential proponents of the notion were Locke and Berkeley. The feeling, as Addison put it, that 'our sight is the most perfect and most delightful of all our senses'[13] was extended by the empiricists to include the belief that it was, in philosophical terms, also the most important of our senses. The sensationalist concept of knowledge was taken over by Scottish philosophers such as Stewart and Alison, and in his *Essay on Taste* (1790) Alison devoted a long section to the importance of the eye in the development of the mind.

The science of psychology which was developed in the mid-nineteenth century depended very heavily on similar ideas. Mid-nineteenth century psychology was a mixture of philosophy, introspection, and experimentation, and was almost entirely sensationalist in its preoccupations. Naturally the senses of hearing, taste, and touch

8 Ibid. iv. 250–1.
9 *LN*, entry 2199; Hardy's transcription of Ruskin, *Works* iv. 251.
10 Ruskin, *Works* iv. 284.
11 Ibid., iv. 278.
12 Cicero, *De Oratore*, and Horace, *Ars Poetica*.
13 Quoted in Paulson, *Emblem and Expression*, p. 48.

were taken very seriously, but by far the greatest importance was attached to the sense of sight. In his *Principles of Psychology* Herbert Spencer said that it was in the human sense of sight,

in the tracts of consciousness produced by the various lights reflected from objects around and concentrated on the retina, that we find the elements of feeling most intimately woven up with the elements of relation. The multitudinous states of consciousness yielded by vision, are above all others sharp in their mutual limitations: the differences that occur between adjacent ones are extremely definite.[14]

Similarly, in the third edition of *The Senses and the Intellect*, Alexander Bain pointed out how important sight was in all fields of psychological investigation. 'The intellectual imagery derived through the eye', he said,

from the forms of still life is co-extensive with the visible creation. For the purpose of discriminating and of identifying natural things, and also for the storing of the mind with knowledge and thought, the sensations of objects of sight are available beyond any other class.[15]

John Stuart Mill, though not a professional psychologist, spoke of the 'commanding influence' of sight from the perspective of philosophy. 'It is', he said

a striking example of the commanding influence of that sense; which, though it has no greater variety of original impressions than our other special senses, yet owing to the two properties, of being able to receive a great number of its impressions at once, and to receive them from all distances, takes the lead altogether from the sense of touch.[16]

The importance to Victorian readers of the principle of *enargeia*—the power of verbal imagery to set objects, persons, or scenes before an audience—can readily be observed in the strongly visual vocabulary of day-to-day reviewing, but its place in more serious criticism is demonstrated by G. H. Lewes's 'Principles of Success in Literature'. This series of essays was first published in the *Fortnightly Review* in 1865—just when Hardy was thinking about a literary career—and throughout, Lewes stresses the importance of the eye in good literary production. This, he says,

[14] Herbert Spencer, *Principles of Psychology*, i. 169–70.
[15] Alexander Bain, *The Sense and the Intellect*, p. 238.
[16] J. S. Mill, *An Examination of Sir William Hamilton's Philosophy*, p. 226.

is because the eye is the most valued and intellectual of our senses that the majority of metaphors are borrowed from its sensations. Language, after all, is only the use of symbols, and Art also can only affect us through symbols. If a phrase can summon a terror resembling that summoned by the danger which it indicates, a man is said to *see* the danger.[17]

Like Ruskin, from whom he derived many of his ideas about expressive vision, Lewes is no simple literalist. As Hugh Witemeyer puts it, Lewes believed that

the images which language evokes in a hearer's mind can never be identical with those in the speaker's mind; they can only be analogous. Lewes, then, avoided a naïve theory of verbal pictorialism. Nevertheless, he strongly favoured the use of distinct and vivid imagery in literature. . . . All description, according to Lewes, requires 'intelligible symbols (clear images).'[18]

It is not surprising, then, that Hardy should have entered wholeheartedly into a literary tradition which stressed visualization so strongly. Ruskin's emphasis on the penetrative power of the visual imagination gained support from psychology, philosophy, and literary criticism, and Hardy must have felt openly encouraged to explore various ways of articulating a visual response which came quite naturally to him. Hardy's early experience in novel-writing gave him considerable confidence in organizing and manipulating visual effects; but in one important respect *Far from the Madding Crowd* represents a qualitative advance over all that Hardy had written before. With the exception of a few unusual moments, all the events and characters of Hardy's first three novels are observed from without. In each there is a relatively sharp separation between the narrator-observer on the one hand and the character-in-action on the other. In *Far from the Madding Crowd* this distinction has to some extent been eroded, and in an important respect characters are understood not simply as they are perceived from without, but also in terms of how they themselves perceive events and other characters. In his book *Distance and Desire* J. Hillis Miller points out how important observation is to the characters of this novel, but even he does not realize how deeply the matrix of the story is penetrated by the moral implications of perception. Hardy's characters are literally obsessed with watching each other, and almost all the events of the book develop immediately out of the act of visual perception. The activity of seeing

---

[17] G. H. Lewes, 'The Principles of Success in Literature', p. 583.
[18] Witemeyer, *George Eliot and the Visual Arts*, p. 40.

or being seen modulates, even within individual sentences, into modes of understanding or misunderstanding; judgements are made on the evidence of what Othello called 'ocular proof', and in scene after scene Hardy brings visual observation and mental perception into close alignment. The very first scene of the book demonstrates this admirably. Superficially it looks like one of those 'tranting' episodes in *Under the Greenwood Tree*, but on closer inspection its style of presentation is seen to be something quite new in Hardy's work. Not only does it contain within it several points of view, it also announces very clearly and precisely one of the major themes of the novel—the relationship between seeing and understanding. Bathsheba Everdene is observed by Gabriel Oak as she is moving her belongings to her aunt's house nearby.

Casually glancing over the hedge, Oak saw coming down the incline before him an ornamental spring waggon, painted yellow and gaily marked, drawn by two horses, a waggoner walking alongside bearing a whip perpendicularly. The waggon was laden with household goods and window plants, and on the apex of the whole sat a woman, young and attractive. Gabriel had not beheld the sight for more than half a minute, when the vehicle was brought to a standstill just beneath his eyes. (*FMC* 3-4.)

Like many scenes from the earlier novels, this one has strong pictorial overtones. 'The picture', says Hardy, 'was a delicate one', but it is also a puzzle-picture. Unaware of Oak's presence, Bathsheba drew out a looking-glass 'in which she proceeded to survey herself attentively'. The details which make up the picture—the colour, the lighting, and the composition—are all perfectly comprehensible. The puzzle lies in the full significance of the picture.

It was a fine morning, and the sun lighted up to a scarlet glow the crimson jacket she wore, and painted a soft lustre upon her bright face and dark hair. The myrtles, geraniums, and cactuses packed around her were fresh and green, and at such a leafless season they invested the whole concern of horses, waggon, furniture, and girl with a peculiar vernal charm. What possessed her to indulge in such a performance in the sight of sparrows, blackbirds, and unperceived farmer who were alone its spectators,—whether the smile began as a factitious one, to test her capacity in that art,—nobody knows; it ended certainly in a real smile. She blushed at herself, and seeing her reflection blush, blushed the more. (*FMC* 5.)

Earlier in his career Hardy would have offered this vignette for its own sake, but now the pictorialism is much richer in meaning. All the genre details are there, but Hardy's description stresses two new elements. First, he emphasizes the part played by observation and by the act of perception: Gabriel Oak *glanced* over the hedge, *saw* the wagon, beheld the sight which was 'just beneath his eyes'; moreover, the little drama takes place in the *sight* of the country animals and (paradoxically) before the 'unperceived' farmer. Furthermore, the point of view is not a single but a multiple one. The reader sees Oak as he secretly spies on Bathsheba, as she in turn contemplates her own image in the glass. The second element is an interpretative one. Bathsheba's response to her own image is highly romantic. She seemed 'to glide into far-off though likely dramas in which men would play a part'. For Gabriel Oak, 'a cynical inference was irresistible' as he observes Bathsheba's narcissism. Finally, the reader is invited to compare the responses of Gabriel Oak and Bathsheba and to make some judgement about their respective characters. Had this episode occurred in *Under the Greenwood Tree*, it would have been merely comic. An imaginary title for the genre original would have been 'Moving House' or 'Tranting in Wessex'; but now there are strong moral overtones, and another title for the picture is buried in the text. The picture is entitled 'Vanity': 'Gabriel, perhaps a little piqued by the comely traveller's indifference, glanced back to where he had witnessed her performance over the hedge, and said, "Vanity".' (*FMC* 7).

'Truly it has been observed', said Hardy at the end of his essay 'The Profitable Reading of Fiction' (1888), that '"the eye sees that which it brings with it the means of seeing".'[19] The 'observation' comes from Carlyle's *French Revolution*:

For indeed it is well said, 'in every object there is inexhaustible meaning; the eye sees in it what the eye brings means of seeing'. To Newton and to Newton's Dog Diamond, what a different pair of Universes; while the painting on the optical retina of both was, most likely, the same![20]

It can be claimed, with no exaggeration, that Carlyle's observation represents one of the major themes of *Far from the Madding Crowd*. Throughout the novel Hardy stresses the qualitative differences between different modes of perception, and between varying interpretations of the optical image. The first scene introduces this idea, and thereafter the text is filled with allusions to the relation between

19 In *Personal Writings*, ed. Orel, p. 125.
20 Thomas Carlyle, *The French Revolution* i. 1. 2.

perception and understanding, to seeing and being seen, to the physiological act of perception and the mental interpretation of what is perceived. The very language of the novel burgeons with metaphors and similes which have their origin in the properties of light and darkness, and which suggest in their turn correlatives in the mental sphere—enlightenment and ignorance.

At the simplest level, all the major characters in *Far from the Madding Crowd* are watchers, observers, or spies. Bathsheba Everdene accurately describes herself as a 'watched woman' (*FMC* 408), and one interpretation of her history is a progression from vain self-contemplation to objective self-assessment. When Gabriel Oak, early in the novel, offers marriage, he describes it to her as a form of benevolent watchfulness—'Whenever you look up, there I shall be—and whenever I look up, there will be you'. (*FMC* 33). But she accepts this offer only after she has passed beneath the much harsher gaze of Frank Troy and Farmer Boldwood. It is Oak, however, who provides Bathsheba with her first audience, and no sooner has he seen her sitting amongst her belongings on the spring wagon in that first scene than he sees her again—this time through the crevices of a shed in which she is working. From his awkward location 'he could form no decided opinion upon her looks, her position being almost beneath his eye, so that he saw her in a bird's-eye view, as Milton's Satan first saw Paradise.' (*FMC* 14). He then sees her a third time as she passes his shepherd's hut. She is on horseback, and Oak 'peeped through the loophole in the direction of the rider's approach.' (*FMC* 17). In their first face-to-face encounter, Bathsheba presents herself to Gabriel as an object of visual contemplation—as a 'portrait' in fact. 'The adjustment of the farmer's hazy conceptions of her charms', Hardy tells us, 'to the portrait of herself she now presented him with was less a diminution than a difference' (*FMC* 19), and his scrutiny of her figure has strong sexual overtones. He 'looked at her proportions with a long consciousness of pleasure. From the contours of her figure in its upper part she must have had a beautiful neck and shoulders; but since her infancy nobody had ever seen them.' (*FMC* 19). For a long time not a word is exchanged between them, yet the dialogue of sight continues and meaning is expressed through the eyes: 'The girl's thoughts hovered about her face and form as soon as she caught Oak's eyes conning the same page.' (*FMC* 19–20). Even when words are eventually spoken, visual perception remains dominant; and the act of looking takes on physical, tangible, almost tactile properties.

Rays of male vision seem to have a tickling effect upon virgin faces in rural districts; she brushed hers with her hand, as if Gabriel had been irritating its pink surface by actual touch, and the free air of her previous movements was reduced at the same time to a chastened phase of itself. Yet it was the man who blushed, the maid not at all. (*FMC* 20.)

Blushing is the physiological consequence of self-consciousness, and grows directly out of the union between seeing and understanding. Bathsheba does blush, but only when she realizes that Gabriel has spied upon her suggestive equestrian gymnastics.

Recollection of the strange antics she had indulged in when passing through the trees was succeeded in the girl by a nettled palpitation, and that by a hot face. It was a time to see a woman redden who was not given to reddening as a rule; not a point in the milkmaid but was of the deepest rose-colour. (*FMC* 21.)

Gabriel's response is to avert his eyes; hers is to make herself invisible to those eyes: 'He heard what seemed to be the flitting of a dead leaf upon the breeze, and looked. She had gone away.' (*FMC* 21). Bathsheba's blush in this scene looks back to her reddening at her own image in the mirror, and it anticipates many more blushes as she becomes progressively aware of the attentions of men. It is a blush which later informs Gabriel of Bathsheba's sensitivity to Boldwood's interest in her.

Gabriel, to whom her face was as the uncertain glory of an April day, was ever regardful of its faintest changes, and instantly discerned thereon the mark of some influence from without, in the form of a keenly self-conscious reddening. He also turned and beheld Boldwood. (*FMC* 139–40.)

Visual perception—seeing—and its consequence in blushing is important in these early scenes, because it is the action of the eye which is such a potent force in all the developing relationships of the book. At this point Boldwood is also drawn into the ocular drama, but he is uncertain of his role, for, as Hardy tells us, Boldwood 'read the pantomime denoting that they were aware of his presence, and the perception was as too much light turned upon his new sensibility.' (*FMC* 140). Boldwood's 'new sensibility' is, of course, his awareness of the existence of Bathsheba, and just as Gabriel Oak's early encounters with the girl were visual ones, so Boldwood's knowledge of her is also gained through a number of 'sightings'. When the farmer first calls on Bathsheba, she is 'invisible' and will not see him, and on

her appearance at Casterbridge market he avoids her eyes, though
she is aware of him through her second sight:

> The numerous evidences of her power to attract were only thrown into greater
> relief by a marked exception. Women seem to have eyes in their ribbons for
> such matters as these. Bathsheba, without looking within a right angle of him,
> was conscious of a black sheep among the flock. (*FMC* 103.)

Piqued that 'the most dignified and valuable man in the parish should
withhold his eyes' (*FMC* 110), Bathsheba decides to send him the
fateful valentine; as she does so, 'Folly in the concrete', says the narrator, 'blushed' (*FMC* 108). The seal on the letter, however, profoundly affects Boldwood's sense of sight; it lingers, we are told 'as a
blot of blood on the retina of his eye' (*FMC* 112). He returns to the
market, and his first encounter with her is like the waking of Adam.

> On Saturday Boldwood was in Casterbridge market-house as usual, when the
> disturber of his dreams entered, and became visible to him. Adam had
> awakened from his deep sleep, and behold! there was Eve. The farmer took
> courage, and for the first time really looked at her. (*FMC* 133.)

Unlike Gabriel Oak, whose initial scrutiny of Bathsheba was direct,
sensual, but uncomplicated, 'Boldwood looked at her—not slily,
critically or understandingly, but blankly at gaze, in the way a reaper
looks up at a passing train—as something foreign to his element, and
but dimly understood.' (*FMC* 133). Hardy describes him as though
he were some primitive astronomer:

> To Boldwood women had been remote phenomena rather than necessary
> complements—comets of such uncertain aspect, movement, and per-
> manence, that whether their orbits were as geometrical, unchangeable, and
> as subject to laws as his own, or as absolutely erratic as they superficially ap-
> peared, he had not deemed it his duty to consider. (*FMC* 133.)

When Boldwood challenges her about the valentine and she confesses
that it was a joke, he detects in her a heartlessness 'which was immediately contradicted by the pleasant eyes' (*FMC* 146). The interview concludes with the return of his blindness: 'Boldwood dropped
his gaze to the ground, and stood like a man who did not know where
he was.' (*FMC* 147).

In the Bible, Bathsheba's namesake is also looked upon and admired. The Second Book of Samuel reads: 'And it came to pass in an
evening-tide that David arose from off his bed and walked upon the

roof of the king's house: and from the roof he saw a woman washing herself; and the woman was very beautiful to look upon.' (11:2.) In the novel neither Oak nor Boldwood confesses to Bathsheba's beauty, but a third character makes a direct and explicit appeal to her vanity. It is Sergeant Troy: '"I've seen a good many women in my time,"' he says to her on their first encounter in the fir plantation, and, regarding her 'critically', continues, 'But I've never seen a woman so beautiful as you. Take it or leave it—be offended or like it—I don't care.' (*FMC* 189). Frank Troy's gaze, his obvious 'frankness' (the pun on Hardy's part is surely intentional), is deceptive. His true nature is better expressed in the 'sly' observation—in the way in which he watches Bathsheba at Greenhill Fair 'peeping from his dressing-tent through a slit' (*FMC* 394), or peering through a hole which he cuts in the canvas as she speaks to Boldwood (*FMC* 398).

Many of the rustic characters cannot look at Bathsheba at all. Poorgrass, one of the farm-hands, 'hardly had strength of eye enough to look in our young mis'ess's face' (*FMC* 64), and when he did, it was 'blush, blush, blush with [him] . . . every minute of the time' (*FMC* 64). Billy Smallberry likewise confesses that he cannot 'look her in the face' (*FMC* 48); so it is left to Gabriel Oak to provide the model of clear-sightedness. In direct contrast to Bathsheba, who contemplates her own image in the mirror to the exclusion of all else, Gabriel Oak, we are told, 'meditatively looked upon the horizon of circumstances without any special regard to his own standpoint in the midst.' (*FMC* 338). The word 'surveillance' is the clue to his role. We learn early in the novel that he is 'the officer of surveillance' over Bathsheba's affairs (*FMC* 182), and when a merger between two farms is proposed, he moves about them 'in a cheerful spirit of surveillance' (*FMC* 380). Gabriel's penetrative insight is a source of irritation to Bathsheba, however, and Hardy, using an appropriate visual metaphor, says of her that 'to be lectured because the lecturer saw her in the cold morning light of open-shuttered disillusion was exasperating.' (*FMC* 153). Bathsheba's own moral partial-sightedness is also expressed in visual terms. Frank Troy's deformities, says Hardy, 'lay deep down from a woman's vision whilst his embellishments were upon the very surface' (*FMC* 215), and her weak moral sensibility is 'dazzled by brass and scarlet' (*FMC* 234). In Oak she sees only his defects, which were 'patent to the blindest', but not his virtues, which 'were . . . as metals in a mine.' (*FMC* 215).

These examples could be supplemented by a multitude of others, but even from this selection it is clear that the business of seeing and being seen is unusually preponderant in the story. Not only is each of the major characters frequently engaged in observing the others, but much of the action grows out of watching and spying. What is also very clear from these examples is that there is no rigid distinction between watching as an act of pure sensation and observation as a form of moral discrimination. In the way in which Hardy chooses to describe his watchers, the literal act of observation often modulates into a metaphor for judging; seeing and understanding are closely related, and frequently the verb 'to see' refers equally to sight and to understanding.

In *Modern Painters* Ruskin is also concerned with the moral implications of perception, and what he says there has an important bearing on the different categories of visualization in *Far from the Madding Crowd*. In the second volume of this work Ruskin develops a psychological theory of vision which involves a number of mental faculties. As Ruskin describes it, seeing—the action of the eye—is merely a mechanical activity; what is important is the way in which the mind interprets the objects of sight. This, he claims, is done by a number of mental faculties which he calls the 'imagination penetrative', the 'theoretic faculty', and the 'aesthetic faculty'. Each of them, he says, acts as 'the intellectual lens and moral retina, by which and on which our informing thoughts are concentrated and represented.'[21]

Of the major characters it is Gabriel Oak whose imagination is most 'penetrative'. Unlike any of the others, he is able to see Bathsheba as she really is: he perceives her strengths as well as her weaknesses, for he is in possession of the kind of imagination which Ruskin describes as 'reaching by intuition and intensity of gaze . . . a more essential truth than is seen at the surface of things'.[22] Hardy explicitly attributes to Gabriel Oak's imagination the ability to penetrate beneath Bathsheba's superficial vanity. It was, says Hardy, at night that

he saw Bathsheba most vividly, and through the slow hours of shadow he tenderly regarded her image. . . . It is rarely that the pleasures of the imagination will compensate for the pain of sleeplessness, but they possibly did with Oak tonight, for the delight of merely seeing her effaced for the time his perception of the great difference between seeing and possessing. (*FMC* 78.)

[21] Ruskin, *Works* iv. 36.
[22] Ibid. iv. 284.

In contrast to Gabriel's 'penetrative imagination', Frank Troy's apprehension of the visible world resembles Ruskin's account of the 'aesthetic faculty'. According to Ruskin, this is a debased version of the 'theoretic faculty', and both respond only to 'ideas of beauty'. The 'theoretic faculty' in man is that part of him which enjoys the perfectly formed, but cannot penetrate beyond the surface of things or appreciate the value of the commonplace. It delights only in the beautiful and the exceptional, and (as the case of the 'aesthetic faculty') has no moral component. It is, he says, 'degraded', and is 'merely the operation of sense, or perhaps worse, of custom'.[23] Ruskin's account of this faculty corresponds closely to the way in which Troy reacts to Bathsheba. His attitude is exclusively sensual, sensuality having become a habit with him. Ruskin says:

We do indeed see constantly that men having naturally acute perception of the beautiful, yet not receiving it with a pure heart, nor into their hearts at all, never comprehend it, nor receive good from it, but make it a mere minister to their desires, and accompaniment and seasoning of lower sensual pleasures, until all their emotions take the same earthly stamp, and the sense of beauty sinks into the servant of lust.[24]

When Troy confesses that he is customarily responsive to beauty in women, Bathsheba is troubled that his attitude to her is, in Ruskin's term, merely 'aesthetic'. In reply, Troy denies the connection between beauty and morality. 'How long is it since you have been so afflicted with strong feeling?' she asks him.

'Oh, ever since I was big enough to know loveliness from deformity.'
''Tis to be hoped your sense of the difference you speak of doesn't stop at faces, but extends to morals as well.'
'I won't speak of morals or religion—my own or anybody else's. Though perhaps I should have been a very good Christian if you pretty women hadn't made me an idolater.' (*FMC* 196.)

In Bathsheba's case, her misjudgements about what she sees are more shortcomings than perversities, and she suffers from what Ruskin calls 'false taste'. False taste, he says, 'is merely that of falseness or inaccuracy in conclusion, not of moral delinquency', and his description of the way in which 'false taste', with its self-preoccupation and subjectivity, clouds the judgement fits Bathsheba to perfection. 'It may be known', says Ruskin,

[23] Ibid. iv. 35–6.
[24] Ibid. iv. 49.

by its fastidiousness, by its demands of pomp, splendour, and unusual combination, by its enjoyment only of particular styles and modes of things, and by its pride also: for it is ever . . . self-exulting; its eye is always upon itself, and it tests all things round it by the way they fit it.[25]

Gabriel Oak's perceptive view, Troy's degenerate aesthetic sense, and Bathsheba's 'false taste' can all be usefully related to Ruskin's moral theory of visual perception, but Boldwood's blindness cannot. The reason is that Oak, Troy, and Bathsheba succeed or fail through the moral judgements they make—through the way in which they interpret and act upon what they see. But Boldwood's failure of vision is not so much moral as pathological, and he must be placed in a different category.

This difference is pointed up in the language which Hardy uses to express Boldwood's blindness. He tends to avoid terms which impute moral failure to the man, and adopts instead the nomenclature of the experimental psychologist. Boldwood, it will be remembered, looked at Bathsheba neither 'slily', nor 'critically', nor 'understandingly'— all terms of moral judgement—but instead, he stared at her 'blankly at gaze . . . as something foreign to his element, and but dimly understood.' (*FMC* 133). For him, women were simply incomprehensible—'remote phenomena'—and to explain how women affected Boldwood, Hardy employs the language of optics. Boldwood, he says, 'had never before inspected a woman with the very centre and force of his glance', and, borrowing a methaphor from the geometry of lenses, he explains that women had 'struck upon all his senses at wide angles.' (*FMC* 134). Such technical terms are a prominent feature of the way in which Hardy describes the farmer's mind. The seal on the valentine becomes 'a blot of blood on the retina of his eye' (*FMC* 112), and his account of Boldwood's attitude to Bathsheba is reminiscent of an experiment in sensationalist psychology. 'The great aids to idealization in love were present here: occasional observation of her from a distance and the absence of social intercourse with her— visual familiarity, oral strangeness. The smaller human elements were kept out of sight.' (*FMC* 141). Boldwood's inability to see Bathsheba clearly is not moral weakness but physiological infirmity. His 'new sensibility' has 'too much light turned upon [it]' (*FMC* 140); he sees shapes and signs but cannot interpret them:

[25] Ibid. iv. 60.

Perhaps in [Bathsheba's] manner there were signs that she wished to see him—perhaps not—he could not read a woman. The cabala of this erotic philosophy seemed to consist of the subtlest meaning expressed in misleading ways. Every turn, look, word, and accent contained a mystery quite distinct from its obvious import, and not one had ever been pondered by him until now. (*FMC* 140.)

We are now in a position to distinguish two separate, but related, visual themes running through *Far from the Madding Crowd*. One is associated with the interpretative power of sight—the morality of perception—and stems from the idea which Hardy took from Carlyle —that 'the eye sees that which it brings with it the means of seeing'—which takes a slightly different form early in the novel where Hardy says that 'in making even horizontal and clear inspections we colour and mould according to the wants within us whatever our eyes bring in.' (*FMC* 16). The other is associated with the optical, rather than the moral, limitations of sight, and finds expression in Hardy's treatment of Boldwood's aberrations. The first theme can be expressed in the question, How do we judge and act according to the data which our eyes feed the mind? The second can be summarized by another question: To what extent can we trust the data of sight? Throughout the novel Hardy dwells on the limitations of sight itself, and the language in which he describes these limitations is drawn from scientific accounts of the effect of light on the eye. Take, for example, this description of Bathsheba's strengths and weaknesses. 'Her emblazoned fault', says Hardy,

was to be too pronounced in her objections, and not sufficiently overt in her likings. We learn that it is not the rays which bodies absorb, but those which they reject, that give them the colours they are known by; and in the same way people are specialized by their dislikes and antagonisms, whilst their goodwill is looked upon as no attribute at all. (*FMC* 171.)

And from whom do we 'learn' this fact? Probably from Helmholtz, who, in 1873, pointed out the paradoxical nature of sight. 'Cinnabar', he said, 'reflects the rays of great length without any obvious loss, while it absorbs almost the whole of the other rays. Accordingly, this substance appears of the same red colour as the beams which it throws back into the eye.'[26] Even in some of the smallest details Hardy allegorizes the limitations of the power of sight. Early in the novel

---

[26] Helmholtz, *Popular Lectures on Scientific Subjects* (1873), p. 263.

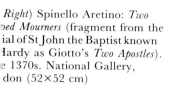

(*Top left*) Antoine Wiertz: *La Belle
ine*. 1847. Belgian Royal
seums of Fine Art, Wiertz
seum, Brussels (140×100 cm)

(*Top right*) Antoine Wiertz: *The
it of the Civilization of the Nineteenth
tury*. 1864. Belgian Royal
seums of Fine Art, Wiertz
seum, Brussels (172×135 cm)

(*Right*) Spinello Aretino: *Two
ped Mourners* (fragment from the
ial of St John the Baptist known
ardy as Giotto's *Two Apostles*).
e 1370s. National Gallery,
don (52×52 cm)

10. Thomas Webster: *A Village Choir*. 1847. Victoria and Albert Museum, London
(61×91.5 cm)

11. Follower of J. B. Greuze:
A Girl. n.d. National Gallery,
London (45.7×38.1)

12. Giovanni Battista Moroni:
Portrait of a Man (*The Tailor*).
National Gallery, London
(97.8×74.9 cm)

Bathsheba and her aunt are supervising the rearing of a young calf. It was

about a day old, looking idiotically at the two women, which showed that it had not long been accustomed to the phenomena of eyesight, and often [turned] to the lantern, which it apparently mistook for the moon, inherited instinct having as yet had little time for correction by experience. (*FMC* 15.)

Like the calf's, Bathsheba's eyesight is corrected by experience, and at the end of the novel she is accredited with the power of adjusting the eyesight of others. Boldwood has shot Troy, and she calmly asks Oak to ride for the surgeon. 'Her statement of the fact in such quiet and simple words came with more force than a tragic declamation, and had somewhat the effect of setting the distorted images in each mind present into proper focus.' (*FMC* 437).

The source of Hardy's interest in the limits of sense perception can be determined, in part, from his reading in these years. When *Far from the Madding Crowd* first appeared, he said that he had been 'latterly reading Comte's *Positive Philosophy*' (*EL* 129), and, sure enough, his literary notes contain many quotations from Comte's writings. Among these are a number which relate to the importance of sensation in the development of human experience. 'Thought', said Comte, 'depends on Sensation,' and Hardy added the *aide-mémoire* that 'Sensations (obj[ective]) more vivid than recollections (subj[ective]).'[27] At this time Hardy may also have read Pater's book *The Renaissance*, for the first time. The edition of 1873 contains the famous passage in which Pater describes the logical conclusion of materialist philosophy. 'Experience,' said Pater, 'already reduced to a swarm of impressions, is ringed round for each one of us by that thick wall of personality through which no real voice has ever pierced on its way to us, or from us to that which we can only conjecture to be without.'[28]

The ultimate source of all these ideas is to be found in the work of Berkeley, Locke, and Hume, and though we do not know when Hardy

---

[27] *LN*, entries 731 and 732; Hardy's additions in brackets.

[28] Walter Pater, *The Renaissance: Studies in Art and Poetry*, p. 187. Describing Gabriel alone in his sheep-hut, Hardy uses terms very similar to those which Pater expresses in the conclusion to *The Renaissance*: 'To find themselves utterly alone at night where company is desirable and expected makes some people fearful; but a case more trying by far to the nerves is to discover some mysterious companionship when intuition, sensation, memory, analogy, testimony, probability, induction—every kind of evidence in the logician's list—have united to persuade consciousness that it is quite in isolation.' (*FMC* 14.)

first read Hume's *A Treatise of Human Nature*,[29] his literary notes show an interest in the problems which these philosophers first raised. He took notes, for example, from G. H. Lewes's essay 'The Course of Modern Thought', in which Lewes outlined the more recent developments stemming from Berkeleian idealism:

Locke, Berkeley, Hume and Kant, directing their analysis exclusively to the subjective aspect of phenomena, soon broke down the barriers between the physical and mental, and gradually merged the former into the latter. Matter and its qualities, hitherto accepted as independent realities, existing where no Mind perceived them, were now viewed as the creations of Mind—their existence was limited to a state of the percipient. The old Dualism was replaced by Idealism. The Cosmos, instead of presenting a problem of Mechanics, now presented a problem of Psychology.[30]

In his book *Thomas Hardy: The Poetry of Perception*, Tom Paulin shows that Hardy knew of Hume's ideas as early as the 1860s, when he read Bagehot's *Estimates of Some Englishmen and Scotsmen*. In this, Bagehot outlines Shelley's debt to Hume, and Paulin points out that Shelley, whom Hardy very much admired, 'repeatedly stressed his agreement with the idea that "nothing exists but as it is perceived".' In his essay 'On Life', which Paulin also quotes, Shelley says:

The view of life presented by the most refined deductions of the intellectual philosophy is that of unity: Nothing exists but as it is perceived. The difference is merely nominal between those two classes of thought which are vulgarly distinguished by the names of ideas and external objects.[31]

Though Paulin gives good reasons on the evidence of the poetry for suggesting that it is Hume's view of mind to which Hardy is closest, it is likely, at least at the time when he was writing *Far from the Madding Crowd*, that the stronger influence was Berkeley's *Essay Towards a New Theory of Vision*. Though it was published in 1709, it was a work which, even in Hardy's day, enjoyed enormous respect. In 1864, for example, Thomas Abbot, one of the principal opponents of Berkeley's ideas was forced to admit that 'if we were challenged to point out a single discovery in mental science which is universally admitted we should at once name the "Theory of Vision".'[32] John Stuart Mill,

[29] Hardy owned a copy of the 1874 edition of Hume's *Treatise*; it is now in DCM.

[30] G. H. Lewes, 'The Course of Modern Thought', *Fortnightly Review* 27 (1877), p. 319; quoted by Hardy in *LN*, entry 899.

[31] Tom Paulin, *Thomas Hardy: The Poetry of Perception*, p. 17.

[32] Thomas K. Abbot, *Sight and Touch: An Attempt to Disprove the Received (or Berkeleian) Theory of Vision*, p. 1.

who endorsed many of Berkeley's views, said that the theory 'constituted a revolution in psychology . . . which [has] . . . determined the whole course of subsequent philosophical speculation'.[33] In 1873 a new edition of Berkeley's works came out and it was reviewed by T. H. Huxley, who supported Mill's views of the *New Theory of Vision*. Huxley formulated Berkeley's primary question thus: 'What are the limits of our faculties?'[34] The relevance of Berkeley's theory to *Far from the Madding Crowd* is that Berkeley is especially concerned with the sense of sight, claiming that 'all the choir of heaven and furniture of the earth—in a word, all those bodies which compose the mighty frame of the world—have not substance without a mind.'[35] Hardy was fully aware of the Berkeleian idea that '*esse* is *percepi*', and wrote into his notebook a summary of Berkeley's views, together with an account of the way in which Hume developed them. Berkeley, he wrote,

established the subjective character of the world of phenomena; that this world I perceive *is* my perceptions, and nothing more. But besides these perceptions there is also spirit, a *me* that perceives them. And to get rid of this imaginary soul or substance was the work of Hume.[36]

That Hardy had more affinity with Berkeley than with Hume can be seen in *Far from the Madding Crowd*. Frequently in the novel Hardy questions the reliability of sense perception; he often points out, both directly and through the use of metaphor, how fallible is our sense of sight. Never does he leave the actual existence of the physical world open to question, however. He shows how wrong human judgements can be when they are based upon the evidence of sight, but, through the personality of Gabriel Oak, he infers that right judgements *can* be made, and that such judgement *should* be made. In this respect Hardy's views resemble those of G. H. Lewes. Lewes reacted against the extremes of idealism, and substituted what he called 'reasoned realism'. Idealism, said Lewes, 'fails to take account of the *Not Self*', and Hardy would have agreed with Lewes when he said: '*My* world may be my picture of it; *your* world may be your picture of it; but there is something common to both which is more than either.[37]

[33] J. S. Mill, *Dissertations and Discussions*, (1859–75), iv. 155.
[34] T. H. Huxley, *Critiques and Addresses* (1873), p. 320 *et seq.*
[35] Quoted by Huxley, *Critiques*, p. 325.
[36] *LN*, entry 1215; the words are those of William Kingdom Clifford.
[37] G. H. Lewes, 'The Course of Modern Thought', p. 321.

Lewes took up a position between the idealism of Kant and the implications of biological materialism, between the notion of all phenomena
as projections of consciousness and the idea of consciousness merely
as the product of biological or chemical forces. When Hardy says in
Far from the Madding Crowd that in 'making even horizontal and clear
inspections we colour and mould according to the wants within us
whatever our eyes brings in' (*FMC* 16), he does not question the
existence of material reality. He merely suggests that the interpretation of visual sensations is intimately dependent upon the temperament, nature, and psychological disposition of the perceiver. In the
essay quoted above, Helmholtz made a similar point. He said:

> The inaccuracies and imperfections of the eye as an optical instrument, and
> those which belong to the image on the retina, now appear insignificant in
> comparison with the incongruities which we have met with in the field of sen-
> sation. One might almost believe that Nature had here contradicted herself on
> purpose, in order to destroy any dreams of a pre-existing harmony between
> the outer and inner world.[38]

In *Far from the Madding Crowd* the continuity between the inner and
outer worlds, the realms of action and moral judgement, is often violated by distortions of visual perception; but in the course of the novel
Hardy makes optical assessments even more difficult for his characters
by his treatment of setting. In a novel in which so much hangs upon
clarity of perception, the number of scenes which take place at times
of day or in climatic conditions in which such clear-sightedness is impossible serves to stress the fallibility of human judgement. Of the
fifty-seven chapters that make up the novel, at least thirty-one are set
in conditions under which vision is partly or totally obscured. For
example, the first event of importance takes place on the eve of St
Thomas's, 'the shortest day in the year' (*FMC* 8), and the novel
closes on the night immediately following the marriage of Gabriel and
Bathsheba. Between the events of these two important nights, many
other episodes are acted out in darkness. Gabriel's sheep are driven
over a precipice at night, Bathsheba's ricks catch fire at night, and
Gabriel Oak meets Fanny Robin, without actually seeing her, on the
same night. Troy converses with Fanny from the window of his bar-
racks in 'a prospect of which the chief constituent was darkness'
(*FMC* 95), the sheep-shearing supper takes place in the twilight, and
on the same night Bathsheba meets Troy in the fir plantation. Gabriel

---

[38] Helmholtz, *Popular Lectures*, p. 269.

warns Bathsheba about Troy during a 'twilight walk', but she steals away to meet the soldier at the dead of night. On his return Troy plays a cruel trick on Boldwood, possible only under the cover of night, and it is night when Gabriel rescues the ricks from the fury of the storm. Fanny Robin meets Bathsheba and Troy on an autumn day which Troy describes as 'black as my hat' (*FMC* 298), and Bathsheba plants flowers on Fanny's grave at night. On his reappearance at Greenhill Fair, Troy plays the part of Dick Turpin on Black Bess in the light of the dying day, then escapes from the fair at the dead of night. Finally, hooded and disguised, he appears at Boldwood's fatal party on a night which one of the farm-hands describes as 'dark as a hedge' (*FMC* 424).

What is so striking about these scenes of darkness is the way in which they are interspersed with other scenes of dazzling brilliance. For example, the sunshine of the sheep-shearing, 'strong enough to blind a weak-eyed man' (*FMC* 165), is followed by a night as dark as 'the ninth plague of Egypt' (*FMC* 183). Similarly, on the night of the tempest the darkness 'so intense that Gabriel worked entirely by feeling' (*FMC* 284) is illuminated by flashes in which 'Gabriel was almost blinded' (*FMC* 287). The fact is that in *Far from the Madding Crowd*, both light and darkness conspire to deceive the senses. In a literal sense, the effects of light can be both illuminating and blinding, and while darkness can obscure, it can also concentrate the eye. At the metaphorical level, mental light can have the effect of distorting the image, while darkness can sometimes reveal more than daylight. For example, though the darkness of the storm was 'impenetrable by the sharpest vision' (*FMC* 288), the chiaroscuro caused by the flashes of lightning irradiated Bathsheba's consciousness, bringing her to an awareness of Gabriel Oak's true worth. Hardy also assigns to light contradictory functions. It, too, can illuminate and deceive; it can be 'kindly' or it can be 'garish'. Gabriel sees Bathsheba in 'the cold morning light of open-shuttered disillusion' (*FMC* 153), and she herself knows 'in her noon-clear sense she never loved [Boldwood]' (*FMC* 231). Gabriel and Bathsheba pass through their 'bright times and dark times' (*FMC* 450), and are reconciled in Weatherbury Churchyard to the accompaniment of a hymn, the words of which bear directly upon this theme: 'Lead, kindly Light, amid the encircling gloom' (*FMC* 448). The second verse of Newman's hymn, which Bathsheba and Gabriel also hear, acts as a reminder of the other kind of light in the novel.

I loved the garish day, and, spite of fears,
Pride ruled my will: remember not past years.

In the early sections of the novel it is Frank Troy who personifies the 'garish' light, the false and deceptive source of illumination. There is no mistaking the 'spot of artificial red' (*FMC* 208) which stands out so against the natural green of the countryside, and beside Troy, Gabriel Oak 'had a melancholy tendency to look like a candle beside gas' (*FMC* 276). Though Bathsheba is described on one occasion as being as 'proud as Lucifer' (*FMC* 48), it is in fact Troy who is the creator of false light. He is 'a man of sin' (*FMC* 255), the 'juggler of Satan' (*FMC* 268); the devil smiles upon him (*FMC* 197), and he creates his pyrotechnic masterpieces, first in Bathsheba's fir plantation, and later in the hollow amid the ferns.

These two scenes embody many of the prominent themes of *Far from the Madding Crowd*. Hardy fully exploits the contrasts between darkness and light as a means of assaulting the senses; both involve the activities of watching and being watched, and in both, judgements are made on the basis of visual information. The scene in the fir plantation, like so many of the episodes in the story, takes place at night. After the harvest supper Bathsheba makes her regular nightly inspection of the farm, and, as 'watching is best done invisibly' (*FMC* 182), she takes with her a 'dark-lantern'. This simple device—a lamp with a shutter—clearly has implications for the nature of Bathsheba's own state of awareness, particularly since it is operated in the spot which was 'the darkest point of her route, even though only just outside her own door.' (*FMC* 184). The lamp is as yet unopened, and the plantation remains shrouded in gloom and as 'black as the ninth plague of Egypt'. In her blindness Bathsheba is unaware that she has become entangled with Troy; it is only when the anonymous 'hand seized the lantern' and opened the door that 'the rays burst out from their prison, and Bathsheba beheld her position with astonishment.' (*FMC* 184).

The man to whom she was hooked was brilliant in brass and scarlet. He was a soldier. His sudden appearance was to darkness what the sound of a trumpet is to silence. Gloom, the *genius loci* at all times hitherto, was now totally overthrown, less by the lantern-light than by what the lantern lighted. The contrast of this revelation with her anticipations of some sinister figure in sombre garb was so great that it had upon her the effect of a fairy transformation. (*FMC* 184–5.)

Of course, this is a brilliant piece of Victorian melodrama, and it depends for its effect on what contemporary psychologists called the Law of Relativity. A sense impression, it was claimed, is known only by its opposite; light is known only by contrast with darkness, since, as Bain explained, 'every mental experience is necessarily *two-fold*.'[39] Yet Hardy is subtle in his management of this *coup de théâtre*; like the young calf at whose birth she assisted earlier in the novel, Bathsheba's sense of sight is undeveloped, and the blindness caused by the darkness is exchanged for a new blindness created by the light. She is dazzled, not by the light from the lantern, but, as Boldwood perceptively notices later in the story, 'by brass and scarlet'. It is the rays reflected from Troy's uniform, not the source of light itself, which prevent her from seeing clearly, and when he looks into her eyes, the effect is complete: 'His gaze was too strong to be received point-blank with her own.' Their entanglement is physical, sexual, and moral. Her good looks instantly bring into operation his 'aesthetic faculty'; his flattery plays upon her 'false taste', and they are united in their mutual misinterpretation of the image of the other.

Hardy does not allow the reader to be deceived by this dramatic illusion, however. When he visited the Royal Academy exhibition in 1870, he was impressed by the 'fine conception' of Gérôme's picture of the Crucifixion (*EL* 100). Gérôme had used the shadows of the crosses symbolically, and in this scene Hardy permits his reader a view, denied to the protagonists, which also exploits the symbolic power of shadows. As the couple attempt disentanglement, the lantern is set on the ground between them, and the image it creates is full of prophetic doom. 'It radiated upwards into their faces, and sent over half the plantation gigantic shadows of both man and woman, each dusky shape becoming distorted and mangled upon the tree-trunks till it wasted to nothing.' (*FMC* 185).

The charm with which Troy began to seduce Bathsheba in the fir plantation completely mesmerizes her in the hollow amid the ferns.[40] The sun is setting, as it often does at moments of crisis in Hardy's novels, and as the aggressive 'bristling ball of gold in the west' suggestively and sensually sweeps 'the tips of the ferns with its long,

---

[39] Bain, *The Senses and the Intellect*, p. 8.
[40] Bain spoke of how, 'in the presence of a light too strong to be agreeable, the eye is worked upon, as by a spell or fascination, and continues gazing on what gives pain or discomfort. . . . Human beings experience, in a small degree, the fascination that in the moth is overpowering, even to self-destruction.' (*The Senses and the Intellect*, pp. 227–8).

luxuriant rays' (*FMC* 208), the nature of this particular crisis is made clear. It was God himself, of course, who originally created light, and it was God, in the form of Jesus Christ, who later brought the 'kindly light' into the world. Holman Hunt's famous picture *The Light of the World*—a picture which Hardy saw at the International Exhibition in 1862—depicts Christ as meek and gentle to the point of androgeny. In the fern hollow Troy challenges God's power to create light, and he does so with demonic aggression—with the blade of his sword. Previously the couple had met on Bathsheba's territory—literally just outside her door. Now the spot is remote, a mile from her dwelling, uncultivated, and removed from the community in which she normally lives. Here, Troy creates a new heaven and a new earth, complete with a rainbow, but it is an inverted rainbow—'a sort of rainbow upside down in the air' (*FMC* 209). The assault on Bathsheba's senses is reminiscent of Cytherea Graye's first meeting with Manston in *Desperate Remedies*, and it anticipates Eustacia Vye's dream about Clym Yeobright in *The Return of the Native*. In each case the heroine's senses are mesmerized, but most especially the sense of sight. As Troy raised his sword, 'the atmosphere was transformed to Bathsheba's eyes,' and before those very eyes Troy generated his 'firmament of light':

Beams of light caught from the low sun's rays, above, around, in front of her, well-nigh shut out earth and heaven. . . . In short, she was enclosed in a firmament of light, and of sharp hisses, resembling a sky-full of meteors close at hand. (*FMC* 211.)[41]

There are two important developments in Hardy's writing which distinguish a scene like this from anything he had previously written. First, the descriptive range has increased in depth and complexity: he has managed to combine an acute and sensitive response to natural details with an almost gymnastic ability to manipulate view point. Second, his use of language is rich in a complex of associations. From the opening scene, through the large set pieces, down to some of the smallest details, Hardy combines a credible and vivid narrative with a metaphorical and symbolic language which generates its own meaning. On the one hand *Far from the Madding Crowd* is about Bathsheba Everdene's history and her relationships with men; on the other, it is

---

[41] Frank Troy anticipates the character of Alec d'Urberville in a number of interesting ways. Not only do they adopt cavalier and swaggering attitudes towards women, they both have explicitly demonic associations (see p. 84 above) and they both generate artificial light (see p. 202 below).

a meditation on the way in which the sense of sight feeds the mind with information about the material world. There is, however, no disjunction between these two levels of writing. Bathsheba's growth towards self-knowledge is expressed in terms of adjusting, focusing, and correcting her sense of sight, and her development serves to bear out one of the central propositions of the book, that 'in making even horizontal and clear inspections we colour and mould according to the wants within us whatever our eyes bring in.'

4

The Return of the Native
Literary Portraiture

> For as from our beginning we run through variety of looks, before
> we come to consistent and settled faces; so before our end, by sick
> and languishing alterations, we put on new visages: and in our
> retreat to earth may fall upon such looks which from community of
> seminal originals were before latent in us.[1]

The theme which Hardy established in *Far from the Madding Crowd*
—the discrepancy between appearance and reality—is one which
crops up frequently in subsequent novels. In *The Mayor of Casterbridge*
Elizabeth-Jane asks herself 'why things around her had taken the
shape they wore in preference to every other possible shape', and
'what that chaos called consciousness . . . tended to, and began
in' (*MC* 135–6); and, commenting on the heroine's feeling of guilt
and alienation after the birth of her child, the narrator in *Tess of
the d'Urbervilles* remarks that 'the world is only a psychological
phenomenon' (*TD* 108). In the later novels, however, Hardy is concerned less with the psychology of perception than with the
philosophy of perception, less with the vagaries and the fallibility of
the eye in yielding the truth about the material or moral realm, than
with the significance of independent modes of perception for belief
and conduct. In this respect *The Woodlanders* is the logical successor to
Far from the Madding Crowd. In this novel the attitudes of individual
characters, and the judgements that they make of each other, are
determined, not by their response to the retinal image, but by the
quality and nature of their respective sensibilities. In *Far from the Madding Crowd* vision can be corrected and adjusted to conform to a
universally accepted norm; in the later novels, particularly *The
Woodlanders*, no such absolute standard exists; here perception is
relative and determined ultimately by the forces of evolution.

It comes as no surprise, then, to learn that the original idea for *The
Woodlanders* came to Hardy as soon as he had finished *Far from the*

[1] Sir Thomas Browne, 'Letter to a Friend' (1690), in *LN*, '1867' Notebook, entry
216.

Madding Crowd; he was deflected from developing it, however, by a set of circumstances connected with his reputation. He was very anxious about the fact that he was being classed as a 'rustic' writer, one who dealt solely with provincial characters in provincial settings; and since the idea for *The Woodlanders* pointed to yet another 'clear, fresh, country piece', at least superficially, he wrote instead *The Hand of Ethelberta*, a society novel set in London and Rouen. It is a weak novel, but fortunately Hardy was capable of enough self-criticism to be aware of the wrong direction he had taken. So in his next book, he returned (imaginatively at least) to his native heath for inspiration. By 1876, however, the year in which he began *The Return of the Native*, Hardy's interest in literary visualization had changed significantly. It is true that, like *Far from the Madding Crowd*, *The Return of the Native* has its spies and its watchers, but in this novel the visual drama does not take place in the eyes of the characters. Now, it is the reader who is the principal spectator, and it is in *his* imagination that the spectacle unfolds. In *The Return of the Native* Hardy develops one of the techniques which he had begun to explore in *Desperate Remedies*. The similarity is pointed up by the moment in *The Return of the Native* when Clym Yeobright realizes that he is committed to marrying Eustacia Vye. The couple wander to the edge of Egdon Heath where 'everything before them was on a perfect level. The sun, resting on the horizon line, streamed across the ground from between copper-coloured and lilac clouds, stretched out in flats beneath a sky of pale soft green.' (*RN* 24). The appearance of the landscape is an emblem of Clym's mental state; it is the visual embodiment of a particular mood, about which Hardy is quite explicit. 'There was', he says, 'something in its oppressive horizontality which too much reminded [Clym] . . . of the arena of life; it gave him a sense of bare equality with, and no superiority to, a single living thing under the sun.' (*RN* 245). If this phrasing is familiar, it is because Hardy has borrowed it word for word from *Desperate Remedies*. At the point at which Cytherea Graye realizes that marriage to Aeneas Manston is inevitable, the water-meadows around Knapwater House are lit by the same sun and in the same colours, and Cytherea, like Clym, feels similarly oppressed. It was in *Desperate Remedies* that Hardy first tentatively explored the idea of employing setting as a vehicle for emotion, of charging the visual image in such a way that it becomes a correlative for feelings experienced by the characters. In Chapter 2 we saw how the episodes in Budmouth Bay, the interview between Cytherea and Miss Aldclyffe, and other points in the narrative were intensified so that the images seemed to be redolent with meaning which lay beyond or behind appearances. In *The Return of the Native* Hardy further develops this technique, creating what might be called a psychological landscape for his characters. The first part of this chapter, then, is concerned with the visual influences and the intellectual constituents which inform Hardy's creation of Egdon Heath; the second part tries to show how he created links between setting and character through an unusual but ingenious visual presentation of character.

Fiction and Landscape

The opening pages of *The Return of the Native* are written with a power and a sense of confidence which are quite new in Hardy's style. The extended account of land and sky populated only by the imaginary 'furze-cutter' provides an overture to a drama of Wagnerian proportions. Though Hardy had not yet heard a Wagner opera,[2] the unhurried, steady, and solemn pace at which the panorama unfolds resembles the overture to *Das Rheingold*, in generating an appropriate mood for the epic which follows. Like Wagner, Hardy was creating a work of art on the Greek model, and like Wagner's operas too, the work has implications which reach beyond the local and particular circumstances of the narrative. Consequently, Hardy was intent not only on presenting a landscape which would be memorable and vivid, but on imbuing that landscape with a significance beyond its material appearance. Ever since 1865 he had been conscious of the fact that the 'poetry of a scene' lies in 'the minds of the perceivers' (*EL* 66). In his account of Egdon Heath he managed, for the first time, to combine in a single entity the objective and the subjective, the observed visual phenomenon and the significance of that phenomenon. He managed to unite his talent for the picturesque with his tendency to interpret form as symbol—to bring together the literal and the abstract.

One of the consequences of the conjunction of these two elements is that each generates a kind of geographical orientation—the physical and the metaphorical—both of which are important, not only in *The Return of the Native*, but in subsequent novels also. First, there is the literal Wessex setting—the sequestered and remote spot in the West Country, inward-looking in its tendencies and old fashioned in its

---

[2] Hardy first heard Wagner's music, which he described as '*weather* and *ghost* music' (*EL* 237) in 1886. In 1906 he compared 'late Wagner' with 'late Turner' (*LV* 117).

manners. But there is also another kind of topographical scheme at work—a setting which is related not to the literal meaning of the novel, but to its more imaginative, subjective side. This other kind of setting is connected specifically with *the appearance* of Egdon Heath, and the way in which, according to Hardy, landscapes with similar appearances were appealing more and more to modern man. 'It is a question', he says in the opening pages of the book,

if the exclusive reign of . . . orthodox beauty is not approaching its last quarter. The new Vale of Tempe may be a gaunt waste in Thule: human souls may find themselves in closer and closer harmony with external things wearing a sombreness distasteful to our race when it was young. The time seems near, if it has not actually arrived, when the chastened sublimity of a moor, a sea, or a mountain will be all of nature that is absolutely in keeping with the moods of the more thinking among mankind. And ultimately, to the commonest tourist, spots like Iceland may become what the vineyards and myrtle-gardens of South Europe are to him now; and Heidelberg and Baden be passed unheeded as he hastens from the Alps to the sand-dunes of Scheveningen. (*RN* 5.)

This is an extremely important passage because it sets out, for the first time in Hardy's writing, a view of the relationship between modern man and ancient landscape—a view which he expressed again and again in the novels right up to *Jude the Obscure*. In his infancy, Hardy suggests, man found greatest satisfaction in the landscape forms of the south of Europe—in parts of the world which are benign, colourful, and sunlit. In his maturity, however, he will look elsewhere for scenery which conforms to his needs, aspirations, and moods. As the race grows older, the mind no longer finds 'poetry' in the south, and turns instead to the north of Europe. From the Alps, Baden-Baden, and the myrtle-gardens of the south of Europe, man will turn more and more to landscape and scenery which previous generations had considered barren, bleak, hostile, and unsympathetic—to Scheveningen, Iceland, and, of course, Egdon Heath. The 'aesthetic of northerness'—or 'beauty in ugliness'[3]—appears frequently in Hardy's writing; he makes reference to it directly or indirectly in *A Laodicean, The Woodlanders, Tess of the d'Urbervilles*, and *Jude the Obscure*, and it plays a significant part in the patterning of *The Return of the Native*. The sources seem to be primarily two.[4] The first derives from

[3] 'To find beauty in ugliness is the province of the poet.' (*EL* 279).
[4] For a third influence on Hardy see Appendix.

Hardy's own experience, and from his personal attitudes to landscape—attitudes which came clearly into focus during a journey which he made with Emma to Holland, Belgium, and the valley of the Rhine. The second can be found in his response to certain kinds of landscape painting—painting which, when Hardy was writing *The Return of the Native*, exemplified for him this special relationship between man and nature.

After finishing *Far from the Madding Crowd*, in 1874, Hardy married Emma Lavinia Gifford, and in 1876 they made a vacation trip through Holland, up the Rhine, and back to England via Brussels. At the time, Hardy was planning his new novel, and, as a 'common tourist', he was observing the scenery of Europe. The couple left London on May 29th, crossed to Rotterdam, visited the resort of Scheveningen on the North Sea coast, and joined the Rhine at Cologne. They travelled southward, visiting various towns on the river, arriving finally at Heidelberg and Baden-Baden. There was something extremely significant about this journey for Hardy, because he rehearses all or part of it in a number of novels. Heidelberg is where Fitzpiers and Felice Charmond first meet in their youth, and Hardy imbues their memories with a false glamour and a specious romance (*W* 233), and it is to Baden-Baden that they flee in an attempt to escape the consequences of their action in the northern woods of Little Hintock. Heidelberg and Scheveningen also play an important part in *A Laodicean*. Captain de Stancy, the impoverished aristocrat, vainly pursues the rich heroine Paula Power as she travels down the Rhine. The route of her party exactly mirrors that taken by Hardy and his wife in 1876, and when they reach Heidelberg, de Stancy, like Hardy himself, climbs to the top of the tower on the Königsstuhl. On the day the Hardys went up, the weather was very hot, and friction had already begun to develop between Hardy and his wife. From the top (so Emma confided to her diary) she 'saw nothing', and she underlined the words 'wish I had not',[5] but for Hardy the view was filled with significance of a personal kind. The sunset produced an optical effect that was, he said, 'almost tragic.' (*EL* 145). In *A Laodicean* the sight of the setting sun had for de Stancy, too, 'something that was more than melancholy, and not much less than tragic' (*L* 377), and he attributes his response to a combination of depression, ageing and the futility of his pursuit of Paula Power. Eventually, however, de Stancy finds a

---

5 *Emma Hardy's Diaries*, p. 84. See also Millgate, *Thomas Hardy: A Biography*, p. 183.

spot in keeping with his mood: it is the beach of Scheveningen, where the Hardys had stopped in 1876.

Unlike Heidelberg, Scheveningen had no picturesque attraction. It is, warned Murray's *Handbook for Travellers* (1868), 'a desert of undulating sand-hills barely covered by coarse grass',[6] and Emma recorded standing 'on a sand hill or dyke—saw red-roofed village beneath us at our right, and the sea and Dutch shipping at our left'. This, she added, 'was a very characteristic view of Holland; grass growing thinly in the deep loose sand: stones laid down in it for a road.'[7] What Hardy himself felt at this spot we do not know, but the world-weary de Stancy found here what he missed at Heidelberg. The dull and featureless beach, the wind and the rain, suited him, and his mind responded to the 'poetry' of the scene. '"It always seems to me"', he says to Paula Power, '"that this place reflects the average mood of human life. I mean, if we strike the balance between our best moods and our worst we shall find our average condition to stand at about the same pitch in emotional colour as these sandy dunes and this grey sea do in landscape."' (L 387). The suggestion, both here and in *The Return of the Native*, is that the modern mind will fail to identify with those scenes which had pleased it at an earlier period, but will find an appropriate vehicle of expression in the sad and desolate landscape, in the 'chastened sublimity' of 'things wearing a sombreness distasteful to our race when it was young.' (RN 5).

Painting had always been important to Hardy, and during the period of *The Return of the Native* he seems to have turned to specific works of art which confirmed for him this idea about 'beauty in ugliness'. He must have been well aware, for example, that the coastal area around Scheveningen had long been a source of inspiration to painters in search of the wild, the dramatic, and the windswept,[8] and in 1878 he made explicit connections between his recent

[6] [John Murray, pub.], *Handbook for Travellers in Holland and Belgium*, 19th edn, p. 36.

[7] *Emma Hardy's Diaries*, p. 74.

[8] In 1870 *The Times* praised the power of James Hook's *Scheveningen Sands* at the Royal Academy (30 Apr. 1877, p. 13), and in 1876 the *Art Journal* gave a detailed account of Hendrik Mesdag's Scheveningen scene *Lifeboat Going to the Rescue* Jan. 1876, p. 13). Mesdag (1831–1915) was a pupil of Alma-Tadema in Brussels. His *Scheveningen Beach* and *Lighthouse at Scheveningen* are in Amsterdam; *Summer Evening near Scheveningen* is in Berlin; *Small boats at Scheveningen* is in Brussels; and *Beach at Scheveningen: Winter* is in the Mesdag Museum, the Hague. The Dutch had for a long time painted this part of their coast, and in 1876 Bingham Mildmay lent his seventeenth-century painting by Ruysdael, *Scheveningen Sands*, to the Royal Academy exhibition of Old Masters. This

trip up the Rhine, his attitude to landscape, and the work of the painters Boldini and Hobbema.[9] 'The method of Boldini,' he wrote,

the painter of 'The Morning Walk' in the French Gallery two or three years ago (a young lady beside an ugly blank wall on an ugly highway)—of Hobbema, in his view of a road with formal lopped trees and flat tame scenery—is that of infusing emotion into the baldest external objects either by the presence of a human figure among them, or by mark of some human connection with them.

This accords with my feeling about, say, Heidelberg and Baden *versus* Scheveningen—as I wrote at the beginning of *The Return of the Native*—that the beauty of association is entirely superior to the beauty of aspect, and a beloved relative's old battered tankard to the finest Greek vase. Paradoxically put, it is to see the beauty in ugliness. (*EL* 157–8.)

Boldini's *The Morning Walk* of 1873 (Plate 13) was for many years thought to be lost, but is now known to be in a private collection in Bologna; Hobbema's *Avenue, Middelharnis* of 1669 (Plate 14) stands where it did in Hardy's day in the National Gallery, purchased as part of the Peel Collection in 1871; and if at first sight their differences seem greater than their similarities, Hardy clearly detected a common motive. Both contain small figures dominated by their surroundings; in both, the light is subdued and the setting undramatic; and it could be argued that both painters have made a virtue of the commonplace. Certainly at least one of Hardy's contemporaries saw a species of beauty in ugliness in the Hobbema. The critic of *The Times* described it as 'a double row of ugly pollard poplars lining a straight road, bordered by the ditches that enclose pollards and market gardens'.[10]

picture was brought for the National Gallery in 1893, and is now known as *The Shore at Egmond-aan-zee*. When Hardy visited the Louvre in 1874, he may well have seen Adrian van der Velde's *The Beach of Scheveningen*, but it is certain that he knew another view of Scheveningen by that artist's brother Willem (1633–1707), which had been bought by the National Gallery as part of the Peel Collection. In the same year that Hardy visited Paris, the Salon boasted no fewer than three pictures of Scheveningen. Hendrik Mesdag, Anton Mauve (1838–88), and Frederik Kaemmerer (1839–1902) each received honourable mention in the English press. See *Athenaeum*, 23 May 1874, p. 704, and 9 May 1874, p. 636. There were, no doubt, many more pictures of Scheveningen painted at this time.

9 Boldini (1842–1931) was an Italian living in Paris. His reputation was made by his rather facile, late nineteenth-century studies of people in Parisian high society. Hobbema's (1638–1709) *Avenue, Middelharnis* was thought, in Hardy's day, to be the scene of the painter's birthplace. See R. N. Wornum, *The Abridged Catalogue of the Pictures in the National Gallery: Foreign Schools*, p. 45.

10 *The Times*, 1 June 1871, p. 4.

1878 —

Nov. 23. Went to private view, Dudley Gallery
— was struck with a picture by an
Italian — "Near Porta Salara" by N.
Mangiarelli — (care of F. Leighton Esq.
2 Holland Park R⁰.) It showed 3
travellers on a dull uninteresting road,
stopping before a gaunt blank walled
inn — the woman of which comes out to
them — In the distance waste &
dreariness.

Figure 1. Thomas Hardy: Diary page showing sketch of Mangiarelli's painting
Near Porta Salara. 1878. Dorset County Museum, Dorchester

At this time Hardy seems to have made a point of mentally collecting similar images with which to furnish his memory and he found at least two more at the Grosvenor Gallery in 1878. Ignoring all the avant-garde and progressive works for which this gallery was the show-case,[11] he selected the academic pieces by Alma-Tadema and Frederick Leighton as examples of the expression of beauty in ugliness. In Alma-Tadema's *Sculpture*,[12] 'men at work carving the Sphinx', as he described it, and Leighton's *Ariadne Abandoned by Theseus*, which he described as 'an uninteresting dreary shore, little tent one corner, etc.', he claimed that 'the principles I have mentioned have been applied to choice of subject' (*EL* 158).[13] The picture which for Hardy most vividly encapsulated the special relationship between man and landscape, however, was called *Near Porta Salara*. It was by Mangiarelli, a little-known Italian painter living in London and was owned by Frederick Leighton; Hardy saw it when he went to a private viewing at the Dudley Gallery in November 1878. Though Hardy's diaries for this date were destroyed, one fragment is preserved in Dorchester County Museum (Figure I). Not only does it contain Hardy's thumb-nail sketch of the painting itself, it also affords a description of the salient features presumably written by him on the spot. The painting, he says, shows 'three travellers on a dull uninteresting road, stopping before a gaunt blank walled inn—the woman of which comes out to them. In the distance waste and dreariness.'[14] The original has been lost but there is enough in Hardy's description to see how it fitted into his thinking about man and his setting, and to perceive the links with his treatment of Egdon Heath. Like some of the other artists Hardy admired, Mangiarelli had managed to take a scene ostensibly lacking in interest and infuse it with vitality and originality through the relationship between the figures and the surroundings. Like Hobbema, Boldini, and the others, Mangiarelli ratified for Hardy the idea that 'the beauty of association is entirely superior to the beauty of aspect' (*EL* 158). The connection between *Near Porta Salara* and the narrative of *The Return of the Native* is not specifically visual, and the verbal rendition of landscape in *The Return of*

[11] For the circumstances surrounding the opening of the Grosvenor Gallery, see J. B. Bullen, 'The Palace of Art, Sir Coutts Lindsay and the Grosvenor Gallery'.
[12] This picture by Lawrence Alma-Tadema (1836–1912) is now known as *The Sculptor's Studio in Ancient Rome*. Collection of Mr George Wildenstein, New York (31.1 × 831.7. cm.). It was engraved for *The Art Journal*, NS 16 (1878), opp. p. 124.
[13] Frederick Leighton's (1830–96) *Ariadne Abandoned by Theseus* was first exhibited at the Royal Academy in 1868, and is now in Salarjung Museum, Hyderabad.
[14] *Diary fragment* in DCM, entry for 23 Nov. 1878.

the Native is based not so much upon the pictorial features of the painting as upon a common emotional register. There is one pictorial image, however, which *is* directly related to Hardy's account of Egdon Heath. It is by Hardy himself, (Plate 15) and shows very clearly 'the swarthy monotony' of his native Puddletown Heath just behind the cottage in which he was born. The activity of painting and drawing in the area around his boyhood home contributed materially to the fictional scenes in *Under the Greenwood Tree* and *Far from the Madding Crowd*. *Rainbarrow and the Heath* was also painted before he wrote *The Return of the Native*, but its pictorial details look forward to his account of Egdon Heath. The tertiary olive greens, browns, and greys, for example (all of which are very close in tone and do not reproduce well in monochrome), bear a close resemblance to the 'antique brown dress' (*RN* 6) of the fictional heath, while the featureless undulating horizon could well be described as 'surfaces which [were] neither so steep as to be destructible by weather, nor so flat as to be the victims of floods and deposits.' (*RN* 7). In accordance with Hardy's mature precepts, there is a figure in the scene—a single character whose presence relieves the monotony of earth and sky. Though not the furze-cutter of Egdon, but a cowhand, it is nevertheless this figure, reclining in the middle-distance, who communicates interest to a landscape which otherwise has little to arrest the attention of the spectator.

If the art of painting contributes surprisingly little to the visual qualities of landscape and landscape description in *The Return of the Native*, it does play an enormously important part in another aspect of the writing of this novel. Strangely, it is the characterization rather than the scenery which has strong connections with the painter's art. We have seen the importance for Hardy of the 'humanization' of landscape—of the human 'mark' made upon the otherwise empty scene. He also had a spontaneous tendency to detect life in inanimate objects—to see 'countenances' in hills, trees, and buildings (*LY* 58) and to regard the objects of nature as 'pensive mutes' (*EL* 150). In *The Return of the Native* he animates the inanimate by means of an altogether unexpected process of stylization: he translates both into verbal 'portraiture'. In this novel, portraiture forms the common ground between the animate and the inanimate, and it is through the visual rendition of human physiognomy that Hardy links man and his setting. This claim requires some explanation, and the remainder of the chapter is concerned principally with the way in which Hardy manipulates the relationship between landscape and character in terms of portraiture.

Verbal Portraiture

The earliest reviewers of *The Return of the Native* identified Egdon Heath as one of the principal dramatis personae of the novel.[15] Even in the first few pages of the story, the heath is described as an 'untameable Ishmaelitish thing' (*RN* 6), whose relationship with its environment resembles relationships within a human family. The storm is its 'lover', and the wind its 'friend' (*RN* 5); it 'fraternizes' with twilight, and is 'a near relation of night' (*RN* 4). Like man, too, the heath has its affections and its hates. As an 'obsolete thing' (*RN* 205) it is the 'enemy' of civilization (*RN* 6), and it is sufficiently animate to be 'hated' by both Wildeve and Eustacia (*RN* 98), but loved by Thomasin, Mrs Yeobright, and Clym, all of whom find 'friendliness and geniality' in its appearance (*RN* 137).

It is that appearance, however, which is most intriguing, since, of all the heath's qualities, it is the one which is most human. It is attributed with 'clothing', albeit only one 'antique brown dress' (*RN* 6), but which 'venerable . . . coat', says the narrator, provides a 'satire on human vanity in clothes.' (*RN* 6). It is the 'face' of the heath, however, which features so prominently in the novel, and the title of the very first chapter—'A Face on which Time Makes But Little Impression'—underlines its importance. The heath has a 'Titanic form' (*RN* 4) and an 'Atlantean brow' (*RN* 13); it is 'haggard' and 'ancient' (*RN* 5); it has a 'wild' face (*RN* 6), a 'grim old face' (*RN* 413), and a 'lonely face' (*RN* 6). Sometimes the face is 'swarthy' (*RN* 6), sometimes as dark as that of a Negro (*RN* 149). It is 'full of watchful intentness' (*RN* 4), and 'solitude seemed to look out of its countenance.' (*RN* 6). Wildeve can make nothing of this face, and its 'subtle beauties [are] lost to Eustacia.' (*RN* 81). In contrast, the natives understand it. At night Mrs Yeobright feels no fear of the heath since 'darkness lends no frightfulness to the face of a friend' (*RN* 38); Clym Yeobright finds 'friendliness and geniality written in the faces of the hills around' (*RN* 137), and his cousin admires the 'grim old face' of the heath (*RN* 413). The mobile and expressive face

[15] In the *Observer* of 29 Jan. 1879, a reviewer said that 'the Heath of Edgon may be considered one of the dramatis personae.'

is framed by the furze which Hardy frequently calls 'shaggy locks' (*RN* 178), and to complete the portrait, the Roman road bisects it 'like the parting-line on a head of black hair' (*RN* 8).

Hardy uses the anthropomorphism of the heath as a way of distinguishing between the moral strengths and weaknesses of certain characters, but his concentration on the physiognomy of Egdon draws attention to one of the principal themes of this novel—the expressiveness of the human face. Visually speaking, the book is a veritable gallery of portrait studies. Faces are looked at, watched, examined, and analysed for signs of feeling, marks of intelligence, and symptoms of anxiety. Not only is the face of the heath persistently scrutinized, sometimes for signs of a change in the weather, more often for a human mark or message, but the faces of both major and minor characters are the subject of a permenent watchfulness. They are watched by each other, but most of all by the narrator. Again and again in this novel, characters are introduced into the story in terms of the appearance of their faces. Their presence is always anticipated by fragments of physiognomy or glimpses of facial features—the profile half-revealed in darkness, obscured, or partially covered by clothing. All the major characters enter the story in mysterious circumstances, and each of those circumstances heightens the desire to see the face. The most outstanding examples of this are the preparations which Hardy makes for the portraits of Eustacia Vye as 'Queen of Night' and of Clym Yeobright with his 'face of the future'; but the lesser characters, Thomasin and Mrs Yeobright, and the rustic characters whom Hardy depicts in a series of miniatures, also emerge slowly and tantalizingly from the darkness of the night. Granfer Cantle, Timothy Fairway and Susan Nonesuch appear around the flickering fire on Rainbarrow as a series of partial and incomplete studies by Dürer: 'The brilliant lights and sooty shades which struggled upon the skin and clothes of the persons standing round caused their lineaments and general contours to be drawn with Düreresque vigour and dash.' (*RN* 18). Granfer Cantle dances by himself, but Timothy Fairway chooses a partner in Susan Nonesuch. Her 'broad form' was 'lifted bodily by Mr. Fairway's arm' in a scene of rustic exuberance. As he 'whirled her round and round', the 'clicking of the pattens, the creaking of the stays, and her screams of surprise, formed a very audible concert.' (*RN* 33). Dürer's own *Dancing Peasants* was described in similar terms by William Bell Scott in an 1869 edition of the engravings. It is, he said, 'a group full of vigour and enjoyment, the sturdy little woman being as strong and frisky as a young bear'.[16] In *Under the Greenwood Tree* Hardy had already exploited the vigour of the genre scene, but the spirited 'dash' of Dürer's engraving stands in strong contrast to the quieter pictures of English and Dutch life which had inspired the scenes of the earlier novel. In *Under the Greenwood Tree* the distortion introduced into the descriptions of the Mellstock choir was simply comic in its effect. Here the strange group portrait is both comic and macabre.

Shadowy eye-sockets, deep as those of a death's head, suddenly turned into pits of lustre: a lantern-jaw was cavernous, then it was shining; wrinkles were emphasized to ravines, or obliterated entirely by a changed ray. Nostrils were dark wells; sinews in old necks were gilt mouldings; things with no particular polish on them were glazed; bright objects, such as the tip of a furze-hook one of the men carried, were as glass; eyeballs glowed like little lanterns. Those whom Nature had depicted as merely quaint became grotesque, the grotesque became preternatural; for all was in extremity. (*RN* 18.)

The stress on the grotesque in this passage, and its connection with the art of Dürer, touches on one of the central themes of *The Return of the Native*. In the 1870s Dürer's work was something of an anomaly for art-historians and critics alike. As with much of the art of northern Europe, it did not conform to classical or Renaissance standards of beauty. 'He fails', wrote J. A. Crowe in the contemporary guide to Dutch, Flemish, and German painting, 'in feeling for beauty',[17] and this failure, said Crowe, was especially observable in his portraits: 'Even in the expression and form of the countenance, Dürer follows a certain form, which cannot be called the normal type of ideal beauty.' For Crowe, Dürer's art is characterized by wilful and deliberate distortion. He fails 'in some instances', says Crowe, to produce 'even a faithful copy of common life after the manner of his contemporaries'. Mary Heaton, in her biography of Dürer, was equally apologetic. Though she felt that his 'strange tendency to the fantastic' was one of his chief charms, she describes his etching of dancing peasants as 'ludicrous and uncouth'.[18]

The tenacious notion that true beauty was the prerogative of the south lies behind Hardy's remark on the popularity of 'the vineyards and myrtle-gardens of South Europe'. It also influenced his choice of

[16] William Bell Scott, *Albert Dürer: His Life and Works*, p. 214.
[17] [*Kugler's*] *Handbook of Painting: The German, Felmish and Dutch Schools*, ed. J. A. Crowe, p. 153.
[18] Mary Margaret Heaton, *The History of the Life of Albrecht Dürer of Nürnberg*, p. 194.

Dürer for this scene. 'Numerous . . . writers . . . all agree', says Heaton, 'that [he] would have been a greater artist had he had Italian training, and had he modelled his art on that of Greece instead of indulging a wild Teutonic imagination.'[19] But it is just the 'ludicrous and uncouth' and the 'wild Teutonic imagination' which attract Hardy. For Hardy, Dürer is a quintessentially northern artist. He is, says Heaton, 'preeminently the representative artist of Germany . . . in its strange love for the weird and grotesque in art'.[20] Pater, too, used the word 'grotesque' to describe Dürer's work. In *The Renaissance* he disparagingly contrasts the 'morbid or grotesque' art of the north of Europe and the 'grim inventions' of Dürer with the serener, Mediterranean work of Michelangelo.[21] Even though Dürer did not conform to conventional standards of beauty, however, he was greatly admired for what Crowe called the 'life and character'[22] of his drawing. In the scene on the Rainbarrow this vitality is most graphically represented in 'the face of an old man' which emerges piece by piece. The portrait, says Hardy, 'was not really the mere nose and chin that it appeared to be, but an appreciable quantity of human countenance.' (*RN* 18). At first it is anonymous, then slowly it is identified; but the full significance of the face of this true native of the heath is made clear only much later in the story, when its grotesque but animate features are compared with Yeobright's worn appearance.

Thomasin Yeobright also enters the story for the first time as an anonymous face. We learn of her recent history through the conversation between Venn and Captain Vye, and by the end of that discussion the reader is as anxious to see into the Reddleman's van as the captain himself. Eventually Venn opens the door at Mrs Yeobright's request, and he illuminates the picture in his mobile 'cabinet' by means of his lantern. Under the light,

a fair, sweet, and honest country face was revealed, reposing in a nest of wavy chestnut hair. It was between pretty and beautiful. Though her eyes were closed, one could easily imagine the light necessarily shining in them as the culmination of the luminous workmanship around. The groundwork of the face was hopefulness; but over it now lay like a foreign substance a film of anxiety and grief. . . . The scarlet of her lips had not had time to abate, and

---

[19] Ibid., p. 166. Similar views were expressed by F. W. Fairholt in 'Dürer', in *Rambles of an Archaeologist* (1871), p. 199.

[20] Heaton, p. 165.

[21] Pater, *The Renaissance*, p. 73.

[22] Crowe, *Handbook of Painting*, p. 153.

just now it appeared still more intense by the absence of the neighbouring and more transient colour of her cheek. (*RN* 41.)

What Hardy has done here with Thomasin Yeobright, he does on a much larger scale with Eustacia Vye and Clym Yeobright. Objective contemplation—the face framed by the hair, the 'luminous workmanship' of the facial features, the soft illumination, the careful annotation of colouring on a pictorial model—gives way to interpretation. The picture speaks of 'hopefulness' overlaid with 'anxiety and grief', and it is through this interpretation that we learn something of Thomasin's character and a little more of the circumstances which have brought her to Diggory's van. A similar pattern is repeated with Eustacia Vye and Clym Yeobright. The faces of each of these major characters are revealed by the author in a protracted and tantalizing way: each of them is likened to painted or sculpted artefacts, and in each case the face is inscribed with what Hardy calls 'legible meanings.' (*RN* 162).

Mystery surrounds Eustacia's first appearance in the story. She is observed by Diggory Venn as a distant and anonymous 'presence' (an important word) rising on the summit of Rainbarrow. The mystery is deepened by her return to the barrow after the departure of the rustics, and the enigma of her behaviour is enhanced by her face which is obscured by clothing. Her form, Hardy tells us, is 'wrapped in a shawl folded in the old cornerwise fashion, and her head in a large kerchief.' (*RN* 59). When the wind blows this kerchief aside, the reader is allowed a glimpse of her profile, but what he sees does nothing to dispel the enigma. The profile was visible 'against the dull monochrome of cloud around her; and it was as though side shadows from the features of Sappho and Mrs. Siddons had converged upwards from the tomb to form an image like neither but suggesting both.' (*RN* 62).[23] The reader's curiosity is heightened by a brief lecture on the importance of physiognomy in the expression of character which Hardy then reads. 'In respect of character', he says,

[23] Both the MS (University College, Dublin) and the serialized version in *Belgravia* read 'Marie Antoinette and Lord Byron'. In the first edition (1878) this became 'Marie Antoinette and Mrs. Siddons'; Sappho was not added until 1893. The 'lost' Marie Antoinette might well be an allusion to *Marie Antoinette On Her Way to the Place of Execution*, which was exhibited by Lord Ronald Gower at the summer exhibition of the Royal Academy in 1876. The critic of the *Art Journal* described 'the white marble form of Marie Antoinette, attenuated and tall, with head erect and face sublimed' as 'startling in its vividness', NS 15 (June 1877), p. 185, and the piece was reproduced in the *Art Journal*, NS 16 (Sep. 1878), p. 184. Gower was a collector of images of Marie Antoinette, and published his collection in the early 1880s.

a face may make certain admissions by its outline; but it fully confesses only in its changes. So much in this the case that what is called the play of features often helps more in understanding a man or woman than the earnest labours of all the other members together. Thus the night revealed little of her whose form it was embracing, for the mobile parts of her countenance could not be seen. (*RN* 62.)

Once again, it is the word 'reveal' which Hardy uses in conjunction with the power of the human face. That revelation comes very soon in the famous chapter entitled 'Queen of Night':

Eustacia Vye was the raw material of a divinity. On Olympus she would have done well with a little preparation. She had the passions and instincts which make a model goddess, that is, those which make not quite a model woman. Had it been possible for the earth and mankind to be entirely in her grasp for a while, had she handled the distaff, the spindle, and the shears at her own free will, few in the world would have noticed the change of government. (*RN* 75.)

There is a touch of irony in this, and it informs the elaborate set piece which follows. Eustacia is not quite a goddess: she just has the makings of one. But neither is she altogether human, for she is determinedly and deliberately aloof. It is not easy to decide whether the ambivalence derives principally from Hardy's attitude to his own creation, or whether it stems from Eustacia's own self-delusions; what is certain, however, is that it is not dispelled by the bizarre constituents of her personality.

At first she appears like a classical bust abandoned in a wild northern place. Her geometric profile and her sinuous proportions are not native to the heath, but derive from a southerly climate and location.

Viewed sideways, the closing-line of her lip formed, with almost geometric precision, the curve so well known in the arts of design as the cima-recta, or ogee. The sight of such a flexible bend as that on grim Egdon was quite an apparition. . . . One had fancied that such lip-curves were mostly lurking underground in the South as fragments of forgotten marbles. (*RN* 76.)

It is not from 'Saxon pirates' and northern stock that Eustacia inherits such lips; they come from her Mediterranean ancestry on her father's side. He was a 'Corfiote by birth' (*RN* 77), heralded 'from Phaeacia's isle' (*RN* 78), and was 'a sort of Greek Ulysses' (*RN* 251). But Eustacia's classicism is entirely superficial, and is shown up by her voluptuous sensuality and her 'sudden fits of gloom, one of the phases of the night-side of sentiment which she knew too well for her years.' (*RN* 76). Her eyes are 'Pagan' rather than classical and they are

full of nocturnal mysteries, and their light, as it came and went, and came again, was partially hampered by their oppressive lids and lashes; and of these the underlid was much fuller than it usually is with English women. This enabled her to indulge in reverie without seeming to do so: she might have been believed capable of sleeping without closing them up. . . . Her presence brought memories of such things as Bourbon roses, rubies, and tropical midnights; her moods recalled lotus-eaters and the march in 'Athalie'; her motions, the ebb and flow of the sea; her voice the viola. (*RN* 76.)

As David J. DeLaura has pointed out,[24] in this account of Eustacia there is the reminiscence of another famous 'presence'—the one which Pater conjured up in his book *The Renaissance* of 1873. It is the *Mona Lisa*, whose 'presence . . . rose thus so strangely beside the waters' and says Pater, is 'expressive of what in the ways of a thousand years men had come to desire'.[25] Eustacia's 'presence' rises on the summit of Rainbarrow; she, too, is a *femme fatale*, and, like the *Mona Lisa* as Pater describes her, has an intense inner life. That life, says Pater, is generated out of 'strange thoughts and fantastic reveries and exquisite passions', while the equally passionate Eustacia, with her 'heavy eyelids', indulges in 'reveries without seeming to do so.' (*RN* 76). According to Pater, *The Gioconda*'s eyelids are 'a little weary';[26] similarly, Eustacia's eyes are 'partially hampered' by her 'oppressive lids and lashes', giving the impression of lassitude. Both Pater and Hardy stress the importance of the female soul. 'Assuming that the souls of men and women were visible essences,' writes Hardy, 'you could fancy the colour of Eustacia's soul to be flame-like', whereas the *Mona Lisa*, says Pater, has a beauty into which 'the soul with all its maladies has passed'. Both women project a curious and exotic set of associations as the visible essence of their presence. The *Mona Lisa* expresses 'the animalism of Greece, the lust of Rome, the mysticism of the middle age, . . . the sins of the Borgias', while Eustacia brings back memories of 'Bourbon roses, rubies and tropical midnights'. In *The Renaissance* Pater uses the *Mona Lisa* as a symbol. 'She might stand', says Pater,

---

[24] David J. DeLaura, 'The "Ache of Modernism" in Hardy's Later Novels', pp. 382–3.
[25] Pater, *The Renaissance*, p. 98.
[26] Ibid., p. 99.

'as the embodiment of the old fancy, the symbol of the modern idea.'
I have tried to show elsewhere[27] what Pater meant by this, and how
he uses Leonardo da Vinci's art to epitomize the romantic spirit in
art. According to Pater, all periods in history have their romantic
side—even classical Greece and the Italian Renaissance. Some of
those periods are more obviously dominated by the romantic spirit
than others; but romanticism, he argues, 'although it has its epochs,
is in its essential characteristics rather a spirit which shows itself at all
times, in various degrees in individuals and their works'.[28] Hardy,
who read Pater's account of romanticism,[29] expressed a very similar
sentiment. 'Romanticism', he said, 'will exist in human nature as
long as human nature itself exists' (*EL* 189); and in Eustacia Vye he
created his own 'symbol of the modern idea'. The word 'romantic' is
frequently associated with her life, her temperament, and her ideas.
Her father was 'a romantic wanderer' (*RN* 251), and from him she
inherited her 'rich, romantic lips' (*RN* 118). She is in constant pursuit of the romantic, 'intense and . . . exceptional'; there was, says
Hardy, 'no middle distance in her perspective', which was filled with
'romantic recollections of sunny afternoons on an esplanade [which]
. . . stood like gilded letters upon the dark tablet of surrounding
Egdon.' (*RN* 78). She is a 'romantic martyr to superstition' (*RN* 212)
and her infatuation with Clym Yeobright is part of her romantic
obsession with the exotic. 'This perfervid woman', says Hardy, 'was
. . . half in love with a vision.' (*RN* 139).[30]

Hardy's debt to Pater's romantic symbol, however, is not specifically visual. His style—the cadences, the associative technique—and
the symbol of the *femme fatale* may well derive from Pater's treatment
of the *Mona Lisa*, but, with the exception of her heavy eyelids,
Eustacia Vye bears no physical resemblance to Leonardo's masterpiece. Yet Hardy is very precise about that appearance:

She was in person full-limbed and somewhat heavy; without ruddiness, as
without pallor; and soft to the touch as a cloud. To see her hair was to fancy

[27] J. B. Bullen, 'Walter Pater's Interpretation of the Mona Lisa as a Symbol of
Romanticism'.

[28] Walter Pater, 'Romanticism', p. 69.;

[29] LN, entry 1736.

[30] Leonardo's taste for the 'bizarre or recherché' (Pater, *The Renaissance*, p. 87) and
his preference for the 'more remote' and 'exceptional' (p. 86), link him with the
modern romantic temper, which, says Pater, constantly seeks 'new impressions, new
pleasures' ('Romanticism', p. 65) and delights in 'things unlikely and remote.' (p. 67).

that a whole winter did not contain darkness enough to form its shadow: it closed over her forehead like nightfall extinguishing the western glow. (*RN* 75.)

The physical characteristics of Eustacia resemble, at least in one of their aspects, those 'love-freighted lips and absolute eyes that wean / The pulse of hearts to the sphere's dominant tune' of Rossetti's *Astarte Syriaca* (Plate 16). Rossetti's Syrian Venus is a deadly goddess, full-limbed and heavy with sensuality; she, too, has hair of blackest night which closes over her forehead, and her extraordinary lips might well be described as 'cima-recta or ogee'. When Graham Robertson met Jane Morris herself, he was struck by the 'carven lips . . . firm and sharp',[31] and Eustacia's are 'clearly cut as the point of a spear.' (*RN* 76). Even the Tartarean setting of Rossetti's portrait is appropriate to the novel, in which the central figure emerges from the swirling darkness flanked by emblems of her victory over the hearts of men. The picture was finished in 1876, the year that Hardy was writing the *Return of the Native*, and even if he did not see this precise image, his account of Eustacia must surely derive from the type of aesthetic beauty which was then in vogue. The female aesthete of the 1870s, according to one contemporary, was 'a pale distraught lady with matted dark . . . hair falling in masses over the brow, and shading eyes full of love-lorn langour, or feverish despair'.[32] This may well have its origins in the wild and mystic beauty of Holman Hunt's illustration of Tennyson's 'The Lady of Shalott' (Plate 17), and was both popularized and parodied in Du Maurier's satires on aestheticism in *Punch* and deified in Rossetti's portraits of Jane Morris. Among the aesthetes themselves, this particular image of woman was highly self-conscious, determinedly individualistic, historically reactionary, and, above all, romantic. If the role of the artist is, as Hardy suggests, 'to adopt that form of romanticism which is the mood of the age' (*EL* 189), he could not have picked a more suitable image for Eustacia; yet his portrait of her concludes with the romantic view of woman from another age:

In a dim light, and with a slight rearrangement of her hair, her general figure might have stood for that of either of the higher female deities. The new moon behind her head, an old helmet upon it, a diadem of accidental dewdrops round her brow, would have been adjuncts sufficient to strike the note of Artemis, Athena, or Hera respectively, with as close an approximation to the antique as that which passes muster on many respected canvases. (*RN* 76–7.)

[31] W. Graham Robertson, *Time Was*, p. 94.
[32] Walter Hamilton, *The Aesthetic Movement in England*, p. 24.

The clue to the identity of those 'respected canvases' is to be found in George Eliot's *Daniel Deronda*. At the archery meeting in Brackenshaw Park, Gwendolen Harleth appears in clothing which 'set off her form to the utmost': 'A thin line of gold round her neck, and the gold star on her breast, were her only ornaments. Her smooth soft hair piled up into a grand crown made a clear line about her brow. Sir Joshua would have been glad to take her portrait.'[33]

As Hugh Witemeyer points out, 'Sir Joshua would have entitled the portrait *Miss Harleth as Diana.*'[34] Sir Joshua Reynolds had already made an anonymous contribution to *The Return of the Native* in the portrait of Eustacia Vye, as 'side shadows from the features of Sappho and Mrs Siddons . . . converged upwards from the tomb to form an image like neither but suggesting both.' (*RN* 62). Here the allusion is almost certainly to Reynold's picture of Sarah Siddons as *The Tragic Muse* (Plate 18)—a picture which Hardy first saw at the International Exhibition of 1862, then again at the Royal Academy in 1870. In it, Sarah Siddons sits regally enthroned in a Tartarean setting, not unlike that in the Rossetti picture, and flanked, this time, not by torch-bearers but by harbingers of death and tragedy—one carrying the poisoned cup, the other the dagger. During the years in which Hardy had been writing novels, Reynolds's reputation had undergone considerable change. In the 1830s and 1840s he had been the 'Sir Sloshua' of the Pre-Raphaelites, and the painter of 'correct taste' but 'little imagination' of Hardy's own *Schools of Painting* notebook;[35] but in subsequent decades he had gradually earned the respect and admiration of the critics. At the International Exhibition, thirty-four of his portraits were on show; it was the annual exhibition of Old Masters at the Royal Academy, however, which set in motion the real vogue for his work. His Sarah Siddons portrait was shown in 1870; twenty-one portraits were on view in 1875, thirty-one in 1876, and a further twenty-one in 1877. His claim on Hardy's attention was his reputed ability to capture the essential psychology of his sitters. 'No one', said one critic, 'has surpassed Reynolds in his profound feeling for the indescribable thoughts of the inward man.'[36] Reynolds, said another, 'saw into the inner character of the sitter'.[37]

---

[33] George Eliot, *Daniel Deronda* i. 170.

[34] Witemeyer, *George Eliot and the Visual Arts*, p. 93.

[35] *Personal Notebooks*, ed. Taylor, p. 113.

[36] *International Exhibition, 1862: Official Catalogue of the Fine Art Department* (1862), p. 4.

[37] *The Magazine of Art*, Dec. 1878, pp. 230–32.

The 'respected canvases' depicting Artemis, Athena, and Hera can all be identified with some certainty. For reasons of consistency, Hardy transports Reynolds's goddesses from Rome to Greece, but at least two of Reynolds's sitters chose Diana or Artemis as their deity. Lady Anne Fermour (Plate 19) has a 'new moon' in her hair and pearls (Hardy's 'accidental dewdrops') decorating her head and wrist, while Elizabeth, Duchess of Manchester, has very similar decorative adjuncts in her role as Diana (Plate 20). Athena, or Minerva, is the subject of the portrait of Lady Charlotte Hill (Plate 21), and Anabella, Lady Blake, posed as Hera or Juno receiving the so-called 'cestus' from Venus—a potent symbol of sexual attractiveness (Plate 22).[38]

Reynolds was not alone in creating these composite portraits, or 'fancy pictures' as they were known, in which fashionable sitters idealized themselves by association with mythical divinities. Jean Hagstrum suggests that the trend in England was started by Van Dyck and was then taken up by Sir Peter Lely, Godfrey Kneller, and many others.[39] The idea, of course, goes back well beyond the eighteenth century, but the tradition itself throws an interesting light on Hardy's own techniques of verbal portraiture in *The Return of the Native*. Edgar Wind tells us that

the Roman Emperor Commodus had his portrait sculpted with lifelike accuracy, yet he surrounded his head with the skin of a lion and held a heavy club in his hand. Being thus vested with the emblems of Hercules, he presented himself as possessed of his virtues, and the honours due to the ancient demi-god were transferred to the emperor in whom he was embodied.[40]

Similarly, Wind adds, 'the Virgin Queen will assume the role of Diana, and the *Roi Soleil* will invest himself with the symbols of Phoebus Apollo.'[41] In his portrait of Eustacia Vye, Hardy is attempting something very similar. In the manner of the classical composite portrait, he surrounds his central figure with emblems derived from romantic images of women. Eustacia Vye is 'composed' of elements from Pater's account of the *Mona Lisa*, Rossetti's fatal Venus, and Reynolds's aristocratic deities. Hardy adopts for Eustacia what Wind

---

[38] See Ellis Waterhouse, *Sir Joshua Reynolds*.

[39] Jean Hagstrum, *The Sister Arts: The Tradition of Literary Pictorialism and English Poetry from Dryden to Gray*, pp. 144 and 146.

[40] Edgar Wind, 'Studies in Allegorical Portraiture—1: (i) In Defence of Composite Portraits', p. 138.

[41] Ibid.

calls 'the method of expressing one's power through a visible sign'.[42]
And though Hardy's signs are both verbal and visual, they co-operate
to invest Eustacia with semi-divine status: she is the 'raw material of
divinity'.

Hardy adopts a very similar technique for the appearance of Clym
Yeobright, but there is a wryness about his account of Eustacia,
which contrasts strongly with his presentation of Clym. Eustacia is
neither wholly goddess nor wholly woman, and she only 'approxi-
mates' to the antique. Wind claims that 'not for one moment does
Reynolds assume that in depicting a woman as Hebe or Juno he is in-
vesting her with some rightful sign of divinity'. Hardy's rendering of
the 'Queen of Night' is also profoundly self-conscious; it is written, as
one early critic perceptively pointed out, in 'the Grosvenor Gallery
style'.[43] Nevertheless, its conjunction of aestheticism, pictorialism,
mannerism, and romanticism creates a sense of incongruity that
reflects Eustacia Vye's position on Egdon Heath.

Clym Yeobright's face is as important as Eustacia Vye's. Before
Yeobright arrives on Egdon Heath, at least two of the major
characters speculate on the appearance of his face. One of these is his
cousin Thomasin. 'Dear Clym,' she says to herself, 'I wonder how
your face looks now?' (RN 130). The other is Eustacia herself,
whose desire to see Clym's face borders on obsession. Warned of his
imminent arrival at Blooms-End Cottage, she goes many times onto
the heath to catch a glimpse of him, and when their first encounter is
frustrated by the twilight, she returns home and dreams about him.
Significantly, this is a dream in which his face plays a crucial role. In
the dream,

she was dancing to wondrous music, and her partner was a man in silver
armour . . . the visor of his helmet being closed. The mazes of the dance were
ecstatic. Soft whispering came into her ear from under the radiant helmet,
and she felt like a woman in Paradise. Suddenly these two wheeled out from
the mass of dancers, dived into one of the pools of the heath, and came out
somewhere beneath into an iridescent hollow, arched with rainbows. 'It must
be here,' said a voice by her side, and blushingly looking up she saw him
remove his casque to kiss her. At that moment there was a cracking noise, and
his figure fell into fragments like a pack of cards. (RN 138.)

Any reader of *Far from the Madding Crowd* will recognize the similarity
between the events of this dream and Frank Troy's sword exercises in

42 Ibid.   43 *The Times*, 5 Dec. 1878, p. 8.

13. Giovanni Boldini:
*Ragazza in Bianco e
Contadini* (*The Morning
Stroll*). 1873. Private
Collection, Bologna
(24×33 cm)

14. Meindert Hobbema:
The Avenue, Middelharnis.
1689. National Gallery,
London
(103.5×141cm)

15. Thomas Hardy:
Rainbarrow and the Heath.
n.d. Dorset County
Museum, Dorchester

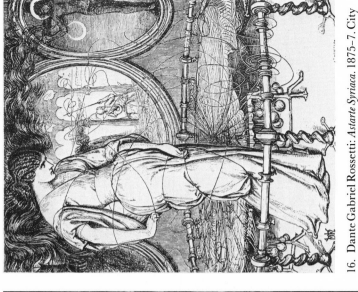

16. Dante Gabriel Rossetti: *Astarte Syriaca*. 1875–7. City of Manchester Art Galleries (182.9×106.7 cm)

17. William Holman Hunt: *The Lady of Shalott*. Engraved by J. Thompson for *Poems by Alfred Tennyson*, 1857

the hollow among the ferns. The warlike appearance, the sequestered location, the blushing, the kiss, even the rainbow, appear in both; and whereas Bathsheba cannot meet Troy's glance, Eustacia is denied the sight of Clym's face. 'O that I had seen his face!' she cries, and wakes herself up. But disappointment increases desire, and the whole mumming incident grows out of her passion to 'behold face to face the owner of the awakening voice.' (*RN* 141).

It is in a chapter entitled 'The Two Stand Face to Face' that Eustacia, dressed as a Turkish knight, gets her first clear view of Yeobright. In this scene, however, the terms of her dream are reversed. It is *she* who wears the visor, and it is *her* face that is obscured. With 'the power of her face all lost' and 'the charm of her emotions all disguised', the fascination of 'her coquetry' is 'denied existence' (*RN* 169). At this point in the novel the face of Clym Yeobright moves into prominence, and it is his face which becomes a 'spectacle' that both Eustacia and the reader are invited to observe. Clym is ensconced in the interior of Blooms-End Cottage, and his face is lit by the nearby fire.

A face showed itself with marked distinctness against the dark-tanned wood of the upper part [of the settle]. The owner who was leaning against the settle's outer end was Clement Yeobright, or Clym, as he was called here. . . . The spectacle constituted an area of two feet in Rembrandt's intensest manner. A strange power in the lounger's appearance lay in the fact that, though his whole figure was visible, the observer's eye was only aware of his face. (*RN* 161.)

Whereas the face of Eustacia Vye was first likened to sculpture, Clym's is rendered in terms of painting. In order to understand why Hardy chose Rembrandt as the author of this portrait, however, we have to know something of Rembrandt's contemporary reputation. Obviously the special lighting played an important part in Hardy's choice. In the *Handbook of Painting* Crowe described Rembrandt's ability to express 'that clear, very warm but limited light, which only seems to dawn through masses of shadow'.[44] Rembrandt's standing in the 1870s, however, was not, as high as it is now. He was not ranked beside the masters of Italian art, in part because his subjects were mainly commonplace domestic and genre scenes, and in part because his treatment was unidealized. He was looked upon as a painter whose work was expressive rather than beautiful, and who concentrated

[44] Crowe, *Handbook of Painting*, p. 367.

on the inner vitality of his sitters rather than on the beauty of form. Like Dürer, Rembrandt was a master, in Hardy's own phrase, of 'beauty in ugliness'.

When, for example, a large number of Rembrandt's drawings and etchings went on show at the Burlington Fine Arts Club in 1877, the critic of the *Saturday Review* praised Rembrandt for his un-Italian qualities and for his ability to capture in paint the less conventionally beautiful aspects of the human countenance. Rembrandt, he said was, 'never more himself than when chronicling the time-worn wrinkles in the face'.[45] In his account of the face of Clym Yeobright, Hardy seems to have taken up a similar idea, since he, too, draws attention to the signs of premature ageing.

To one of the middle age the countenance was that of a young man, though a youth might hardly have seen any necessity for the term of immaturity. But it was really one of those faces which convey less the idea of many years as its age than of so much experience as its store. The number of their years may have adequately summed up Jared, Mahalaleel, and the rest of the antediluvians, but the age of modern man is to be measured by the intensity of his history. (*RN* 161.)

Clym's face gives palpable evidence that 'thought is a disease of the flesh' (*RN* 162), and like the figure of St Jerome in Rembrandt's *St Jerome in Meditation*—a picture shown at the Burlington Fine Arts Club—Clym's face is eroded by his 'wearing habit of meditation' (*RN* 161).

The appropriateness of Rembrandt's name on Clym's portrait is increased by the geographical explanation which Crowe gives for his style. Like Dürer's, his work was interpreted as peculiarly northern; and his genius for creating comfortable, dimly lit interiors, it was argued, stemmed from the climatic conditions of northern Europe.

Various conditions attending a northern climate and life, it must be remembered, are expressed in his works, and expressed also with an earnestness and intensity belonging to a genuine Dutch nature. In contrast with the rawness and inhospitality of the climate, which in its cold, damp, and darkness renders an open-air existence, for the greater part of the year, not only unattractive but injurious, a Northman's great object is to create a household climate, warmed and lighted by himself, which, in the compactness of the apartments containing it, in the ornamental objects which accompany it, and in his very consciousness of the difference between the external

[45] *Saturday Review*, 16 Jan. 1875, p. 83.

and internal atmosphere, gives a feeling of comfort and ease which a Southerner can never imagine, and which has remained unknown to those nations which are descended from the Latin races. This feeling speaks aloud from many of the pictures and etching of Rembrandt.[46]

It can be no coincidence that Hardy chose to place his own 'Rembrandt' portrait in what must be one of the cosiest interiors in all his novels. Outside, the mummers stand in the 'cold and frosty night' (*RN* 165); inside, near the fire, 'not a symptom of draught disturbs the air', and the backs of the men 'are as warm as their faces' (*RN* 161). Here are men who live in the north with what Crowe describes as its 'cold damp and darkness'; but beside the fire 'songs and old tales are drawn from the occupants [of the settle] by the comfortable heat, like fruit from melon-plants in a frame.' (*RN* 161).

The stress on the warmth of the interior, and the allusion to the work of Rembrandt, both serve to emphasize once again the north–south axis which runs like a leitmotif through the novel. Eustacia's profile is reminiscent of fragments of sculpture 'lurking underground in the South' (*RN* 76), while Clym's appearance is closely identified with the northerness of the heath. Clym, says Hardy, 'had been so inwoven with the heath in his boyhood that hardly anybody could look upon it without thinking of him.' (*RN* 198). He is further linked to the heath in the appeal that his face makes to the modern sensibility. Like the face of 'haggard Egdon', which 'appealed to a subtler and scarcer instinct, to a more recently learnt emotion, than that which responds to the sort of beauty called charming and fair' (*RN* 5), Clym's face is 'in keeping with the moods of the more thinking among mankind', and its strength lies not in its conventional beauty and outward form, but in its expressiveness and 'inner meaning'.

In Clym Yeobright's face could be dimly seen the typical countenance of the future. Should there be a classic period to art hereafter, its Pheidias may produce such faces. The view of life as a thing to be put up with, replacing that zest for existence which was so intense in early civilizations, must ultimately enter so thoroughly into the constitution of the advanced races that its facial expression will become accepted as a new artistic departure. People already feel that a man who lives without disturbing a curve of feature, or setting a mark of mental concern anywhere upon himself, is too far removed from modern perceptiveness to be a modern type. Physically beautiful men—the glory of the race when it was young—are almost an anachronism now; and

---

[46] Crowe, *Handbook of Painting*, p. 367.

we may wonder whether, at some time or other, physically beautiful women may not be an anachronism likewise. (*RN* 197.)

Just as the 'vineyard and myrtle-gardens of South Europe' may have satisfied 'our race when it was young' (*RN* 5), but now men turn to the 'chastened sublimity' of places like Egdon, so Clym's face is similarly 'haggard' and unconventionally beautiful.

What the Greeks only suspected we know well; what their Aeschylus imagined our nursery children feel. That old-fashioned revelling in the general situation grows less and less possible as we uncover the defects of natural laws, and see the quandary that man is in by their operation. (*RN* 198.)

The defects in 'natural laws' were discovered by both biological scientists and geologists—by Darwin, Huxley, and Spencer, and by Lyle—and it is these 'defects' which explain the strange features of Clym Yeobright: 'The lineaments which will get embodied in ideals based upon this new recognition will probably be akin to those of Yeobright.' (*RN* 198). The idea that the modern face was expressive of the sum total of its experience was not uncommon in the nineteenth century, and at least two of Hardy's contemporaries expressed the idea in writing.[47] But a more potent image of the expressive countenance was provided by sculpture, and the work of one sculptor in particular may well have furnished Hardy with several 'faces of the future'. The sculptor was Thomas Woolner. In the 1870s Woolner had built himself a considerable reputation for busts of intellectuals, scientists, and statesmen; these were noted not for their classical or conventional beauty, but for the sense of nervous energy and mental vitality they conveyed.

In the portraits of Newman (1867), Carlyle (1868), Darwin (1870), Dickens (1872), Kingsley (1876), Tyndall (1877), and Huxley (1878), Woolner created a series of faces which bore evidence of deep thought, the 'wearing habit of meditation', and an active inner life. F. G. Stephens pointed out how in Woolner's bust of John Stuart

---

[47] F. G. Simcox in 'The Transformation of the British Face', *Art Journal*, NS 13 (June 1874), wrote that 'the face is of the nature of a palimpsest: every generation writes its own story there; and . . . the history of a long past may be written underneath.' (p. 21). He also anticipated Hardy's view that the modern face reflects the modern sensibility, saying that 'the rate of the intellectual movement has varied, the accumulation of positive knowledge of various kinds has continued without important interruptions, and . . . our life, which is reflected in our faces, has been gradually transformed by our growing knowledge.' (p. 21). There is a hint of a similar idea in Pater's account of the *Mona Lisa*.

Mill the face was merely 'an expressive mask for his intelligence'.[48] But by general consent, Woolner's masterpiece was his bust of Tennyson (Plate 23). It was shown with a number of his other works at the Royal Academy exhibition of 1876, which Hardy almost certainly visited before making his journey to Holland and the Rhine. Woolner's *Tennyson* received considerable attention as an example, in the words of *The Athenaeum*, of 'sculptural art of the finest kind',[49] but attention was directed in particular to the expressive quality of the portrait and to the 'deep ploughed traces of age'.[50] It was William Michael Rossetti, writing in *The Academy*, who saw in this piece something of the 'countenance of the future'. Rossetti described 'the noble facial line and fine features, the onward look which, as age advances, seems almost as much that of a seer or apostle as of a poet, the rich beard, and hair . . . are given with the full force of truth and of art in conjunction.[51] Hardy suggested that Clym's face might be read 'as a page', and the critic of the *Saturday Review* said that Woolner's bust 'reads as the epitome of a life; the poems of many years seem to write their lines across cheek and brow.'[52]

Hardy did not meet Woolner until 1880, but that meeting has interesting implications for the connection between the countenance of Clym Yeobright and Woolner's bust of Tennyson. They spent the evening together at the Rabelais Club in London, and on the following day Hardy sent the sculptor a copy of *The Return of the Native*, to which he attached a note. 'I hoped', Hardy wrote,

that I should have been able to say a few more words to you on the interesting subject of the art of the future which we began at the Rabelais Club dinner. As I scarcely expressed my meaning clearly I leave here for you a copy of my 'Return of the Native' where, at p. 171, I have embodied my ideas on the matter.[53]

The page to which Hardy referred Woolner was the one on which he described Clym's 'countenance of the future' as created by the new Phidias. He clearly hoped that his views would strike a sympathetic chord in Woolner.

---

[48] F. G. Stephens, 'Mr. Woolner's Sculptures', *Athenaeum*, 25 Dec. 1875, p. 884.
[49] *Athenaeum*, 20 May 1876, p. 704.
[50] *Academy*, 3 June 1876, p. 542.
[51] Ibid.
[52] *Saturday Review*, 41 (June 1876), p. 747.
[53] *Letters* i. 73.

The Articulate Look

The invitation to 'read' the meaning of Clym Yeobright's face is developed in the narrative through use of the visual metaphor. His anxiety and his trouble transform him into a 'picture of wretchedness,' 'If any man wants to make himself immortal by painting a picture of wretchedness,' he cries, 'let him come here' (*RN* 366). Sometimes this picture is classical: 'The Pupils of his eyes, fixed steadfastly on blankness, were vaguely lit with an icy shine; his mouth had passed into the phase more or less imaginatively rendered in studies of Oedipus.' (*RN* 384); sometimes it is biblical. After his escape from the weir pond he appears, as Alastair Smart has noticed,[54] like a figure from Sebastiano's *The Raising of Lazarus* (Plate 24): he is 'a thin, pallid, almost spectral form, wrapped in a blanket, and looking like Lazarus coming from the tomb.' (*RN* 447-8).

But the human face yields up its meaning more readily in movement than in stasis—'fully confesses', as Hardy himself points out, 'only in its changes' (*RN* 62)—so once the portraits of the first half of the novel have been clearly delineated, they are abandoned in favour of something more mobile and more in keeping with the drama of the narrative. Throughout the second half, Hardy consistently exploits the expressive power of the face, alternately covering and uncovering it, placing it in strange and unaccustomed lights, and filling it with strong emotion. Eustacia's beauty is 'cloaked and softened' by her outdoor attire, 'so that her faced looked from its environment as from a cloud, with no noticeable lines of demarcation between flesh and clothes' (*RN* 305-6), while at the same time Clym covers his face with goggles to protect his eyes. The face which had so fascinated Eustacia on their first meeting is now unrecognizable, and 'this man from Paris was . . . so disguised by his leather accoutrements, and by the goggles he was obliged to wear over his eyes, that his closest friend might have passed by without recognizing him.' (*RN* 298). There are many such episodes, but none more graphically illustrates Hardy's stress on the power of physiognomy than Clym Yeobright's discovery of the circumstances of the death of his mother. The discovery takes place when Clym goes to question Johnny Nonesuch—the only witness of the tragic events on that hot summer's day. 'How was her

54 Alastair Smart, 'Pictorial Imagery in the Novels of Thomas Hardy', p. 271. *The Raising of Lazarus* was part of the original Angerstein Collection which formed the nucleus of the National Gallery collection in 1827.

face?' Clym asks the child. 'Like yours now,' he replies. Susan Nonesuch looked at Clym and 'beheld him colourless, in a cold sweat.' (*RN* 383). The child had indeed scrutinized Mrs Yeobright's face after she had been turned away from Clym's cottage, but at the time he had been unable to 'read' what he saw there. He looked at her 'in a vague, wondering manner, like that of one examining some strange old manuscript the key to whose meaning is undiscoverable.' (*RN* 342). Unlike the child, however, Clym *is* able to interpret that meaning, and that meaning causes his own face to resemble the study of Oedipus. In a state of desperation he returns home, and on the way he sees another face. It is 'the imperturbable countenance of the heath, which, having defied the cataclysmal onsets of centuries, reduced to insignificance by its seamed and antique features the wildest turmoil of a single man.' (*RN* 384). When Clym returns to his cottage, the drama in terms of human physiognomy continues. Preparing himself to challenge Eustacia about the death of his mother, Clym 'came behind her, and she saw his face in the glass. It was ashy, haggard, and terrible.' (*RN* 386). They contemplate each other's image silently in the mirror, and those images communicate more than words. 'While she looked, the carmine flush with which warmth and sound sleep had suffused her cheeks and neck, dissolved from view, and the death-like pallor in his face flew across into hers.' Clym is able to read her face. ' "You know what is the matter," he said huskily, "I see it in your face".' (*RN* 386). As he accuses Eustacia of driving away his mother, Clym invites her to 'call to mind' another face—the face of Mrs Yeobright. ' "Think of her",' he urges Eustacia,

'what goodness there was in her: it showed in every line of her face! Most women, even when but slightly annoyed, show a flicker of evil in some curl of the mouth or some corner of the cheek; but as for her, never in her angriest moments was there anything malicious in her look.' (*RN* 390.)

Even now, however, Eustacia's face has not lost its power over Clym. 'For once . . . in her life she was totally oblivious of the charm of her attitude' (*RN* 392–3), but *he* was not, and as he tied the strings of her bonnet, 'he turned his eyes aside, that he might not be tempted to softness'.

The real drama of the novel ends as it began—with a series of portraits. Clym Yeobright, as mentioned earlier, rises from the dead like a figure from a painting by Sebastiano, while Eustacia finds in death something of the peace, dignity, and tranquility of the funerary monuments with which Hardy, as a church architect, was so familiar. 'Death', says Hardy, 'eclipsed all her living phases.'

Pallor did not include all the quality of her complexion, which seemed more than whiteness; it was almost light. The expression of her finely curved mouth was pleasant, as if a sense of dignity had just compelled her to leave off speaking. Eternal rigidity had seized upon it in a momentary transition between fervour and resignation. Her black hair was looser now than . . . [ever] before, and surrounded her brow like a forest. The stateliness of look which had been almost too marked for a dweller in a country domicile had at last found an artistically happy background. (*RN* 448.)

Once again in the novel, the stasis of portraiture asserts itself. Eustacia Vye—passionate, romantic, aesthetic—finds her true artistic context only in death. She has, in the course of the novel, literally set her face against the primitive, barbaric, and untamed face of the heath, and the heath has claimed her.

In a very real sense Hardy gives visual expression to the narrative of *The Return of the Native* in terms of human physiognomy. The three principal faces of the novel—Eustacia Vye's, Clym Yeobright's, and that of the heath—are surrounded by a number of miniatures—the rustics, Thomasin, and Mrs Yeobright—faces all of which contain 'legible meanings', though, surprisingly, the facial appearance of Wildeve and Venn receive very little attention, and Captain Vye's none at all. The immediate inspiration for the use of portraiture in *The Return of the Native* may well have come from a revival of interest in the genre which took place in the years immediately preceding the writing of this novel. The summer exhibition of the Royal Academy of 1876—the exhibition which contained the sculptures by Thomas Woolner—also contained an unusually large number of portraits. The critic of the *Saturday Review* pointed this out. Portraiture, he said, 'though often deemed a monotonous art', seemed to have undergone a renaissance. 'At the Academy,' he said, 'faces that are far from fair' had acquired 'style through treatment'. He praised the portraits by Millais, Leighton, Orchardson, and many others for their 'grace and persuasive manner', saying that they seemed to have 'inherited the palette and pencil of Reynolds'.[55] As for the work of Reynolds himself, that too underwent radical reassessment. The large number of portraits by him in the exhibitions of Old Masters during the decade increased public

[55] *Saturday Review*, 3 June 1876, p. 713.

interest. It was said that he 'animated portraiture . . . by poetry',[56] or that he 'painted biographies'.[57] The same critic suggested that his paintings 'are biographies in themselves, and are almost indispensable adjuncts to writers of written biography'.[58]

The encouragement to use portraiture as an 'adjunct' to literature also came from Thomas Carlyle. Hardy was familiar with Carlyle's views on the value of portraiture, because he quoted Carlyle in his preface to Jonathan Foster's *Wessex Worthies*. 'In all my poor historical investigations', said Carlyle,

it has been and always is, one of the most primary wants to procure a bodily likeness of the personage enquired after—a good portrait if such exists; failing that, even an indifferent if sincere one. In short, any representation made by a faithful creature of that face and figure which he saw with his eyes, and which I can never see with mine, is now valuable to me, and much better than none at all.[59]

Hardy's response to this idea was a daring one. Instead of using the portrait as an 'adjunct' to characterization, he incorporated the portrait itself in the text. Through his direct and indirect allusions to the methods and techniques of Dürer, Rembrandt, and Reynolds, and to the work of the moderns—Woolner, Rossetti, and others—he transformed his characters into symbols; his individuals become types, and even his landscape participates in the symbolic drama of the story. When the critic of the *Saturday Review* said in 1876 that 'the genius of our generation [is] given up to portrait painting',[60] he was referring to the paintings of the summer exhibition of that year. He might, however, with no incongruity, have extended his remarks to Hardy, and to *The Return of the Native*.

[56] *Saturday Review*, 3 June 1875, p. 149.
[57] *The Magazine of Art*, Dec. 1878, p. 230.
[58] Ibid.
[59] *Personal Writings*, ed. Orel, p. 88. Hardy also reported the words of Leslie Stephen, who, when planning the *Dictionary of National Biography*, said that he 'was making it his object to get hold of the personal appearance of his characters whenever he could do so, holding that a few words on the look of a man as he walked and talked, so far as it could be gathered from portraits and traditions, was worth a page of conjecture on his qualities'.
[60] *Saturday Review*, 3 June 1876, p. 713.

5

A Laodicean: Architecture as Symbol

'The New Renaisance: the dispute between Greek and Gothic—or
Gk. [*sic.*] and Hebraic [or] Naturalistic and ascetic [or] secular and
monastic [or] mediaeval and renaissance—are all names for contradictory views of life.'[1]

A Laodicean is one of Hardy's most curious exercises in literary form.
It provides little evidence of the imaginative fire which characterizes
Hardy at his best, and the second half of the novel fits uneasily with
the first. Yet, even though this work does not have the power of his
major fiction, it possesses an intrinsic interest to any student of his
mind and methods of writing. Its very rawness and the presence in
the text of unresolved and unassimilated ideas provide unusual evidence of Hardy's literary practices—a kind of writer's 'workshop
manual'—but what is more important is that a number of the technical problems which he set himself, but failed to solve here, found
more complete and satisfying expression in *The Mayor of Casterbridge*
and *Jude the Obscure*.

This novel is Hardy's most extensive experiment in *ecphrasis*—
verbal rendition of actual works of visual art for prophetic reasons,
or to give expression to moral or psychological ideas. Nathaniel
Hawthorne's *Marble Faun* (1860) employs the technique extensively,
as do George Eliot's *Romola* (1863) and Henry James's *The Story of a
Masterpiece* (1868) and *Madonna of the Future* (1873). The most famous
text to use a work of art in this way, of course, is Oscar Wilde's *Picture
of Dorian Gray*, in which the changing appearance of the portrait acts
as a commentary on the state of Dorian's soul.

Hardy rarely uses this technique. The statue which Barbara in
Barbara of the House of Grebe brings to England to worship after her
husband's death provides one example, and the d'Urberville portraits
provide another. Other instances are few and far between, except,

---

[1] 'Debased Hellenism and the New Renaissance', *The Church Quarterly Review*, 10
(Apr. 1880), p. 107, in *LN* entry 1189.

that is, in *A Laodicean*, where portraits, furnishings, and particularly architectural objects have considerable emblematic significance. Of course, Hardy had used both portraits and buildings in his novels before, but the portraits were usually employed either allusively or metaphorically, and buildings simply as appropriate settings for a specific set of incidents. In *The Return of the Native*, for example, though Hardy relies heavily on similes and metaphors borrowed from painting and sculpture to point up the appearance of Clym and Eustacia, the canvases themselves never appear on Egdon Heath; in *Under the Greenwood Tree* Mr Penny's workshop is '*like* a framed portrait . . . by some modern Moroni' (*UGT* 68); and in *Desperate Remedies* Cytherea's pose is reminiscent of a picture by Greuze. In *A Laodicean*, however, when George Somerset visits de Stancy Castle, he sees on the walls many of the paintings which Hardy himself had enjoyed in the nearby house of Kingston Lacy. Somerset is amazed to see works by 'Holbein, Jansen, and Vandyck; Sir Peter [Lely], Sir Geoffrey [*sic*] [Kneller], Sir Joshua [Reynolds], and Sir Thomas [Lawrence]' (*L* 27). In *The Return of the Native* the references to Dürer and Rembrandt ask the reader to respond to the visual techniques—subject, composition, and colouring—of works by each painter. In *A Laodicean* these things are much less important, and the list of works by famous artists serves principally to ratify the antiquity and nobility of the de Stancy family. For example, when Charlotte de Stancy, a member of the decayed aristocracy, stands on the battlements of de Stancy Castle, she appears as a Holbein portrait. In spite of the allusion to shape and colour, the purpose is to establish beyond all doubt her identity as a member of the nobility. Somerset saw

the dinted nose of the de Stancys outlined with Holbein shadowlessness against the blue-green of the distant wood. It was not the de Stancy face with all its original specialities: it was, so to speak, a defective reprint of that face. (*L* 29.)

Similarly, when Captain de Stancy dresses in armour and stands before a portrait of one of his ancestors, the visual similarity serves only to amaze Paula Power, and to reinforce the power over her mind of de Stancy's family tree.

Going then and placing himself in front of a low-hanging painting near the original, so as to be enclosed by the frame while covering the figure, arranging the sword as in the one above, and setting the light that it might fall in the right direction, he recalled [Paula Power and Charlotte de Stancy] when he put the question, 'Is the resemblance strong?' (*L* 215.)

The same portraits reappear at the end of the novel, when de Stancy, in a mood of desperation and depression, makes a bonfire and destroys them. Once again, however, their function is not a visual one; it merely symbolizes the final dissolution of the de Stancys. Hardy's use of *ecphrasis* in terms of portraiture and painting in this novel is a fairly simple matter. His extension of the device to include architecture and building styles, however, is, much more complex. The text of the novel is replete with elaborate descriptions of actual buildings, from Gothic churches to railway tunnels and from noncon-formist chapels to modern villas, and each of these buildings is associated with certain sentiments and ideas, some of which Hardy explains, some of which he does not. In the novel, however, Hardy uses the connections between building style and the prevailing ideology of that style—Gothic, neo-Hellenic, utilitarian—to express, or at least attempt to express, a much wider debate going on in Vic-torian society, of which the battle between architectural styles was but one manifestation.

Hardy's personal involvement with the architectural profession hardly needs stressing, and his sixteen years of day-to-day contact with builders and architects left its mark on his novels. Many of his most admirable characters have architectural connections, from Owen Graye and Edward Springrove in *Desperate Remedies* to Jude Fawley in *Jude the Obscure*, and almost all the stories contain sym-pathetic accounts of individual buildings. It was not, however, the technical details which most concerned him. Though he was extremely familiar with the utilitarian and practical aspects of the building trade, what interested him about architectural form was its expressive potential. 'The human interest in an edifice', he once wrote, 'ranks before its architectural interest, however great the latter may be.'[2] Hence the very 'bricks and mortar' in the diary at Talbothays 'throb with a burning sensibility' to the mind of the infatuated Angel Clare (*TD* 198), and in the 'reverberations' of Mr Melbury's house, 'queer old personal tales were yet audible if properly listed for.' (*W* 25). In *The Mayor of Casterbridge* Hardy develops an intimate relationship between buildings and their inhabitants: between, for example, the ancient and four-square house and its occupier, Michael Henchard; between the subversive style of building in Mixen Lane and its equally

[2] Hardy, 'Memories of Church Restoration' (1906), in *Personal Writings*, ed. Orel, p. 207.

subversive inhabitants. In *Jude the Obscure* the romantic skyline of Christminster becomes the palpable and visible embodiment of Jude Fawley's equally romantic personal aspirations. But it is in *A Laodicean* that architecture plays the most prominent role, and it was *A Laodicean* which, Hardy confessed, contained 'more facts of his own life than anything he had ever written'.[3]

As the full title, *A Laodicean: A Story of Today*, suggests, the novel deals with intellectual doubt, religious uncertainty, and ideological hesitancy—in short, modern Laodiceanism. It centres on the architect George Somerset and his pursuit of the rich young heiress Paula Power. Somerset, who is trying to make a career in architecture, is invited by Paula to do extensive remodelling of a Norman castle which she has inherited from her father John Power. Paula is a mixture of strange, and apparently contradictory, modern impulses. Her wealth comes from recently built railways, yet she is deeply attached to her ancient and dilapidated castle. Living with just one female companion, she exercises great personal freedom. She exploits to the full the benefits of a telegraph system whose intricacies she has mastered, and keeps abreast of European and American fashions; but at the same time she is committed to the past. She is fascinated by neo-Hellenism of a Swinburnian kind, and takes delight in all forms of medieval antiquity. When Captain de Stancy, a descendant of the former owners of the castle, comes back from abroad, she is attracted by his ancient lineage and aristocratic background. The Captain exploits her romantic disposition, and nearly gets her to marry him. He pursues her throughout Europe, but her affection for George Somerset finally triumphs.

Paula Power and George Somerset are both modern Laodiceans. Paula in particular is constantly faced by difficult choices—not only choices between lovers, but choices between religious attitudes and between divergent ways of life. Somerset, too, has to make important choices in the course of his career. He has to make up his mind about the style in which he will build, and his bewilderment is, in architectural terms, the equivalent of Paula Power's dilemma about her own life. Consequently, when the novel opens, we find Somerset in the grip of what the narrator calls 'the modern malady of unlimited appreciativeness' (*L* 9).

---

[3] William Archer, *Real Conversations*, p. 4.

When quite a lad, in the days of the French-Gothic mania which immediately succeeded to the great English-pointed revival under Britton, Pugin, Rickman, Scott, and other medievalists, he had crept away from the fashion to admire what was good in Palladian and Renaissance. As soon as Jacobean, Queen Anne, and kindred accretions of decayed styles began to be popular, he purchased old-school works as Revett and Stuart, Chambers, and the like, and worked diligently at the Five Orders; till quite bewildered on the question of style, he concluded that all styles were extinct, and with them all architecture as a living art. (*L* 6.)

Somerset's bewilderment was shared by many of Hardy's architectural contemporaries, and was the inevitable response to a situation which T. L. Donaldson described in 1842 as follows: 'We are wandering', he said, 'in a labyrinth of experiments, and trying by an amalgamation of certain features in this or that style of each and every period . . . to form a homogenous whole with some distinct character of its own.'[4] In *A Laodicean*, however, the choice of architectural styles—a choice which both Paula and Somerset have to make— is but a symptom of a multiplicity of other choices. The 'modern malady of unlimited appreciativeness' is not confined to architectural styles: it extends to intellectual and religious beliefs, concerns man's view of his relationship with the past, and profoundly affects his style of life in the present.

In the early part of the nineteenth century, historical scholarship, biblical criticism, and scientific exploration had all tended to undermine old-fashioned ontological certainties, and had contributed substantially to the relativism of contemporary intellectual life. In the discipline of architecture, stylistic eclecticism was frequently related to philosophical relativism. According to historian Peter Collins, architects G. E. Street and Robert Kerr both pointed to similarities between the multiplicity of styles from which the builder might choose and a theological indifferentism which had its roots in France.[5] Victor Cousin, in *The True, The Beautiful and the Good* (1853), helped form the

[4] T. L. Donaldson, *Preliminary Discourse* (1842), p. 30. Donaldson presented Hardy with the silver medal of the Royal Institute of British Architects on 16 March 1863 for his essay 'On the application of coloured brick and terra-cotta to modern architecture'. C. J. P. Beatty points out in his unpublished dissertation 'The Part Played by Architecture in the Life and Work of Thomas Hardy', p. 620, that Hardy was mistaken in the belief that it was Gilbert Scott from whom he received the prize (*LY* 210). Hardy also won a prize offered by William Tite to the Architectural Association. See Beatty, *Thomas Hardy's Career in Architecture, 1856–1872* p. 5.

[5] Peter Collins, *Changing Ideals In Modern Architecture*, pp. 117–8.

basis of 'unlimited appreciativeness' by developing a composite of views selected and adapted from other systems. In *A Laodicean* Hardy fully exploits this connection between intellectual indifferentism and architectural eclecticism, with its inherent assumption that one can choose one's religious beliefs or adopt a moral or intellectual position with as much arbitrariness as one might choose the style of a house or a church. Expressed like this, choice was not a matter of conviction, but an expression of taste. One might adopt nonconformism, high Anglicanism, or Catholicism, not out of deeply held beliefs, but as the expression of personal temperament, determined primarily by romantic impulses. And, as Collins suggests, architectural eclecticism and philosophical indifferentism were equally 'an expression of un-committed romanticism'.[6] Hardy seems to share this belief, and in his preface to *A Laodicean* he states that his novel will explore the many and unusual sides of modern 'romantic issues' (*L* vii).

In the course of the book, Laodiceanism, or the conflict between the numerous 'romantic issues', is expressed in a series of tableaux vivants. They take the form of contrasting images, the visual com-ponents of which generate a number of clearly defined ideas or sen-timents whose meaning is often modified and changed by contrast with similar tableaux. When the novel opens, Somerset is discovered in the act of drawing an English parish church near the village of Sleeping Green.

The sun blazed down, till it was within half-an-hour of its setting; but the sketcher still lingered at his occupation of measuring and copying the chevroned doorway, a bold and quaint example of a transitional style of architecture, which formed the tower entrance to an English village church. The graveyard being quite open on its western side, the tweed-clad figure of the young draughtsman, and the tall mass of antique masonry which rose above him to a battlement parapet, were fired to a great brightness by the solar rays, that crossed the neighbouring mead like a warp of gold threads, in whose mazes groups of equally lustrous gnats danced and wailed incessantly. (*L* 3.)

Here is a picture within a picture. Somerset makes an architectural study similar in type to those in Hardy's own *Architectural Notebook*,[7] while Hardy creates a verbal picture, and both are imbued with rest and tranquility appropriate to a setting in Sleeping Green. Yet, as so

---

[6] Ibid.
[7] Now in DCM.

often with Hardy's sunset passages, there is also a hint of sadness. 'There are few', says the narrator, 'in whom the sight of a sunset does not beget as much meditative melancholy as contemplative pleasure, the human decline and death that it illustrates being too obvious to escape the notice of the simplest observer.' (*L* 3–4). The presence of the gnats, who live out their brief lives and die with the sun, anticipates a very similar effect in *Tess of the d'Urbervilles*,[8] and suggests that the source of melancholy in this scene is intimately related to decay, change, and the passing of old orders. This is confirmed by the second scene of the novel. Nearby, Somerset comes upon another ecclesiastical building of a very different caste. It was

a recently-erected chapel of red brick, with pseudo-classic ornamentation, and the white regular joints of mortar could be seen streaking its surface in geometrical oppressiveness from top to bottom. The roof was of blue slate, clean as a table, and unbroken from gable to gable; the windows were glazed with sheets of plate glass, a temporary iron stove-pipe passing out near one of these, and running up to the height of the ridge, where it was finished by a covering like a parachute. (*L* 11.)

Everything about this building stands in sharp contrast to the Gothic church which Somerset has just left. Whereas the church is medieval, the chapel is an imitation of the classical style. The church is mellow, mature, even crumbling, whereas the chapel is new, clean-cut, even brash. The church is irregular in its shape, whereas the line of the chapel is unbroken and perfect. Whereas traditional materials were used in the construction of the church, the chapel is furnished with a new ugly iron pipe for its heating system. It is no wonder that Somerset, who had spent the afternoon in the presence of antiquity should murmur to himself: 'Shade of Pugin, what a monstrosity!' (*L* 11). Pugin, of course, loathed modern buildings of this kind, and Pugin's name on Somerset's lips provides an important clue to the source of the dominant visual effect in *A Laodicean*—the contrasted images.

Many Victorian writers had used the idea of graphic juxtapositions and comparisons to show up the poverty of modern life when compared with that of the past. One thinks of Carlyle's verbal images of the slums of the industrial north contrasted with the dignity of medieval St Edmundsbury in *Past and Present* (1843), or Ruskin's indictment of the spiritual state of modern England when compared

---

[8] See Ch. 8 below.

with that of medieval Venice in *The Stones of Venice* (1851–3). But no writer had succeeded in creating a more vivid and telling juxtaposition of old and new than Augustus Welby Pugin in his book *Contrasts*. Pugin first published this famous work in 1836, to provide what he called 'a parallel between the noble edifices of the fourteenth and fifteenth centuries and similar buildings of the present day; shewing the present decay of taste'.[9] The strength of Pugin's argument lay not so much in the text as in the illustrations. By placing on the same page pictures of medieval buildings and buildings of later date, he set out to demonstrate in simple, graphic terms how architectural taste had been corrupted by spiritual and moral decline. The almshouses, churches and dignified buildings of an age of faith are set beside the prisons, preaching-houses, and squalid slums of the nineteenth century, and in one of Pugin's plates, showing the contrast between the ideal beauty of the Perpendicular style of St Augustine's at Skirlaw and the mean architecture of St Pancras in London (Plate 25), we find an analogue for the church and chapel at Sleeping Green. Pugin, in common with many architectural writers of the time, used building style as the physical embodiment of social, intellectual, and moral values. For Pugin, religious sectarianism and economic expediency went hand in hand with utilitarianism in modern building. 'Government preaching-houses, called churches', he says, 'start up at the cost of a few hundreds each, by the side of Zion Chapels, Bethel Meetings, New Connexions and Socialist Halls.'[10] The sense of utilitarian meanness also forms part of Somerset's response to the new chapel. It had, he thought, 'neither beauty, quaintness, nor congeniality to recommend it', and he makes an explicit mental contrast between chapel and church. 'The dissimilitude between the new utilitarianism of the place and the scenes of venerable Gothic art which had occupied his daylight hours could not', he thought, 'well be exceeded.' (*L* 12–13). In *Contrasts* Pugin stressed the economic rapaciousness of the rich in their desire to build churches at the cheapest rate, and he condemned those speculators who

ponder between a mortgage, a railroad, or a chapel, as the best investment of their money, and who, when they have resolved on relying on the persuasive eloquence of a cushion-thumping popular preacher, erect four walls . . . cram the same full of seats, which they readily let.[11]

[9] A. W. Pugin, the subtitle of *Contrasts* (1836).
[10] A. W. Pugin, *The True Principles of Pointed or Christian Architecture*, p. 56.
[11] Pugin, *Contrasts* 2nd edn, p. 50.

Hardy's new chapel had been erected at the expense of a railroad
magnate, John Power, and Hardy, too, has his 'cushion-thumping'
preacher in the form of Parson Woodwell: Woodwell was a man, says
Hardy, 'who could move some of the hardest men to tears.' (*L* 230).

There is a striking similarity between Pugin's use of medieval and
modern architecture and the images of *A Laodicean*, but Hardy's
values are subtly different from Pugin's. The Catholic in Pugin
sacrificed, as Nikolaus Pevsner puts it, 'at the altar of Perpendicular',[12] but Hardy did not share this single-minded devotion to
one style. Pugin could envisage no modern architecture for which
Gothic was not the model, and the series of illustrations in *Contrasts*
culminates in the picture of a balance in which modern architecture is
weighed against Gothic and is found wanting. Hardy's images, however, are far more ambiguous. For Pugin, Gothic style is a living form;
but in the opening scene of *A Laodicean* the sun sets on the Gothic
church, thereby suggesting the 'decline and death' of a style that is no
longer alive. The nonconformist chapel, on the other hand, is brilliantly
lit 'from within'. Somerset notices 'the intense and busy energy'
around the chapel, and though it stands on a 'shabby plot of ground',
the grass has been 'trodden away by busy feet'. In short, the chapel
had 'a living human interest that the numerous minsters and churches
knee-deep in fresh green grass . . . often lacked.' (*L* 13)

Though Hardy does not share Pugin's ideals, he employs Pugin's
technique of contrasts throughout *A Laodicean*. For Pugin the choice
between medieval and modern was a simple one, as simple as the
choice between Catholicism and apostasy. Since 1836 the weeds of
doubt had grown up and choked such idealism, and the changes
which had come about in architectural taste provided Hardy with a
metaphor for similar changes which had taken place in the intellectual
life of the period. When he first entered the profession in 1856 in Dorchester, the Gothic style was accepted as unquestioningly as the Ten
Commandments; by the time Hardy came to build Max Gate in the
1880s, the authority of Gothic was as uncertain as the authority of the
Bible, and the 'loss of faith' in architectural circles paralleled other
revolutions which had taken place in the life of both mind and spirit.

Hardy's own training as an architect had been almost exclusively
in the neo-medieval style.[13] In the Dorchester office of John Hicks in

---

12 Nikolaus Pevsner, *Some Architectural Writers of the Nineteenth Century*, p. 113.

13 Though as Beatty points out, Hardy's *Architectural Notebook* in DCM contains a
wide variety of material from 'Gothic details to drains'. *Thomas Hardy's Career in
Architecture*, p. 8.

the late 1850s, he had become familiar with the techniques of church restoration, and when he went to London, he was employed in the office of Arthur Blomfield specifically as a 'Gothic draughtsman' (*EL* 48). Blomfield's business evolved into one of the largest architectural practices of the nineteenth century, and almost all the work Hardy did there, and later for Raphael Brandon, G. R. Crickmay, and R. T. Smith, was some variation of Gothic. Yet even when Hardy entered the profession that style was going into decline. The enthusiasm for Gothic work generated first by Pugin (father and son), and later by Ruskin, had been largely dissipated, and a reaction had set in against what was seen to be the pedantic dullness of mere reproduction. The change was marked by an event which took place in the very year Hardy went to London. In 1862, Gilbert Scott, by now the high priest of revivalism, suffered a great blow to his ideals and reputation when Palmerston rejected his plans for the new government buildings in favour of a more sobre, more serviceable Italianate design. This was the first round in what came to be known as 'the battle of the styles', and it was a battle that continued throughout Hardy's professional career. It culminated in G. E. Street's much-despised Gothic-style lawcourts in the Strand, and like many of his contemporaries, Hardy was critical of the inappropriateness of the ornamental detail. It seemed to him to embody a particular kind of hypocrisy and sham which violated many of the ideals of the early revivalists. 'Everywhere', said Hardy, 'religious art-forces [are] masquerading as law symbols! The leaf, flower, fret, suggested by spiritual emotion, are pressed into the service of social strife.' (*EL* 240). Hardy was equally critical of Street's soulless Gothic creation of St Mary's at Great Fawley in Berkshire.[14] In *Jude the Obscure* he refers to Street as a 'certain obliterator of historic records' who had 'run down from London and back in a day' to design a new church for Marygreen (*JO* 6). By the 1880s Hardy's youthful enthusiasm for Gothic architecture had evaporated. 'Mediaevalism', as he said in *Jude the Obscure*, was 'as dead as a fern leaf in a lump of coal' (*JO* 99), and Gothic architecture, he said on another occasion, has been 'a dead art for the last three hundred years, in spite of the imitations broadcast over the land'.[15] Hardy was equally doubtful about the wisdom of restoration. He felt that a great

[14] Pevsner describes the church of St Mary which Street built in 1866 as 'a serious, almost forbidding church'. Nikolaus Pevsner, *The Buildings of England: Berkshire* (Hardmondsworth: Penguin Books, 1966), p. 148.
[15] Letter to *The Times*, 7 Oct. 1914, p. 10.

deal of damage had been done to ancient buildings in the name of restoration, but in fact 'it was impossible to restore the grey carcases of medievalism whose spirit has fled'.[16] Consequently in 1881, Hardy joined the Society for the Protection of Ancient Buildings as a gesture of penance for what he viewed as his early acts of architectural vandalism.[17]

Many of these misgivings about the nature of Gothic—misgivings which represent doubts and uncertainty at many levels—are incorporated in *A Laodicean*, and find expression in the visual contrasts which abound in it. In the first example the apparently straightforward opposition between medievalism and modernism is complicated by an underlying relativism. The Gothic church is beautiful, and the modern building ugly; but one is dead and inert, whereas the other is bustling with human life. This ambiguity becomes clearer in the second major contrast of the book, in which medievalism is represented by a castle, and modernism, not by a building this time, but by the telegraph system. The substitution of the secular for the ecclesiastical takes place when George Somerset makes his way to his lodgings following the line of the telegraph wire. He expects that it will lead to a nearby hamlet, but instead it runs right into a medieval castle—de Stancy Castle. The new contrast is as surprising as the previous one. Modern invention here has its home in a 'fossil of feudalism', and Hardy spells out two possible interpretations of this odd juxtaposition. Seen in one way,

there was a certain unexpectedness in the fact that the hoary memorial of a stolid antagonism to the interchange of ideas, the monument of hard distinctions in blood and race, of deadly mistrust of one's neighbour in spite of the Church's teachings, and of a sublime unconsciousness of any other force than a brute one, should be the goal of a machine which beyond everything may be said to symbolize cosmopolitan views and the intellectual and moral kinship of all mankind. (*L* 22.)

But seen in another way,

the modern fever and fret which consumes people before they can grow old was also signified by the wire; and this aspect of today did not contrast well

[16] Preface to *A Pair of Blue Eyes*, p. vii.

[17] Hardy said that 'much beautiful ancient Gothic, as well as Jacobean work, he was passively instrumental in destroying or altering beyond identification; a matter for his deep regret in later years' (*EL* 41), and he told William Archer that he 'used to be sent round to sketch village churches as a preliminary to their restoration—which mostly meant destruction'. William Archer, *Real Conversations*, p. 33. See also *Personal Writings*, ed. Orel, pp. 214–5, and *LY* 145.

with the fairer side of feudalism—leisure, light-hearted generosity, intense friendships, hawks, hounds, reveals, healthy complexions, freedom from care and such a living power in architectural art as the world may never again see. (*L* 22.)

The view is entirely relativistic, and the relativism which was implicit in the first contrast is made explicit in the second. Pugin would have offered unqualified condemnation of the style of life represented by the telegraph, as opposed to that represented by the castle; but now, says Hardy, you may choose any interpretation which suits your temperament. The problem of choice serves to introduce Paula Power, the heroine of the story, for it is she who has brought the telegraph to de Stancy Castle. Paula, Hardy tells us, is 'emphatically a modern type of maidenhood' (*L* 15), and her modernity lies precisely in this issue of choice. Even more than Somerset, she suffers from the malady of 'unlimited appreciativeness', and her crisis of identity is reflected in the multiplicity of styles of life which she adopts. She is the daugher of a rich railway magnate, and has decided to invest her inheritance in de Stancy Castle. The original de Stancy fortune had been squandered by Sir William, and he had been forced to sell the castle to the highest bidder. The elder brother, Captain de Stancy, had gone into the army, while the younger sister, Charlotte, had struck up a friendship with Paula, to whom the castle now belonged. Paula's interest in her castle, however, is not archaelogical; it is part of a desire to be 'romantic and historical.' (*L* 123). De Stancy Castle, 'irregular, dilapidated, and muffled in creepers' (*L* 21) perfectly suits her 'fanciful *prédilection d'artiste* for hoary medieval families' (*L* 371),[18] and the interior resembles the contents of the South Kensington Museum:

There was a great collection of old movables and other domestic art-work . . . suites of tapestry hangings, common and fine; green and scarlet leather work, on which the gilding was still but little injured; venerable damask curtains; quilted silk table-covers, ebony cabinets, worked satin window-cushions, carved bedsteads, and embroidered bed-furniture. (*L* 27–8.)

The comparison with the teaching collection in London is appropriate here because they are both the creation of nineteenth-century historicism, a historicism which claims everything from the past as

[18] Hardy borrowed the phrase 'prédilection d'artiste' from Karl Hillebrand's theological article, 'Familiar Conversations on Modern England', *Nineteenth Century*, 8 (1880), p. 1008. See *LN*, entry 1203.

equally interesting. It reflects that type of life which Pater, in *The Renaissance*, described as quintessentially modern. 'To regard all things and principles of things as inconstant modes or fashions', said Pater, 'has more and more become the tendency of modern thought,'[19] and the essays which go to make up his book bear out that proposition. They are historical in content, but are characterized by their perplexing multiplicity of viewpoints. For Pater, history has become a matter of taste: the re-creation of the past in the image of the self. The aesthetic critic, he says, is 'ever curiously testing new opinions and courting new impressions';[20] he moves promiscuously between those historical and modern styles which best express his own temperament. Paula Power is Hardy's version of that same sensibility, and her bedroom is the palpable working-out of the Paterian view of life.

On the tables of the sitting-room were most of the popular papers and periodicals . . . not only English, but from Paris, Italy and America. Satirical prints, though they did not unduly preponderate, were not wanting. Besides these there were books from a London circulating library, paper-covered light literature in French and choice Italian and the latest monthly reviews. (*L* 39–40.)

Here is an image of 'unlimited appreciativeness' and of the modern desire (again in Pater's words) 'to bring into connection with each other modes of thought and feeling, periods of taste, forms of art and poetry'.[21] But if the physical conditions of Paula's life are Paterian, then her mental constitution is Arnoldian, for she considers herself simultaneously 'medieval' and 'Greek'. Her neo-paganism—a style which strikes horror into the heart of the Baptist minister (*L* 79)—is as fanciful and bizarre as her love of the Middle Ages. She engages Somerset to build a 'Greek colonade' in the precincts of the Norman castle; she wants a fountain in the middle, and 'statues like those in the British Museum.' (*L* 91). Not content with bringing the Elgin Marbles to Wessex, Paula also wishes to start a Greek pottery in the neighbourhood. This, too, is a nebulous idea derived from her wanderings in museums. Apparently she has 'visited the British Museum, continental museums and Greece and Spain: and hopes to imitate the old fictile work . . . especially the Greek work of the best period' (*L* 38).

[19] Pater, *The Renaissance*, p. 186.
[20] Ibid., p. 189.
[21] Ibid., p. 2.

All this might seem like a parody of Grecomania were it not for the fact that both the medieval strain in Paula's temperament and the desire for the pagan way of life come straight from the pages of Matthew Arnold's essay 'Pagan and Medieval Religious Sentiment'. In this essay, which Hardy read in preparation for writing the novel,[22] Arnold sets up two contrasting views of life, which he calls 'paganism' and 'medievalism'. Paganism, which he identifies with the idylls of Theocratus, is characterized by the operation of 'the senses and understanding'; medievalism, on the other hand, for which Arnold takes St Francis of Assisi as the representative figure, is characterized by the 'heart and the imagination'.[23] For Arnold 'medievalism' and 'paganism' represent complimentary human needs, and in *Culture and Anarchy* he elaborates this theory in social terms by rechristening them Hebraism and Hellenism. The question for Arnold, however, is how, in the modern world, we are to choose between these apparently contradictory 'views of life', and he suggests a tentative answer in the phrase 'imaginative reason'. 'The main element of the modern spirit's life is neither the senses and understanding, nor the heart and imagination; it is the imaginative reason.'[24]

By the time Hardy was writing that reconciliation had not been effected. On the contrary what one writer called 'the standing dispute between Greek and Gothic philosophy of life' had settled into a fixed opposition. The same writer summarized it thus: 'Professor Arnold calls it Greek and Hebraic. Naturalist and Ascetic, or secular and Monastic, Medieval and Renaissance, are all names for contradictory views of life.'[25]

Hardy's version of this apparent contradiction is expressed through Paula Power's desire to build a Greek courtyard in a Norman castle, in her love of Greek gymnastics and medieval lineage, in her flirtation with Roman Catholicism and her androgynous sexuality. But Hardy proposes an explanation of this dilemma which is quite different from Arnold's. Paula's paganism and medievalism are both subsumed by her highly romantic temperament. She has a '*prédilection d'artiste*' for

[22] Hardy copied large extracts from this essay into his notebook in 1880. See *LN*, entry 1176.

[23] 'Pagan and Medieval Religious Sentiment', in Matthew Arnold, *The Complete Prose Works* iii. 226.

[24] Ibid. iii. 230.

[25] 'Debased Hellenism and the New Renaissance', p. 107. Hardy copied passages of this review into his notebook. See *LN*, entry 1189.

many styles and modes of life. She wants to be, above all, 'romantic and historical', and as Hardy noted while writing *A Laodicean*, 'Romanticism will exist in human nature as long as human nature itself exists.' (*EL* 189). Hardy's explicit aim in *A Laodicean* was to 'adopt that form of romanticism which is a mood of the age.' (*EL* 189). Paula Power's commitment to the Middle Ages and to Greece is one of those forms; Somerset's intellectual eclecticism is another—what Collins calls 'uncommitted romanticism'. But the varieties of modern romanticism do not end there. In his preface to *A Laodicean* Hardy points out that the only kind of romanticism 'formerly recognized by novelists' had been a turning back to the past. 'Romantic issues', however, were not necessarily 'restricted to a change back to the original order' (*L* vii), and just as the 'mood of the age' had changed, so had those issues. Hardy recognized that as there had been a romanticism of the Middle Ages, so there was a romanticism of the railway and the telegraph, and through the life and work of Paula's father, John Power,[26] he explored yet another version of the romantic temper.

When Somerset is told that John Power, the famous railway engineer, had recently discovered de Stancy Castle while building a nearby tunnel, he interprets the event as 'a clash between ancient and modern' (*L* 35)—quite wrongly, for, like all the other apparently simple contrasts in the novel, this one, too, is ambiguous. At first sight, Power, the embodiment of what Hardy calls 'the march of the mind—the steamship, and the railway' (*L* 101), should be opposed to the romantic way of life. But through a series of 'visual aids', Somerset is led to see that this is not so. John Power's works are introduced into the novel in a contrast between two architectural forms which are once again reminiscent of Pugin. 'Do you think it a thing more to be proud of that one's father should have made a great tunnel and railway like that', Paula asks Somerset, 'than that one's remote ancestor should have built a great castle like this?' (*L* 102). Though he chooses his words diplomatically, the architect in Somerset feels impelled to judge in favour of the ancestor. 'From a modern point of view,' he says, 'railways, are no doubt, things more to be proud of than castles . . . though I myself, from mere association, should

---

[26] John G. Cox is probably correct in identifying Power with the wealthy Baptist railway-builder Samuel Morton Peto. Peto funded the building of Bloomsbury Central and Regent's Park Baptist churches. See Cox, 'John Power was Sir Samuel Morton Peto', p. 15.

decide in favour of the ancestor who built the castle.' Nevertheless, he feels forced to add that, 'to design great engineering works . . . requires no doubt a leading mind. But to execute them, as he did, requires of course only a following mind.' (*L* 102).

The distinction between the leading and the following mind, between the true artist and the mere mechanic, reflects an issue that was widely debated in Hardy's day. When he was a young architect, his fellow architects tended to adopt an attitude of superiority towards the utilitarian constructions of engineers. The engineers themselves, however, had consistently argued that their work was eminently more in keeping with the times than the imitative tendencies of nineteenth-century architectural style. In his introduction to *The Encyclopaedia of Civil Engineering*, for example, Edward Cresy wrote in 1847 that 'the future historian of Britain will not refer to her architectural remains, but to the vast works of the engineer by which to judge the habits of the civilization of the age.[27] During Hardy's time architects suffered two major blows to their pride. The first occurred when William Paxton, a landscape gardener, was engaged to design the huge glass and steel construction of the Crystal Palace for the 1851 Great Exhibition, and the second came when the design of Francis Fowke, a military engineer, was adopted for the building to house the International Exhibition of 1862—a building which Hardy himself often visited.

In this battle between 'romantic' architect and 'hard-headed' engineer, railway engineering was especially controversial. It was explicitly modern, it had no precedent, and, unlike traditional building, it was free of the trammels of historicism. It could afford to be unconventional, and it was, above all, highly profitable. Both its detractors and its supporters associated it with modern materialism, modern religious nonconformity, and political liberalism. In his writings about the problems created by the new railway style, Robert Kerr, for example, wondered what architecture would be most suitable for a 'railway travelling Reform-Bill people', and just as Hardy had identified the telegraph with 'the intellectual and moral kinship of all mankind', so Cardinal Newman perceived a connection between railway travel, the spread of intelligence, and the dissipation of ignorance.[28] It was quite in keeping with the spirit of railway-building that

[27] Edward Cresy, quoted in Collins, *Changing Ideals in Modern Architecture*, p. 190.
[28] Kerr and Newman, quoted in Pevsner, *Some Architectural Writers of the Nineteenth Century*, p. 219.

John Power should be an active Nonconformist. He was responsible for chapel and railway, both of them hives of modern activity. In *Jude the Obscure* Sue tells Jude that she would rather meet him in the Melchester railway station than in the cathedral, because, she says, the railway station has become 'the centre of the town life now' (*JO* 160).

A number of architectural historians stressed the blend of daring and imagination in the new railway architecture. Viollet-le-Duc, whose work Hardy knew,[29] commented favourably on the style of modern bridges. 'Our engineers have struck out a new path,' he said, and he warned that architects 'have up to now not ventured farther than a timid adaptation of new techniques to old forms'.[30] It is appropriate that the test-case of John Power's imaginative genius should have been the tunnel near de Stancy Castle, for in 1862, the year that Hardy went to London, James Fergusson praised the simple grandeur of tunnels in his *History of the Modern Styles of Architecture*. 'Some of the entrances to the tunnels which are found on most railways in England, are', he said, 'as grand as any city gates, and grander than many triumphal arches that are to be found in Europe', but he pointed out that simplicity was essential for this effect. They achieve this beauty he said, when 'they depend for expression on their own mass and dimensions, relieved only by a few simple but appropriate mouldings'.[31] When Somerset inspects Mr Power's tunnel, he is surprised by a similar monumentality and simplicity. 'The tunnel that had seemed so small from the surface was a vast archway when [Somerset] reached its mouth' (*L* 105–6), and he found himself conscientiously admiring 'the construction of the massive archivault, and the majesty of its nude ungarnished walls'. What Somerset had previously considered merely practical and utilitarian begins to assume the majesty of ancient ruins, and he mentally balances in his

[29] Hardy said that Violett-le-Duc 'probably knew more about French architecture than any man of his time'. *The Times*, 7 Oct. 1914, p. 10. See n. 15.

[30] Violett-le-Duc, quoted in Pevsner, *Some Architectural Writers of the Nineteenth Century*, pp. 212–3.

[31] James Fergusson, *History of the Modern Styles of Architecture*, p. 477. Surprisingly, Pugin expressed similar views, though he felt that a great opportunity had been missed in railway architecture. 'The Railways,' he said, 'had they been naturally treated, afforded a fine scope for grand massive architecture. Little more was required than buttresses, weathering, and segmental arches, resistance to *lateral* and *perpendicular pressure*. I do not hesitate to say, that, by merely following out the work that was required to its natural conclusion, building exactly what was wanted in the simplest most substantial manner . . . grand and durable masses of building could have been produced.' *An Apology for the Revival of Christian Architecture in England* (1843), p. 10.

mind 'the grandeur of this fine piece of construction against that of the castle'. Once again the simple terms of Pugin's *Contrasts* are complicated by subtle alternatives, and Somerset wonders 'whether Paula's father had not, after all, the best of it' (*L* 106).

Paula's father has the 'best of it' by doing to the tunnel what the work of ages had taken to do to the castle. He had naturalized the massive but simple stonework by turning the cutting into a grotto. 'The popular commonplace', says Hardy, 'that science, steam, and travel must always be unromantic and hideous, was not proven by this spot.' (*L* 104). One of those people who thought that railways were 'unromantic and hideous' was Ruskin. He hated the restless bustle of railway travel,[32] and thought that it was inimical to the working of the imagination; never, he said, would it produce an architecture which could contribute to man's 'mental health, power and pleasure'. 'Better bury gold in the embankments', he wrote in *The Seven Lamps of Architecture*, 'than put it in the ornaments on the stations.'[33] In 1880 he reissued the book adding a note which distinguished true architectural form from 'a wasp's nest, a rat hole or a railway station'.[34] In the following year, Hardy took up this animal image, and turned it from a 'rat hole' into a romantic 'little blue-black spot like a mousehole'.

On either slope of the deep cutting, green with long grass, grew drooping young trees of ash, beech, and other flexible varieties, their foliage almost concealing the actual railway which ran along the bottom, its thin steel rails gleaming like silver threads in the depths. The vertical front of the tunnel, faced with brick that had once been red, was now weather-stained, lichened, and mossed over in harmonious rusty-browns, pearly greys, and neutral

---

[32] Going by railroad I do not consider as travelling at all; it is merely "being sent" to a place, and very little different from becoming a parcel; the next step to it would of course be telegraphic transport.' *Modern Painters* iii, in Ruskin, *Works* v. 370. In the chapter entitled 'The Lamp of Beauty' in *The Seven Lamps of Architecture*, Ruskin delivered a diatribe against railway travel and railway architecture. 'Another of the strange and evil tendencies of the present day', he wrote, 'is to the decoration of the railroad station. Now, if there be any place in the world in which people are deprived of that portion of temper and discretion which is necessary to the contemplation of beauty, it is there. It is the very temple of discomfort, and the only charity that the builder can extend to us is to show us, plainly as may be, how soonest to escape from it. . . . No one would travel in that manner who could help it—who had time to go leisurely and between hedges, instead of through tunnels and between banks: at least, those who would, have no sense of beauty so acute as that we need consult it at the station.' Ruskin, *Works* viii. 159.

[33] Ruskin, *Works* viii. 160.

[34] Ruskin, *Works* viii. 28.

greens, at the very base appearing a little blue-back spot like a mousehole—the tunnel's mouth. (*L* 104–5.)

The reaction of Mrs Goodman, Paula's companion, to the romance of this spot is almost Wordsworthian. 'If it were not a railway,' she said, 'we should call it a lovely dell.' (*L* 105).

So the physical appearance of the tunnel and the cutting suggests that even modern utilitarianism has its romantic side, and that 'romantic issues are not necessarily restricted to a change back to the original order' (*L* vii). In spite of his devotion to 'the march of the mind', to railways, and to engineering, Mr Power's modernism is tinged with 'that form of romanticism which is the mood of the age' (*EL* 189). Even his religious beliefs have strong romantic overtones. Hardy describes Parson Woodwell's nonconformity as the 'Wertherism of the uncultivated' (*L* 230), and Power's support of the Baptist cause is not so far removed from his daughter's '*prædilection d'artiste*' for Catholicism (*L* 110).[35]

The contrasts of *A Laodicean* which at first seem like stark oppositions are in fact different sides of the romantic spirit. The 'clash between ancient and modern', Greek and Gothic, imaginative utilitarian, and are not in fact the simple opposites of Pugin's *Contrasts*. Hardy never worked out the full implications, since he fell ill after completing thirteen chapters, but the last few pages sketch out the intended resolution. Captain de Stancy, the child of a highly unromantic family,[36] having failed in his pursuit of Paula Power, returns to the castle bent upon destruction. He gathers together the paintings which had so impressed Somerset on his first visit:

Included in the group were nine by Sir Peter Lely, five by Vandyck, four by Cornelius Jansen, one by Salvator Rosa . . . many by Kneller, and two by Romney. . . . [He] also brought a Raffaelle Virgin-and-Child, a magnificent Tintoretto, a Titian, and a Giorgione. (*L* 475.)

De Stancy sets light to the pile, and the conflagration is enormous. The castle is left uninhabitable—only the sturdy Norman walls being

---

[35] The phrase 'Wertherism of the uncultivated' also comes from Karl Hillebrand's 'Familiar Conversations on Modern England'. See n. 18. Hillebrand suggests that in Germany conversions to Catholicism were 'common under the influence of the Romantic school, whose members had almost all been sceptics before they embraced the Roman faith, more out of a *prédilection d'artiste* . . . than out of a deeper conviction' (p. 1014).

[36] Captain de Stancy suffers from rootless 'taedium vitae'; his sister cares no more for the past than 'a sparrow', and Sir William, whose only considerations are financial ones, lives in Myrtle Cottage, an emblem of 'mushroom modernism' (*L* 47).

proof against the flames. But the effect of the fire is to raise once again the question of style. Paula Power and George Somerset intend to marry and build a house in the grounds of the castle. ' "We will build a new house," ' says Somerset, ' "eclectic in style" ': ' "We will remove the ashes, charred wood, and so on from the ruin, and plant more ivy. . . . You, Paula, will be yourself again, and recover . . . from the warp given to your mind . . . by the medievalism of that place.' " (*L* 481). The former contrasts of the novel are resolved in a highly Arnoldian marriage in which Somerset's 'senses and understanding' serve to temper Paula's 'heart and imagination'. I shall become, says Paula 'a perfect representative of "the modern spirit" . . . representing neither the senses and understanding, nor the heart and imagination; but what a finished writer calls "the imaginative reason".' (*L* 481). Theoretically, the scheme is a good one, but alas for Arnold, Hardy knows that 'romanticism will exist in human nature as long as human nature itself exists', and Paula's last words echo the persistent theme of the novel:

'Very well, I'll keep straight on; and we'll build a new house beside the ruin, and show the modern spirit for evermore. . . . But, George, I wish—.' And Paula repressed a sigh.
'Well?'
'I wish my castle wasn't burnt; and I wish you were a de Stancy!' (*L* 481.)

The idea of exploring various 'romantic issues' in a modern context—'a story for today'—probably occurred to Hardy while he was writing *The Return of the Native*. In one of its aspects the earlier novel is also about varieties of romanticism—the wild, unbridled romanticism of Eustacia Vye, the nympholeptic romanticism of Wildeve, and the modern idealistic romanticism of Clym Yeobright. It would appear that Hardy wished to develop these ideas in *A Laodicean*, to abstract still further the working of the romantic spirit in modern life. In *The Return of the Native* this spirit is very much a function of personal temperament; in *A Laodicean* it informs and underlies many sides of intellectual life in such a way that what at first sight appear to be conflicting trends in belief, style, and aesthetic attitudes are at bottom no more than varieties of 'uncommitted romanticism'. Fortunately, Hardy dropped the idea, and never returned to it in this form. Romanticism is a nebulous and insufficient basis for fiction; the ideas are too rarefied, and the architectural vehicle for those ideas carries little conviction. The views of Arnold and Pater on the one hand and the debates taking place in the architectural press on the other are un-promising materials for a novelist, and in his next important novel, *The Mayor of Casterbridge*, Hardy wisely placed image before idea, and character before concept.

6

Visual Appearance and Psychological Reality in *The Mayor of Casterbridge*

'It is a man's sincerity and *depth of vision* that make him a poet.'
'The gifted man is he who *sees* the essential point, and leaves all the rest aside as surplusage.'
'Penetrate through obscurity and confusion to seize the characteristic features of an object.'[1]

When, in the autumn of 1880, Hardy reached Chapter 13 of *A Laodicean*, he fell ill, and the remainder of the novel had to be dictated from his bed. He was not happy with the result, and ascribed the failure of the book, at least in part, to his living in London. 'Residence in or near a city', he claimed, 'tended to force mechanical and ordinary production from his pen' (*EL* 193). So in the next few years he set about trying to find a location better suited to his temperament. First, he and his wife went to Wimbourne in Dorset, where they rented a house and Hardy began writing *Two on a Tower*. The move was not a success, and, according to Hardy's biographer Michael Millgate, the couple failed to become integrated into the local community.[2] This book, too, was less than successful. It was written hurriedly and never received Hardy's full attention, and even before he had finished it, he felt that he had 'lost his way' as a novelist. Neither *A Laodicean* nor *Two on a Tower* had been shaped by Hardy's intuition. Each is dominated by abstract ideas, and the settings, which had played such a successful and important part in his earlier work, had become far-flung and exotic. What he needed, he said, was 'an ample theme', but one which was related to 'the intense interests [and] passions . . . that throb through the commonest lives' (*EL* 199). He was quite right, and eventually the pursuit of the commonplace brought him

---

[1] Thomas Carlyle, 'The Hero as Poet', in *Heros and Hero Worship*, in *LN*, entries 1404, 1405, and 1406; Hardy's emphasis.
[2] Michael Millgate, *Thomas Hardy*, p. 234.

back to the scenes of his childhood and youth; in 1883 he and Emma moved back to the Borough of Dorchester.

There is no doubt that one of the strengths of *The Mayor of Casterbridge* is the conviction with which Hardy portrays Wessex provincial life. The richness of the texture of that life comes principally from Hardy's sharp eye for detail, and from his feel for the social structures of small-town existence. In *A Laodicean* and *Two on a Tower*, idea took precedence over image, so the characters remained flat and their lives shadowy. In *The Mayor of Casterbridge* the ideological patterning is more carefully hidden, and is never allowed to assume greater importance than narrative or character. This is achieved in part through a proliferation of visual detail and in part through Hardy's unwavering attention to the significance of observed phenomena. Casterbridge itself, for example, is seen from all angles. As Susan Henchard and Elizabeth-Jane approach it for the first time, Hardy presents the little community, not only from afar and close to, but also from above:

> To birds of the more soaring kind Casterbridge must have appeared on this fine evening as a mosaic-work of subdued reds, browns, greys, and crystals, held together by a rectangular frame of deep green. To the level eye of humanity it stood as an indistinct mass behind a dense stockade of limes and chestnuts, set in the midst of miles of rotund down and concave field. (*MC* 30.)

This sense of a strong, physical presence extends even to the smallest details of Casterbridge life. When Elizabeth-Jane visits Michael Henchard, the furnishings of his room are rendered with a similar conviction.

> The dining-room to which he introduced her still exhibited the remnants of the lavish breakfast laid for Farfrae. It was furnished to profusion with heavy mahogany furniture of the deepest red-Spanish hues. Pembroke tables, with leaves hanging so low that they well-nigh touched the floor, stood against the walls on legs and feet shaped like those of an elephant, and on one lay three huge folio volumes—a Family Bible, a 'Josephus', and a 'Whole Duty of Man.' (*MC* 76–7.)

There is no doubt that Hardy's move to Dorchester played a major part in the development of this style of writing. Not only did he involve himself in Dorchester society and renew his interest in local traditions and customs, but there was one event above all others which helped him rediscover his creative roots. After years of wander-

3. Sir Joshua Reynolds: *Sarah Siddons as 'The Tragic Muse'*. 1784. Huntington
Foundation, San Marino, California (599.5×370.8 cm)

19. Sir Joshua Reynolds: *Lady Anne Fermour, Wife of Thomas Dawson.* 1753–4. Private Collection, London (312.4×251.5 cm)

20. Sir Joshua Reynolds: *Elizabeth, Duchess of Manchester, and her son, George Viscount Mandeville.* 1769. The National Trust, Wimpole Hall, Cambridgeshire (629.5×461 cm)

21. Sir Joshua Reynolds: *Lady Charlotte Hill, Countess Talbot.* 1762. Tate Gallery, London (499.4×370.8 cm)

22. Sir Joshua Reynolds: *Anabella Lady Blake, as 'Juno Receiving the Cestu from Venus'.* 1769. Present whereabout unknown (691.4×370.8 cm)

ing about the country, he found a permanent residence which served
to express his personality and embody many of his aspirations.[3]
   Almost as soon as Hardy moved to Dorchester, he made up his
mind to build a house. From a temporary residence in Shire-Hall
Place, he began negotiations with the Duchy of Cornwall for a one-
and-a-half-acre site on the outskirts of the town. By November 1883
the well had been dug, the trees planted, and the foundations laid out.
The symbolic significance of this house is hard to overstate. For
Hardy, who had always lived in rented accommodation, such a dwelling was a monument to his success; but what is even more important
is that the design itself was entirely his own. The physical labour was
carried out by his father and brother, but Hardy oversaw everything
from the foundations to the roof; he was responsible for the details of
the plumbing and the layout of the heating; he decided on the disposition and construction of the windows and doors; and he even super-
vised the planting of the garden. It was as if his life, which had
previously been so rootless and nebulous, suddenly materialized in
bricks, mortar, and stone.
   It comes as no surprise to learn that the building of Max Gate coin-
cides exactly with the writing of *The Mayor of Casterbridge*. The morn-
ings would be spent constructing piece by piece the material life of fictional Casterbridge, and in the afternoons Hardy would be intimately
involved with the paraphernalia of building. Just as the form of the
novel took shape in Hardy's mind, so his new house rose before his
eyes.
   The influence of material things—their design, shape, and colour
—can be felt everywhere in *The Mayor of Casterbridge*. No other novel
by Hardy presents the physical constituents of life so vividly. From
the feel and texture of garments to the design of furniture and interiors, from the details of agricultural implements to the shape and
quality of building materials, the text is filled with references to utilitarian and decorative objects. Yet it would be quite wrong to assume
that Hardy had merely transcribed what he saw around him, or that
he had abandoned abstract issues and ontological concerns. He never
looked upon himself as a realist, and stressed that Casterbridge was
in no way a replica of Dorchester. 'Casterbridge', he said, when he
was offered the freedom of the Borough of Dorchester in 1910, 'is not

---

[3] Hardy said that 'the worst of taking a furnished home is that the articles in the
rooms are saturated with the thoughts and glances of others.' (*LY* 17).

Dorchester—not even Dorchester as it existed sixty years ago'. Rather, he had taken many liberties with its 'ancient walls, streets, and precincts' to create 'a dream-place that never was outside an irresponsible book.' (*LY* 143–4). Yet at the same time he argued for an imaginative connection between life and fiction: 'When somebody said to me that "Casterbridge" is a sort of essence of the town as it used to be, "a place more Dorchester than Dorchester itself", I could not absolutely contradict him,' and to explain the nature of this 'dream-place', Hardy concluded with a visual metaphor: 'At any rate,' he said, 'it is not a photograph in words' (*LY* 144). The figure of speech is important in defining Hardy's techniques in *The Mayor of Casterbridge*, because it relates to two statements which he made when he was writing the novel. In the first he said that the activity of a novelist is like 'looking at a carpet', where, 'by following one colour a certain pattern is suggested, by following another colour, another' (*EL* 198). This process, he said, though it is 'quite accurately, a going to Nature' is not a mimetic act, because the result 'is no mere photograph, but purely the product of the writer's own mind'. The second statement also involves a visual reference, and helps to define even more precisely the way in which Hardy envisaged the process of transformation from the literal to the imaginative. Not long after he had finished writing *The Mayor of Casterbridge*, he wrote in his diary that 'his art' was 'to intensify the expression of things, as is done by Crivelli, Bellini, etc., so that the heart and inner meaning is made vividly visible.' (*EL* 231–2).

The Pictorial Analogue

To understand what Hardy meant by this, and its relevance to *The Mayor of Casterbridge*, it is necessary to know what the work of Crivelli and Bellini meant to his contemporaries. Hardy was most familiar with the examples of their painting in the National Gallery—Crivelli's *Pietà* and Bellini's *Agony in the Garden* (Plates 2 and 1), for example—and undoubtedly he knew of the way in which they both appeared as transitional figures in contemporary art history. According to the authorities, Bellini inherited something of the harshness of Mantegna's style, yet at the same time anticipated 'the golden age of Venetian colourists'.[4] The words 'sharp' and 'primitive' occur frequently in the accounts of Bellini's works, and Crowe and Cavalcaselle claimed that the 'sculptural aspect' of the drapery in *The Agony in the Garden*

---

[4] J. A. Crowe and G. B. Cavalcaselle, *A History of Painting in North Italy* i. 139.

'display[s] much of Mantegna's spirit'.[5] This suggestion of a simple, but forceful, expressiveness attached itself even more strongly to the work of Crivelli. He might have created some of 'the rudest and most unattractive pictures in art', said Sir Henry Layard, yet other paintings border on 'the grandest character'. Above all, said Layard, though his forms are often grotesque, his paintings are never 'expressionless',[6] and R. N. Wornum said something very similar when he pointed out that though Crivelli's pictures are often 'exceedingly hard' and 'almost invariably ugly', they never 'want expression'.[7] Crivelli's paintings, said Crowe and Cavalcaselle, invariably surprise the spectator 'by the life which he concentrated into their action and expression'.[8]

It is this recurrent word 'expression' which is so important, since Hardy, too, wished to 'intensify the expression of things'. What Crivelli and Bellini did was to transform the natural world and the human body into expressive images—images which expressed the peculiar temperaments of their creators. They managed, through the intensity of their gaze, to find a 'beauty in ugliness', to change inert natural form and fill it with personal meaning.[9]

In *The Mayor of Casterbridge* Hardy also endows his images with expressive life. He observes and transcribes the features of Victorian Dorchester in such a way that they partake of a significance which is greater than that apparent on their surface; Hardy manages to reveal the 'heart and inner meaning' of things by visible means, and though his model is not directly the painting of Crivelli or Bellini, pictorialism features prominently in bringing the salient features of his images to the mental eye of the reader. This is nowhere clearer than in the opening sequences of the book. The first scene appears at first to be a straightforward rural episode—three travellers on the road to Weydon-Priors—but the manner in which Hardy accounts for the episode suggests not so much a directly observed event as an image in art.

One evening of late summer, before the nineteenth century had reached one-third of its span, a young man and woman, the latter carrying a child, were approaching the large village of Weydon-Priors, in Upper Wessex, on foot.

---

[5] Ibid., p. 142.
[6] *The Italian Schools of Painting Based on the Handbook of Kugler*, ed. A. H. Layard, 4th edn, i. 342.
[7] R. N. Wornum, *The Epochs of Painting* (1864), p. 117.
[8] Crowe and Cavalcaselle, *A History of Painting in North Italy*, i. 85.
[9] In 1888 Hardy wrote: 'To find beauty in ugliness is the province of the poet.' (*EL* 279). See also *EL* 158.

They were plainly but not ill clad, though the thick hoar of dust which had accumulated on their shoes and garments from an obviously long journey lent a disadvantageous shabbiness to their appearance just now. (*MC* 1.)

The whole stress of this passage lies on externals and their significance; the narrator assumes the role of a passive and ignorant spectator scanning the image before him for its meaning. He notices the way in which the figures are grouped on the highway, shifts his viewpoint, moves in closer, and reinterpets what he sees. 'They walked side by side in such a way as to suggest afar off the low, easy, confidential chat of people full of reciprocity; but on closer view it could be discerned that the man was reading' (*MC* 2). The static, pictorial quality of the image is enhanced by the use of a technical vocabulary. It is the eye of the draughtsman that sees the anonymous male figure in 'profile', with 'a facial angle so slightly inclined as to be almost perpendicular'; and it is the eye of the painter which perceives the female face as flesh lit by sunlight when she 'caught slantwise the rays of the strongly coloured sun, which made transparencies of her eyelids and nostrils and set fire on her lips.' (*MC* 2). The vagueness of the landscape—it is a place which 'might have been matched at almost any spot in any county in England'—and the anonymous road, reminiscent of the 'dull uninteresting road' of Mangiarelli's *Near Porta Salara*,[10] serve to strengthen the focus on the central figures. But what emerges most prominently from this opening passage is the appearance of the male figure, and particularly the details of his clothing and the tools of his trade:

He wore a short jacket of brown corduroy, newer than the remainder of his suit, which was a fustian waistcoat with white horn buttons, breeches of the same, tanned leggings, and a straw hat overlaid with black glazed canvas. At his back he carried by a looped strap a rush basket, from which protruded at one end the crutch of a hay-knife, a wimble for hay-bonds being also visible in the aperture. (*MC* 1.)

Once again in Hardy's work we have an image derived from the genre study of rural life, but its use in this context is quite distinct from the genre paintings of *Under the Greenwood Tree*.[11] In the earlier novel,

10 Diary fragment in DCM. See Figure I opp. p. 95.
11 Norman Page, in *Thomas Hardy*, pp. 77–82, points to many of the pictorialist techniques in *The Mayor of Casterbridge*, and makes some excellent connections with contemporary genre painting. He does not fully develop the significance of these pictures, however, or suggest why Hardy uses pictorialist techniques so extensively in this novel.

the static, pictorial quality of the scenes was comic in its effect, and was frequently employed to illustrate the sociability of rustic life. Here, the manifold details of the image are charged with secondary meaning, and are expressive of much more than were the pictures of Mellstock society. The differences between the pictorialism of *Under the Greenwood Tree* and that of *The Mayor of Casterbridge* can be illustrated with reference to Thomas Webster's *The Village Choir* (see Plate 10) and Sir Hubert von Herkomer's picture *Hard Times* (Plate 26). As Christopher Wood suggests, *The Village Choir* could well 'illustrate the easy-going eccentricity that survived in rural parishes',[12] and Hardy's text, too, stresses the jovial eccentricity of English rural life. Herkomer's picture is quite different, however, in both technique and effect. It was painted in 1885, just after Hardy had written *The Mayor of Casterbridge*, and though it was not the model for Hardy's opening scene, there are striking similarities. The grouping of the figures is suggestive of their respective mental attitudes—the weariness of the woman and child and the stoicism of the man. Like Henchard, the male figure is unemployed, and the tools of his trade (here thrown down at the side of the road) make his occupation clear, and in both picture and text the clothing of the figures speaks of hardship and penury. In the Herkomer painting, as well as in Hardy's account of the three travellers, all the information is communicated through the visual presentation of physical objects. In Hardy's opening scene, and elsewhere in *The Mayor of Casterbridge*, objects—the material stuff of life—are vested with an importance and a significance which is far greater than their superficial appearance. The rush basket, hay-knife, and curious 'wimble' certainly lend an authenticity to the picture of rural life, but, more important, they serve to define very precisely Henchard's occupation in life and his social standing in the rural community. Even more dramatically, his character, personality, and disposition are announced not in any conscious mode of self-expression, but rather in his manner of walking, which in turn is 'made visible' in the simple folds in his trousers:

His measured, springless walk was the walk of the skilled countryman as distinct from the desultory shamble of the general labourer; while in the turn and plant of each foot there was, further, a dogged and cynical indifference personal to himself, showing its presence even in the regularly interchanging fustian folds, now in the left leg, now in the right, as he paced along. (*MC* 1.)

---

[12] Christopher Wood, *Victorian Panorama: Paintings of Victorian Life*, p. 90.

Henchard's clothing and the tools of his trade serve to establish the primary relationship between the visual and the conceptual in *The Mayor of Casterbridge*. At one level the novel is about the meaning of clothing—not just the garments which man places on his body, but the objects with which he surrounds himself, which in their turn consciously or unconsciously express his inner nature. Hardy's primary source for the idea is Carlyle, and particularly Carlyle's investigation of the 'world in clothes' in *Sartor Resartus*, but he may also have known about the theories of Gottfried Semper, who stressed the idea that all the physical extensions of *Homo sapiens*, from simple forms of ornament to the most elaborate architectural structures, are essentially an expression of man's spirit.

The Metaphorical Function of Clothing

Henchard's hay-knife, 'wimble', leggings, waistcoat, and breeches all recur towards the end of *The Mayor of Casterbridge*. When Henchard leaves the town for the last time, he vainly tries to re-establish his former identity by cleaning up his 'old hay-knife and wimble', setting himself up in 'fresh leggings, knee-naps and corduroys' (*MC* 360), and once again the narrator adopts the pictorial mode. 'Though she [Elizabeth-Jane] did not know it Henchard formed at this moment much the same *picture* as he had presented when entering Casterbridge for the first time nearly a quarter of a century before' (*MC* 361; my emphasis). It is against the opening picture that Henchard's changing appearance is constantly measured. After a gap of sixteen years Susan sees her former husband dining in the Kings Arms at Casterbridge, and immediately that original image asserts itself in her mind. 'When last she had seen him he was sitting in a corduroy jacket, fustian waistcoat and breeches and tanned leather leggings, with a basin of hot furmity before him.' (*MC* 37). Now, the 'old-fashioned evening suit [and] an expanse of frilled shirt' announce Henchard's new-found fortune, and the 'heavy gold chain' eloquently proclaims his status; but his subsequent fall from respectability is accompanied by a further series of sartorial changes. When he begs to be allowed to participate in the reception for the Prince of Wales, his petition to the Council is conducted in 'the very clothes which he had used to wear in the primal days when he had sat among them.' (*MC* 303), though those clothes are now 'frayed and threadbare'. Even when he appears in the Royal Presence, he clings pathetically to the trappings of his former status, 'doggedly [retaining] the fretted and weather-beaten garments of bygone years.' (*MC* 306). And when, towards the end of the novel, Henchard takes on the work of general labourer, his image as skilled countryman again reasserts itself in the text. He once wore 'clean, suitable clothes, light and cheerful in hue; leggings yellow as marigolds, corduroys immaculate as new flax, and a neckerchief like a flower garden' (*MC* 264)—emblems of simplicity, dignity, and naturalness—but in his fallen state 'he wore the remains of an old blue cloth suit of his gentlemanly times, a rusty silk hat, and a once black satin stock, soiled and shabby.' (*MC* 264).

The changes which take place in Henchard's appearance as a result of his shifting status are unconscious ones, and his attitude to clothing, like his attitude to most things, is spontaneous and unpremeditated. This is not true of all the characters in the novel, many of whom are acutely conscious of their appearance. Within the text, the discussion of fashions, the numerous references to details of dress, and the persistent allusions to the sartorial appearance of other characters act as a constant reminder to the reader that clothing here has a significance which lies beyond appearances. The two most important characters in this respect are undoubtedly Elizabeth-Jane and Lucetta Templeman, and both their similarities and their differences focus specifically on their respective attitudes to dress and clothing and, in consequence, to the larger issues of appearance and reality.

Elizabeth-Jane first comes to Casterbridge as part of her mother's plan to free them from what Hardy (in an undoubtedly self-conscious metaphor) calls 'the strait-waistcoat of poverty' (*MC* 28). It is no accident that her entry into the novel, which takes place on 'the highroad to Weydon-Priors', reproduces many of the features of the very first 'picture' of the novel, and focuses sharply on matters of dress. Susan Henchard 'was dressed in the mourning clothes of a widow. Her companion, also in black, appeared as a well-formed young woman of about eighteen.' (*MC* 20). Under the auspices of Henchard, Elizabeth-Jane and her mother prosper, and that prosperity is marked by outward changes. 'It might have been supposed', says the narrator, 'that . . . a girl rapidly becoming . . . comfortably circumstanced . . . would go and make a fool of herself by dress' (*MC* 100), but Elizabeth-Jane formed instead 'curious resolves on checking gay fancies in the matter of clothes' (*MC* 109). A momentary lapse in those resolves, however, provides an important clue to the central position which clothes occupy in this novel. One day Henchard gave Elizabeth-Jane some 'delicately tinted' gloves:

> She wanted to wear them to show her appreciation of his kindness, but she had no bonnet that would harmonize. As an artistic indulgence she thought she would have such a bonnet. When she had a bonnet that would go with the gloves she had no dress that would go with the bonnet. It was now absolutely necessary to finish; she ordered the requisite article, and found that she had no sunshade to go with the dress. In for a penny, in for a pound; she bought the sunshade, and the whole structure was at last complete. (*MC* 109.)

The 'structure', or artefact, which Elizabeth-Jane creates is not the natural expression of her personality, but the result of 'an artistic indulgence', and its effect on those around her is dramatic and immediate. She becomes 'visible' to the inhabitants of Casterbridge, who, 'as soon as [they] thought her artful . . . thought her worth notice' (*MC* 110), and when even Donald Farfrae is moved by her appearance, Elizabeth-Jane decides to recreate the same structure before the mirror to test its effect. Putting on the 'muslin, the spencer, the sandals, [and] the parasol', she looked at her reflection. What she sees, however, is not her real self but 'a picture'—a false image: 'The *picture* glassed back was, in her opinion, precisely of such a kind as to inspire that fleeting regard, and no more.' (*MC* 128; my emphasis). Unlike most women, whose eyes, says the narrator in a cynical aside, are 'ruled . . . so largely by the superficies of things' (*MC* 305)—one thinks of Bathsheba Everdene in this context— Elizabeth-Jane is conscious of the discrepancy between her inner self and the artefact which she has created. This is important, since throughout *The Mayor of Casterbridge*, 'art'—whether it is the art of the fashion-designer or even the skill of the painter—is always associated with 'artfulness', with false appearances, personal cunning, and ultimately moral duplicity, and Elizabeth-Jane's clear-sightedness in these matters is emphasized by contrast with that 'artful little woman' (*MC* 171) Lucetta Templeman.

Lucetta enters the story as Elizabeth-Jane's *doppelgänger*. Like Elizabeth-Jane on the road to Weydon-Priors, 'the personage was in mourning . . . was about her age and size, and she might have been her wraith or double, but for the fact that it was a lady much more beautifully dressed than she.' (*MC* 153). It is significant that Elizabeth-Jane's eyes 'were arrested by the artistic perfection of the lady's appearance' (*MC* 153), since that 'artistic appearance' is to play an important part in Lucetta's development as a character *vis-à-*

vis Elizabeth-Jane. Lucetta is a complete 'art-work', and her faith in the value of appearances is her undoing. In a passage which Hardy subsequently deleted from the manuscript, he makes this very clear—probably too clear for his purposes. When Elizabeth-Jane first visits Lucetta, she asks her, ' "How did you know the way to dress so well?" ' Lucetta explains how she bought and paid for her appearance:

I went to Paris to the largest Magazin, and said, 'Make me fashionable,' holding out some bank-notes.' They half stripped me, and put on me what they chose. Four women hovered round me, fixed me on a pedestal like an image, and arranged me and pinned me and stitched me and padded me. When it was over I told them to send several more dresses of the same size, and so it was done.[13]

In the final version of the novel, two dresses arrive at High Place Hall, not from Paris but from London, and Lucetta spreads them on the bed in the form of two 'images', each suggesting a human figure. Her choice between them is a measure of the difference in attitude between herself and Elizabeth-Jane: ' "You are that person" ' (pointing to one of the arrangements), "or you are *that* totally different person" (pointing to the other) "for the whole of the coming spring." ' (*MC* 191). Unlike Elizabeth-Jane, Lucetta believes that clothes make the woman, and Lucetta's misplaced faith in the value of appearances is the immediate cause of her death. As Penelope Vigar points out, 'Lucetta's flimsy vanity is parodied by the bawdy fantasy of the skimmity-ride which blazons noisily and "with lurid distinctness" the scandal of her former relationship with Michael Henchard.'[14] ' "How folk do worship fine clothes" ', comments one of the jealous and disaffected rustics, while another, Nance Mockridge by name, would ' "like to see the trimming pulled of such Christmas candles" ' as Lucetta (*MC* 308). Carefully dressed 'images' of Lucetta and Henchard are paraded back to back in a second *doppelgänger* episode. The figure of Lucetta is 'dressed as *she* was dressed when she sat in the front seat at the time the play-actors came to the Town Hall', exclaims one of the spectators of the skimmity-ride; 'her neck is uncovered, and her hair in bands, and her back-comb in place; she's got on a puce silk, and white stockings, and coloured shoes.' (*MC* 321). For the first time Lucetta sees herself as she really is, and reality breaks

[13] DCM, *Mayor of Casterbridge* MS, fol. 218. The serialization prints this in a slightly modified version. See *The Graphic*, 33 (March, 1886), p. 270.
[14] Penelope Vigar, *The Novels of Thomas Hardy: Illusion and Reality*, p. 163.

through appearance. '"She's me—she's me—even to the parasol— my green parasol,' (*MC* 321) cries the bewildered girl, and unable to stand so much reality, falls into a paroxysm from which she never recovers.

The 'double' is extremely important in *The Mayor of Casterbridge* in pointing up the discrepancy between illusions of all kinds and the often cruel nature of reality which those illusions conceal. Elizabeth-Jane is herself the double of her dead stepsister; the living Newsome is a replica of the Newsome supposed dead; and Henchard himself has his doubles. His own image floats before him in the weir at the Ten Hatches. It prevents the quick death he is planning for himself and preserves him for a lingering one; finally, he leaves Casterbridge to all appearances the double of the figure who entered it. Many of these replicas are created through similarities of sartorial appearance; the images look alike because they are dressed alike, and, as Penelope Vigar suggests, throughout the story, 'details of dress and appearance are made to function both as overt representations of character, and as a symbolic commentary on the novel's theme'.[15] Lucetta believes that garments express a meaning which can be manipulated by artifice, but she is unable to read the 'inner meaning' of their forms. Elsewhere, Abel Whittle's breeches provide the immediate cause of the first major struggle between Henchard and Farfrae (*MC* 113); Elizabeth-Jane's expensive muff tells Henchard that a new relationship has been struck up between Farfrae and her (*MC* 349); and when Henchard leaves Casterbridge for the last time, he takes with him some 'cast-off belongings' of Elizabeth-Jane 'in the shape of gloves [and] shoes' (*MC* 366). Throughout the novel clothing acts as a means of recording both personal and communal life. Even a detail like the state of the furmity woman's apron expresses the changes in her personal fortunes. She was 'once thriving [and] cleanly white aproned', but returns to the story in 'a shawl of that nameless tertiary hue which comes, but cannot be made.' (*MC* 229). At the communal level, the life of the Casterbridge townsfolk can be read in their garments. The market-place, says the narrator, is 'a little world of leggings, switches and sample bags', where 'suits . . . were the historical records of their wearers' deeds . . . and daily struggles for many years past.' (*MC* 174–5).

Consequently, clothes and clothing in *The Mayor of Casterbridge* have a double role. As visual objects they impart to the narrative a sense of

---

[15] Ibid., p. 160.

materiality; their form, substance, design, and texture lend a palpability to the character of their wearers, and communicate a strong sense of the quotidian and the commonplace. But clothes are also highly symbolic in their nature, and each of the sartorial details points to aspects of character or social status which are essentially intangible and abstract in quality. In this way, not only is the daily life of Casterbridge communicated through the physical objects which constitute that life, but those same objects express some of the moral values, aspirations, and ambitions of the inhabitants of the town. Casterbridge is literally a 'world in clothes', and the metaphorical use which Hardy makes of the material substance of Casterbridge life strongly resembles the ideas of another writer who attached great importance to the symbolic function of dress. This was, of course, Thomas Carlyle, who, in *Sartor Resartus* of 1833, claimed, through the words of his imaginary Professor Teufelsdröckh, that, 'clothes, as despicable as we think them, are so unspeakably significant'.[16] *Sartor Resartus* is an extended investigation and analysis of this central idea, and throughout the book Carlyle uses the metaphor of clothing to explore the relationship between appearance and reality in human life. 'Men', says Carlyle,

are properly said to be clothed with Authority, clothed with Beauty, with Curses, and the like. Nay, if you consider it, what is Man himself, and his whole terrestrial Life, but an Emblem; a Clothing or visible Garment for that divine ME of his, cast hither, like a light-particle, down from Heaven?[17]

According to Carlyle, clothing has both a utilitarian and an expressive role in the life of the individual. On the one hand, as 'the tatters raked from the Charnel-house of Nature',[18] clothing covers his brute nakedness, but on the other, it acts as the symbolic expression of his spirit. 'Clothes', he says, 'gave us individuality, distinctions, social polity; Clothes have made Men of us.' But if we are unaware of the distinction between reality and mere appearance, he says, or are deceived into taking the garment for the man, then clothes will 'make Clothes-screens of us'.[19]

Though Hardy's admiration for Carlyle was qualified, Carlyle remained a powerful influence throughout his life.[20] He often read and

---

[16] Thomas Carlyle, *Sartor Resartus*, in *Collected Works* i. 70.
[17] Ibid. i. 70.
[18] Ibid. i. 54.
[19] Ibid. i. 39.
[20] Hardy seems to have admired Carlyle as a prose stylist, but had reservations

reread his copy of Carlyle's *Works*, and *Sartor Resartus* was one of his favourite texts.[21] He alludes to it in his account of Egdon Heath in *The Return of the Native*, where the 'venerable one coat' of the heath provides a 'satire on human vanity in clothes' (*RN* 6), and when asked by the editor of the *Fortnightly Review* to nominate a favourite passage of prose for an article 'Fine Passages in Verse and Prose, Selected by Living Men of Letters', Hardy chose something from *Sartor Resartus*.[22]

In both *Sartor Resartus* and *The Mayor of Casterbridge*, clothing is an emblem of man's status among his fellows. '*Man*', says Carlyle, '*is a Spirit* . . . bound by invisible bonds to *All Men*', and his clothes are 'the visible emblems of that fact'.[23] 'Society', he adds, 'is founded upon cloth;'[24] 'clothes . . . are like a tissue woven by men as an emblem of the connection between them.'[25] In *The Mayor of Casterbridge* Henchard's massive gold chain is a symbol of his standing in society; he is, as Carlyle put it, 'clothed with Authority'. Yet Carlyle warns just how ephemeral and insubstantial such symbols can be. 'On a sudden,' he says, 'as by some enchanter's wand . . . the Clothes fly-off . . . and Dukes, Grandees, Bishops, Generals, Annointed Presence itself . . . stand straddling there, not a shirt on them.'[26] Henchard's chain of authority is similarly insubstantial; he violates the socially accepted bond between himself and his wife, he is stripped of his chain and his other symbols of office, and his own nakedness is suggestively prefigured in his insistence that Abel Wittle should appear at work *sans culottes*.

Though *Sartor Resartus* starts out as a disquisition on clothes and clothing, as it progresses, Carlyle expands and extends the meaning of these words to take in much more than the materials that adorn the body. He conceives of the body itself as a form of clothing for the

about his ideas. The clothes metaphor seems to have captured Hardy's imagination, nevertheless, and he exploits it to the full in *The Mayor of Casterbridge*. By the time he came to write *The Woodlanders*, however, he felt that Carlyle's transcendentalism was considerably outmoded by recent scientific findings, that and his 'natural supernaturalism' could not be reconciled with Darwin's theories. See ch. 7 below.

[21] See Lennart Björk's remarks in *LN*, 94 n.

[22] He also chose a passage from the French Revolution. See *Personal Writings*, ed. Orel, pp. 106–10.

[23] Carlyle, Works, i. 58.

[24] Ibid. i. 49.

[25] Ibid. i. 58.

[26] Ibid. i. 59.

spirit; furthermore, in the physical world all those objects which man creates and uses—his tools, his furnishings, his buildings, his very towns and cities—fall under Carlyle's definition of clothing, each being the symbolic expression of man's inner nature. In *The Mayor of Casterbridge* Hardy employs a similar principle. Take tools, for example. The prominence of tools—the hay-knife and 'wimble'—in the first picture of Henchard has already been pointed out, and it is those same tools which he 'refurbishes' when he leaves Casterbridge. 'Man', Carlyle points out, 'is a Tool-using Animal.'

Weak in himself, and of small stature, he stands on a basis, at most for the flattest-soled, of some half-square foot, insecurely enough. . . . Nevertheless he can use Tools, can devise Tools . . . without Tools he is nothing, with Tools he is all.[27]

The inhabitants of Casterbridge realize that 'without Tools they are nothing', and the shop windows of the town proclaim the importance of implements. There were

scythes, reap-hooks, sheep-shears, bill-hooks, spades, mattocks, and hoes at the iron-monger's; bee-hives, butter-firkins, churns, milking stools and pails, hay-rakes, field-flagons, and seed-lips at the cooper's; cart-ropes and plough-harness at the saddler's; carts, wheelbarrows, and mill-gear at the wheelwright's and machinist's; horse-embrocations at the chemist's; at the glover's and leather cutter's, hedging-gloves, thatchers' kneecaps, ploughmen's leggings, villagers' patterns and clogs. (*MC* 32.)

This list, which Hardy says is 'endless', is much more than a picturesque detail. The elaborate gear and tackle embody a whole way of life, rich and diverse. It is a traditional, old-fashioned life, and the plethora of tools which symbolize it stands in marked contrast to the single piece of machinery which appears so starkly one day in Casterbridge market-square—Farfrae's horse-drill. 'It was', says Hardy, '[a] new-fashioned agricultural implement . . . till then unknown, in its modern shape, in this part of the country' (*MC* 191). It is a vivid object whose primary and secondary colours are quite unlike the tertiary hues of Casterbridge. There is also a hint about it of the unnatural and the grotesque. 'The machine', says Hardy, 'was painted in bright hues of green, yellow, and red, and it resembled as a whole a compound of hornet, grasshopper, and shrimp, magnified enormously.' (*MC* 191). The implements in the shop windows are the

[27] Ibid. i. 39.

product of a slow and natural evolution; the horse-drill is emphatically the creation of an age of machinery. Between the two there is
both gain and loss. Carlyle speaks ironically of the great 'progress'
man has made in 'the interval between the first wooden Dibble
fashioned by man, and those Liverpool Steam-carriages',[28] and
Hardy suggests that with the advent of newfangledness, 'the rugged
picturesqueness of the old method disappeared with its inconve-
niences.' (MC 103). In the text of the novel, the literal depiction of
tools merges with their symbolic significance. When, for example,
Farfrae takes over the corn trade, his new and ferocious efficiency is
expressed through the instruments of measurement: 'The scales and
steelyards began to be busy where guess-work had formerly been the
rule' (MC 256), while at an even more metaphorical level, the conflict
between Farfrae and Henchard is likened to the opposition between
primitive instruments. 'It was', says Hardy, 'the dirk against the
cudgel.' (MC 132).

In *Sartor Resartus*, Carlyle, in the persona of Professor Teufelsdröckh, observes the 'clothing' of man's existence from a double perspective. Sometimes it is the substantial projection of man's
spirit; at other times it is ephemeral and phantasmagoric. On some
occasions Teufelsdröckh sees 'clothing' as charged with inner significance. He looks 'into the mystery of the World; recognising in the
highest sensible phenomena . . . fresh or faded raiment', observing
that 'all objects are as windows, through which the philosophic eye
looks into Infinitude itself'.[29] Yet at other times the professor declares
that material things are illusive, and that 'a whole immensity of
Brussels carpets, and pier-glasses, and or-molu . . . cannot hide from
me that such Drawing-room is simply a section of Infinite space'.[30]
The substantial and the palpable melt into nothingness, and 'we sit in
a boundless Phantasmagoria and Dream-grotto [where] . . . sounds
and many-coloured visions flit round our sense'.[31] A very similar
dualism operates in *The Mayor of Casterbridge*. Elizabeth-Jane, for example, is sensitive to the true significance of appearances, and to the
way in which outward appearances can convey inner meaning, yet
she, like Teufelsdröckh, is troubled by the insubstantiality of material
existence. As she nurses her dying mother,

28 Ibid. i. 40.
29 Ibid. i. 70.
30 Ibid. i. 28.
31 Ibid. i. 51.

the subtle-souled girl [was] asking herself why she was born, why sitting in a room, and blinking at the candle; why things around her had taken the shape they wore in preference to every other possible shape. Why they stared at her so helplessly, as if waiting for the touch of some wand that should release them from terrestrial constraint; what that chaos called consciousness, which spun in her at this moment like a top, tended to, and began in. (*MC* 135–6.)

'In that strange Dream,' says Teufelsdröckh, 'how we clutch at shadows as if they were substances; and sleep deepest while fancying ourselves most awake.' Similarly, as Elizabeth-Jane contemplates the insubstantially of things, 'her eyes fell together; she was awake, yet she was asleep.' (*MC* 136).

The events of *The Mayor of Casterbridge* lend support to Elizabeth-Jane's anxiety about 'the wand' which might touch material things and 'release them from terrestrial constraint', or, in Carlyle's words, the 'enchanter's wand' which makes the clothes 'fly-off', reducing man to a naked animal. Henchard, for example, surrounds himself which objects which reflect a solid, substantial way of life. His belongings are massive in the simple, physical sense. The 'profusion [of] . . . heavy mahogany furniture of the deepest red-Spanish hues', the 'Pembroke tables, with leaves hanging so low that they well-nigh touched the floor' and 'with legs and feet shaped like those of an elephant' (*MC* 77), together with the 'lofty' rooms and 'wide' landings (*MC* 99) of his house all contribute to the illusion of permanence and size. In his account of Henchard's belongings, Hardy dwells on visual details, using images in which antiquity and affluence mingle to create an aura of timeless stability: 'the old pier-glass, with gilt columns and huge entablature, the picture-frames, sundry knobs and handles, and the brass rosette at the bottom of each riband bell-pull on either side of the chimney-piece.' (*MC* 139). Carlyle had warned against trusting to 'a whole immensity of Brussels carpets, and pier-glasses and ormolu', and sure enough, the certainties of Henchard's life are destroyed as if by supernatural agency: 'Like Prester John's, his table had been spread, and infernal harpies had snatched up the food.' (*MC* 145). The mayoral chain passes to Farfrae, who not only moves into Henchard's house, but also marries the woman whom Henchard had assumed was his. Appropriately, it is Henchard's furniture which most vividly symbolizes his ruin. Farfrae buys it all, then offers a few pieces to the former mayor as a gift.

The play on the relationship between the substantial and the illusory extends to other interior scenes in the novel. Lucetta, for example, creates an elaborate setting for herself at High Place Hall which is a reflection of her 'artfulness'. In contrast to the dark and massive objects in the mayor's house, the light and airy High Place Hall is 'prettily furnished'. The 'little square piano with brass inlayings' (*MC* 173) and the 'sofa with two cylindrical pillows' (*MC* 172) speak of an advanced taste in furnishings. '"I didn't know such furniture as this could be bought in Casterbridge,"' says Henchard, who is more familiar with Pembroke tables and pier-glasses. '"Nor can it be,"' replies Lucetta, '"nor will it till fifty years more of civilization have passed over the town."' (*MC* 202). When Henchard describes Lucetta as 'an artful little woman' (*MC* 171), he means that she is cunning, but, as we have seen, the word also implies that she is the creator and manipulator of artifice. The inhabitants of Casterbridge wrongly thought that Elizabeth-Jane was 'artful' (*MC* 110) when she dressed brilliantly, but the term is in fact totally appropriate for Lucetta. Not only is she someone who gazes upon Casterbridge life 'as a picture merely' (*MC* 181), she actually strikes poses reminiscent of famous works of art. On the occasion of Elizabeth-Jane's visit to High Place Hall, Lucetta 'deposited herself on the sofa in . . . [a] flexuous position, and throwing her arm above her brow—somewhat in the pose of a well-known conception of Titian's—talked up at Elizabeth-Jane invertedly across her forehead and arm.' (*MC* 172–3). Hardy may well have seen Titian's *Rape of Europa* which was shown at the Academy in 1876 (Plate 27) and Lord Sutherland's *Diana and Acteon* (Plate 28). He may have been thinking of *Jupiter and Antiope*, otherwise known as the *Pardo Venus* which he would have seen in the Louvre, for each of them employs this distinctive pose. In both the *Diana* and the *Pardo Venus* the mythological females recline seductively in attitudes of languid sexuality, and in both they are being 'discovered' by prospective lovers. When Lucetta thinks that she, too, might receive a male visitor, she prepares to be similarly 'discovered'. Giving orders that any gentleman should be admitted to her room immediately,

she arranged herself picturesquely in the chair; first this way, then that; next so that the light fell over her head. Next she flung herself on the couch in the cyma-recta curve which so became her, and with her arm over the brow looked towards the door. (*MC* 178.)

Lucetta is no more a real Diana, however, than Farfrae is a real Acteon, and, hearing footsteps on the stair, Lucetta, 'forgetting her curve (for Nature was too strong for Art as yet), jumped up and ran and hid herself behind one of the window-curtains in a freak of timidity.' (*MC* 179). In *Desperate Remedies* Cytherea Graye's 'master-piece of movement' is modelled on Greuze's *Head of a Girl*, and in *A Pair of Blue Eyes* Elfride Swancourt appears to Stephen Smith like the picture of a saint from a medieval painting, but both Cytherea and Elfride adopt poses spontaneously and unconsciously.[32] Lucetta Templeman is obsessed with appearances, however, and like George Eliot's Gwendolen Harleth, she is fully aware of her stylized atti-tudes. '"How do I appear to people?"' she asks Elizabeth-Jane. '"Well—a little worn,"' replies the astute girl, and treating her friend more in the spirit of art than life, eyes her 'as a critic eyes a doubtful painting.' (*MC* 198).

Lucetta also tries to arrange the lives of others according to the dic-tates of art, and her particular 'masterpiece' forms one of the most curious episodes in the novel. Henchard and Farfrae, who are both courting her, are invited to tea at High Place Hall. The atmosphere is formal and frigid, and the studied artifice is modelled this time not on Titian, but on early Italian art.

They sat stiffly side by side at the darkening table, like some Tuscan painting of the two disciples supping at Emmaus. Lucetta, forming the third and haloed figure, was opposite them; Elizabeth-Jane, being out of the game, and out of the group, could observe all from afar, like the evangelist who had to write it down. (*MC* 208.)

Though the analogy with painting is not Lucetta's but the narrator's, the unnatural stiffness of the image forms an integral part of the arti-fice with which Lucetta surrounds herself. The whole episode has been carefully engineered by Lucetta, and the frozen formality of what she has created contrasts strongly with the sounds that the four protagonists hear through the windows of High Place Hall. Inside, all is reduced to stasis, and is perceived through the eye; outside the vitality of life is experienced through the ear, as they hear

the click of a heel on the pavement under the window, the passing of a wheel-barrow or cart, the whistling of the carter, the gush of water into householder's buckets at the town-pump opposite; the exchange of greetings among their neighbours, and the rattle of the yokes by which they carried off their evening supply. (*MC* 208.)

Elizabeth-Jane is the passive spectator of all this, 'the evangelist who had to write it down'. She watches as Henchard courts Lucetta, and

[32] See Ch. 2 above.

is forced to watch when Lucetta shifts her affection to Farfrae. She is the most speculative and philosophical member of Casterbridge society, and in this respect is not unlike Professor Teufelsdröckh. But just as Henchard and Lucetta create interiors expressive of their character, so Elizabeth-Jane inhabits rooms which reflect her temperament, and it is surely no coincidence that those rooms resemble in certain important respects Teufelsdröckh's accommodation. The professor inhabits a 'speculum or watch-tower' from which 'he might see the whole life-circulation of [his] considerable City';[33] similarly, Elizabeth-Jane's room in Henchard's house was 'rather high . . . so that it . . . afforded her opportunity for accurate observation' (*MC* 103). With Lucetta by her side, she surveys the town from another vantage-point—a window in High Place Hall—and what is merely 'a picture' for Lucetta is full of human meaning for Elizabeth-Jane as she explains the identity of each of the townsfolk (*MC* 176). Elizabeth-Jane's final lodgings are also located on high. She takes an 'upper room no larger than the Prophet's chamber . . . nearly opposite her stepfather's former residence', from which she can see 'Donald and Lucetta speeding in and out of the door.' (*MC* 262).

There are correspondences, too, between the meditative activity of Teufelsdröckh and Elizabeth-Jane and the furnishings of their vantage-points. The professor's 'Wahngasse watch-tower' '. . . was a strange apartment; full of books and tattered papers, and miscellaneous shreds of all conceivable substances. . . . Books lay on tables, and below tables.'[34] Though Elizabeth-Jane is a much tidier creature, she, too, spends 'hours . . . devoted to studying such books as she could get hold of.' (*MC* 262). When she moves to join Henchard in his seed and grain shop, she creates another 'Prophet's chamber' characteristic of her desire for learning. Henchard strays in one day, and 'what struck him about it was the abundance of books lying everywhere. Their number and quality made the meagre furniture that supported them seem absurdly disproportionate.' (*MC* 349). Elizabeth-Jane's furniture is 'meagre', and Henchard's is substantial and has all the appearance of permanence, whereas Lucetta's is a small collection of lightweight artworks. All these furnishings, however, fall into the category of 'clothing' in Carlyle's definition of the term. Henchard, with his naive belief in the permanence of things, resembles Carlyle's noble but naked anthropophagus who fails to dis-

---

[33] Carlyle, Works i. 19.
[34] Ibid., 22.

tinguish between appearance and reality; Lucetta is Carlyle's 'clothes-screen', for whom life is a matter of externals or a series of self-conscious artifices. Only Elizabeth-Jane, from 'the crystalline sphere of a straightforward mind' (*MC* 205), is fully aware of the significance of the material world, and can interpret the language of 'clothes'. She alone perceives their true symbolic import, and she alone refuses to encumber her life with what is ultimately ephemeral. But in *The Mayor of Casterbridge*, the clothes metaphor does not rest here; it is not confined to those aspects of material life over which men and women have decisive control. It extends to include the structure of Casterbridge itself—its houses, buildings, inns, and taverns—and extends even to the design of the town, the special topographical features of which are expressive of the lives of its inhabitants past and present.

The Architectural Metaphor

In *Sartor Resartus* Carlyle said that 'not a Hut [man] builds but is the visible embodiment of a Thought; but bears visible record of invisible things; but is, in the transcendental sense, symbolical as well as real'.[35] Hardy had already experimented with a similar idea in *A Laodicean*. George Somerset's devotion to Gothic building and Paula Power's desire to build a Greek courtyard in a medieval castle are the 'visible embodiment' of a historicist view of architecture on the one hand, and a romantic, but confused, set of attitudes, on the other. The failure of the novel stems in part from Hardy's inability to use architectural form as a genuine expression of temperament. The relationship between the characters and the ideas is not an integral one, and the romantic affair between Paula and Somerset has no real connection with the interaction between medievalism and modernism.

In *The Mayor of Casterbridge*, the connection between the building and its occupier is far more imaginatively organic. Henchard's house provides such an apt visual metaphor for his solid, old-fashioned principles that one tends to forget that it is the residence of *all* mayors of the borough. Faced with 'red-and-grey old brick' (*MC* 70), it is massive and dignified, and, like Henchard himself, its design is open and frank. From the front door passers-by could 'see through the passage to the end of the garden—nearly a quarter of a mile off.' (*MC*

<hr />

[35] Ibid., 213.

70–1). For Henchard there is a continuity between life and labour, and in his house there is a little door which opens directly into the garden, '[permitting] a passage from the utilitarian to the beautiful at one step.' (*MC* 88).

Perhaps more than with any other character, Henchard's rise and fall is mirrored in his various dwellings. His first abode within the novel is a furmity tent, where he wakes wifeless, homeless, and rootless. The contrast between this tent and the substantial Georgian house in Casterbridge is a palpable sign of his rise through that society, and his downward path through Casterbridge is marked by a whole series of dwellings. First, he is forced to surrender the mayoral residence to Farfrae and take up lodgings with Jopp, a man whom he had formerly 'employed, abused, cajoled, and dismissed by turns' (*MC* 255). Situated in one of the precincts which 'embodied the mournful phases of Casterbridge life' (*MC* 145), Jopp's house is suggestive of ruin. Indeed, its very stones speak of ruin, since it is constructed 'from the long dismantled Priory, [and] from scraps of tracery, moulded window-jambs, and arch-labels . . . mixed in with the rubble of the walls.' (*MC* 255). Henchard tries to reconstruct the ruins of his own life, and moves into a seedman's shop 'not much larger than a cupboard'—a cruel parody of his former flourishing business. But it is his final resting-place which symbolizes his total dissolution. It is Abel Whittle's cottage, of which

the walls, built of kneaded clay originally faced with a trowel, had been worn by years of rain-washings to a lumpy crumbling surface, channelled and sunken from its plane, its grey rents held together here and there by a leafy strap of ivy which could scarcely find substance enough for the purpose. The rafters were sunken, and the thatch of the roof was in ragged holes. (*MC* 382.)

Similarly, Lucetta's house, High Place Hall, embodies salient features of her personality:

It had . . . the characteristics of a country mansion—birds' nests in its chimneys, damp nooks where fungi grew, and irregularities of surface direct from Nature's trowel. At night the forms of passengers were patterned by the lamps in black shadows upon the pale walls. (*MC* 159–60.)

As Penelope Vigar suggests, the description of High Place Hall 'parodies all the bewildering façades of its owner in epigrammatic succession'.[36] On one side it is Palladian with a 'reasonableness

36 Vigar, *The Novels of Thomas Hardy*, p. 150.

[which] made it impressive' (*MC* 160); on the other, where it opens into 'one of the little-used alleys of the town', its design strongly suggests 'intrigue'—suggestive, as Vigar points out, of Lucetta's own life with its 'discreetly veiled but dubious past'.

Unlike the architectural forms of *A Laodicean*, the significance of which is primarily ideological or conceptual, the buildings of Caster-bridge convey an exclusively human meaning, and are everywhere redolent with human feelings and associations. The two bridges at the end of the High Street, for example, possess 'speaking countenances', and the story they tell is one of intimate human contact. On these bridges,

every projection . . . was worn down to obtuseness, partly by weather, [but] more by friction from generations of loungers, whose toes and heels had from year to year made restless movements against these parapets, as they stood there meditating on the aspect of affairs. (*MC* 257.)

Buildings in the High Street also take on human features, where 'the overhanging angles of walls, . . . originally unobtrusive, had become bow-legged and knock-kneed.' (*MC* 68). The relationship between men and buildings in Casterbridge is a reciprocal one, and is most clearly seen in the non-verbal language adopted by the yeoman farmers of the borough. They often spoke, says the narrator, 'in other ways than by articulation', using the face, the hat, the stick, and the body, and the syntax of this language is an architectural one. 'Satisfaction' is expressed by 'a broadening of the cheeks, a crevicing of the eyes' (*MC* 69); 'tediousness announced itself in a lowering of the person by spreading the knees to a lozenge-shaped aperture'; and, most remarkable of all, the very substance of the building is brought into play. 'Deliberation', says the narrator, finds expression in 'sundry attacks on the moss of adjoining walls with the end of . . . [the] stick' (*MC* 70).

This notion of an intimate connection between society and building style was common in the nineteenth century. Carlyle's view that architecture is 'the visible embodiment of Thought' has its roots in the eighteenth century, but was developed to a considerable degree by architectural writers like Ruskin and Pugin. For Pugin the cathedrals and abbeys of England and France represent the superiority of the medieval over the modern way of life, while for Ruskin it was the churches and palaces of Venice which spoke of spiritual greatness and subsequent decay. Hardy's notebook entries and the various remarks he made both suggest that he was in sympathy with this view,[37] but unlike Pugin and Ruskin, he was concerned less with monumental and extraordinary buildings than with the domestic and the commonplace. During the years Hardy spent in London, a generation of architects arose who believed in what Pevsner calls 'the intimate and serviceable'.[38] Nesfield's lodge in Kew Gardens (1866), Thackeray's house in Kensington Palace Gardens (1861), and Philip Webb's Red House (1858) are all testimony to the growing interest in domestic design. Perhaps what most distinguishes Hardy's use of architectural forms in *The Mayor of Casterbridge* from the approach of earlier writers, however, is his treatment of buildings as just one of many ways by which a community expresses its collective values. In this respect Hardy is closer to the Henry Cole circle at Marlborough House, and their interest in what Owen Jones called the 'grammar of ornament'.[39] It was William Morris who explicitly linked textile design, furniture design, interior decoration, and building, by describing them all as forms of 'architecture'.[40] Hardy was undoubtedly familiar with Morris's views, which are distantly related to those expressed by Carlyle in *Sartor Resartus*. But whereas Carlyle perceives a symbolic link between what Morris calls 'the lesser arts', Morris's interest is fundamentally practical. He firmly believes in the coherence of the domestic arts, but he has nothing to say about the significance of those arts in any symbolic context.

There is one writer in this period, however, who views the consistency of man's material and spiritual life in a way which closely resembles Hardy's treatment of a similar relationship in *The Mayor of Casterbridge*. Gottfried Semper, in the two volumes of his work *Der Stil*, put forward an evolutionary theory of the arts in terms of man's need for expression. Semper wrote these books while he was teaching at the newly established Department of Practical Art in Marlborough House,

---

[37] In 1876 he copied into his notes a remark from Balzac to the effect that 'architecture is the expression of morals' (*LN* entry 262). He joined the Society for the Protection of Ancient Buildings in 1881 in order to preserve what he later called 'chronicles in stone' ('Memories of Church Restoration', in *Personal Writings*, ed. Orel, p. 204), and he is reported to have said that 'people make buildings in their own image' (C. J. P. Beatty, 'The Part Played by Architecture in the Life and Work of Thomas Hardy', p. 2).

[38] Pevsner, *Some Architectural Writers of the Nineteenth Century*, p. 268.

[39] The title of a book by Owen Jones published in 1856.

[40] Morris, who was one of the founders of the Society for the Protection of Ancient Buildings, delivered his paper to the society in 1882. See William Morris, 'The Lesser Arts of Life', in *The Collected Works of William Morris* xxii. 253–69.

and they appeared in 1861 and 1863 respectively, while Hardy was working in the office of Arthur Blomfield. Hardy may well have known of Semper's ideas not from *Der Stil*, but from a source closer to home. In 1884, when he was writing *The Mayor of Casterbridge*, there was a flurry of interest in Semper's theories of architecture and ornament. It was reported in *The Architect* and *The Builder*—journals which he would undoubtedly have consulted while he was designing Max Gate—and the way in which Semper's ideas were described by his pupils and followers would have held considerable interest for him.[41] In *The Architect*, for example, Lawrence Harvey, one of Semper's students from the Marlborough House days, summarized the German professor's views in terms very similar to those underlying *The Mayor of Casterbridge*. 'Art', said Semper, 'began with adorning and clothing our bodies, and branched out later on in adorning and clothing all the objects we use—weapons, tools, dwellings'.[42]

The similarity between Hardy's use of artefacts in *The Mayor of Casterbridge* and Semper's evolutionary history of human decoration lies in the common assumption that all objects in use are both expressive and utilitarian. Everything that man invents, builds, creates, designs, and uses is in some way expressive of a personal or collective mind, and the paradigm for all material objects is the form taken by human clothing. Semper detects a continuity between textile arts, ceramic arts, tectonic art (carpentry and joinery), and stereometric arts (masonry and carving), all of which act as a covering for the human spirit. Architecture, he says, 'borrows some of its ornament from dress', and it 'bears with dress the impression of analogous influences, such as the taste, character, and civilization of a people'.[43] In Hardy's Casterbridge, not only is the status and the temperament of individuals expressed through their clothing and their furniture, but the temper of the borough is proclaimed in the dress of the

---

[41] Gottfried Semper was born in Hamburg in 1803, and came to teach at Marlborough House, London, between 1851 and 1855. He returned to the Continent in 1855 as Professor of the Polytechnic, Zurich. When he died in 1879, T. L. Donaldson, who had presented Hardy with the prize awarded him by the Architectural Association, wrote Semper's obituary in *The Builder* 37 (Aug. 1879), p. 880. The two volumes of *Der Stil in den technischen und tektonischen Kunsten* (1861 and 1863) were to have been completed by the addition of a third. For Semper's evolutionary theories of architectural form, see L. D. Ettlinger, 'Science, Industry and Art: The Theories of Gottfried Semper', and Pevsner, *Some Architectural Writers of the Nineteenth Century*, pp. 252–68.
[42] Lawrence Harvey, 'Gottfried Semper', p. 244.
[43] Anon., 'Semper's Theory of Architectural Ornament', p. 821.

market-goers, and the history of the town is recorded in its buildings. 'When textile products are used in the form of surfaces, they serve the purpose of covering, of protecting, of enclosing,' says Semper, and 'from them language borrows its words, religion its symbols, and architecture its ornamentation.'[44]

One detail in the contemporary discussion of Semper's work would have had a particular claim on Hardy's attention. On two occasions, in The *Architect* of 18 October 1884 and in that of 20 December 1884, parallels were drawn between what Semper said about the function of architecture as a form of 'ornament' and what Carlyle had said about the symbolism of clothing in *Sartor Resartus*.[45] On both occasions it was suggested that *Sartor Resartus* was a commentary on Semper's ideas, and one writer even hinted that Professor Teufelsdröckh was modelled on Semper himself. Though the dates of publication make both these theories unlikely,[46] the fact that Semper was connected with Carlyle might well have been enough to rouse Hardy's curiosity. Carlyle's influence can be clearly detected in Hardy's treatment of the clothes, tools, and furnishings of Casterbridge. Carlyle, however, has relatively little to say about architecture or building in any technical sense, so it must have been what Hardy read of Semper's ideas that encouraged him to extend the 'clothes' metaphor to the architectural fabric of Casterbridge. But there is one further aspect of the material existence of the town which has not yet been touched upon—its physical layout and topography—and that takes us back to Carlyle.

Casterbridge is precariously located in both place and in time. It is an integral part of the surrounding countryside, yet separated from that countryside; it has its roots in the past, but is forced to look to the future. Similarly, the group which goes to make up Casterbridge society is both tightly knit, living in a town 'compact as a box of dominoes' (*MC* 30), yet divided against itself, individual against individual, group against group. In *Sartor Resartus* Carlyle views the community of man in rather similar terms. On the one hand man is a

---

[44] 'Semper's Theory of Evolution in Architectural Ornament', p. 37.

[45] Harvey wrote that 'Semper first gave out his theory of the art of clothing as the basis of art about the year 1831. Carlyle . . . wrote his "Sartor Resartus" in 1832.' ('Gottfried Semper', p. 244). A member of The Institute of British Architects called Stannus thought that this was 'most likely correct'. See *The Architect*, 32 (Dec. 1884), p. 407. But see note 46 below.

[46] Since *Sartor Resartus* was published in 1831 and Semper's first published work did not appear until 1834, it is very unlikely that Carlyle owed anything to the German. A more plausible view was expressed by a third writer in *The Architect*, who suggested that the idea of the clothes metaphor had its origin in Fichte.

creature at war with his fellow man, from whom he is divided by creed, race, and nationality. On the other hand, behind the spectacle of struggle and conflict, says Carlyle, there are other forces at work—forces which draw men together and serve to establish their underlying brotherhood.

In the novel the two-sidedness of Casterbridge society is nowhere more clearly seen than in the topographical features of the town; and, depending upon the point of view, those features are suggestive either of unity or of conflict. The struggle between Henchard and Farfrae is the most prominent source of strife in the novel, but the monuments of Casterbridge make it clear that their battle is just a small part of a continuing story of conflict. The Roman amphitheatre, once the scene of gladiatorial combats, is haunted not only by the victims of the Roman games, but also by those executed on the town gibbet and those who have taken part in 'pugilistic encounters almost to the death' (*MC* 81). The old arena has lost none of its aura of conflict, even though this may no longer be crude physical combat, and it is here that Henchard arranges to meet first Susan and later Lucetta. The more violent struggles, however, now take place in a modern arena; the nearby market-place is explicitly the 'centre and arena of the town' (*MC* 207), and it is here that 'spectacular dramas' are staged. Farfrae and Henchard repeatedly encounter each other at the 'car-refour' (*MC* 190) of Casterbridge life, and what is initially 'mortal commercial combat' (*MC* 132) with 'dirk against cudgel' (*MC* 132) develops into an actual physical gladiatorial battle in Farfrae's hay-loft. Seen through the eyes of a ruined man, life itself is a mortal combat, and when Henchard leaves Casterbridge for the last time, he declares that he has 'no wish to make an arena a second time' of his life there (*MC* 369).

There are a number of other locations in Casterbridge the placing or physical attributes of which suggest division and strife. Durnover, for example, the most rural and idyllic spot in Casterbridge, lies immediately alongside the sinister area known as Mixen Lane. In Durn-over, the 'wheat-ricks overhung the old Roman street, and thrust their eaves against the church tower; green-thatched barns, with doorways as high as the gates of Solomon's temple, opened directly upon the main thoroughfare.' (*MC* 105). 'Though the upper part of Durnover', says the narrator, 'was mainly composed of a curious congeries of barns and farmsteads, there was', he adds, 'a less picturesque side to the parish. This was Mixen Lane' (*MC* 293). It is 'the Adullam of all the surrounding villages, . . . the hiding-place of those who were in distress, and in debt, and trouble of every kind.' (*MC* 293). Durnover represents the plentiful, Arcadian side of rural life—Mixen Lane the distress and hardship of country life that Hardy alluded to in his essay 'The Dorsetshire Labourer'. The language in which Hardy describes one side of the parish abounds in images of bounty and dignity; but on the other side of the same parish, the very architecture declares the presence of moral poverty: 'Recklessness dwelt under the roof with the crooked chimney; shame in some bow-windows; theft . . . in the thatched and mud-walled houses by the sallows.' (*MC* 293-4.)

Beyond these symbols of strife, conflict, and disorder, however, there is something about Casterbridge which suggests historical continuity and social community. The very 'compactness' of the town, its existence as the 'pole, focus, or nerve knot of the surrounding countryside', serves to preserve the sense of social cohesion in spite of local disharmony. Carlyle expressed a similar view of man's life in *Sartor Resartus*. 'Nature', he says, is not 'an Aggregate but a whole',[47] and the fire that glows in the smithy is not a 'separated speck, cut-off from the whole Universe [but] . . . a little ganglion, or nervous centre, in the great vital system of Immensity'.[48] Casterbridge is also a 'nervous centre'—it suffers its shocks but it remains intact because its parts are organically related. Mixen Lane may be 'a mildewed leaf in the sturdy and flourishing Casterbridge plant' (*MC* 294), but, as Carlyle pointed out, 'all, were it only a withered leaf, works together with all.' The leaf

is borne forward on the bottomless, shoreless flood of Action, and lives through perpetual metamorphoses. The withered leaf is not dead and lost, there are Forces in it and around it, though working in inverse order; else how could it *rot*?[49]

What Hardy failed to do in *A Laodicean*, he achieved with total success in *The Mayor of Casterbridge*: he created a setting which was both credible and expressive. The material aspects of Casterbridge life, from clothing to buildings, from tools to furnishings, give the illusion of permanence and concreteness, yet there is no detail, no object of clothing or item of furniture, which does not express something of the

[47] Carlyle, Works i. 68.
[48] Ibid. i. 69.
[49] Ibid. i. 69.

discrepancy between appearance and reality. The illusion of permanence which physical objects give to the flux and change in life is not just a convention of fiction. As Hardy designed Max Gate, as he scoured the pages of *The Architect* and *The Builder* for accounts of the latest ventilation systems or water-closets, the words of Carlyle on the ephemeral nature of such things must have come back to him. Both Semper and Carlyle spoke of the way in which the material affects of life operated as modes of decoration, of adornment for man's inner nature. They also spoke of how these things are ultimately as 'phantasmagoric' as the spirit itself. In *A Laodicean*, images, ideas, and characters never achieved full integration; the architectural forms, the ideologies which they represent, and the lives of the characters remain to the end distinct and separate. In *The Mayor of Casterbridge* this is not so. Lucetta Templeman's identity is vested in the clothes she wears and the settings which she self-consciously creates, but she is also the personification of the false belief that the garment makes the woman. Hardy achieves this integration in part through concentration—by limiting his drama to the narrow confines of a market town, and by giving each detail its special place in the tightly knit web of life there. He also does it by picturing the episodes in a much more vivid and convincing way than he had managed to do in *A Laodicean*. In one important respect many of the scenes in *The Mayor of Casterbridge* employ the conventions of contemporary narrative painting. Paintings like the first panel of Augustus Egg's *Past and Present* or Holman Hunt's *The Awakening Conscience* or even Hubert Herkomer's *Hard Times* (see Plate 26) locate their subjects in unexceptional surroundings which are then painted with considerable verisimilitude. On closer inspection, however, these surroundings— the middle-class interior, the spot on the country road—yield meanings which relate to the central subject, but extend its significance emblematically. The tottering house of cards in the Egg, the cat with the bird in the Hunt, the collection of tools discarded by the side of the road in the Herkomer all serve to identify more precisely the human dilemma at the heart of the picture. In other words, in these pictures, objects which at first appear arbitrary and commonplace are vested with a special meaning beyond their function as mere decorative adjuncts.

In his essay 'The Profitable Reading of Fiction' (1888), Hardy discussed the function of such 'accessories' in novels. He was critical of social realists who were faithful to 'life garniture and not life', and he supported his views with a quotation from Taine's *History of English Literature*. Novelists of social minutiae, said Taine, who 'paint clothes and places with endless detail', are far removed from those authors who 'create and transform', but Hardy qualified this view of realism with an important proviso. One should not, he said, dismiss as a matter of course novelistic fidelity to externals. 'We must not,' he said, 'as enquiring readers, fail to understand that attention to accessories has its virtues when the nature of its regard does not involve blindness to higher things; still more when it conduces to the elucidation of higher things.'[50] This idea is especially germane to *The Mayor of Casterbridge*, since in this novel the accessories function in two ways. The dark, heavy furniture in Henchard's house, the fashionable decorations in High Place Hall, and the meagre objects in Elizabeth-Jane's lodgings not only lend conviction to the settings, they also elucidate higher things. They invest each scene with the kind of credibility expected from novelists of social minutiae, but they also serve to communicate something of the temperament, disposition, status, and values of each character. One of Hardy's achievements in *The Mayor of Casterbridge* is his development of language of material forms. From the very first page of the book, the vocabulary, syntax, and structure of this language are slowly and imperceptibly built up, so that by the end, the language lends a powerful rhetorical force to Henchard's severance with Casterbridge life. By means of a remarkable and creative act, Hardy managed to transform some of the conventions of contemporary realist literature in the context of his reading of Carlyle and Semper in such a way that the 'accidental' (as he calls it in his essay) becomes 'the essential', and those things which might be dismissed as ephemeral or as mere accessories become what Carlyle described as 'unspeakably significant'.[51]

[50] 'The Profitable Reading of Fiction', in *Personal Writings*, ed. Orel, p. 119.
[51] See n. 16.

7

The Woodlanders: Impressionism and Modernism

'Last century it was the glorification of Nature. . . . Now we find ourselves depreciating Nature, and finding in her alleged imperfections and apparent cruelties.'[1]

Though *The Woodlanders* was started only seven months after *The Mayor of Casterbridge* was finished it is a very different kind of novel. There is no hero—no 'man of character'—who dominates the story; moreover, compared with Henchard, Farfrae, Lucetta, and Elizabeth-Jane, Giles Winterborne, Marty South, and Felice Charmond are relatively shadowy presences. Part of the difference is connected with Hardy's techniques of characterization. In *The Mayor of Casterbridge* the reader 'sees' the protagonists in all their minute particulars. He knows how they dress, how they walk, how they live. This is not so in *The Woodlanders*. It would be very difficult to mentally reconstruct the appearance of Giles Winterborne; Mr and Mrs Melbury have no outstanding physical characteristics, and apart from her once magnificent head of red hair, we know almost nothing of Marty South's looks or demeanour. Even a colourful and romantic figure like Felice Charmond has none of the striking physical attributes of similar women in Hardy's other novels. In fact, Hardy's reaction against the techniques of *The Mayor of Casterbridge* is so strong that he actually resists fulfilling the reader's expectation of a detailed exposition of the physical appearances of his major characters. This is most apparent in the case of Grace Melbury, and at the point at which she is introduced into the story, Hardy actually delivers a lecture on the inadequacy of appearances as a true guide to character. When Grace is met for the first time by Giles in the market-place of Sherton Abbas, the narrator says:

There was nothing remarkable in her dress just now beyond a natural fitness, and a style that was recent for the streets of Sherton. But had it been quite striking it would have meant just as little. For there can be hardly anything

[1] Anon., 'Mr Footman on Modern Unbelief', The *Spectator*, 55 (Apr. 1883), pp. 514–15, in *LN* entry 1301.

less connected with a woman's personality than drapery which she has neither designed, manufactured, cut, sewed, nor even seen, except by a glance of approval when told that such and such a shape and colour must be had because it has been decided by others as imperative at that particular time. (*W* 42.)

At first sight, this is a curious claim coming from the pen of a writer who, in *The Mayor of Casterbridge*, seemed to have learned Carlyle's lesson on the 'unspeakably significant' importance of the correct interpretation of appearances. But the clue to Hardy's new interest in character and characterization is contained in a sentence a little earlier. 'It would have been difficult', he says, 'to describe Grace Melbury with precision, either then or at any time. Nay, from the highest point of view, to precisely describe a human being, the focus of a universe, how impossible!' (*W* 41-2). The important phrase here is 'a human being, the focus of a universe', since it is this which determines Hardy's mode of characterization in *The Woodlanders*. Between the two novels, Hardy's interest in fictional characters has shifted from matter to mind. In *The Mayor of Casterbridge* the inner life of characters is understood by the way it impinges on the material world. Psychology is, as it were, externalized. Appearances are important because they act as a guide to temperament. Of all the characters in the novel, Elizabeth-Jane is the most conscious of this, and realizes that her appearance should reflect her inner life. In *The Woodlanders* this is no longer an issue; the physical differences between Fitzpiers and Giles Winterborne are immaterial, and what now distinguishes them and their values is something quite different.[2]

In *The Woodlanders*, each of the major characters and many of the minor ones are distinguished by their mental attitudes, rather than by their physical attributes. Each one is a subtly different 'focus of a universe', and each one has a distinct set of values with regard to his fellow human beings, and to the woodland setting of Little Hintock. The 'universe' of which each is a 'focus' is made up of a complex of social attitudes, sexual mores, integrity, honour, probity, and so on, and the differences between these universes are most clearly apparent in the ways in which each of the major protagonists respond to the natural world in this sequestered portion of Wessex. Giles Winterborne, for example, is perfectly at home in the woods, and moves

---

2 In February 1887, Hardy wrote: 'The material is not the real—only the visible, the real being invisible optically. That it is because we are in a somnabulistic hallucination that we think the real to be what we see as real.' (*EL* 243).

easily through the forest. Fitzpiers does not, and for him the woods are a threat. Similarly with the other characters. Mr South has a pre-rational, totemistic fear of tree spirits, whereas his daughter, like Giles, is at ease in the woods. Mr Melbury is a timber merchant, and for him the groves of Hintock are merely a source of income, but his daughter, Grace, lives divided between two worlds, one alienated from 'the good old Hintock ways' (*W* 49), the other deeply sym-pathetic to the unaffected simplicity of woodland life. Finally, for Felice Charmond, the woods are just a source of unpleasantness and anguish: they offer nothing to her mind and spirit, and her one idea is to be away and out of them.

The effect of this new perspective on the form and structure of the novel is enormous. Gone is the stable, substantial world of the Wessex market town which provided a solid frame of reference for the characters within it; instead change and flux prevail in the woodlands. Sunshine, shadow, fog, mist, storm, and the cycle of the seasons all contrive to create a shifting and constantly changing set-ting for the narrative. One cannot get lost in Casterbridge: the streets and buildings are all too clearly marked for that. But in *The Woodlanders* characters are for ever losing their way, and the erratic wanderings of Grace, Fitzpiers, and Mrs Charmond are prefigured by the loss of direction suffered by the very first character to be intro-duced into the novel—Barber Percombe.

Perhaps the most important single factor distinguishing the tone of *The Woodlanders* from that of *The Mayor of Casterbridge*, however, is the relationship between the narrator and his story. In the earlier novel that relationship is epitomized by the pictorialism of the opening scene. Here, and throughout the text, a distance is preserved between the narrator and the events which he observes. In this first scene he appears to be scanning a picture. He regards it objectively, and coolly registers the details of an anonymous family group in an anonymous landscape. Though he offers interpretations of what he sees, there is no suggestion that he is the creator of what he sees. His role is that of the interested bystander. This is not the case in *The Woodlanders*, and each observation and event is deeply permeated with the con-sciousness of the narrator himself. He is no longer the objective witness of events; instead, his way of looking at things implicates him in the creation of the events he records. Again, the opening scene of the book is indicative of what is to follow, and it aligns the narrator with his characters as yet another 'consciousness' in the narrative. In the mind of the narrator, the trees of Little Hintock are not just trees: they are transformed into quasi-human presences. They are 'timber or fruit-bearing as the case may be, [and] . . . make the wayside hedges ragged by their drip and shade, their lower limbs stretching in level repose over the road, as though reclining on the insubstantial air' (W 1), and the 'deserted highway' which winds through these trees is populated not, as in *The Mayor of Casterbridge*, by substantial human forms, but by the figments of the narrator's imagination.

> The spot is lonely, and when the days are darkening the many gay charioteers now perished who have rolled along the way, the blistered soles that have trodden it, and the tears that have wetted it, return upon the mind of the loiterer. (W 1.)

Eventually the woodlanders themselves appear, but, like the figures on the deserted highway—the pedestrians and charioteers from the past—they are relatively insubstantial. There is none of the firm and clear-cut distinction between narrator and character found in *The Mayor of Casterbridge*; instead, the inhabitants of Little Hintock are far more intimately bound up with the author's own modes of perception.

The development in Hardy's attitudes to characterization, setting, and the relationship between narrative and narrator almost certainly grew out of his ideas on the function of the novel. In the early months of 1886 he began to formulate a theory about the modern novel which placed the emphasis on ideas rather than characterization. The novel, he said, should deal with society not as an aggregate of separate individuals but as 'one great network or tissue' which 'quivers in every part when one point is shaken, like a spider's web' (*EL* 232). Henceforth, he suggested, fiction should concern itself not so much with the visible world, reproducing 'optical effects' or the commonplaces of ordinary experience; instead, it should deal more with abstractions and philosophical ideas. Inevitably characters would become more shadowy and less palpable: they would take the form of 'Spirits, Spectral figures, etc.' (*EL* 232), and they would be the expression of what he called 'abstract realisms'. Hardy did not realize these ambitions fully until he came to write *The Dynasts*, but in *The Woodlanders* he goes some way to putting his new ideas into practice. When, for example, Giles and Marty South walk out in the twilight of morning early in the novel, the 'optical view' registers them as distinct and separate entities; from a superficial standpoint, 'hardly anything could be

23. Thomas Woolner: *Alfred Lord Tennyson*. 1876. Art Gallery of South Australia (height, 70 cm)

24. Sebastiano del Piombo: *The Raising of Lazarus*. 1517–19. National Gallery, London (381×289.6 cm)

25. Augustus Welby Pugin: (*left*) *St Pancras Chapel and* (*below left*) *Bishop Skirlaw's Chapel, Yorkshire.* Engraving from *Contrasts.* 1841

26. Sir Hubert von Herkomer: *Hard Times.* 1885. Manchester City Art Galleries (85×110.5 cm)

more isolated or more self-contained than the lives of these two.' (*W* 21). But seen in another, more penetrating way, 'their lonely courses formed no detached design at all;' instead, they were 'part of the pattern in the great web of human doings when weaving in both hemispheres from the White Sea to Cape Horn.' (*W* 21). According to Hardy, contemporary realism overlooked the pattern in the web of human affairs. By confining itself to externals and appearances, it neglected the 'true realities' of life. In future, he argued, these true realities, hitherto called 'abstractions', would take their place in the foreground of the novel, while the 'old material realities' would 'be placed behind the former, as shadowy accessories.' (*EL* 232). At least one of the principal sources for these 'realities' was to be found in modern speculative thought, and the novel would reflect the prevailing ontology 'by rendering as visible essences, spectres, etc., the abstract thoughts of the analytical school.' (*EL* 232).

This was not the first time that the notion of 'visible essences' had occurred to Hardy. It was hinted at in *The Return of the Native*, where he used the term to refer to the essential qualities of Eustacia Vye's temperament. 'Assuming that the souls of men and women were visible essences,' he wrote, 'you could fancy the colour of Eustacia's soul to be flame-like.' (*RN* 76). In *The Woodlanders*, however, the operation of the visible essence is far more widespread. Throughout the novel there is the sense that the visible, the external, and the corporeal are merely the carapace for some underlying reality, and that the phenomenal is merely the visible essence of the noumenal. On at least one occasion Hardy lapses into the technical language of this theory. When Mr Melbury sits anxiously wondering whether Fitzpiers will marry his daughter, the narrator says:

Could the real have been beheld instead of the corporeal merely, the corner of the room in which [Mr Melbury] sat would have been filled with a form typical of anxious suspense, large-eyed, tight-lipped, awaiting the issue. (*W* 195.)

It is not difficult to identify some of the 'abstract thoughts of the analytical school' which go to make up the underlying pattern of *The Woodlanders*. Hardy's creation of Little Hintock is very clearly influenced by contemporary writing on metaphysics, evolutionary theory, anthropology, and ethnology. In his *First Principles*, a book which Hardy recommended as a 'patent expander' for the intellect,[3]

[3] *Letters* ii. 24–5.

Herbert Spencer's account of the response of primitive tribes to the incursion of outside forces closely resembles the social changes which take place in Hardy's own rustic community. Spencer wrote that 'a tribe whose members have held together for a generation or two reaches a size at which it will no longer hold together; and on the occurrence of some event causing unusual antagonism among its members, divides.'[4] The arrival of Fitzpiers in Hintock, the division of society, and the subsequent departure of Timothy Tangs and Suke Damson to New Zealand and Fitzpiers and Grace to a northern town has its equivalent in Spencer's description of what he called 'social dissolution'. 'Social dissolution which follows the aggression of another nation,' he says, 'and which . . . is apt to occur when social evolution has ended and decay has begun, is, under its broadest aspect, the reception of a new external motion. . . . It is a decrease of integrated movements and an increase of disintegrated movements.'[5] The consequent 'decline in numbers', he adds, 'is brought about by emigration'.

The choice of a woodland setting must also have been determined, in part, by Hardy's knowledge of primitive myths and rites associated with tree people—myths which were later collected together in J. H. Philpot's *The Sacred Tree, or The Tree in Religion and Myth* (1897),[6] and many incidents in the novel seem to have been inspired by contemporary anthropological literature. The felling of Mr South's tree by Fitzpiers, for example, has a close affinity with C. F. Keary's account of the destruction of the tribal totem by missionaries in Germany. He wrote:

The *village tree* of the German races was originally a tribal tree, with whose existence the life of the village was involved; and when we read of Christian saints and confessors that they made a point of cutting down these half-idols, we cannot wonder at the rage they called forth, nor that they often paid the penalty of their courage.[7]

[4] Herbert Spencer, *First Principles* (1860; 2nd edn, 1867), p. 512. For a summary of the extensive influence of Spencer on Hardy see Björk *LN* entry 882 n.

[5] Spencer, *First Principles*, p. 520.

[6] Max Müller, in 'Solar Myths', an article which Hardy read and annotated, pointed out how important tree myths and legends are in primitive cultures.

[7] C. F. Keary, *Outlines of Primitive Belief*, p. 65. In his section on tree worship in *Primitive Culture* (1871, 2nd end, 1873) ii. 215, Tylor spoke of the way in which 'some trees are noted for the malignity of their demons. Among the Dayabs of Borneo, certain trees possessed by spirits must not be cut down.' See also *LN* entry 1335, where Hardy notes that Spencer (quoting Tylor) says that 'souls of the dead are supposed to haunt the neighbouring forests (by many tribes).'

Such examples could be multiplied many times from the writings of Grimm, Tylor, and Spencer, and both David Lodge and Mary Jacobus draw attention to the anthropological and Darwinian flavour of the narrative.[8] What is important for our purposes, however, is not so much the sources of the anthropological ideas in *The Woodlanders*, interesting though these are, but Hardy's interpretation of the connections between primitive and modern man. In translating 'abstract thoughts' into fiction, Hardy colours and changes them. The anthropological pastoral of *The Woodlanders* is permeated, as Lodge points out, by a mood of resignation and melancholy—a mood reminiscent of the classical elegies of Theocritus, Moschus, and Bion, which reasserts itself in modern times in Milton's *Lycidas* and Arnold's *Balder Dead*. Like these earlier elegies, *The Woodlanders* resembles an act of mourning for some kind of loss. But it is not for the loss of an individual or even a way of life: it is for the loss of a simple, primitive mode of perception—for a change which has come over the face of nature. This change is located not so much in nature itself, however, as in man's failure to respond to the transcendent beauty of nature and his incapacity to take an uninhibited, unqualified joy in what had once been a source of pleasure and solace.

This same sense of loss is expressed in a number of the poems which Hardy wrote in the 1880s, and two in particular—'To Outer Nature' and 'In a Wood'—are especially useful in helping to identify the source of a similar mood in *The Woodlanders*. In both, Hardy speaks of his changed relationships with the natural world, and he tells of the way in which he is no longer able to perceive and respond to nature as he once did. In the first, he appeals to nature to 'show thee as I thought thee / When early I sought thee'—when nature appeared to the young poet, as it had to Wordsworth in his youth,—'apparelled in celestial light'. As a mature man, Hardy sees things differently, and

> . . . such readorning
> Time forbids with scorning—
>   Makes me *see* things
>   Cease to be things
> They were in my morning.
>   (11. 16–20)

---

[8] David Lodge, introduction to *The Woodlanders*, New Wessex Edition, p. 25, and Mary Jacobus, 'Tree and Machine: *The Woodlanders*', in *Critical Approaches to the Fiction of Thomas Hardy*, ed. Dale Kramer, p. 118.

Consequently, nature has 'faded' for him:

> . . . glow forsaken,
> Darkness-overtaken!
> Thy first sweetness,
> Radiance, meetness,
> None shall re-awaken.
> (11. 21–25)

In the second poem, 'In a Wood', which Hardy explicitly identified with the novel by subtitling it 'From "The Woodlanders"', he defines this process more precisely. He explains what it is that he seeks in nature, what he fails to find, and why he fails to find it. In the first stanza he appeals to the trees of the woods not to mar the 'sweet comradeship' of the forest, and in the second he explains how he had come to the wood in search of rest, tranquility, and a balm for the wounds inflicted by urban competitiveness and restlessness:

> Heart-halt and spirit-lame,
>   City-opprest,
> Unto this wood I came
>   As to a nest.
> (11. 9–12)

It is not a 'nest' which he finds, however; instead, the woodlands bear all the marks of violence and destructiveness that he thought he had left behind in the city:

> But, having entered in,
>   Great growths and small
> Show themselves to men akin—
>   Combatants all!
> Sycamore shoulders oak,
> Bines the slim sapling yoke,
> Ivy-spun halters choke
>   Elms stout and tall.
> (11. 16–23)

In the final verse he finds 'no grace . . . / Taught [him] of trees', and he turns again to his own kind where 'at least smiles abound'. Society might be violent and destructive, but that violence and destructiveness is relieved by the personal qualities of individuals.

In *The Woodlanders* nature presents itself to the eye of the narrator sometimes in 'radiance' and 'meetness'—one thinks of the brilliant and colourful episodes on High Stoy Hill (*W* 247–8)—but more often as savage, brutal, and competitive. Trees, animals, and men are locked in a circle of violence: the 'overcrowded branches' rub each other 'into wounds' (*W* 15); trees wrestle 'for existence', their 'branches disfigured with wounds' (*W* 367) or torn from their trunks like dismembered limbs (*W* 263). Plant lives at the expense of plant, and the ivy 'strangles' the promising sapling (*W* 59); animals prey on animals —stoats suck the blood of rabbits, owls hunt the mice (*W* 28)—and man not only destroys animals (*W* 100), he also hunts other men, for which the mantraps decorating Hintock House provide gruesome evidence. Both poet and narrator detect the same force at work in town and country—among the slums and the trees of the forest. Both city and wilderness testify to the operation of 'the Unfulfilled Intention, which makes life what it is' and which is 'as obvious' in the woods 'as it could be among the depraved crowds of a city slum. (*W* 59). This rather unassimilated abstraction derives in part from Hegel's notion of the 'Idea', about which Hardy had been reading in the library of the British Museum (*EL* 234), and which he gently satirizes in Fitzpier's response to Grace Melbury (*W* 154). It also owes something to Herbert Spencer's definition of 'The Unknowable' as an inscrutable noumenal force whose out-workings are perceptible in phenomena.[9] But, most of all, it has its origins in the impersonal operation of the evolutionary principle outlined by Darwin.

In *The Origin of Species*, Darwin described man's double vision of the natural world in terms very similar to those of *The Woodlanders*. Before we were aware of the universal operation of evolutionary forces, he says, we were able to 'behold the face of nature bright with gladness . . . [and] see superabundance of food', but knowledge brings a change of perspective; the significance of the 'shows' of nature alters when we realize that 'the birds which are idly singing round us mostly live on insects or seeds, and are thus constantly destroying life; and we forget how largely these songsters, their eggs, or their nestlings, are destroyed by birds and beasts of prey.[10] This double perspective helps to explain a great deal about the tone and techniques of *The Woodlanders*. The elegiac mood of the novel derives from the author's personal disillusionment, and from the way in

[9] *LN*, '1867' Notebook, entry 10.
[10] Charles Darwin, *The Origin of Species*, ed. Morse Peckham, p. 146.

which a view of nature 'bright with gladness' slowly gave way to a more sombre view of the internal workings of organic life, coloured and moulded by the 'abstract realities' of the 'analytical school'. It also helps to explain the characterization in *The Woodlanders*—a series of relatively shadowy figures dominated by the authorial consciousness. Giles Winterborne is strongly identified with the woods of Hintock, and Felice Charmond is alienated from those same woods; and between these extremes each of the other major characters represents a different stage in the process of disillusionment. Each one is not so much a clear-cut and independent individual as a focus of perception in a spectrum of responses to the natural environment. The underlying principle, both here in *The Woodlanders* and in the poetry, is that it is not nature which has changed, but man; it is not the forms of organic life which have altered, but the way in which man perceives and interprets those forms. This is an important principle in Hardy's thinking, and it grows, in turn, out of his long-standing belief that it is the mind itself which creates its own reality.

As early as 1865 Hardy had noted that 'the poetry of a scene varies with the minds of the perceivers. Indeed, it does not lie in the scene at all.' (*EL* 66). In 1892 he was meditating upon a similar idea: 'We don't always remember', he said, 'that in getting at the truth, we get only at the true nature of the impression that an object, etc., produces on us, the true thing in itself being still, as Kant shows, beyond our knowledge.' (*LY* 9). As we saw in chapter 3, one of the dominant themes of *Far from the Madding Crowd* was the discrepancy between the 'impression' and the reality, between the visual image and the mind's interpretation of that image, or, as the narrator himself put it, how 'in making even horizontal and clear inspections we colour and mould according to the wants within us whatever our eyes bring in.' (*FMC* 16). In the years which led up to the writing of *The Woodlanders*, Hardy's reading suggests that he was still pondering the relationship between perception and consciousness, for he copied into his commonplace book a number of quotations bearing upon the issue. Richard Proctor's article 'The Photographic Eye of Science', for example, taught him that the sensitivity of the human eye was strictly limited to the visible sections of the electromagnetic spectrum, and that there are vast tracts of that same spectrum which are as 'real' as the visible elements but to which the eye is insensitive.[11] A more

11 Richard A. Proctor, 'The Photographic Eyes of Science', *Longman's Magazine*, 1 (1883), pp. 454–5. *LN*, entry 1293.

philosophical account of the limitations of perception was to be found in a review of Lange's *History of Materialism*, from which Hardy copied the sentence: 'No thought is so calculated to reconcile poesy and science as the thought that all our "reality", without prejudice to its strict connection, undisturbed by any caprice, is only *appearance*.'[12] Moreover, as a preliminary to writing *The Woodlanders*, Hardy studied and annotated Edward Caird's complex article on metaphysics in the *Encyclopaedia Britannica*. In this, Caird made the point that it is possible to regard all phenomena as the creation of consciousness. 'The immediate expression of the observer's consciousness', said Caird,

is not 'I think the object,' but it, the object, is. . . . The voice of nature to which he listens is for him not his own voice but the voice of a stranger, and it does not occur to him to reflect that Nature could not speak to anyone but a conscious self.[13]

The implication that 'the world', as he wrote later in *Tess of the d'Urbervilles*, is 'only a psychological phenomenon' (*TD* 108) seems to have had a depressing influence on Hardy. In November 1885 he 'went back', as he put it, to the 'original plot' of *The Woodlanders*—a plot which he had abandoned not long after finishing *Far from the Madding Crowd*—but returned to 'in a fit of depression, as if enveloped in a leaden cloud' (*EL* 230). The reason for this depression is linked to that sense of loss and disillusionment which he describes in the poetry, combined with the growing conviction that the 'whole scope of observation', as Pater so graphically put it, 'is dwarfed into the narrow chamber of the individual mind'.[14] 'Nature', Hardy wrote in a diary entry in December 1885, 'is an arch-dissembler. . . . *nothing* is as it appears.' (*EL* 231).

What Mary Jacobus, in her article 'Tree and Machine', calls the 'depletion of energy' in *The Woodlanders*, the 'attenuation of vigour into quiescence, passion into elegy, endurance into renunciation',[15] is surely connected with Hardy's solipsistic frame of mind, and it is that same frame of mind which so deeply colours the characterization of the novel. Broadly speaking, Hardy brings into play two views of the

[12] 'Lange's History of Materialism—Vol. 11', The *Spectator*, 54 (1881), p. 900. *LN*, entry 1229.

[13] Edward Caird, 'Metaphysic', in *The Encyclopaedia Britannica*, 9th edn, 16 (1883), p. 97. *LN*, entry 1372.

[14] Pater, *The Renaissance*, p. 187.

[15] Jacobus, 'Tree and Machine', p. 120; see n. 8.

natural world, two kinds of consciousness, each with its own perceptions and values. On the one hand, there is the unsophisticated, simple, 'primitive' consciousness of the indigenous woodlander—represented by Giles Winterborne and Mary South—whose 'clear gaze'
(*W* 399) upon the world of Hintock is untramelled by the distorting
effects of modern 'nerves'. On the other hand, there is the more
highly developed view of things, a view which is coloured by introspection and subjectivism. Grace Melbury, who 'combined modern
nerves with primitive feelings' (*W* 358), is pulled now one way, now
another, but it is Fitzpiers and Mrs Charmond who most explicitly
represent variations of the modern view. Fitzpiers, with his experimentation, his preoccupation with metaphysics, his Shelleyan disposition, and his 'modern, unpractical mind' (*W* 145), is, as the narrator points out, almost exclusively attentive to his 'inner visions' (*W*
148), and to the cultivation of the 'inner eye' (*W* 147). He disdains all
'outer regard' (*W* 147), prefers the 'ideal world to the real' (*W* 135),
and looks upon Grace Melbury less as a woman than as the embodiment of a philosophical ideal (*W* 154 and 171). His relationship with
Felice Charmond is modelled on one of the French romances that he
reads in his leisure hours, and when he pursues Felice through the
'gorgeous autumn landscape of White-Hart Vale' (*W* 245), he sees
nothing beyond 'some impassioned visionary theme'. It is in Felice
herself, however, that modern subjectivism takes its most extreme
form, and she is a veritable taxonomy of solipsism. Hintock has for
her the 'effect of bottling up the emotions till one can no longer hold
them.' (*W* 228). She hates the woodlands (*W* 282), cannot tell one tree
from another (*W* 298), and lives in the 'fitful fever' of an inner 'impassioned . . . life' (*W* 404). Such is her loss of contact with objective
existence that she is subject to 'fierce periods of high tide and storm'
in which 'her soul [is] being slowly invaded by a delirium' (*W* 281).
Her universe is a compound of nerves and passion, and as the story
develops, she becomes 'an animated impulse only' (*W* 281).

This binary mode of perception is established early in the novel,
when Barber Percombe is seeking out Marty South with the idea of
purchasing her hair. As he perceives her through the window of her
cottage, the narrator offers the reader two views of the scene within.
The first is the 'clear gaze', detailed and objective, in which each element in the description places the young girl socially and economically
within the Hintock community.

Beside her, in case she might require more light, a brass candlestick stood on
a little round table curiously formed of an old coffin-stool, with a deal top

nailed on, the white surface of the latter contrasting oddly with the black carved oak of the sub-structure. The social position of the household in the past was almost as definitively shown by the presence of this article as that of an esquire or nobleman by his old helmets or shields. (*W* 7.)

The descriptive mode of this passage is reminiscent of the genre study in painting, and its style resembles many of the scenes in *The Mayor of Casterbridge*, in which appearances are 'read' for the multiplicity of their significance. The second view of Marty is that of Percombe himself, and differs substantially from the first. What he is after is her hair, and his eyes focus on that to the exclusion of everything else. The result is not a genre study but an Impressionist sketch:

In her present beholder's mind the scene formed by the girlish spar-maker composed itself into an *impression-picture* of extremest type, wherein the girl's hair alone, as the focus of observation, was depicted with intensity and distinctness, while her face, shoulders, hands, and figure in general were a blurred mass of unimportant detail lost in haze and obscurity. (*W* 9; my emphasis.)

Hardy's first-hand experience of Impressionism probably coincided with a visit he made to London between April and July of 1886—a visit which has important implications for *The Woodlanders*. He may well have read about Impressionist techniques in the periodical literature, and as early as 1883 Frederick Wedmore had written a sympathetic account of the new movement in the *Fortnightly Review*.[16] By 1886, however, Impressionism was making itself strongly felt in the work of English painters. Hardy would not have missed the first exhibition of The New English Art Club which was held in April of that year and which included paintings by Wilson Steer, Edward Stott, and Fred Brown, whose 'gods' according to one contemporary were 'Degas, Manet, Monet and his fellow "Impressionists"'.[17] In the following month Dowdeswell's Gallery put on a one-man show of Whistler's work, and Whistler's influence was felt, too, at the Society of British Artists, of which he had recently become president. Hardy's account of Percombe's view of Marty South's hair had originally been entitled 'post-Raphaelite', but he almost immediately changed this to 'impression-picture'—a change which was confirmed in his mind by a visit to the Society of British Artists on December

---

[16] Frederic Wedmore, 'The Impressionists', p. 77.

[17] Alfred Thornton, *Fifty Years of the New English Art Club* (London: Curwen Press, 1935), p. 7.

7th, 1886. At this exhibition he was much struck by Whistler's *Harmony in Red, Lamplight (Mrs Beatrix Godwin)* (Plate 29), and when he visited Mary Jeune on the evening of the same day, he carried Whistler's image in his mind. He wrote in his diary that 'she was in a rich pinky-red gown, and looked handsome as we sat by the firelight *en tête-à-tête*: she was, curiously enough, an example of Whistler's study in red that I had seen in the morning at the Gallery.' (*EL* 241).

The significance of Impressionist technique to Hardy was that not only was it a quintessentially modern style of painting, it was also one which embodied a highly subjective response to visual stimuli. In his article Wedmore had stressed the modernity of Impressionism, and how in Monet's work 'his impression is his own . . . recorded while it is still vivid, and recorded fearlessly.'[18] Similarly Hardy responded enthusiastically to the highly personal aspects of the new movement. Impressionism for him meant 'that what you carry away with you from a scene is the true feature to grasp', and that you record '*what appeals to your own individual eye and heart in particular* amid much that does not so appeal, and which you therefore omit to record.' (*EL* 241; Hardy's emphasis). The idea, he thought, was 'even more suggestive in the direction of literature than in that of art', because it expressed an individual mode of perception, which seemed to him characteristic of modern consciousness. As in Percombe's perception of Marty South's hair, Impressionist technique focused on some elements in the visual matrix to the exclusion of others, but it reflected, above all else, the characteristics, the prejudices, and the disposition of the perceiving mind.

Impressionism, is only one of the visual techniques whose influence can be detected in *The Woodlanders*, however, and another event which took place in London in 1886 not only put Hardy's attitude to Impressionism in perspective: it, too, left its mark on the novel. In April of that year Hardy was concurrently visiting the London galleries, staying in Bloomsbury, and reading in the library of the British Museum. On April 10th something happened in the Museum which created considerable interest among the British public. A new wing was opened, where, for the first time, visitors were able to see artefacts from the Solomon and Sandwich Islands—sculpture, utensils, masks, and so on—which had been left to the nation in 1865 by Henry Christy. This collection, when added to the artefacts which the Museum already possessed, was one of the largest in the world, and it

[18] Wedmore, 'Impressionism', p. 77.

received an enthusiastic reception in the press. *The Times* correspondent said that though 'the quaint dresses and weapons and the grotesque carvings of South Sea islanders . . . must necessarily be strange sights to a great proportion of the visitors', people would undoubtedly find them more interesting than any other section of the Museum's holdings.[19] The South Sea Island art was certainly new to Hardy, and the contrast between the primitivism which these objects represented and the ultra-modern Impressionist work on show elsewhere in London is clearly registered in the text of *The Woodlanders*.

Throughout the novel the simple, primitive view of life is contrasted with the modern view. Giles Winterborne was one 'whose life had been so primitive, and so ruled by household laws' (*W* 350) that he was no match for the subtler wiles of Fitzpiers, and when Mr Melbury interviews Felice Charmond at Hintock House, he feels 'as inferior as a savage with his bows and arrows to the precise weapons of modern warfare.' (*W* 257). Even more explicitly, the contrast between the galleries of Bond Street and the new wing of the British Museum finds expression in an early account of the seasonal changes in the woods around Hintock,

that change from the handsome to the curious which the features of a wood undergo at the ingress of the winter months. Angles were taking the place of curves, and reticulations of surfaces—a change constituting a sudden lapse from the ornate to the primitive on Nature's canvas, and comparable to a retrogressive step from the art of an advanced school of painting to that of the Pacific Islander. (*W* 58.)

In the novel, the difference between the primitive mind and the modern mind is often expressed in visual terms—sometimes metaphorically, sometimes literally. Grace Melbury's expensive education, for example, is described in terms of a shift in her mental perspective. She had been, says the narrator, 'mentally trained and tilled into foreignness of view', and her subsequent 'passionate desire for the primitive life' (*W* 248) is expressed as a kind of readjustment and refocusing of vision. Her return to the autumn woods of Hintock was for her 'as an old painting restored' (*W* 58), and in the same pictorial vein, her love for Giles Winterborne grew out of a belief in the solid virtues of simple, even primitive, 'unvarnished men' (*W* 264). But her moment of greatest insight occurs when Fitzpiers has left her one evening on High Stoy Hill for his rendezvous with Felice

19 *The Times*, 28 Apr. 1886, p. 8.

Charmond, and is accompanied by literal visual clarity. As he rides away to the east, he forms an alien spot on the beautiful landscape: he resembles 'a Wouvermans eccentricity reduced to microscopic dimensions' (*W* 246).[20] Suddenly Giles Winterborne appears, looking and smelling like 'Autumn's very brother' (*W* 246), and instantly Grace's 'heart rose from its late sadness like a released bough; her senses revelled in the sudden lapse back to Nature unadorned. . . . The veneer of artificiality which she had acquired at the fashionable schools [was] thrown off.' (*W* 247). This momentary lapse back to nature, Grace's retrogressive move in the direction of primitivism, finds expression for both Grace and Giles in an experience of intense, direct visual pleasure. As they walk over High Stoy Hill, the sun is setting, and there

the whole west sky was revealed. Between the broken clouds they could see far into the recesses of heaven as they mused and walked, the eye journeying on under a species of golden arcades, and past fiery obstructions, fancied cairns, logan-stones, stalactites and stalagmite of topaz. Deeper than this their gaze passed thin flakes of incandescence, till it plunged into a bottomless medium of soft green fire. (*W* 247–8.)

Such moments of visual exaltation are rare in *The Woodlanders*, but when they do occur, they are explicitly associated with Giles Winterborne. Once, for example, in the spring, Grace and her father catch a glimpse of the orchards which lie just outside the Hintock woods.

It was the cider country. . . . There the air was blue as sapphire—such a blue as outside that apple-region was never seen. Under the blue the orchards were in a blaze of pink bloom, some of the richly flowered trees running almost up to where they drove along. At a gate, which opened down an incline, a man leant on his arms regarding this fair promise so intently that he did not observe their passing.
'That was Giles,' said Melbury, when they had gone by. (*W* 164.)

On another occasion, in autumn, Winterborne is observed operating his cider press, while behind him 'were to be seen gardens and orchards now bossed, nay encrusted, with scarlet and gold fruit, stretching to infinite distance under a luminous lavender mist.' (*W* 208).

Generally in *The Woodlanders*, such moments of sensuously direct and unsophisticated visual perception are connected with the 'primitive' sensibility, while the elaborate and the subjective view is related to a

---

[20] Philips Wouverman (1619–68) specialized in views of hilly country which frequently included white horses. The National Gallery has a number of his works.

more modern sensibility—the art of the South Sea Islander versus the art of the Impressionist. This duality is complicated by the influence of the narrator's own viewpoint, which is unequivocally of the modern variety. Except at the moments mentioned above, the narrator rarely takes any spontaneous visual delight in nature. He is most keenly aware of the deformed and the crippled, and persistently selects for attention the hideous growths, unpleasant fungi and strange mosses which abound in the woods. In Little Hintock the seasons are deprived of their traditional associations, and the visual imagery depends heavily on the grotesque. The first dawn of the novel breaks like a 'bleared white visage', and the 'sunless day' emerges 'like a dead-born child.' (*W* 24). The roots of trees are 'like hands wearing green gloves' (*W* 58), while the trees themselves are 'haggard, grey phantoms' (*W* 270). In winter the frosts make the leaves fall in 'degraded mass[es] under foot' (*W* 261), and even at the height of summer the sunshine fails to penetrate the undersea world of the woods (*W* 170). Winter creates 'puddles and damp ruts' with a 'cold corpse-like luminousness' (*W* 382), and in the summer the plantations were

more spectral far than in the leafless season, when there were fewer masses and more minute lineality. The smooth surfaces of glossy plants came out like weak, lidless eyes: there were strange faces and figures from expiring lights that had somehow wandered into the canopied obscurity. (*W* 360.)

The narrator's view of the natural world is truly 'Impressionist' in Hardy's definition of the term. The narrator records only those things in nature which impress his 'own individual eye and heart', and just as Barber Percombe generates an 'impression-picture' out of his *idée fixe* about Marty South's hair, so the narrator paints an intense, but highly subjective, picture of the natural environment around Little Hintock. The innocent eye is able to respond spontaneously to the beauty of nature; the eye of the narrator sees the workings of the 'unfulfilled intention'. Schooled in the writings of Darwin, Huxley, and Spencer, the narrator has lost that primitive innocence, and his 'impression' is conditioned by his knowledge of the constant struggle for survival which takes place beneath the surface of things. The prevailing elegiac, postlapsarian tone of *The Woodlanders* derives, at least in part, from Hardy's realization that 'Nature', as he wrote in his diary, 'is an arch-dissembler', and that '*nothing* is as it appears.' (*EL* 231).

Though there is a strong sense of personal anguish in this remark, there is no reaon to suppose that the elegiac tone of *The Woodlanders* is generated exclusively by the failure of Hardy's own 'vision' of nature. On the contrary, there is evidence in the book to suggest that Hardy felt that he was giving expression to a change of attitude which had affected all thinking people. It centres on the relationship between Giles and Marty and their woodland setting; for the way Hardy describes this connection indicates strongly that these two represent types as much as individuals, and that their mode of perception is by no means confined to themselves alone.

Giles and Marty can be distinguished from the other characters in the novel, and even from the narrator himself, in possessing the capacity to read the more arcane signs and the hidden meanings of nature. When others bestow 'casual glimpses' on the 'world of sap and leaves', these two fix upon it their 'clear gaze' (*W* 399). Their view is neither that of the Impressionist with his selective eye, nor that of the Darwinian with his eye for conflict and struggle. Living in perpetual communion with the woods, they

had been possessed of its finer mysteries as of commonplace knowledge; had been able to read its hieroglyphs as ordinary writing. . . . Together they had, with the run of years, mentally collected those remoter signs and symbols which seen in few were the runic obscurity, but all together made an alphabet. (*W* 399.)

For the Impressionist the 'author' of appearances is the perceiving eye; for the evolutionist it is the 'unfulfilled intention'. Who, then, is the author who writes in the hieroglyph, or the alphabet, which Giles and Marty can read? The answer is supplied by Carlyle, who said:

We speak of the Volume of Nature: and truly a Volume it is,—whose author and Writer is God. To read it! Dost thou, does man, so much as well know the Alphabet thereof? With its Words, Sentences, and grand descriptive Pages, poetical and philosophical, spread out through Solar Systems, and Thousands of Years, we shall not try thee. It is a Volume written in celestial hieroglyphs, in the true Sacred-writing.[21]

This passage occurs towards the end of *Sartor Resartus*, in which 'the Philosophy of Clothes attains to Transcendentalism'. The intuitive, perceptive, ability of Giles and Marty to read the symbols of Nature is a species of transcendentalism, and, as C. F. Harrold has pointed out, the idea of nature as a Divine hieroglyph was a common one

[21] Carlyle, Works i. 249.

among early nineteenth-century German transcendentalists.[22] It is significant, however, that it is a woodland setting of which Giles and Marty possess the 'finer mysteries'. We saw the way in which Hardy's choice of such a setting was determined in part by the prominence of the woodlands in anthropological thinking, but the woods played an important part also in the intuitive naturalism of one well-known transcendentalist with whose work Hardy was familiar —Ralph Waldo Emerson.[23]

In 1885 Hardy read Emerson's essay entitled 'Nature' (1836), to which he may have been directed by Arnold's *Discourses in America*, published earlier in the same year. In his essay on Emerson, Arnold had written:

As Wordsworth's poetry is, in my judgement, the most important work done in verse, in our language, during the present century, so Emerson's *Essays* are, I think, the most important work done in prose. His work is more important than Carlyle's.[24]

When Hardy turned to Emerson's work, it was Emerson's remarks on the 'philosophy of insight' which attracted his attention. In this essay on nature, Emerson put forward the view that nature is an encyclopaedia with the capacity of answering any question which man might ask of it. 'Of Nature', he says,

[22] Carlyle, *Sartor Resartus*, ed. C. F. Harrold (New York: Odyssey Press, 1937), p. 36 n. In his book *Carlyle and German Thought*, 1819–1834 (New Haven: Yale Univ. Press, 1934), pp. 106–7, Harrold quotes Schiller, who said: 'Everything . . . within me and without me, is the hieroglyphic expression of a power analogous to my own being. The laws of Nature are figures which a thinking being combines for the purpose of rendering itself intelligible to other thinking beings, the alphabet by means of which all spirits hold intercourse with the most perfect One.' Harrold also points out that a similar idea is to be found in Sir Thomas Browne, who said in *Religio Medici* that, 'Surely the Heathens knew better how to joyn and read these mystical letters than we Christians, who cast a more careless Eye on these common Hieroglyphicks.' (Quoted by Harrold, p. 276). Hardy was reading Browne sometime after 1886: see *LN*, '1867' Notebook, entries 214–34.

[23] In 1882 Hardy made some notes from an article in the *Spectator* (60 (May 1882, p. 591), which compared Emerson and Carlyle (*LN*, entries 1274–7)). In *The Early Life* he recalls an anecdote about Emerson which was told to him in 1883 (*EL* 208), and in 1885 he copied into his notebook a passage from Emerson's introduction to 'Nature' (*LN* entry 1360).

In his *Puritan Temper and Transcendental Faith: Carlyle's Literary Vision* (Cleveland: Ohio State Univ. Press, 1972), pp. 209–13, A. Abbott Ikler points out the numerous stylistic and conceptual similarities between Carlyle's *Sartor Resartus* and Emerson's 'Nature'. He is unable to decide, however, whether Emerson's debt is to German philosophy itself or to Carlyle's interpretations.

[24] Arnold, 'Discourses in America' (1885), in *The Complete Prose Works of Matthew Arnold* x. 182.

we have no questions to ask which are unanswerable. We must trust the perfection of the creation so far as to believe that whatever curiosity the order of things has awakened in our minds, the order of things can satisfy. Every man's condition is a solution *in hieroglyphic* to those inquiries he would put. He acts it as life, before he apprehends it as truth.[25]

According to Emerson, nowhere is that hieroglyphic more vividly perceived, or more accurately read, than amongst the trees of the woods and forests; it is in the woods that one receives the impression of 'the primitive sense of the permanent objects of nature', and it is here 'that the world shall be . . . an open book'. Amongst the trees, he says,

a man casts off his years, as the snake his slough, and at what period soever of life, is always a child. In the woods, is perpetual youth. Within these plantations of God, a decorum and sanctity reign, a perennial festival is dressed, and the guest sees not how he should tire of them in a thousand years. In the woods, we return to reason and faith.[26]

Emerson waxes lyrical about the benefits of the woodland environment, where 'all mean egotism vanishes', and where the very trees speak of the concord and harmony between man and nature. 'The greatest delight which the fields and woods minister', he says, 'is the suggestion of an occult relation between man and the vegetable'. In the poem 'In a Wood' Hardy speaks of the way in which he, too, had gone to the wood in search of that 'occult relation', 'Dreaming of that sylvan ease / Offered the harrowed sense . . . from man's unrest'. What he finds, however, is a measure of the difference between his perspective and Emerson's, between his response to nature in the 1880s and that of the transcendentalists in the 1830s. Instead of 'decorum and sanctity', he discovers 'great growths and small . . . combatants all'; he finds ivy choking 'elms stout and tall', and 'rank poplars . . . cankering in blank despair'.

Similarly, in the novel the woods are not dressed in a 'perennial festival', but tree wars with tree, saplings fear to be 'born', and the 'face of Nature' is not, to use Darwin's words, 'bright with gladness', but is disfigured by growths and wracked by storms. In her essay 'Tree and Machine' Mary Jacobus feels that Marty South's fidelity to the memory of Giles Winterborne 'partially heals the breach between Nature and Imagination', and that 'it alone transcends the

[25] *The Complete Works of Ralph Waldo Emerson* ii. 140; my emphasis.
[26] Emerson, *Works* ii. 142.

limitations of Nature and mortality',[27] but surely Marty's mourning is ultimately sterile. In reality, it is a dirge for the demise of an optimistic transcendentalism no longer possible in the 1880s. The sympathetic, intuitive bond between man and nature, symbolized in Gile's death, has been irrevocably broken, and no amount of mourning can re-establish it. On the night which Giles spends languishing outside his own hut, the 'unfulfilled intention' creates a storm which causes the natural world to rise in vindictive force and crush the one character who was most able to read its transcendent hieroglyphs:

Sometimes a bough from an adjoining tree was swayed so low as to smite the roof in the manner of a gigantic hand smiting the mouth of an adversary, to be followed by a trickle of rain, as blood from the wound. To all this weather Giles must be more or less exposed. (*W* 372.)

When, in 1892, Hardy reminded himself that 'in getting at the truth, we only get at the true nature of the impression that an object . . . produces on us' (*LY* 9), he quoted Kant as his authority, but of course the idea was a familiar one in the nineteenth century. Pater, whom he had met in May of 1886 had made a similar point in the conclusion to *The Renaissance*, but it was Shelley who, above all, others, gave expression to the idea in poetry. There is no doubt that Hardy knew 'The Sensitive Plant' in which Shelley speaks of the subjective nature of experience in a context which strongly resembles that of *The Woodlanders*.[28] The garden in this poem is at first an 'undefiled Paradise' in which every living thing 'was interpenetrated/With the light and odour its neighbour shed'. But with the death of the *genius loci*, the garden, once fair, 'became cold and foul'.

And plants, at whose names the verse feels loath,
Filled the place with a monstrous undergrowth,
Prickly, and pulpous, and blistering, and blue,
Livid, and starred with a lurid hue.'
(11. iii. 58-61)

In *The Woodlanders* Giles Winterborne's death is accompanied by a similar burgeoning of 'monstrous undergrowth'. From the window of his hut Grace could see 'stemless yellow fungi . . . and tall fungi with more stem than stool . . . rotting stumps . . . rising from their mossy

[27] Mary Jacobus, 'Tree and Machine', pp. 132-3.
[28] In his *Primitive Culture* ii. 215, E. B. Tylor quotes Shelley's 'The Sensitive Plant' as exposing a 'conception familiar to old barbaric thought' concerning tree spirits.

setting like black teeth from green gums.' (*W* 376). In Shelley's poem, however, the message is a hopeful one. Since 'nothing is, but all things seem', the beauty of the garden has not really passed away; it is just our perception which has altered. ''Tis we, 'tis ours, are changed; not they', he says. Hardy inherited Shelley's relativism—the belief, as Bagehot put it, 'that there was no substantial thing, either in matter or mind; but only "sensations and impressions" flying about the universe, inhering in nothing and going nowhere'[29]—but he did not inherit Shelley's optimism. When he was writing *Far from the Madding Crowd*, he seemed to believe that we 'colour and mould according to the wants within us whatever our eyes bring in' (*FMC* 16), but in *The Woodlanders* he has gone one stage further, by suggesting that the 'colouring and moulding' of things are determined by forces and ideas beyond our control. Darwinian philosophy had killed the *genius loci* of Hardy's garden: nature was no longer a divine book filled with benevolent meanings. And where once man had exulted in the sheer beauty of visible phenomena, his 'impressions' were now irreversibly determined by the 'abstract thoughts of the analytic school'.

29 Walter Bagehot, *Literary Studies*, ed. R. H. Hutton (London: Longmans, 1902), i. 269–70. Hardy first read this in 1859 (see *EL* entry 43).

8

Patterns of Light and Dark in
Tess of the d'Urbervilles

'All the hues, all the emotions of the sky.'[1]

'Modern Art wants.—The deepest want and deficiency of all modern Art lies in the fact that the Artists have no mythology.'[2]

When Hardy finished *The Woodlanders* in February of 1887, he and Emma set off on their first journey to Italy. The depression which he had felt while writing this novel seems to have lifted and he threw himself energetically into visiting galleries, museums, and churches in Genoa, Milan, Florence, Rome, and Venice. Italy was a 'visionary place' for Hardy, to which he brought 'solidly in (his) person Dorchester and Wessex life' (*EL* 253), and it was a place which thronged with kindred English spirits that had been moved by the vision—Browning, Shelley, Byron, Ruskin, and Turner. Above all, Italy was a land of sunlight, and Venice in particular, in which he 'found more pleasure . . . than in any Italian city' (*EL* 252), was, for him, a creation of that sunlight. 'Venice', he wrote, 'is composed of blue and sunlight. Hence I incline, after all, to "sun-girt" rather than "sea-girt". . . . Venice requires *heat* to complete the picture of her.' (*EL* 254). Hardy did not begin writing *Tess of the d'Urbervilles* for another two years, but not only does it contain numerous references to Italian art, many of the scenes of the new novel recall the amplitude and warmth of the south, where the sun itself had provided the inspiration for many myths and legends. In *The Woodlanders*, Little Hintock had been a shadowy, 'embowered' place, and the woodlanders had lived beneath the crowded branches of trees, which shut out the light even at the height of summer. In *Tess of the d'Urbervilles* the agricultural workers are 'children of the open air' (*TD* 84): they inhabit the fields of Blackmoor Valley, the wider spaces of the

---

[1] Emile Zola, *Abbé Mouret's Transgression* (1886), in *LN*, '1867' Notebook, entry 186.

[2] F. Schlegel, quoted by G. H. Lewes in his *Life of Goethe* (1873), in *LN*, entry 118, and his *Memoranda*, entry for 16 June 1875.

valley of the Froom, and the wind-swept chalk uplands, all of which stand open to the influence of the sky and the sun.

'Dazzling' is the word which Hardy uses repeatedly to describe sunlight in this novel. It makes the white-coated cows in the Froom valley reflect 'rays almost dazzling' (*TD* 133); it shines on the river 'with a molten-metallic glow that dazzled' the eyes of Tess and Angel Clare (*TD* 249); and in the morning sunlight Tess herself is a 'dazzlingly fair dairymaid' (*TD* 169). But the light is not just a visual effect, it is also highly emotive. It acts as a potent force, animating landscape and character alike, transforming and transfiguring all that comes within its ambience. Light serves to generate mood and feeling, and the special quality of light fundamentally alters the quality and the appearance of objects. In *Far from the Madding Crowd* Hardy had explored the limitations of the sense of sight; *what* was seen was less important than *how* it was seen. In *The Mayor of Casterbridge* objects themselves took on a significance irrespective of the way in which they were observed. In *Tess of the d'Urbervilles* the meaning which Hardy attributes to objective phenomena lies neither in the sense of sight nor within the things themselves, but almost entirely in the way in which they are illuminated.

The importance which Hardy attributes to light in this novel derives principally from two sources. The first is the painting of Turner, whose effects of light and colour deeply impressed him in the years between his Italian journey in 1887 and the writing of the novel. The second is the Contemporary interpretation of primitive myth and legend, which suggested that the sun and its movement through the sky provided the inspiration and the primary impulse for all the stories of the ancient divinities. The link between Turner and myth was supplied by Ruskin. In *Modern Painters*—to which Hardy frequently referred in the mid-1880s—Ruskin suggested that Turner's treatment of sun and sunlight in his paintings was actually a modern version of an ancient Greek attitude to solar phenomena.

Hardy, Turner, and Landscape

Together with *The Return of the Native*, *Tess of the d'Ubervilles* is the work in which Hardy most actively exploits the Wessex landscape. In the course of the novel diminutive characters are frequently dwarfed by the immensity of their surroundings. One thinks of Alec d'Urberville crossing the 'joyless monotony' of a swede field like a 'black speck' (*TD*

400), or Tess like a fly on the 'billiard-table' of the Froom valley (*TD* 136). Sometimes the scene is claustrophobically enclosed, as in the wild garden at Talbothays, where there is 'no distinction between the near and the far' (*TD* 157). Sometimes the landscape is redolent with a quiet, intense beauty, as in the sunrises over Talbothays. Sometimes it is dramatic and tumultuous, as in the snowstorm at Flintcomb-Ash. But what characterizes all the landscapes of this novel is the intimate connection between figure and scene, the reciprocity between the visual appearance of a landscape and the human being contained within it.

Ever since Hardy had visited the picturesque woods of Baden-Baden in 1876, he had been convinced that the power of landscape lay not in nature itself, but in what the human mind brought to nature; that 'an object or mark raised or made by man on a scene is worth ten times any such formed by unconscious Nature' (*EL* 153); and that 'the beauty of association is entirely superior to the beauty of aspect' (*EL* 158). After Hardy's trip to Italy his interest in the significance of landscape revived, and he invited the painters Rosamund Thomson and Alfred Parsons to Max Gate, to record Wessex scenes. During these years he became more and more convinced that his original intuition was correct, and that landscape in art was of importance only as a vehicle for human imagination and human emotion. In 1887 he declared that the ' "simply natural" ' was 'interesting no longer', and illustrated his point by comparing the work of two artists. 'After looking at the landscape ascribed to Bonington in our drawing room', he said, 'I feel that Nature is played out as a Beauty, but not as a Mystery.' (*EL* 242). The so-called Bonington *Landscape of Down and Stream* given to Emma by Thomas Woolner is now lost,[3] but for Hardy it summed up the treatment of nature as 'a Beauty'—the 'merely natural' reproduction of scenic effects which he had outgrown. Now, he said, he no longer wished to see 'the original realities —as optical effects', but instead he looked for 'the deeper reality underlying the scenic, the expression of what are sometimes called abstract imaginings.' (*EL* 242). What he could not find in the Bonington he found in Turner, or rather in what he called 'the much decried, mad, later-Turner rendering', where 'the exact truth as to material fact ceases to be of importance' (*EL* 243).

Between 1886 and 1889 interest in Turner's work had been greatly stimulated by a series of important exhibitions. Early in 1886 there

[3] See Ch. 1, n. 29.

were two shows devoted to Turner's graphic work, one at the Burlington Fine Arts Club, the other at the Royal Academy; then in 1887 and 1888 the winter exhibitions of the Royal Academy continued to feature Turner's painting. The series culminated in an exhibition of his water-colours at the Royal Academy in 1889. Many of Turner's late works were shown on the walls of the Academy, and Hardy was absolutely correct when he described them as 'much decried'. Ruskin was one of the very few critics who openly championed Turner's late canvases; for most critics this was the period of Turner's 'decline', and the paintings were regarded, in the words of W. P. Frith, as being 'as insane as the people who admired them'.[4] In his late work Turner was accused of exploiting landscape, light, and colour for his own idiosyncratic purposes—for giving 'uncurbed license . . . to his imagination',[5] and for trying to paint 'visions of pure sunlight which, even to such a Titan as he, was impossible'.[6] He was castigated for failing to paint what Hardy had derisively described as the 'merely natural', and for using nature 'rather as a medium to be moulded and adapted according as his mood swayed him, than as an external reality' which it was his duty, so it was claimed, to 'reproduce and interpret'.[7]

So what attracted Hardy to the 'mad, late-Turner renderings' was exactly what repelled the professional critics. For Hardy, Turner's late work was successful precisely because he imaginatively transformed landscape and endowed it with human meaning. Turner, Hardy said, avoided the 'student style', that is,

the style of a period when the mind is serene and unawakened to the tragical mysteries of life; when it does not bring anything to the object that coalesces with and translates the qualities that are already there,—half hidden, it may be—and the two are depicted as the All. (*EL* 243.)

In the years between the first Turner exhibition in 1886 and the writing of *Tess of the d'Urbervilles*, Hardy sought a theoretical basis for his own intuitions, and his literary notes record the fruits of that search. He reread Ruskin, who argued that the 'simple statement of the truths of nature' in art was limited and banal. The 'highest art', he said, was the expres-

---

[4] Frith's remark was made at the Whistler v. Ruskin trial in 1878, and is quoted in Ruskin, *Works* xxix. 584.

[5] W. G. Rawlinson, 'Turner's Drawings at the Royal Academy', *The Nineteenth Century*, 19 (1886), p. 403.

[6] Ibid.

[7] Claude Phillips, 'Old Masters at the Royal Academy', *The Academy*, 31 (1887), p. 82.

sion of personal insight and is based 'on sensations of peculiar minds, sensations occurring to *them* only at particular times'.[8] From Francis Palgrave he learned that 'the secret of our great landscapists from Gainsborough to Turner' lay in the power of 'the artist's soul' to make itself articulate in 'the forms and colours of his canvas'.[9] But it was from contemporary French criticism that Hardy gained the most substantial support for his views on the treatment of landscape in art. He read and translated an article in the *Revue des deux mondes* in which Georges Lafenestre offered an interpretation of art which effectively inverted the English attitude to the late paintings of Turner. Whereas many English critics had accused Turner of using nature as a motif for his own imaginings, Lafenestre said that 'one cannot repeat too often that what makes a work of art is the force of the sentiment that an individual fixes in it, and eternizes in it'.[10] For the artist, he said, 'nature is only an arsenal, always open, where he goes to look for his means of expression'. Most important, however, was Frédéric Brunetière's detailed account of the Symbolist treatment of landscape, which, again, Hardy translated from the pages of the *Revue des deux mondes*. Arguing against the literal transcription of nature in realist art, Brunetière suggested that Symbolism provided a richer and more complex view of the natural world. Naturalism, he said, merely imitates the 'exterior contour of things'; the Symbolists, on the other hand,

teach that things have also a soul, of which the bodily eyes only seize the envelope, or the veil, or the mask. 'A landscape is a state of the soul'—one recalls that *mot* of Ameil. . . . This does not mean . . . that a landscape changes its aspect with the state of the soul, to-day melancholy and tomorrow smiling, according as we are glad or joyous ourselves. . . . But it means, on the contrary, that independently of the sort or species of emotion that it awakens within us . . . a landscape is in itself 'sadness,' or 'gaiety,' 'joy,' or 'suffering,' 'anger,' or 'peacefulness.'[11]

The idea that 'things . . . have a soul' must have been a very attractive one to Hardy, who spontaneously animated the inanimate

[8] Ruskin, *Works* iii. 135; quoted in *LN*, entry 1381.
[9] F. T. Palgrave, 'The Decline of Art', *The Nineteenth Century*, 23 (1888), pp. 71–2; quoted in entry 1482.
[10] Georges Lafenestre, 'La Peinture étrangére a l'Exposition Universelle', *Revue des deux mondes*, 96 (1889), p. 159; quoted in entry 1674.
[11] Frédéric Brunetière, 'Symbolistes et Decadens', *Revue des deux mondes*, 90 (1888), pp. 217–18; quoted in *LN* entry 1639.

—who, as he said, could not help 'noticing countenances and tempers in objects of scenery' (*LY* 58)—and who claimed that 'realism' in art meant not literal transcription, but 'seeing into the *heart of a thing* (as rain, wind, for instance)' (*EL* 190; Hardy's emphasis). In *Tess of the d'Urbervilles* he frequently draws analogies between the physical properties of a landscape and the human drama enacted within it.[12] The two girls, Tess and Marian, 'crawling over the surface' of the impersonal brown face of the swede field at Flintcomb-Ash, 'like flies' form a visual emblem of their featureless and monotonous life (*TD* 364), just as the lushness of the Froom corresponds with the plenitude of life in the valley. The Symbolist principle, as Hardy understood it from Brunetière, was that 'between (external) nature & ourselves there are "correspondences" "(latent) affinities," mysterious "identities," & that it is only so far as we seize them that, penetrating to the interior of things, we can truly approach the soul of them.'[13]

Brunetière's theory of symbolic 'correspondences' applied principally, of course, to the relation between artist and artwork, in that the artist himself discovered in natural forms a rapport between his emotions and the forms and patterns in the physical world; but on at least one occasion in *Tess of the d'Urbervilles* Hardy allows his heroine to interpret landscape as a symbol of her predicament. As Tess crosses the high ground on her way to Emminster, she looks down upon Blackmoor Valley. In spite of what Brunetière had said, she *does* invest what she sees with the state of her soul; on the chalky surface of the ridge, says the narrator, 'the landscape was whitey-brown; down there, as in Froom Valley, it was always green. Yet it was in that vale that her sorrow had taken shape, and she did not love it as formerly. Beauty to her, as to all who have felt, lay not in the thing, but in what the thing symbolized.' (*TD* 378).

With regard to the creative process of writing itself, however, French Symbolist theories confirmed one important view about the

---

12 Hardy may also have been encouraged by the example of Zola. He copied into his *'1867' Notebook* passages from *Abbé Mouret's Transgression* in the recent translation of 1886, including the following: 'Far off, on the edge of the horizon, the hills, still hot with the setting luminary's farewell kiss, seemed all tremulous and quivering, as though shaken by the steps of some invisible army. Nearer . . . all the pebbles in the valley seemed animated with a throbbing life.' (*LN*, *'1867' Notebook*, entry 192; Hardy's ellipsis). See also the epigraph for this chapter. For the influence of this novel on Hardy see Lennart Björk's remarks in the *'1867' Notebook*, entry 187 n.

13 Brunetière, see n. 11.

role of the imagination which Hardy already held—that the role of the author was not to reproduce natural effects for their own sake, or even to lend verisimilitude to the action, but, instead, to 'bring out the features which illustrate [his own] idiosyncratic mode of regard' (*EL* 294). What the theories did not provide, however, were the technical means by which this act of imaginative re-creation or penetration might be achieved; none of the articles or books, either in French or in English, which Hardy was reading at this time offered any practical or specific advice on the processes of transformation, and none of them had much to say about the actual vehicle of expressiveness in literature. The solution to the problem came only months before he started to write *Tess of the d'Urbervilles*, and it came not from literary theory, but from the direct and immediate experience of painting. In January 1889 Hardy visited a dazzling exhibition of Turner's water-colours at the Royal Academy. 'Seldom if ever', wrote one critic, 'has the art of Turner, even in the galleries of the Academy, been more splendidly illustrated,'[14] and Hardy recorded his enormous excitement in his diary. As on previous occasions, he was struck by Turner's capacity to shape, mould, and transform the features of landscape according to the dictates of his imagination. Each water-colour, said Hardy, 'is a landscape plus a man's soul'. Turner, he said, 'first recognizes the impossibility of really reproducing on canvas all that is in a landscape; then gives for that which cannot be reproduced a something else which shall have upon the spectator an approximative effect to that of the real.' (*EL* 283). What is new in Hardy's response to these pictures is that he seems to have fully recognized for the first time the actual means by which Turner activates the process of transformation. 'What he paints', Hardy wrote, 'is chiefly *light as modified by objects*.' (*EL* 283). As Hardy's own underscoring suggests, the recognition of this fact came to him as an important revelation.

In Turner, Hardy had found a painter who revealed the inner meaning of landscape by painting not objects, but the effect of light on objects. It is light which is Turner's vehicle for imaginative expressiveness, and he communicates 'the deeper reality underlying the scenic', not by painting trees, mountains, rocks, and lakes, but by painting light itself. Here, in Turner's depiction of 'light modified by objects', is surely the source of so many of the brilliant scenes in *Tess*

[14] Claude Phillips, 'The Winter Exhibition of the Royal Academy', *The Academy*, 35 (1889), p. 101.

of the d'Urbervilles in which the landscape dissolves in the glow of light and sunlight. In an early episode at Chaseborough, for example, Hardy uses an effect by which physical objects are replaced entirely by the aerial play of light and colour. It was 'a fine September evening, just before sunset, when yellow lights struggle with blue shades in hair-like lines, and the atmosphere itself forms a prospect without aid from more solid objects.' (*TD* 76). Here, the landscape, or 'prospect', is composed solely of illumination. Elsewhere in the novel, Hardy focuses less on the constituent elements of the landscape than on the illuminative medium through which they are seen. Aerial perspective, or 'atmosphere', is especially important. On the high ground overlooking Blackmoor Valley, 'the lanes are white, the hedges low and plashed, the atmosphere colourless' (*TD* 9), while on the lower ground, the atmosphere is 'languorous, and is so tinged with azure that what the artists call the middle distance also partakes of that hue . . . [and] the horizon is of the deepest ultramarine.' (*TD* 10).

The presence of the artist and his palette point to the pictorial source of light and colour, but even when the painter is not prominent, the stress on light remains. The 'clear and bracing air' of the valley of the Froom lacked 'the intensely blue atmosphere' of Blackmoor Valley (*TD* 133), but that very clarity contributes to the intense power of the sun shining down upon Talbothays. As Tess descends for the first time into the valley what she sees is indeed what Hardy had perceived in Turner's water-colours—light as modified by objects. The cows that were 'spotted with white reflected the sunshine in dazzling brilliancy, and the polished brass knobs on their horns glittered with something of a military display.' (*TD* 137). The courting of Angel and Tess in the dawn light of the water-meadows is played out not so much on terra firma but amongst a multiplicity of lights and shadows. Hardy carefully defines the exact quality of that light, pointing out that 'the grey half-tones of daybreak are not the grey half-tones of the day's close, though the degree of their shade may be the same.' (*TD* 166). And the evening landscape in which they walk is shaped by the light of the setting sun. Tess and Angel move amongst 'the beams of the sun, almost as horizontal as the mead itself', and the light forms 'a pollen of radiance over the landscape.' (*TD* 247).

The relationship between these effects and Turner's painting is analogous rather than imitative. From Turner, Hardy learned that light could be more than an external influence upon landscape: it could be used as the single most potent force, shaping landscape from within. But Hardy also realized that Turner used light to endow his paintings with meaning. Unlike Bonington, who painted the 'merely natural', Turner managed to communicate 'the tragical mysteries of life', and this, too, was achieved by manipulating the source of illumination. In *Tess of the d'Urbervilles* Hardy creates a literary equivalent for this technique. The pattern of light and dark, of natural illumination and artificial illumination, generates a meaning which is related to, but essentially independent of, the narrative.

Light and Darkness in *Tess of the d'Urbervilles*

The principal source of light in the novel is the sun, and in the numerous scenes which take place in sunlight Hardy carefully records its effect. The very first meeting of Angel and Tess is conducted in the rays of the setting sun, and they part for the last time on Salisbury Plain in the rays of the rising sun. Tess sees Angel on the evening of the 'club-walking' at Marlott, and 'it was not until the rays of the sun had absorbed the young stranger's retreating figure on the hill that she shook off her temporary sadness' (*TD* 18); moreover, it is 'in the growing light' of the sun, with 'their faces and hands as if they were silvered' (*TD* 505) that the couple wait at Stonehenge for the arrival of the police. The rising and setting of the sun mark out significant points in the narrative. The sun rises over the dead body of the horse Prince, creating 'a hundred prismatic hues' (*TD* 36) in the pool of blood in the road, and when the sun sinks over the village dance at Chaseborough, it signals the end of Tess's life as a virgin. Her return to agrarian life is accompanied by a sunrise which drives away the darkness of the night. It is a 'hazy sunrise in August', when 'the denser nocturnal vapours, attacked by the warm beams, were dividing and shrinking into isolated fleeces within hollows and coverts' (*TD* 109). A period of darkness marks the death of Tess's child, but her 'rally'—her determination to make a new life at Talbothays—is acted out in brilliant sunshine. As she entered the valley of the Froom, 'her hopes mingled with the sunshine in an ideal photosphere which surrounded her as she bounded along against the soft south wind.' (*TD* 133–4).

The courtship of Angel and Tess follows precisely the movement of the solar day and rhythm of the solar year. Their affection is born in the 'spectral, half-compounded, aqueous light' of dawn; it grows to a pitch of feverish physical intensity in the noonday July heat, in which passion comes 'like an excitation from the sky' (*TD* 193). Their formal engagement and move towards marriage is marked by the sun's decline from the zenith. They develop an 'unreserved comradeship out of doors', lit by the rays of the autumn sun whose beams were 'almost as horizontal as the mead itself' (*TD* 247), and as they are married on New Year's Eve, the sun sinks to the horizon. It was 'so low on that short last afternoon of the year' that it formed a 'golden staff' (*TD* 277) across the floor at Wellbridge.

The presence of the sun in this novel is so marked that its absence or withdrawal is highly dramatic. The terrible events of the wedding night and the resurrection of the past are prefaced by both the death of the day and the death of the year.

With the departure of the sun the calm mood of the winter day changed. Out of doors there began noises as of silk smartly rubbed; the restful dead leaves of the preceding autumn were stirred to irritated resurrection, and were whirled about unwillingly. . . . It soon began to rain. (*TD* 278.)

The mood of the novel also changes, and for Tess, whose life had previously been illuminated by love and sunlight, 'the gold of the summer picture was now grey, the colours mean, the rich soil mud, and the river cold.' (*TD* 321). She now spends her days in self-imposed exile in sunless Flintcomb-Ash where, on the chalk upland, everything was 'in colour a desolate drab', and the sunless sky 'a white vacuity of countenance with the lineaments gone.' (*TD* 363–4). The winter sets in; the wind and rain lash the young girl; then comes the frost, and finally the snow carried on winds from 'behind the North Pole' (*TD* 367). When the sun does appear it comes with light but no warmth. The 'low winter sun' illuminates the form of Alec d'Urberville as he preaches in the barn (*TD* 386); the 'cold sunlight' peers 'invidiously upon the crocks and kettles, upon the bunches of dried herbs shivering in the breeze' (*TD* 462), as Tess's family are evicted from their cottage after the death of Mr Durbeyfield and it comes as a vengeful deity to claim its most recent human sacrifice at Stonehenge. ' "Did they sacrifice to God here?" ', Tess asks Angel on their last night together. ' "No", ' he replies. ' "Who to?" ', she asks again. ' "I believe to the sun" .' (*TD* 503). When Tess is hanged at Wintoncester, the sun makes one last appearance. As Angel and 'Liza-Lu take their leave of the place, the 'sun's rays smiled on pitilessly.' (*TD* 506).

Sun and sunlight have strong emotional connotations throughout *Tess of the d'Urbervilles*, and though those connotations vary—sometimes sunlight is cheering, sometimes it is cruel or indifferent—its opposite, darkness or obscurity, is uniformly sinister and threatening. Hardy had already employed the symbolism of the contrast between light and darkness, night and day, in a number of previous novels. The darkness of Bathsheba Everdene's fir plantation in *Far from the Madding Crowd* is symptomatic of her own lack of self-awareness, which the dazzling light of the lantern does nothing to dispel, and the obscurity of Egdon Heath in *The Return of the Native* provides an appropriate Tartarian setting for Eustacia Vye. But in *Tess of the d'Urbervilles* darkness is far more all-encompassing, as it persistently threatens to engulf the tenuous hold the mind has on light, hope, and reason.

Many of the journeys in this novel—journeys created by the contingencies of the plot—take place at night. It is the obscurity of darkness which causes the death of Prince at the beginning of the novel, and at the end, Tess and Angel grope their way blindly through the 'black solitude' (*TD* 501) as they fly from the arm of the law. The darkest journey of all is the one which leads Alec and Tess to Cranborne Chase. Amongst the trees, 'the obscurity was . . . so great' that Alec 'could see absolutely nothing but a pale nebulousness at his feet. . . . Everything else was blackness alike.' (*TD* 90). Moreover, Tess's violation in 'darkness and silence' is an act of instinctual blindness. Everywhere darkness is filled with the forces of destruction. Tess's flight from Flintcomb-Ash takes place in a 'chilly equinoctial darkness' populated by an 'impish multitude' (*TD* 441) of creatures associated with black magic, and on the night of Prince's death, little Abraham, Tess's brother, sees in 'the strange shapes assumed by the various dark objects' a 'tree that looked like a raging tiger' and another 'which resembled a giant's head.' (*TD* 32). The night often takes the form of a predatory animal. It 'swallows up' Tess's brother (*TD* 25) in a metaphor innocent enough until, after the marriage of Angel and Tess, the night returns with a ravenous appetite:

The night came in, and took up its place . . . unconcerned and indifferent; the night which had already swallowed up [Angel's] happiness, and was now digesting it listlessly; and was ready to swallow up the happiness of a thousand other people with as little disturbance or change of mien. (*TD* 301.)

The metaphor extends to the 'darkness' of Tess's past life which is inhabited by 'gloomy spectres', or 'wolves' (*TD* 249) kept at bay only by the light of her love for Angel. She knew 'that they were waiting like wolves just outside the circumscribing light, but she had long spells of power to keep them in hungry subjection there.' (*TD* 249).

Throughout the novel sunlight and darkness are engaged in a battle for supremacy. 'Yellow lights struggle with blue shadows' (*TD* 76) in the sunset at Chaseborough, but in the sunrise at Marlott the 'nocturnal vapours' are successfully 'attacked by the warm beams' of the morning light. Sometimes light triumphs; sometimes darkness is the victor: 'In the twilight of the morning light seems active, darkness passive; in the twilight of the evening it is darkness which is active and crescent, and the light which is the drowsy reverse.' (*TD* 166). This daily warfare between light and dark has an analogy in the human world. When the light of love burned strongly for Tess, she 'walked in brightness' (*TD* 249), but it is a brightness which is fragile and vulnerable, since 'in the background those shapes of darkness were always spread.' (*TD* 249).

The opposition between sunlight and darkness is absolute; the two are mutually exclusive, and represent contradictory states. The contrast between sunlight and artificial light, however, is rather different. Here there is no 'struggle'; instead, artificial light is offered as the deceptive, even demonic, alternative to the light of the sun. It usually comes in the form of firelight, and Hardy exploits the infernal associations of fires as they cast their lurid and unnatural glow over the events of the narrative.

As Tess feeds a bonfire at Marlott, Alec d'Urberville suddenly appears in its light as a figure recently escaped from hell. ' "A Jester" ', he says ironically, ' "might say this is just like Paradise. You are Eve, and I am the old Other One come to tempt you in the disguise of an inferior animal".' (*TD* 445). Throughout the novel the 'red coal' of Alec d'Urberville's cigar acts as a permanent reminder of his Satanic origins (*TD* 79 and 59). Satan makes another appearance in the story, this time taking the form of a 'creature from Tophet' (*TD* 415) mechanically stoking the primum mobile of the threshing-machine 'in a sort of trance, with a heap of coals by his side.' (*TD* 415). The agricultural workers are children of organic life, and they 'serve vegetation'; the anonymous black figure of the threshing-machine, however, is the slave of 'fire and smoke' (*TD* 415), acting in accordance with the demands of his 'Plutonic master'.

It is during the wedding night at Wellbridge, however, that firelight is more explicitly demonic. It is in the light of the fire that

Angel urges Tess to put on the necklace, ear-rings, and bracelets sent as heirlooms by his godmother. At Talbothays, nature herself had supplied all Tess's jewellery in the form of 'minute diamonds of moisture' which 'hung upon Tess's eyelashes, and drops upon her hair, like seed pearls.' (*TD* 168). Now the 'steady glare' from the fire replaces the light of the sun and transforms the jewellery about her face and neck 'into an Aldebaran or a Sirius—a constellation of white, red, and green flashes, that interchanged their hues with her every pulsation.' (*TD* 284).[15] Artifice has usurped the place of nature, and Hardy sets the scene for Tess's confession in the apocalyptic glow of the fire.

> The ashes under the grate were lit by the fire vertically, like a torrid waste. Imagination might have beheld a Last Day luridness in this red-coaled glow which fell on his face and hand, and on hers, peering into the loose hair about her brow, and firing the delicate skin underneath. . . . She bent forward, at which each diamond on her neck gave a sinister wink like a toad's; and pressing her forehead against his temple she entered on her story of her acquaintance with Alec d'Urberville. (*TD* 287.)

Light and darkness, sunlight and shadow, the illumination from fires and the illumination from the sky, are treated both literally and symbolically in this novel. On the one hand, they help to create a credible setting for the pastoral tragedy, and on the other, they generate what Brunetière termed the 'latent affinities' and 'mysterious identities' between 'external nature and ourselves'— between character and environment. Hardy creates these affinities in part by employing the archetypal power of light and darkness to suggest joy and sorrow, life and death, but he also draws on a more specific set of meanings related to sun and sunlight, darkness and night. At almost every point in *Tess of the d'Urbervilles* the solar symbolism which Hardy uses has close connections with the mythical properties of light and darkness. He was familiar with the current nineteenth-century view that the source of all primitive legends, even primitive religions, was to be found in the path of the sun through the sky. In early mythology the real, objective sun merges with the divinities which it inspired. In *Tess of the d'Urbervilles* the sun, which plays such a prominent part in the action, is imaginatively linked with the main protagonists, and

---

[15] The constellation Aldebaran 'shone with a fiery red glow' above the head of Gabriel Oak at midnight on St Thomas's Eve at the beginning of *Far from the Madding Crowd* (*FMC* 9).

the connection between them is derived from the ancient, mytho-poetical power of solar illumination.

Solar myth and *Tess of the d'Urbervilles*

In his book *Fiction and Repetition*, J. Hillis Miller says that the sun in *Tess of the d'Urbervilles* is, 'as in tradition generally, the fecundating male source, a principle of life, but also a dangerous energy able to pierce and destroy.'[16] Using Tony Tanner's observations about Hardy's use of the colour red in this novel,[17] Miller goes on to link the multiplicity of red objects mentioned in the story with this generative principle. The red ribbon in Tess's hair, her red mouth, the red strawberry given to her by Alec d'Urberville, the red stains on her arms in the garden at Talbothays, the red painted sign, the red of blood itself, are all, Miller suggests, 'incarnated in one form in the sun'. For Miller the importance of this theme is the way in which redness creates a repeated 'mark' throughout the text of the novel, imprinting itself again and again on the story. What he says is un-doubtedly correct, but this view overlooks the fact that Hardy's allu-sions to redness are just one aspect of his much more extensive employment of the themes, the patterns, and the imagery associated with solar myth. Redness is certainly allied to the creative and destructive power of the sun in the novel, but what is more important is that the sun is also an emblem for a complex set of religious and cultural values. The persistent and ubiquitous struggle between sunlight and shadow is the visual equivalent, or visible essence, of a moral conflict within the novel—a conflict between a religious im-pulse which is primitive, simple, and untramelled by the demands of conventional orthodoxy and religious dogmas which are deeply en-trenched in an ethical code.

The sun is the source of life and light, and in its benevolent form rises as a god in the August dawn—a 'golden-haired, beaming, mild-eyed' creature. It is 'god-like' in appearance, 'gazing down in the vigour and intentness of youth upon an earth that was brimming with interest for him.' (*TD* 109). This same appearance 'explained the old-time heliolatories in a moment', and 'one could feel', says the nar-rator, 'that a saner religion had never prevailed under the sky'. It is the sun which is the deity presiding over the 'aesthetic, sensuous,

---

[16] J. Hillis Miller, *Fiction and Repetition*, p. 122.
[17] See Introduction, n. 19.

27. Titian: *The Rape of Europa*. 1561. Isabella Stewart Gardner Museum, Boston (178×205 cm)

28. Titian: *Diana and Acteon*. 1556–9. Collection of the Duke of Sutherland, National Gallery of Scotland (188×203 cm)

29. James McNeill Whistler: *Harmony in Red Lamplight* (Mrs Beatrix Godwin). 1886. University of Glasgow, Birnie Philip bequest (189.8×88.9 cm)

pagan pleasure in natural life' (*TD* 203) of Talbothays; it presides, too, over the religion of Greece, which, Angel argues, would have had a better influence on mankind than the religion of Palestine (*TD* 203). The sun is the heart of 'the great passionate pulse of existence', and it is solar worship which stands in opposition to the 'geocentric view of things' of dogmatic Christianity, with its 'zenithal paradise' and 'nadiral hell' (*TD* 203).

It is amongst the pagan customs of the remote areas of the countryside that ancient sun-worship has survived. At Marlott in the 'clubwalking' episode—itself a survival of fertility rituals—each girl, we are told, was 'warmed without by the sun', while at the same time 'each had a private little sun for her soul to bask in.' (*TD* 12). Chaseborough is deeply pagan in both appearance and customs. Here, the rustic girl Car, with her Greek form 'beautiful as some Praxitelean creation' (*TD* 82), dances with the other country folk in an Ovidian revel—'satyrs clasping nymphs—a multiplicity of Pans whirling a multiplicity of Syrinxes' (*TD* 77), but it is amongst the 'impassioned, summer-steeped heathens' (*TD* 201) of Talbothays that solar worship is most prominent, and there it has become absorbed into the rites of primitive Christianity. It is largely the women of the community who unconsciously perpetuate the old forms of religion, because women, living in the companionship of 'outdoor Nature', 'retain in their souls far more of the Pagan fantasy of their remote forefathers than of the systematized religion taught their race at later date.' (*TD* 134–5). This is particularly true of Tess herself, and though she is pursued by the 'moral hobgoblins' of orthodoxy, she yields spontaneously to the influence of the sun.

It is under the influence of the sun that Angel and Tess fall in love. The 'rush of juices' and the 'hiss of fertilization' (*TD* 190) created in the organic world by the July sun carry over to the human world, and mutual affection comes 'like an excitation from the sky' (*TD* 193). Consequently, when Tess embraces Angel, she not only embraces a man, she also opens herself to the power of the sun, which lights up her whole being:

There they stood upon the red-brick floor of the entry [to the dairy house], the sun slanting in by the window upon his back as he held her tightly to his breast; upon her inclining face, upon the blue veins of her temple, upon her naked arm, and her neck, and into the depths of her hair. (*TD* 218.)

The identification in Tess's mind between Angel and the sun transforms her love for him into a kind of sun-worship: she lifts her heart to him 'in devotion' (*TD* 246); he is a 'divine being' (*TD* 258); he is 'god-like in her eyes' (*TD* 233); he is her 'Apollo' (*TD* 493). Her affection for Angel is generated by emotional solar radiation; it becomes for her 'the breath and life of [her] being', which 'enveloped her as a photosphere, irradiated her into forgetfulness of her past sorrows, keeping back the gloomy spectres that would persist in their attempts to touch her.' (*TD* 249). The word 'photosphere' here suggests both the aura of light which surrounds the sun and the halo which envelops the head of the blessed, and as Tess's marriage approaches, so the suggestions of religious veneration increase. Her one desire is 'to call [Angel] her lord . . . then, if necessary, to die.' (*TD* 270). Her love for him is described as a kind of 'idolatory' (*TD* 273), and when she tries to pray to God, it was 'her husband who really had her supplication.' (*TD* 273).

It is the wedding day that completes the apotheosis of Angel in Tess's eyes, and one powerful image blends the pagan and Christian sentiments of the event, uniting solar worship with Scriptural language. Immediately after the wedding service, says Hardy, Tess 'felt glorified by an irradiation not her own, like the angel whom St. John saw in the sun.' (*TD* 272). At one level her feelings are inspired by her memory of the Book of Revelation from which she has conflated two episodes. In Chapter 12, a woman appears 'clothed with the sun', 'travailing in birth, and pained to be delivered'. In this episode a dragon waited 'to devour her child as soon as it was born', but the woman 'fled into the wilderness' to a place prepared for her 'by God'. In the second episode, in Chapter 19, St John records having seen 'an angel standing in the sun' who 'cried with a loud voice, saying to all the fowls that fly in the midst of heaven, Come and gather yourselves together unto the supper of the great God'.

At another level this image derives not from Tess's experience, but from Hardy's. His visits to the National Gallery had familiarized Hardy with Turner's late painting *The Angel Standing in the Sun* (Plate 30).[18] This is an interpretation of the second episode from Revelation, and in the form in which Turner illustrates it, the painting fits well with Tess's situation. Unlike the author of the biblical account, Turner has chosen to depict the event as a struggle between the forces of light and the forces of darkness. So not only is the angel irradiated by the sun, but the aura of light drives away 'gloomy spectres—dark

18 This was a picture which did not meet with Ruskin's approval. See Ruskin, *Works* viii. 167.

skeletal creatures not mentioned in the Bible. Turner's picture is sub-titled 'The Flight of the Angel of Darkness', and the visual antithesis, which is entirely Turner's invention, provides an admirable analogy to one of the principal themes of *Tess of the d'Urbervilles*.

Turner's influence on the novel, both here and elsewhere, extends beyond Hardy's admiration for his use of light as an expressive medium. We know for certain that Hardy was deeply impressed by the way in which Turner employed light symbolically, but he must also have known of Turner's leanings towards solar mythology. According to Ruskin, Turner's treatment of light and colour was not simply aesthetic, it was also an act of worship. In Turner's painting, said Ruskin, 'nothing is cheerful but sunshine; whenever the sun is not, there is melancholy and evil.' For Turner, 'Apollo is God; and all forms of death and sorrow exist in opposition to him.'[19] For Tess, too, light is life, darkness is melancholy, and Angel is Apollo. Like Tess, Turner, in Ruskin's words, was a 'Sun-worshipper of the old breed' who 'meant it, as Zoroaster meant it'.[20] And Ruskin told the story that shortly before his death Turner had unequivocally asserted that 'the Sun is God'.[21]

Ruskin's conception of Turner as a modern heliolator was closely related to his views on Greek myth. In the closing chapters of the last volume of *Modern Painters*, Ruskin describes Turner as not just the finest landscape painter of recent times, but also as the most articulate exponent of Greek myth; and in the years which followed *Modern Painters*, Ruskin began to attach more and more importance to the function of myth as the repository of an ancient and intuitive wisdom about man's relationship with the natural world. Ruskin's study of myth culminated in *The Queen of the Air* of 1869, in which he makes it clear that the correct interpretation of myth yields a species of knowledge to which the modern eye has become blind. The senses of modern man, Ruskin argues, have become dulled to the inner work-ings of nature, but the fables of the Greek deities, if carefully studied, can place us in a new and vital relationship with nature and its power. Among the most important of these stories are the myths of Apollo, for it is this god who represents the *primum mobile* of the natural

---

[19] Ruskin, *Ariadne Florentina* (1872), in *Works* xx. 489–90;

[20] Ruskin, *Fors Clavigera* (1874), in *Works* xxviii. 147.

[21] In a letter to Henry Acland in 1867, Ruskin wrote: 'If the nation can heartily believe even that the Sun is God (like poor Turner) and act on such belief . . . it may see its way to better things.' *Works* xxxvi. 543.

world. 'It may be easy to prove', says Ruskin, 'that the ascent of Apollo in his chariot signifies nothing but the rising of the sun.' 'But what', he asks, 'does the sunrise itself signify to us?'

If only languid return to frivolous amusement, or fruitless labour, it will, indeed, not be easy for us to conceive the power, over a Greek, of the name of Apollo. But if, for us also, as for the Greek, the sunrise means daily restoration to the sense of passionate gladness, and of perfect life—if it means the thrilling of new strength through every nerve . . . the purging of evil vision and fear by the baptism of its dew; if the sun itself is an influence, to us also, of spiritual good—and becomes thus in reality, not in imagination, to us also, a spiritual power,—we may then . . . with the Greek rise to the thought of an angel who rejoiced as a strong man to run his course.[22]

According to Ruskin, Turner responded intuitively to the spiritual power of light and sunlight, and with a mythological subject like *The Python Slayed by Apollo* he gives a precise symbolic form to the subject which recurs perennially in his paintings—the struggle between light and darkness, of 'purity with pollution', of 'life with forgetfulness', and of 'love with the grave'.[23] This attitude to light and sunlight, Ruskin argued, is 'no metaphor', nor has it 'ever been so'. 'To the Persian, the Greek and the Christian, the sense of the power of the God of Light had been one and the same,'[24] and in 1876 he summed up his growing conviction of the seriousness of solar worship even in a modern context. 'All up and down my later books', he wrote in *Fors Clavigera* 'you will find references to the practical connection between physical and spiritual light',[25] and, speaking to the 'workmen and labourers of Great Britain', he said that 'you cannot love the real sun, that is to say, physical light and colour, rightly, unless you love the spiritual sun, that is to say justice and truth, rightly.'[26]

Although Hardy was familiar with Ruskin's views, the way in which he uses the principles underlying solar myth in *Tess of the d'Urbervilles* differs significantly from Ruskin. As orthodox Christian beliefs began to lose their hold upon Ruskin, he took a more and more sympathetic view of Greek mythology. Nevertheless, his reading of myth is still subsumed under a fairly strict ethical code, and he never abandons himself to the unfettered paganism of the

[22] Ruskin, *Queen of the Air* (1869), in *Works* xix. 302–3.
[23] Ruskin, *Modern Painters*, in *Works* vii. 420.
[24] Ruskin, *The Eagle's Nest* (1872), in *Works* xxii. 204.
[25] Ruskin, *Fors Clavigera* (1876), in *Works* xxviii. 614.
[26] *Ibid.*

Greek ethos. In spite of his love of Greek legend and its naturalistic impulses, Ruskin could never be counted among those 'sun-steeped heathens' of Hardy's Froom Valley. Consequently, Hardy turned to others amongst his contemporaries who offered a more exclusively pagan interpretation of mythology, and for whom the Greek experience stood in sharp contrast to the rigid demands of Victorian Christian orthodoxy.

The myth of Apollo

In 1889 Hardy was delighted to receive an appreciative letter from John Addington Symonds sympathizing with his paganism, since Hardy had long admired Symonds's *Studies of the Greek Poets*, and had studied minutely his essays on Greek myth and culture in the *Essays Speculative and Suggestive* (1890). Symonds reinforced for Hardy the prevailing belief in the essentially natural sources of myth and the importance of Apollo. Nature, said Symonds,

is the first, chief element by which we are enabled to conceive the spirit of the Greeks. The key to their mythology is here. Here is the secret of their sympathies, the well-spring of their deepest thoughts, the primitive potentiality of all they have achieved in art. What is Apollo but the magic of the sun, whose soul is light?[27]

But both Ruskin's ethical interpretation of solar myth and Symonds's celebration of Greek antinomianism would have been impossible without the scholarship of the philologist Max Müller, who in the 1850s radically altered the English interpretation of the significance of mythology. Müller's work was based on a comparative method of analysis, as he submitted his extensive knowledge of primitive myths from many cultures to linguistic analysis. In 1856 he began to publish his findings, all of which corroborated his single most important intuition—that all myth and legend, indeed the primary religious impulse in man, could be traced back to the response of the primitive mind to the rising and setting of the sun. 'How often we felt incredulous', he wrote in 1885, 'when, in tracing Greek, Roman, and Vedic myths back to their original source, we always found that they applied to the sun in his ever varying aspects.'[28] In spite of his own

[27] John Addington Symonds, *Studies of the Greek Poets* (1873), p. 404.
[28] Max Müller, 'Solar Myths, p. 906; quoted in *LN* entry 1359. In *Fors Clavigera* Ruskin quoted Müller's remark that amongst the Zoroastrians, 'the vital principle of

incredulity, however, Müller was forced to the conclusion that the sun acted as the most important influence on the human imagination, and what he says about its significance in the modern world closely anticipates what Ruskin said some years later. 'We, with our modern ways of life', he wrote,

are not aware how everything we think or speak or do is dependent on the sun, and it is only the true man of science who by the latest discoveries has been brought back to that full conviction of his solar dependence which the son of nature has never lost.[29]

Hardy knew Müller's work in the 1870s,[30] and in 1886 he followed a debate between Müller, Spencer, Lang, and Gladstone on methodological procedures in the analysis of myth.[31] Nor was *Tess of the d'Urbervilles* the first novel in which he had harnessed the power latent within the myth of the sun. In *The Woodlanders*, as Mary Jacobus points out, Giles Winterborne bears a close relationship to the Teutonic hero Balder, the 'sun-god and source of natural regeneration'.[32] Jacobus writes of the way in which Matthew Arnold's treatment of the myth of Balder in his poem 'Balder Dead' very much resembles the failure of the powers of natural regeneration following

their religion is the recognition of one supreme power; the God of Light—in every sense of the word—the Spirit who creates the world, and rules it, and defends it against the power of evil.' Ruskin, *Works* xxvii. 217.

[29] Müller, 'Solar Myths', p. 906.

[30] *LN*, entry 166, is a quotation, in Emma Hardy's hand, from 'Max Müller's *Chips from a German Workshop*', *Saturday Review*, 41 (Jan. 1876), p. 52; and *LN*, entry 578, is a quotation from J. P. Mahaffy's *Social Life in Greece* (1874), which refers to von Müller's ideas. Michael Millgate in 'Hardy's Fiction: Some Comments on the Present State of Criticism', *English Literature in Transition*, 14 (1971), p. 233, suggests that Hardy might have been familiar with Müller and his views on solar myth.

[31] W. E. Gladstone, 'The Dawn of Creation and of Worship', *The Nineteenth Century*, 18 (1885), pp. 685–706; T. H. Huxley, 'The Interpreters of Genesis and the Interpreters of Nature', *The Nineteenth Century*, 18 (1885), pp. 849–60; Müller, 'Solar Myths' pp. 900–22; W. E. Gladstone, 'Proem to Genesis', *The Nineteenth Century*, 19 (1886), pp. 1–21; Andrew Lang, 'Myths and Mythologists', *The Nineteenth Century*, 18 (1885), pp. 50–65; T. H. Huxley, 'Mr Gladstone and Genesis', *The Nineteenth Century*, 19 (1886), pp. 191–205; Henry Drummond, 'Mr Gladstone and Genesis', *The Nineteenth Century*, 19 (1886), pp. 206–14. See *LN*, entries 1359 and 1361. By the time that Hardy was writing *Tess of the d'Urbervilles*, von Müller's position with regard to the interpretation of myth—a position based upon comparative linguistics—had been successfully challenged by Andrew Lang, whose methods were those of the comparative anthropologist. See especially Richard M. Dorson, 'The Eclipse of Solar Mythology', pp. 25–63; James Kissane, 'Victorian Mythology'; and Janet Burstein, 'Victorian Mythology and the Progress of the Intellect'.

[32] Mary Jacobus, 'Tree and Machine', p. 119.

in the wake of Giles's death, but the details of the narrative of *The Woodlanders* suggest that Hardy is as much dependent on Müller as Arnold. Müller, who quotes from Arnold's poem, suggests that 'there is much suffering in nature to those who have eyes for silent grief, and it is this tragedy—the tragedy of nature—which is the lifespring of all the tragedies of the ancient world.'[33] As we saw in the last chapter, *The Woodlanders* derives much of its tragic tone from what Müller calls 'the tragedy of nature', and the story of Giles Winterborne fits well with Müller's description of the archetypal solar hero. This, he said, involves 'the idea of a young hero, whether he is called Baldr, or Sigurd, or Sîfrit, or Achilles, or Meleager, or Kephalos, dying in the fulness of youth'. Like Giles, these heroes are forced to 'leave their first love' and perish by 'the hand or by the unwilling treachery of their nearest friends or relatives', and, according to Müller this myth was 'first suggested by the Sun, dying in all his youthful vigour either at the end of the day, conquered by the powers of darkness, or at the end of the sunny season, stung by the thorn of winter'.[34]

In *Tess of the d'Urbervilles* Hardy turns from one solar deity to another, from Balder to Apollo. The sun-god rises 'in the vigour . . . of youth' (*TD* 109), wrestles with the powers of darkness, and dies on the day of Angel's and Tess's marriage, at a point in the novel which is simultaneously the 'end of the day' and the 'end of the sunny season'. In the novel, Apollo's acolytes are the 'impassioned . . . heathens in the Var Vale' (*TD* 201) who possess 'the bold grace of wild animals' (*TD* 222), and resemble in many respects the 'youthful race' described in Müller's work. The worshippers of Apollo, he says, are 'free to follow the call of their hearts,—unfettered by the rules and prejudices of a refined society, and controlled only by those laws which nature and the graces have engraved on every human heart'.[35] In Talbothays, Angel felt for the first time the 'great passionate pulse of existence, unwarped, uncontorted, untrammelled by those creeds which futilely attempt to check what wisdom would be content to regulate.' (*TD* 203).

Tess's love comes to her as an impulse, and it comes in the moments between sleep and waking—first in the Apollonian light of dawn at Talbothays, then when she rises from her afternoon nap 'like

---

[33] Max Müller, 'Comparative Mythology', in *Chips from a German Workshop*, 2nd ed. (1868), ii. 110.
[34] Ibid.
[35] Max Müller, *Chips* ii. 132.

a sunned cat'. Müller describes the connection between love and solar worship, when

such hearts [are] suddenly lighted up by love,—by a feeling of which they knew not either whence it came and whither it would carry them; an impulse they did not even know how to name. . . . Was not love to them like an awakening from sleep?[36]

Both Tess and her primitive antecedents look for a name for that love, and like the Greeks who, in Müller's account, were pervaded by a 'glowing warmth, purifying their whole being like a fresh breeze, and illuminating the whole world around them with a new light', they identify their love with Apollo. 'There was but one name by which they could express love,' Müller says, 'there was but one similitude for the roseate bloom that betrays the dawn of love,' and his account of the creation of mythological language fits exactly with Tess's own experience: ' "The sun has risen," they said, where we say, "I love"; "the sun has set," they said, where we say, "I have loved".'[37]

Angel Clare, of course, is not Apollo. He is the youngest son of Parson Clare of Emminster, and has voluntarily given up a university career in order to train himself as a farmer. Yet he carries in him enough of the attributes of his mythological counterpart to make it clear that Tess's likening him to Apollo is not simply a figment of her imagination. His harp-playing, his role as herdsman, his power to bring both light and destruction, are all reminiscent of the god of the Greeks. But in Angel the power of Apollo is weak. He is like a lesser god who finds himself in a country where, and at a time when, a new religion and a new morality hold sway; consequently, the positive virtues for which he stands are suddenly and brutally eclipsed.

It was Heine who, in *The Gods in Exile*, developed the idea of the pagan gods taking refuge in the countryside at what he called 'the definite triumph of Christianity' in the third century. 'Deprived of shelter and ambrosia', he wrote, they were forced to take to 'vulgar handicrafts as a means of earning their bread'. Apollo in particular, said Heine in Walter Pater's translation, 'seems to have been content

<hr/>

[36] Ibid.
[37] Ibid. In his article 'Astrology? Stars, Sun and Moon as Symbols in Hardy's Works', p. 219, J. O. Bailey points out that 'Hardy's sun usually symbolizes hope and happiness, blessing whatever it shines upon and prophesying good fortune. His poem "The Sun's Last Look on a Country Girl" treats his beloved sister Mary [and] in "Coming up Oxford Street, Evening" Hardy calls the evening sun a "warm god" brightening the darkness of London.'

to take service under graziers, and as he had once kept the cows of Admetus, so he lived now as a shepherd in Lower Austria'.[38] Pater quoted Heine in his study of Pico della Mirandola in *The Renaissance*, and they represent an idea which continued to fascinate Pater throughout his life. In *A Study of Dionysus* (1876) he traced the palingenesis of the myth of Bacchus; his study of Raphael of 1892 refers again to Heine's version of the legend, and his character Duke Carl of Rosenmold, in the imaginary portrait of the same name (1887), is one who wished to bring 'Apollo with his lyre to Germany', and to set about transforming himself into 'the Apollo of Germany'.[39]

Hardy's familiarity with Pater's view of the persistence of paganism is beyond question. Hardy first met Pater in the summer of 1886; then, when Pater moved from Oxford to Earl's Terrace in Kensington, and Hardy took lodgings in Upper Philimore Place nearby, their meetings were frequent (*EL* 275 and 278), and there can be no doubt that they discussed Pater's enthusiasm for the subject. It is not entirely surprising, then, that Angel resembles these latter-day solar deities. In Pater's translation of Heine's story, Apollo is seized by monks, confesses that he is indeed Apollo, and before his execution,

begged that he might be suffered to play once more upon the lyre, and to sing a song. And he played so touchingly, and sang with such magic, and was withal so beautiful in form and feature, that all the women wept, and many of them were so deeply impressed that they shortly afterwards fell sick.[40]

Angel, too, is a musician, and is so beautiful that the girls of the dairy 'writhed feverishly' in their beds with a 'hopeless passion' for him (*TD* 187).

What is most striking about Pater's treatment of the Apollo myth and Hardy's use of the same myth in *Tess of the d'Urbervilles* is that the influence of the god is deeply ambiguous. Unlike Müller in his scholarly account of primitive religion and myth, or Ruskin in his imaginative rendering of the stories of the old gods, Pater emphasizes the power of Apollo to bring both love *and* destruction. The double-

---

[38] Pater, *The Renaissance*, p. 24.
[39] Pater, 'Duke Carl of Rosenmold', in *Imaginary Portraits*, pp. 124 and 135. On Pater's interest in the survival of the ancient gods, see J. S. Harrison, 'Pater, Heine and the Old Gods of Greece'; William Shuter, 'History as Palengenesis in Pater and Hegel', *PMLA*, 86 (1971), pp. 411–21; and Steven Connor, 'Myth as Multiplicity in Walter Pater's *Greek Studies* and "Denys L'Auxerrois" '.
[40] Pater, *The Renaissance*, p. 25.

sidedness of Apollo's role was an integral part of the legend as it appears in Greek tragedy. He is the god of fertility and generation, but he is also the bringer of plagues and 'sudden death'. He resembles Christ as the Good Shepherd who watches over his flock, but he is also an evil one, the Devil even, a hunter who destroys the very animals he befriends. He returns bearing his lyre and his bow. It is in his story 'Apollo in Picardy' that Pater makes the most of this powerful duality, making it clear that the influence of Apollo is a 'violent beam, a blaze of new light', but also 'a curse . . . to its receiver'.[41]

'Apollo in Picardy' tells the story of the appearance in medieval France of a strange figure with apparently supernatural powers. He is nominally in charge of the animals at a religious retreat, but whereas 'the other herdsmen of the valley are bond-servants', he is 'a hireling at will'. He comes once a year, 'singing his way meagrely from farm to farm, to the sound of his harp'.[42] Similarly, Angel freely goes 'the round' of farms, 'his object being to acquire a practical skill in the various processes of farming' (*TD* 147). He, too, plays on a harp, though his is 'an old harp which he had bought at a sale' (*TD* 151). Angel's playing—'though both instrument and execution were poor' (*TD* 158)—is at its most necromantic when it lures Tess into the wild garden at Talbothays. Here, 'the floating pollen seemed to be his notes made visible,' and on two occasions in 'Apollo in Picardy', Pater uses the same phrase, 'music made visible'.[43] Tess is transfixed by the sound which has the power to drive away her troublesome thoughts: ' "*You*, sir," ' she says to Angel, ' "can raise up dreams with your music, and drive all . . . horrid fancies away" ' (*TD* 160), while Pater's strange deity 'charmed away other people's maladies' through his music, calming 'the respiration of the troubled sleeper'.[44]

Pater's hero is both Christ-like and demonic. He 'seemingly loved his sheep; was an "affectionate shepherd"; cured their diseases . . . and if they strayed afar would bring them back tenderly upon his shoulders'.[45] Yet he is also violent and savage. His name, Apollyon, 'came nearest to a malignant one in Scripture,'[46] and after his games with wild animals he 'breaks the toy; deftly snaps asunder the fragile back'.[47]

[41] Pater, 'Apollo in Picardy', in *Miscellaneous Studies* (1895), 2nd edn, p. 143. Though *Tess of the d'Urbervilles* was published in 1891, and 'Apollo in Picardy' not until 1893, the rate at which Pater usually worked makes it quite possible that he discussed his ideas for 'Apollo' even before Hardy began writing his novel.

[42] Pater, *Miscellaneous Studies*, pp. 151–2.   [43] Ibid., pp. 145 and 154.

[44] Ibid., p. 155.   [45] Ibid., p. 158.   [46] Ibid., p. 152.   [47] Ibid., p. 157.

Though all alike would come at his call, or the sound of his harp, he had his preferences. . . . The small furry thing he pierced with his arrow fled to him nevertheless caressingly, with broken limb, to die palpitating in his hand.[48]

In Pater's story, Apollyon, driven by a force greater than himself, violates the pigeon-house, destroying 'the bright creatures in a single night';[49] but it is the accidental killing of his closest companion, Hyacinth, which forms the climax of the piece. In one of the versions of the original myth, the god inadvertently kills Hyacinth with a discus, a symbol of the sun, and in Pater's story the discus is discovered in a grave and is 'wrested . . . with difficulty from the hands of the half-crippled gravedigger'.[50] The discus is known as one of the Devil's penny-pieces, and when Apollyon throws it, it strikes the young boy, 'crushing in the tender skull upon the brain'.[51]

Like one of the wild animals in Pater's story, Tess is attracted by Angel's playing, and, 'like a fascinated bird, could not leave the spot' (*TD* 158). In the course of the novel she is frequently likened to some trapped and hunted creature—a bird in a 'clasp net' (*TD* 370), 'a bird in a springe' (*TD* 251), a 'wounded animal' (*TD* 279)—and her affinity with the wounded and dying pheasants bespeaks her own fate—she is, like Hyacinth, the close companion of a destructive divinity.

Like Pater's Apollyon, Angel is both the Good Shepherd—or at least the good herdsman—who by his love and his light keeps in 'subjection' the 'wolves'[52] that seek to devour Tess, and he is also the bringer of plagues, violence, and sudden death. Both Pater and Hardy exploit the duality of the Apollo legend, but Hardy, unlike Pater, extends that duality to the Christian myth.

In *Tess of the d'Urbervilles* Christianity has benevolent and retributive aspects. Just as the worship of Apollo is both life-giving and destructive, so the worship of Christ is a source of love and a source of judgement. In their simple spontaneous modes, pantheism and Hebraism are easily reconciled. As Tess bounds along in her 'ideal photosphere', the psalm she sings is an invocation to the sun and the

---

[48] Ibid., p. 157.
[49] Ibid., p. 160.
[50] Ibid., p. 166.
[51] Ibid., p. 168.
[52] In *Myth Ritual & Religion* (1887), Andrew Lang pointed out that in *Electra* Sophocles calls Apollo 'the wolf-slayer'. 'The ancients,' said Lang, 'explained the fact indifferently by calling the deity the protector or the destroyer of the beasts in question.' *Myth Ritual and Religion*, ii. 201.

moon to 'bless me Lord', and there is nothing incongruous about the 'Fetichistic utterance in a Monotheistic setting.' (*TD* 134). Often, however, the mysticism of Christianity degenerates into a set of moral imperatives, most graphically illustrated by the itinerant evangelical sign-writer, who decorates the countryside with the hideous red slogans of 'the last grotesque phase of a creed which had served mankind well in its time.' (*TD* 101). 'THY, DAMNATION, SLUMBERETH, NOT' are the words which catch Tess's attention, and they encapsulate a religion more preoccupied with judgement than with worship, and represent a belief which has hardened into dogma.

Tess's tragedy lies in the fact that, as a child of nature, she has been born into that 'grotesque phase' of Christianity in which moral precept is more important than worship. Hardy's reading of J. C. Morison and T. H. Huxley seems to have convinced him of the idea that the true religious spirit—whether pagan or Christian—is fundamentally independent of ethical systems, and that only at a later date in the evolution of society was worship tainted by its association with moral codes.[53] In *Tess of the d'Urbervilles* this is made plain in a conversation between Tess and Alec d'Urberville. He insists on the identity between religious dogma and 'loving kindness and purity'. For her part, 'she tried to argue, and tell him that he had mixed in his dull brain two matters, theology and morals, which in the primitive days of mankind had been quite distinct.' (*TD* 421). Like Hardy, she had been reading Leslie Stephen, who, in *Belief and Conduct*, had claimed that 'it is hopeless to assert that morality is caused by a belief in Christianity'. 'To me', Stephen argued, 'it seems that the dogmatic declarations of the dependence of morality upon theology are not only gratuitous, but essentially illogical'.[54] Ironically, however, the greatest offender in this respect is not Alec d'Urberville at all, but Angel. In spite of the fact that he has no orthodox religious belief, in his attitude to Tess he perpetuates all the ethical imperatives related to the 'grotesque phase' of Christianity—he has, as the narrator puts it, 'an ethical system without any dogma' (*TD* 421).

A novel, however, as Hardy pointed out in the preface to *Tess of the d'Urbervilles* is 'an impression, not an argument'. It was, he said,

[53] From James Cotter Morison, *The Service of Man*, Hardy noted that 'primitive religion had little or no connection with morals—oftener evil than good' (*LN*, entry 1464); and in 'Evolution and Theology', *The Nineteenth Century*, 19 (1886), p. 346, Huxley wrote about the arbitrary connection between religious belief and human conduct.

[54] Leslie Stephen, 'Belief and Conduct', pp. 382–3.

'intended to be neither didactic nor aggressive', but to be 'oftner charged with impressions than with convictions' (*TD* xviii). The achievement of this novel is that, in spite of the seriousness of the issues with which it deals, it rarely loses its momentum in mere polemic. The narrative maintains its freshness to the end, and though it may frequently verge on melodrama, it is never dull. The key to Hardy's success lies in the vitality of his 'impression'—in never letting the 'vividly visible' escape him—and in managing to create a constant stream of analogues—visible essences—for the relationship between belief and conduct. The synthesis between idea and image can be most graphically illustrated by two complimentary episodes in the book, episodes which have outward similarities but inner contrasts. They are both sunrise scenes—one at Talbothays, the other at Stonehenge—and they both bring out the way in which Hardy uses a pattern of imagery to illustrate the two faces of paganism and the double-sided nature of Christianity.

In keeping with the traditions of solar myth, the love of Angel and Tess takes shape in the dawn light over Talbothays, 'that strange and solemn interval, the twilight of the morning' (*TD* 166). Nocturnal fears are dispersed by the beneficent agency of light—which is 'active'. But dawn is also the moment of generation in man's religious impulses. 'Sunrise', said Müller, 'was the revelation of nature, awakening in the human mind that feeling of dependence, of helplessness, of hope, of joy and faith in higher powers, which is the source of all wisdom, the spring of all religion.'[55] Consequently, the meads around Talbothays are the nursery of both love and religion. They are Paradise; they are the garden of Gethsemane; and they are Arcady. Tess and Angel are 'impressed . . . with a feeling of isolation, as if they were Adam and Eve', and the 'singular, luminous gloom' makes Angel 'think of the Resurrection hour' (*TD* 167). He is Adam and he is Christ, but the narrator's tone is tinged with irony. The comment, 'He little thought that the Magdalen might be at his side' represents a sardonic reflection on Angel's later un-Christ like rejection of Tess for sexual 'impurity'. At Talbothays all is yet innocent, pure, and undefiled; yet there is something unreal, even false about this pastoral. Angel idealizes his companion, and as he sees her in the white light of dawn, 'a whole sex condensed into one typical form', biblical myth merges with classical myth; he calls her 'Artemis, Demeter, and other fanciful names, half teasingly'.

[55] Max Müller, *Chips* ii. 99–100.

Here are Pater's ancient divinities, glimpsed for a moment in a modern setting, but it is Ruskin who provides the visual ambience for the return of the gods. In one of his lectures on Greek painting, Ruskin compares a picture of Artemis, 'moon of the morning, walking low on the hills', and Apollo 'walking on the earth, god of the morning'[56] with a picture by Turner. Turner, he says, uniquely among modern artists, senses the presence of the classical deities in English landscape: 'even near Leeds', Turner feels the influence of 'Apollo, and Artemis and Athena', and in his picture *Farnley Hall* he has 'given us the very effect of morning light', which corresponds to that influence: 'the glittering of sunshine on dewy grass, half dark; and the narrow gleam of it on the sides and head of the stag and hind'.[57]

At the scene in Talbothays, Hardy reproduces the 'grey moisture of the grass' and the 'general sea of dew', and though the stag and hind have become the sleeping forms of the cattle, the classical divinities are physically present in Tess and Angel. But Angel is hardly aware of the appropriateness of his choice of names. First he calls her Demeter, the Arcadian goddess of fertility and procreation who lost her child Persephone to the Underworld, but when he calls her Artemis, he also (unwittingly) casts himself in a classical role. Artemis, the presiding deity of the dawn light was also the virgin twin sister of Apollo, sharing with him many of his aspects and attributes, including those of hunter and bringer of death.

The dawn light over Talbothays endows all the events which take place in it with an other-wordly quality—the world not of reality, but of dreams, in which the imagination is allowed full play. As the sun rises, the 'commonplace' reasserts itself (*TD* 168), and Tess's features become 'simply feminine', changing from 'those of a divinity who could confer bliss to those of a being who craved it.' (*TD* 168). This period in the life of Tess and Angel, when the creation of light is identified with the creation of love in an Arcadian setting of pastoral innocence, bears all the marks of a 'golden age'—a period beautiful, transient, and mythical. By presenting the events of dawn in this way, Hardy once again seems to be following Pater, who, in one of his many stories about the return of the gods, says that

almost every people, as we know, has had its legend of a 'golden age' and of its return . . . and yet in truth, since we are no longer children, we might well question the advantage of the return to us of a condition of life in which, by

56 Ruskin, 'Lectures on Art', in *Works* xx. 148.
57 Ibid., xx. 151–2.

the nature of the case, the values of things would, so to speak, lie wholly on their surfaces, unless we could regain also the childish consciousness, or rather unconsciousness, in ourselves.[58]

At Talbothays, neither Tess nor Angel are able to see beyond the 'surfaces', and though their innocence is undoubtedly attractive, it depends for its existence on the preservation of an attitude of mind, a whole set of values, and a way of life which is at odds with the moral and religious climate of the modern period. The sunrise over Talbothays illuminates a 'golden age' in the life of Tess and Angel; but when the sun rises over Stonehenge, they are no longer children, and they are forced to come to terms with the harsh and pitiless light of common day.

This last great sunrise scene of the novel repeats, but changes, some of the elements which helped to create the Arcadian landscape of Talbothays. The lush floor of the Arcadian Froom Valley has given way to the wide, houseless, and empty plain, and the light which falls upon it from the sky is not the light of the Resurrection, but the light of the Apocalypse—of retribution and of judgement. Both Apollo and Christ are present, but now as the dim shadows of their former selves. The wind, playing on the supposedly Druidic temple, creates the sound of Apollo's lyre 'like the note of some gigantic one-stringed harp' (*TD* 501), but it is a harp which plays no melody, and when Tess questions Angel about the possibility of an afterlife, 'like a greater than himself, to the critical question at the critical time he did not answer.' (*TD* 504). There is a reminiscence, too, of the pagan and Christian legend of the Good Shepherd, when Tess remembers that 'one of my mother's people was a shepherd hereabouts, now I think of it. And you used to say at Talbothays that I was a heathen. So now I am at home.' (*TD* 502). But the shepherd has departed, and for Tess, the pagan innocence of Talbothays is no more. At Talbothays one kind of 'heathenism' reigned; at Stonehenge another kind comes into prominence, as Tess lies on the Druidical stone of sacrifice.

Druidical symbols have pursued Tess throughout the book. Mistletoe hung from the trees in Cranbourne Chase when she conceived her child by Alec d'Urberville (*TD* 42); it hung above her bed

---

[58] Pater, 'Denys L'Auxerrois', p. 47. In his essay 'Nature Myths and Allegories,' John Addington Symonds also pointed out that 'we cannot return to the state of thought about the world, out of which the primitive myths sprang,' but goes on to suggest that the same myths might be 'reinterpreted in a modern context' (*Essays Speculative and Suggestive* ii. 131).

at Wellbridge; and it was 'under the mistletoe' (*TD* 305) that she contemplated suicide. In solar mythology the mistletoe has special significance, since it is a spear of mistletoe by which Loki the Malicious kills Balder the sun-god. But Hardy's choice of the Druidical monument for the climax of his story may also have been intimately connected with his visit to the Turner exhibition in 1889.

One of the most dramatic water-colours in the exhibition was a study of Stonehenge (Plate 31). It was already known to admirers of Turner's work because it had been published as an engraving in his *Picturesque Views in England and Wales* in 1832, but it received special attention from the critics in 1889 because the original water-colour, which was privately owned, rarely went on public display. Ruskin knew it well, but what links Hardy's use of Stonehenge with Ruskin's account of Turner's painting is that Ruskin interprets the painting as a Druidical emblem of vengeance and retribution. In the fifth book of *Modern Painters*, the book in which Ruskin elaborates his idea of Turner as the great exponent of myth, he makes a comparison between two illustrations in the *Picturesque Views*, each of which exemplifies Turner's response to the 'two great religions of England— Druidical and Christian'.[59] The first is the Christian image. It is a view of Salisbury, dominated by its cathedral (Plate 32). It is raining, but the rain, says Ruskin, is full of 'blessing—abundant but full of brightness', and in the foreground the whole scene is presided over by the figure of the Good Shepherd. The other picture—the study of Stonehenge—is the Druidical image. 'That, also,' says Ruskin,

stands in great light; but it is the Gorgon light—the sword of Chrysaor is bared against it. The cloud of judgement hangs above. The rock pillars seem to reel before its slope, pale beneath the lightening. And nearer, in the darkness, the shepherd lies dead, his flock scattered.[60]

In the climactic scene of *Tess of the d'Urbervilles* Hardy uses the same two monuments—Salisbury Cathedral and Stonehenge—in a context which invokes their respective religious functions. Like Adam and Eve, with whom Hardy several times compares them, Tess and Angel are compelled to abandon the terrestrial paradise of their life in the Froom valley and to till the 'thorns and thistles' of the wilderness. After Angel's return from South America and Alec d'Urberville's

[59] Ruskin, *Modern Painters*, v (1860), in *Works* vii. 190.

[60] Ibid., vii. 190-1. In his *Outlines of Primitive Belief*, C. F. Keary speaks of the similarity between the solar god Balder and 'Apollo Chrysaôr, girt with a sword' (p. 370).

murder, the couple are pursued across the country by the forces of law. Their journey might have led them anywhere in England, but Hardy chooses to take them through 'the steepled city of Melchester' (*TD* 500), where 'the graceful pile of cathedral architecture rose dimly on their left hand'. Significantly, however, in a novel where light and darkness are so sharply opposed, their journey takes place at night, with the consequence that the beautiful form of the cathedral 'was lost upon them'. In Ruskin's account of the engraving, Salisbury cathedral, the rain, and the good shepherd all confer a Christian blessing on the land; but Tess and Angel, who are denied a view of that same monument, are also excluded from the blessing which it represents. Instead, they grope their way through the darkness into the 'open loneliness and black solitude' (*TD* 501) of Salisbury Plain, and to the foot of Stonehenge.

In the Turner water-colour which Hardy saw at the Royal Academy, Stonehenge stands in the aftermath of a great storm, and in keeping with the solar imagery of the novel, Hardy transforms this into a sunrise episode. But he preserves much of what Ruskin called 'the Gorgon light' of the picture. At Talbothays, the beams of the rising sun were 'active' in generating love, life, and worship; at Stonehenge, the early morning rays bring vengeance and judgement, creating strong contrasts of light and darkness: 'The eastward pillars and their architraves stood up blackly against the light, and the great flame-shaped Sunstone beyond them; and the Stone of Sacrifice midway.' (*TD* 504). As Glen Wickens points out, in this incident 'Tess knows, like the pagan speaker in [Swinburne's] "Hymn to Properpine" that, "Yea, is not even Apollo, with hair and harpstring of gold / A bitter god to follow, a beautiful god to behold?"' [61]

One of the remarkable achievements of *Tess of the d'Urbervilles* is the way in which Hardy gives concrete and visible expression to abstract ideas about the relationship between contrasting views of religious worship and the ethical implications of religious belief. His model was Turner, who, by painting the ever-changing appearance of light, was able to communicate 'the tragical mysteries of life' (*EL* 243); but for his material he drew on Müller's interpretation of solar myth, Ruskin's view of Greek legend, and perhaps most of all, Pater's fascination with the return of the ancient gods. Even more remarkable, perhaps, is the way in which Hardy synthesizes ideas and images with unobtrusive consistency throughout the narrative. The solar symbolism, the frag-

[61] G. Glen Wickens, 'Hardy and the Aesthetic Mythographers: The Myth of Demeter and Persephone in *Tess of the d'Urbervilles*', p. 103.

ments of myth and legend, and the careful manipulation of light and colour are not confined to the large set pieces, but inhere even in passing effects. One final example will show how Hardy, through a precise use of diction and vocabulary, manages to create a symbolic 'correspondence' between the simple natural effect of small insects flying in the sun, Tess's love for Angel, and the larger mythological structure of the novel. Just before naming the day of their marriage, Tess and Angel walk together in the setting November sun around Talbothays.

Looking over the damp sod in the direction of the sun, a glistening ripple of gossamer webs was visible to their eyes under the luminary, like the track of moonlight on the sea. Gnats, knowing nothing of their brief glorification, wandered across the shimmer of this pathway, irradiated as if they bore fire within them, then passed out of its line, and were quite extinct. (*TD* 256.)

9

The Well-Beloved:
The Renunciation of Art

Sculpture. 'The ideality of the art of Sculpture—each object presenting beauty or passion in an immortal abstraction from all that is
temporary and accidental—appealed in a peculiar degree to
Shelley's imagination.'[1]

In Hardy's classification of his own fiction, *Tess of the d'Urbervilles* and
Jude the Obscure appear as 'Novels of Character and Environment',
whereas *The Well-Beloved* is placed in the group entitled 'Romances
and Fantasies'. The first group, he said, 'claim a verisimilitude in
general treatment and detail', whereas in *The Well-Beloved*, 'the interest aimed at is of an ideal or subjective nature, and frankly imaginative' (*WB* viii). The similarities in plot, characterization, and
structure between *The Well-Beloved* and Hardy's other novels have
often been pointed out, and Hardy's distinction between the two
groups seems to suggest not so much a new departure, as an unusual
'subjective' treatment of themes which have occurred before. J. Hillis
Miller mentions the similarities in the relationships between Pierston
and the three Avices in *The Well-Beloved*, between Tess and her lovers
in *Tess of the d'Urbervilles*, or again between Jude and his women in
Jude the Obscure,[2] whereas Michael Millgate mentions the shared
Shelleyan obsession of Fitzpiers and Pierston—two characters with
similar surnames.[3] The idea of the wraith, 'double', or *doppelgänger*,
plays an important part in *The Mayor of Casterbridge*, but is even more
prominent in *The Well-Beloved*, and just as the action of *The Return of
the Native* is limited to the remote narrow confines of the 'Thule' of
Egdon Heath (*RN* 5), so Hardy sets the important events of *The Well-
Beloved* on the 'Ultima Thule' of Portland (*WB* 98). It is *A Pair of Blue
Eyes*, however, that is most relevant as an antecedent for *The Well-
Beloved*. Proust noticed 'the parallelism between *The Well-Beloved*,

---

[1] Dowden, The Life of Bysshe Shelley (1886), in *LN*, entry 1964.
[2] J. Hillis Miller, introduction to *The Well-Beloved*, New Wessex Edition, pp. 13–14.
[3] Michael Millgate, *Thomas Hardy*, p. 330.

where the man loves three women, [and] *A Pair of Blue Eyes*, where the woman loves three men',[4] but the similarities do not end there. Like *A Pair of Blue Eyes*, *The Well-Beloved* is a highly stylized narrative in which repetition, re-enactment, and rehearsal take precedence over 'verisimilitude'. Both novels are about erotic experience, refined and distilled in the minds of their protagonists, and both are intensely 'subjective', to use Hardy's own word, in that they express not so much events in the author's life as his attitudes of mind or emotional experiences. Perhaps the most important feature of *The Well-Beloved*, however, is that the hero is a creative artist, for one of the themes of the novel is the relationship between the erotic life and the creative life. Erotic fantasy—the endless pursuit of a female ideal—and the act of creation come together within the eye of the beholder, since it is the eye of Jocelyn Pierston which searches for the forms of the inspirational 'well-beloved', and it is that same eye which translates the forms into works of sculpture. The denouement of the story concerns the onset of Pierston's 'blindness' concurrent with what Hardy calls 'the strange death of the sensuous side of Jocelyn's nature' (*WB* 209), and it is here that *The Well-Beloved* comes close to *Jude the Obscure*. Though the former is 'subjective' in its tone, and the latter polemical and 'objective', there is common ground between them in Hardy's treatment of visual experience. Both are concerned with the effect on the mind of 'loss of sight', and both deal—one subjectively, the other objectively—with Hardy's turning away from a sensuous delight in visual forms. In the final chapter of this book we shall see that Hardy's treatment of visual experience is markedly different in *Jude the Obscure* from that in previous novels. Part of the reason for this is provided by the narrative of *The Well-Beloved*, and most especially by the different endings—one written in 1891, the other in 1897.

Physical Appearances in *The Well-Beloved*

Compared with the visual plenitude of the preceding novels, *The Well-Beloved* is spare, economical, and stylized. The stress upon repetition and parallelism in the narrative is supported by the repetition of visual motifs; Hardy emphasizes certain physical characteris-

---

[4] Quoted by Miller, introduction to *The Well-Beloved*, pp. 15–16. See also Ch. 2, n. 31.

tics of the 'Isle of Slingers' to the exclusion of others, and he draws attention to the shared physical properties of his characters at the expense of their differences. Throughout the novel, form—shape, outline, direction—is more prominent than colour; little attention is paid to local or atmospheric, aerial perspective, and where Hardy employs pictorialism, the 'pictures' resemble two-dimensional diagrams or charts. The scene in which Pierston watches the burial of the first Avice from a distance has much in common with some of the scenes in *A Pair of Blue Eyes*.

The level line of the sea horizon rose above the surface of the isle, a ruffled patch in the mid-distance as usual marking the Race, whence many a Lycidas had gone, 'visiting the bottom of the monstrous world'; but had not been blest with a poet as a friend. Against the stretch of water, where a school of mackerel twinkled in the afternoon light, was defined, in addition to the distant lighthouse, a church with its tower, standing about a quarter of a mile off, near the edge of the cliff. The churchyard gravestones could be seen in profile against the same vast spread of watery babble and unrest. . . . The coffin, with its twelve legs, crawled across the isle, while around and beneath it the flashing lights from the sea and the school of mackerel were reflected; a fishing-boat, far out in the Channel, being momentarily discernible under the coffin also. (*WB* 78–9.)

In this extract the juxtaposition of island and sea by the reduction of perspective distance, in the context of Milton's 'Lycidas', suggests a kind of mental foreshortening in which image and idea are closely related. This intimate connection between the visual and the conceptual is maintained throughout the story, in such a way that the repeated visual motifs gradually become less important as observed phenomena and more important as elements within the mental experience of Jocelyn Pierston. This is particularly clear in the presentation of the physical appearance of characters. Pierston's first response to women is always a visual one, but his observations are idealized through reference to works of art. Marcia, for example, appears to him as 'A Juno': 'Nothing more classical', adds the narrator, 'had he ever seen.' (*WB* 19–20). The 'perfect and passionless repose' of the face of the second Avice 'imparted a Minerva cast to ' the profile' (*WB* 90), and she shows a profile 'not unlike that of one of the three goddesses in Rubens's 'Judgement of Paris,' while the 'curve of sound' made by her voice 'was as artistic as any line of beauty ever struck by his pencil—as satisfying as the curves of her who was the World's Desire.' (*WB* 96–7).

As for the physical properties of the 'island' itself, they are most important in defining its role in the creative life of the sculptor. The island is both connected yet separated from the mainland. The perilous pebble-bank, the 'precarious' wooden bridge (*WB* 21), and later, the lines of the railway, provide fragile links with the shore, which are frequently broken by storms and tempests. In stormy weather, the narrator assures the reader, 'the "Island" was an island still.' (*WB* 25). Yet the connections with the mainland are important, since the island provides Pierston, both literally and metaphorically, with the raw material of his art. It affords not only the rock in which he sculpts the shape of the 'well-beloved', it is also the source, the spring, or the 'well', from which he derives the inspiration for that sculpture. The activity of sculpting itself is practised exclusively in the metropolis, yet the links back to the island are always present. Pierston's ghostly father, for example—one of many ghostly fathers in the book whose presence is felt but not seen—sends the geometrically fashioned 'cubes' of raw material to London from the island, just as in a more obscure way he communicates to his son the characteristic feature of the island temperament through the laws of heredity. Since the island itself is a 'single block of limestone' (*WB* 3), the stone pieces quarried from it are themselves miniature islands. Each one comes to London, like Pierston himself, as a hereditary 'chip off the old block'; each is 'imbued with' its island 'associations'; each calls up the '*genius loci* whence it came' (*WB* 85); and each contains the typical island 'shape'. In the case of the rock, the single most prominent feature is its verticality, its 'steepness':

The towering rock, the houses above houses, one man's doorstep rising behind his neighbour's chimney, the gardens hung up by one edge to the sky, the vegetables growing on apparently almost vertical planes, the unity of the whole island as a solid and single block of limestone four miles long, were no longer familiar and commonplace ideas. All now stood dazzlingly unique and white against the tinted sea, and the sun flashed on infinitely stratified walls of oolite, 'the melancholy ruins of cancelled cycles'. (*WB* 3–4.)

The quotation from Shelley's *Prometheus Unbound*—'The melancholy ruins / Of cancelled cycles'—helps to identify something of the meaning which Hardy attributes to the frequently repeated references to the rising stratification of the island. Layer upon layer of rock, the 'infinitely stratified walls of oolite', suggest the passing of great spans of geological time, and the human habitations rising one above the other represent the most recent 'cycle'. Historical time, like geological time, is cyclical as men from 'Norman, Anglian, Roman, Balearic-British times' (*WB* 76) have built their houses on the island. But these houses are all constructed from the rock, and to complete 'the unity of the whole', even the people themselves derive their temperament from the same rock. Pierston understands the character of the third Avice because, as he says, he knows 'the perfect and pure quarry she was dug from.' (*WB* 111). In other words, the visual presentation of sheer rock-face, 'the steep whereon the houses at the entrance to the Isle were perched like grey pigeons on a roof-side' (*WB* 148), provides a permanent physical record of the passage of time: on this island time has become materialized in stone, and age upon age is petrified in the very substance from which Pierston creates his images of the 'well-beloved'.

Set against the strong vertical of the island rock stands the equally strong horizontal of the sea—'the level line of the sea horizon'—and the sea, whose presence permeates the action as prominently as the rock, is also connected with the passage of time. On one side of the island is Deadman's Bay, the resting-place of 'those who had gone down in vessels of war, East Indiamen, barges, brigs, and ships of the Armada' (*WB* 12), and on the other side is the 'tameless', 'never pacified' Race, 'whence many a Lycidas had gone' (*WB* 78). In contrast to the rock of the island, Deadman's Bay, The Race and The Shambles provide no permanent record of the men and women who have disappeared beneath the waves; here the dead are merely rolled 'to oneness on [the] . . . restless sea-bed.' (*WB* 13). Whereas the rock is still and unchanging, the sea is ever moving, ever in a state of flux, and the sea, like time itself, threatens to devour Pierston in the first ending of the novel and to destroy the two lovers in the second ending. The novel offers, then, two concepts of time: the 'repeated cycles' of time, represented by the verticality of the rock, and the destructive 'fast' time, represented by the flow of water, and these two concepts have a direct bearing on Hardy's treatment of the 'well-beloved'. In one of her aspects the 'well-beloved' is related to the theme of repetition. Her characteristics are permanently recorded in the faces of many women; but those same characteristics are transmitted from mother to daughter, daughter to granddaughter. Hardy's note on the original idea for the novel supports this reading. 'The story of a face', he wrote in 1889, 'which goes through three generations or more, would make a fine novel or poem on the passage of

Time. The differences in personality to be ignored.' (*EL* 284). This idea, he added, 'was to some extent carried out in the novel *The Well-Beloved*, [and] the poem entitled "Heredity", etc.' In the poem, heredity is conceived of as a time-defying force, passing unchanged from generation to generation; it is 'the eternal thing in man, / That heeds no call to die.'

The destructive power of time, on the other hand, represented visually in the novel by the sea, also has its influence on the 'well-beloved' and corresponds to the passing corporeal frame in which the immortal hereditary power is temporarily lodged. The bodies of the three Avices are young, grow old and die, Pierston and Marcia wither; but the inherited characteristics continue to be transmitted.

The Significance of Repetition

In *A Pair of Blue Eyes* Hardy explored a similar theme. It describes the career of Elfride Swancourt as she passes through, and fundamentally changes, the lives of four men. For the two most prominent of these, Steven Smith and Henry Knight, Elfride exists principally as an 'image', and that image is summed up most vividly in the way in which her face (especially her eponymous 'blue eyes') occurs again and again in the drawings of Steven Smith. There is, however, a strong suggestion of metempsychosis in the story. Elfride and her grandmother are 'alike as peas' (*PBE* 286), and Elfride re-enacts many of the events of her grandmother's life, and becomes, like her grandmother before her, Lady Luxellian. In *The Well-Beloved* the roles are reversed, and the single male character pursues a feminine ideal as it inhabits the bodies of a number of women. In both novels the relationships are highly stylized and all involve repeated motifs, but even in other novels there is the strong suggestion of a similar kind of repetition. Seen in one way, the romantic involvements of Ethelberta, Eustacia, and Lucetta can be interpreted as a series of repeated patterns; and in both *Tess of the d'Urbervilles* and *Jude the Obscure*, the triangular relationships between male and female characters are based upon an arrangement of complements, contrasts, and parallels.

We can discover one source of this patterning in Hardy's own temperament and his life-long mental pursuit of an intangible ineffable female ideal—'professional beauty chases' as he calls them. His diaries and notebooks record the way in which, like Pierston, he was moved to an unusual degree by casual glimpses of women. One diary entry for May 29th, 1888, will stand for many similar ones:

That girl in the omnibus had one of those faces of marvellous beauty which are seen casually in the streets but never among one's friends. It was perfect in its softened classicality—a Greek face translated into English. Moreover she was fair, and her hair pale chestnut. Where do these women come from? Who marries them? Who knows them? (*EL* 288.)

The hints of nympholeptic and racial preoccupations in this entry suggest a close link with the themes of *The Well-Beloved*, but it is Hardy's spontaneous narrative impulse, an impulse expressed in the biographical questions which express the close link between the erotic and the creative in Hardy's mind. In this respect *The Well-Beloved* comes closer to the sources of Hardy's own creative life than his other novels. In this story romantic involvement and creativity are intimately associated, and undoubtedly Hardy's inner life once again provided the main stimulus for the connection. Yet the idea may well have received encouragement from elsewhere. Hardy certainly knew the work of Rossetti, and a substantial part of Rossetti's *œuvre* was related to an impulse very similar to that which Hardy describes in *The Well-Beloved*.

Rossetti died in 1882, and almost immediately the Royal Academy and the Burlington Fine Arts Club put on large retrospective exhibitions of his graphic work. The public had never seen Rossetti's painting and drawing on this scale before, and many of the critics were struck by the recurrence of similar facial features in the paintings of the later years. Some were 'repelled by an insistent monotony of facial type; a facial type too unusual to be generally considered ideally beautiful',[5] and Sidney Colvin felt that Rossetti had 'become the slave of his own predelictions', who, having found 'a particular cast of beauty' which 'he repeats again and again', had created 'a series of mystic and symbolic . . . fanciful, female incarnations'.[6] *The Times* critic, however, described Rossetti's achievement in terms which closely resemble those which Hardy attributed to his fictional artist. The later work, he said, 'had given rise to the prejudice that [Rossetti] actually could paint but one face, and in consequence kept repeating himself with little change or modification', but the same critic went on to explain how Rossetti had 'concentrated all his energy on the development of a type of female loveliness which in the history of art will remain identified with his name'.[7] The many records and

---

[5] 'Exhibitions', *The Art Journal*, NS 21 (1883), p. 61.
[6] Sidney Colvin, 'Rossetti as a Painter', *Magazine of Art*, 6 (1883), p. 183.
[7] *The Times*, 13 Jan. 1883, p. 4.

reminiscences published in this period express differing attitudes to, and give different explanations for, Rossetti's obsession with a single female type. William Sharp, in an early study published in 1882, said that although Rossetti 'became almost a slave to one type . . . his invariable defence of this was that it was to him an ideal face, or at any rate the highest in all qualities that appealed to him which he had ever seen'.[8] Reviewing the large London exhibition of 1883, F. G. Stephens recognized the connection between the repeated motif of the later paintings and the creative impulse itself: 'Rossetti's "mystery"', he said, 'was the secret of Beauty, and his later works attest him searching it and illustrating it in many ways'.[9] His principal example was the *Astarte Syriaca* (see Plate 16) the torch-bearers of which 'may have been intended to represent the artist himself as poet and as a painter, thus doubly an acolyte of Beauty', he suggested. Rossetti's brother claimed that Rossetti regarded this painting 'as his most exalted performance' because it repeated and summed up many of his aims and aspirations. It contained, said William Michael, 'his utmost intensity of thinking, feeling, and method'; it was 'an ideal of the mystery of beauty, offering a sort of combined quintessence of what he had endeavoured in earlier years to embody in the two several [*sic*] types of *Sibylla Palmifera* and *Lilith*.'[10] The connection between the mental attitudes of Jocelyn Pierston and Rossetti himself is strengthened by the themes of the two prose pieces *Hand and Soul* and *St Agnes of the Intercession* which were reprinted in his brother's edition of the *Collected Works*. In the first, a medieval painter, Chiaro dell'Erma, discovers in dream the true fount of creative inspiration. His own soul appears to him in female form, and admonishes him to 'paint me thus, as I am, to know me'.[11] Joseph Knight was quick to point out the connection between fiction and reality, and the fact that much of what Rossetti 'ascribes to Chiaro dell'Erma is . . . [in reality] his own experience'. 'The aspirations', he said, 'which drove his hero to be a painter are those by which he was himself stirred', and Rossetti, like Chiaro (and, of course, like Pierston), was, Knight said, motivated exclusively by 'a revelation from within'.[12] The second, *St Agnes of the Intercession*, is a fragment, but it, too, bears upon the themes of *The*

[8] William Sharp, *Dante Gabriel Rossetti: A Record and a Study* (1882), p. 196.
[9] F. G. Stephens. 'The Early Works of Rossetti', *The Portfolio*, 8 (1883), p. 115.
[10] William Michael Rossetti, *Dante Gabriel Rossetti as Designer and Writer*, p. 99.
[11] *The Collected Works of Dante Gabriel Rossetti*, ed. William M. Rossetti (1901), i. 394.
[12] Joseph Knight, *Life of Dante Gabriel Rossetti*, p. 51.

Well-Beloved. It is a story of metempsychosis, in which the hero discovers that he and his wife are reincarnations of a Renaissance artist and his lover.

Of course, Pierston is not a portrait of Rossetti, but there are sufficient correspondences between the life of the sculptor and the life of the painter to suggest an analogy. Like Rossetti, Pierston becomes 'a one-part man' (*WB* 64); he compulsively repeats an image in sculpture, and the titles of those pieces are strongly reminiscent of Rossetti's works; they are 'Liliths' (*WB* 101), 'Aphrodite', and Astarte figures. Like Rossetti's Chiaro dell'Erma, and like Rossetti himself, Pierston pursues relentlessly the image of his own soul or 'Psyche' (*WB* 116), and like Chiaro who saw his own soul in a dream, Pierston's creations are similar 'dream figures' (*WB* 49)—it is his 'dreams he translated into plaster' (*WB* 51). The transmigration of the soul, already touched on in *A Pair of Blue Eyes*, was a theme which also preoccupied Rossetti. One of its forms is that of the *doppelgänger* so powerfully embodied in an early drawing entitled *How They Met Themselves*, and in Hardy's novel the identity of the 'well-beloved' migrates from body to body as 'his wraith in a changed sex' (*WB* 158).

The Failure of Inspiration

He would not have stood where he did in the ranks of an imaginative profession if he had not been at the mercy of every haunting of the fancy that can beset a man. It was in his weaknesses as a citizen and a national unit that his strength lay as an artist. (*WB* 101.)

Hardy's remark about the source of Pierston's creativity is strangely applicable to Rossetti, and bears closely upon Hardy's own dilemma. Pierston's obsession is both a blessing and a disease. It is related in an indirect way to his creative life, and it provides him with 'sober business' (*WB* 51); but it is also 'his doom—his curse' (*WB* 156). The *Well-Beloved* can be read, like Shakespeare's *Tempest*, as an allegory of the abandonment of the 'sober business' of creating art, but it can also be interpreted as a comment on the release from an obsession or a 'curse'. This is most clearly evident in the form of the two endings. When Hardy first conceived the plot of *The Well-Beloved*, the 'sobre business' upon which he was currently engaged was the writing of *Jude the Obscure*, and the first ending was completed before Hardy began the later novel. The second ending, however, was added after *Jude the Obscure* had been published. J. Hillis Miller would have us believe that the conclusions to *The Well-Beloved* are alternatives; each, he suggests, is of equal status, and the 'problem of endings is thematised in the story'.[13] His thesis is an ingenious one, but it is not strictly in accordance with the facts. Whereas Hardy included a 'ghostly' ending in *The Return of the Native*, he never, at any time, offered his reader alternative conclusions to *The Well-Beloved*. They remain mutually exclusive ways of drawing the book to a close, each providing a quite separate interpretation of the central theme of the novel, and standing in a different relationship to the novel written between them.

In the version of the *The Well-Beloved* which appeared in 1892 in the *Illustrated London News*, Pearston (as his name is spelt in this version) marries Marcia, parts from her, and, assuming she is dead, marries the third Avice. When Henri Leverre, a former lover of Avice, returns to the island, Pearston (rather like Philotson in *Jude the Obscure*) decides to give her up rather than force her to stay against her will. He announces that he will go in search of Marcia, but instead attempts suicide in The Race. The attempt fails, and Marcia mysteriously returns to nurse him, though her classical features are now reduced to 'a parchment-covered skull'.[14] Cynical laughter provides the 'ending to [Pearston's] would-be romantic history'.[15]

In the 1897 ending Pierston does not marry the third Avice. Instead, she elopes with Henri, Marcia's son. Meanwhile, the sculptor, who has caught a chill at the burial of the second Avice, hangs uncertainly between life and death. Marcia returns to nurse him, and at this point there is a major thematic change. In the later ending, Pierston slowly recovers his health, and as he does so, he comes to the realization that his artistic powers have deserted him. As he returns to normal life, he discovers that he can 'no longer attach a definite sentiment to images of beauty recalled from the past', and that 'his appreciativeness was capable of exercising itself only on utilitarian matters' (*WB* 209). Though it would be inappropriate to insist upon too rigid a parallel, Pierston's spontaneous renunciation of art seems to have some general correspondence with Hardy's own decision to abandon novel-writing. Pierston's sculpture, like Hardy's novels, had brought him public acclaim, but for both sculptor and author, late middle-age was the time to abandon the old profession.

[13] Miller, introduction to *The Well-Beloved*, p. 19.
[14] Ibid., p. 248.
[15] Ibid., p. 249.

It is the terms of Pierston's withdrawal from the springs of his own inspiration, however, which have such an important bearing on *Jude the Obscure*. The final proof of his change in artistic sensibility comes when he returns from the private domain—the 'Island'—to the public domain—London. He goes to his studio, where he is repelled and revolted by the creations of his own hand, and when he visits the National Gallery, his response to the productions of other artists is similar:

On another afternoon they went to the National Gallery, to test his taste in paintings, which had formerly been good. As she had expected, it was just the same with him there. He saw no more to move him, he declared, in the time-defying presentations of Perugino, Titian, Sebastiano, and other statuesque creators than in the work of the pavement artist they had passed on their way. (*WB* 213.)

It is as if Pierston has lost the capacity for sensuous visual pleasure, and is no longer able to 'live in the eye' as he once did. Though this is undoubtedly a metaphor for the general loss of vital energy, it is significant that Hardy has chosen this particular manifestation of creativity to stand for something more general. Here, once again, the techniques and preoccupations of *The Well-Beloved* comes close to those of *Jude the Obscure*. For many of Hardy's characters, visual pleasure is a source of insight and delight; in *Jude the Obscure* this is not so. The world which they inhabit is drained of light and colour, and their loss of 'vision' parallels in the 'objective' realm the 'strange death of the sensuous side of Jocelyn's nature' (*WB* 209) in *The Well-Beloved*.

10

Jude the Obscure: The Retreat from the Light

'"One must be able", Millet said, "to make use of the trivial for the expression of the sublime." They (Millet and Whitman) both insisted that the artist must deal with the average and typical, not with the exceptional.'[1]

Jude the Obscure is Hardy's farewell to the art of novel-writing. It was serialized in *Harper's Magazine* in 1894, and appeared in book form the following year. Though Hardy himself suggested that it bore a resemblance to 'former productions of [his] pen' (*JO* viii), its mood of unrelieved gloom and sense of desperation set it apart from his previous novels. This is particularly true of the way in which he treats the visible world. In *The Woodlanders* and *Tess of the d'Urbervilles* the pessimistic view of human relationships is counteracted to some extent by moments of joy and exaltation—moments which often take the form of a positive delight in external visible phenomena. Scenes of active visual pleasure—Giles Winterborne observing the golden abundance of the apple orchards or revelling in the colours of the sunset on High Stoy Hill, Tess's joyful arrival in the bright sunshine of the valley of the Froom or her courtship of Angel in the sunny meadows around Talbothays—offset sombre periods of pain and unhappiness. In *Jude the Obscure* there are very few, if any, such moments; and it is as if, in this final novel, Hardy had deliberately excluded his characters from experiences of visual pleasure. The title of the novel is important in this respect. The word 'obscure', usually taken as a description of Jude Fawley and his social status, is also applicable to the visual tone of the book. The dictionary offers a number of meanings, many of which involve the deprivation of visual sensation. 'Enveloped in darkness', 'approaching black, dark, sombre', 'hardly perceptible to the eye', 'devoid or deficient in light; dark, dim, hence gloomy, dismal'[2] are some of them, and there is evidence

---

[1] Havelock Ellis, 'Whitman', in *The New Spirit* (1890), p. 107, in *LN*, entry 1701.
[2] *Oxford English Dictionary*.

in the novel itself that this was one set of meanings which Hardy wished to invoke by this choice of title. For example, as Little Father Time travels to his new home at Marygreen, Hardy tells us that for him, the houses, the willows, the *obscure* fields beyond, were apparently not regarded as brick residences, pollards, meadows; but as human dwellings in the abstract, vegetation, and the *wide dark* world (*JO* 334; my emphasis). The whole setting of *Jude the Obscure* is so 'wide' and 'dark' that when Edmund Gosse reviewed the novel in 1896, he thought that Hardy 'wilfully deprives himself of a great element of his strength'[3] by restricting his imaginative palette.

Darkness, of course, is not the prerogative of this novel, and many of the others contain powerful nocturnal effects. Much of the action in *Far from the Madding Crowd* takes place in darkness; in *The Return of the Native*, Egdon Heath is frequently swathed in shadow, and Eustacia Vye presides over the heath as Queen of Night; the woods of Little Hintock have about them a sinister primeval darkness, and many of the climactic moments in *Tess of the d'Urbervilles*—Tess's seduction, for example—take place under the cloak of night. In each of these novels, however, darkness and light stand in sharp contrast to each other, and the brightness of the sunlight is all the more vivid for the presence of the darkness which threatens to envelop it. The psychologist Alexander Bain described this effect as 'The Law of Relativity', suggesting that the human mind only comprehends sensations through a process of comparison and contrast—that we only understand light through its removal or withdrawal.[4] As early as *Far from the Madding Crowd* Hardy extended the application of this law from the physical to the moral realm. In that novel and in subsequent ones, darkness and night are often suggestive of moral blindness and human failing—of a lack of en*light*enment. The clear light of day, on the other hand, often suggests moral clear-sightedness, and frequently sunlight is associated with joy, vitality, and exuberance—a delight in consciousness itself. The capacity for seeing, for interpreting correctly what 'the eye brings in', is simultaneously visual and moral, and characters like Cytherea Graye, Diggory Venn, Elizabeth-Jane Newsome, and Giles Winterborne are all gifted with considerable insight as well as sharpness of eyesight. Cytherea Graye possesses the freshness of youthful perception (*DR* 18), but Gabriel Oak takes a more philosophical

---

[3] Edmund Gosse, 'Cosmopolis', in *Thomas Hardy: The Critical Heritage*, ed. R. G. Cox, p. 265.

[4] Alexander Bain, *The Senses and the Intellect*, p. 8.

stance, 'meditatively [looking] upon the horizon of circumstances without any special regard to his own standpoint in the midst.' (*FMC* 338). Diggory Venn is more active as an observer, and has an 'eye which glared . . . strangely through his stain', and which was 'keen as that of a bird of prey, and blue as autumn mist' (*RN* 9). Elizabeth-Jane combines penetration with meditation, and this is perceptible in her eyes. As she watches Farfrae dancing, she is 'thoughtful yet much interested, her eyes beaming with a longing lingering light, as if Nature had been advised by Correggio in their creation.' (*MC* 121). The watching of Giles Winterborne and Marty South is intuitive rather than analytical. They bestow upon the woods of Little Hintock a 'clear gaze', whereas others give the woods only 'casual glimpses', and the clarity of that gaze allows them insights into the working of nature which may be denied to the casual observer. *Jude the Obscure* is unusual among Hardy's novels in having no observer or intelligent watcher who actively contemplates the unfolding of events. On the contrary, in this novel none of the characters is endowed with a well-developed visual sensibility, and even though at various stages of their lives both Jude and Sue are involved with aspects of the crafts and techniques of design, neither takes any spontaneous pleasure in visual effects. The reason is that they are both, in their different ways, prey to what Hardy calls 'the modern vice of unrest' (*JO* 98). Watching, as every artist knows, is best done silently and statically, and the watchers of the previous novels were often still and taciturn. Not so Jude Fawley and Sue Bridehead. Their personal problems are so great that their life together is divided by incessant discussion and perpetual motion.

In Hardy's novels it is stillness rather than travel which broadens the mind. Travel—the desire for movement, whether it is merely to Budmouth or to Paris—is often (as in the case of Eustacia Vye or Felice Charmond) associated with escapism, while the necessity for it, as in the case of Tess Durbeyfield, is linked with a species of hunting or being hunted. The method of conveyance is also important. Travel by horse, wagon, or on foot at least allows characters to see or be seen. Giles and Grace can observe the countryside on their journey from Sherton Abbas, and Gabriel Oak can see Bathsheba clearly whether she is on her wagon or her horse. The railway train is a very different matter, and it is significant that Sue and Jude spend such a high proportion of their time in railway carriages. The railway station, as Sue points out, is now the centre of town life rather than the

30. J. M. W. Turner: *The Angel Standing in the Sun*. 1846. Tate Gallery, London,
Turner bequest (785×785 cm)

31. J. M. W. Turner: *Stonehenge, Wiltshire. c.* 1827. Engraved by R. Wallis for H. L. Lloyd, *Picturesque Views of England and Wales from Drawings by J. M. W. Turner.* 1832-8

32. J. M. W. Turner: *Salisbury, Wiltshire. c.* 1827. Engraved by R. Wallis for H. L. Lloyd, *Picturesque Views of England and Wales from Drawings by J. M. W. Turner.* 1832-8

cathedral (*JO* 160). Their constant recourse to this mechanical and utilitarian form of transport is a symbol of their modernity, but it is also symptomatic of an indifference to visual beauty. 'No one', said Ruskin, 'would travel in that manner who could help it,' because 'it transmutes a man from a traveller into a living parcel.'[5] In *Jude the Obscure* the list of towns through which the two 'Ishmaelites' (as Hardy calls them) pass, reads like a gazeteer of the south of England. For Ruskin such travel deprived man of his humanity, because it deprived him of his eyes; it forced him to part 'with the nobler characteristics of his humanity for the sake of a planetary power of locomotion'. 'Do not ask him to admire anything', he said; 'you might as well ask the wind.'

If Sue's and Jude's responses to visual stimuli are inhibited by incessant movement, they are further frustrated by introspection and discussion, for again, of all Hardy's characters, they are the most articulate and talkative, *Jude the Obscure* having the highest proportion of dialogue of any of his novels. Hardy had previously hinted at the contrast between watching and talking. Oak is silent and observant; Yeobright is talkative but 'blind'. Winterborne with his 'clear gaze' is taciturn, whereas Fitzpiers, who cultivates his 'inner visions', has a tendency to lecture his listeners. In the case of Sue and Jude, existential anxieties, problems about faith, and doubt about action and moral judgement, and above all about the value and status of marriage, are expressed in debate, discussion, and argument, all of which allow no time to observe or contemplate those things lying beyond the immediate sphere of interest. It is as if their anxieties actually generate a form of sensory deprivation, which forces them to exist in a kind of limbo, cut off and remote from external sources of pleasure and joy.

An episode late in the novel demonstrates this very clearly when set against a similar event in *Tess of the d'Urbervilles*. In the earlier novel Tess and Angel, having decided to marry, walk together in the water-meadows which surround Talbothays. The strength of Tess's feelings for Angel is expressed indirectly through the intensity and brilliance of the light and the colour of the surroundings.

Her feelings almost filled her ears like a babble of waves, and surged up to her eyes. She put her hand in his, and thus they went on, to a place where the

---

[5] Ruskin, 'The Lamp of Beauty', in *The Seven Lamps of Architecture* (1849), in *Works* viii. 159.

reflected sun glared up from the river, under a bridge, with a molten-metallic glow that dazzled their eyes, though the sun itself was hidden by the bridge. . . . Upon this river-brink they lingered till the fog began to close round them —which was very early in the evening at this time of the year—settling on the lashes of her eyes, where it rested like crystals, and on his brows and hair. (*TD* 248–9.)

The couple are silent; they enjoy each other's company through a shared pleasure in the sights around them. Visual excitement and emotional excitement are closely allied, and the couple's attachment is celebrated in a kind of natural coronation when the crystals of mist settle upon them. In *Jude the Obscure* Sue and Jude take a very similar walk. As in *Tess of the d'Urbervilles*, it takes place in the countryside, and it celebrates a possible forthcoming marriage. Sue and Jude, while staying at Albrickham, have received word of their respective divorces. They are now free to marry again, and Sue

proposed that they should take a walk in the fields, even if they had to put up with a cold dinner on account of it. Jude agreed, and Sue went upstairs and prepared to start, putting on a joyful coloured gown in observance of her liberty; seeing which Jude put on a lighter tie.

'Now we'll strut arm and arm', he said, 'like any other engaged couple. We've a legal right to.' (*JO* 311.)

What is spontaneous with Tess and Angel has become studied with Sue and Jude. Their desire to be like 'any other engaged couple' is deeply self-conscious, and the celebration fails.

They rambled out of the town, and along a path over the low-lying lands that bordered it, though these were frosty now, and the extensive seed-fields were bare of colour and produce. The pair, however, were so absorbed in their own situation that their surroundings were little in their consciousness.

'Well, my dearest, the result of all this is that we can marry after a decent interval.' (*JO* 311.)

Here is a double perspective, that of the characters and that of the reader. Sue and Jude are so obsessed by their problems that the sights of the natural world fail to penetrate their consciousness; they are effectively denied the pleasure of sight. The reader is permitted to see, however, that even were they endowed with the power of observation, they would derive little pleasure in a world which is barren, fruitless, and without colour. In the episode in *Tess of the d'Urbervilles* the vibrancy of light and colour is simultaneously *seen* by the characters and *interpreted* by the reader as the objectification of powerful feeling. In *Jude the Obscure* there is no such continuity. The landscape, though unseen by Sue and Jude, is, nevertheless, a potent symbol of their desolation.

Though *Jude the Obscure* is not especially memorable for its landscape settings, architectural forms play an important part in its visual patterning. In certain respects, Hardy's use of architecture is reminiscent of *A Laodicean*, and many of the conversations between freethinking Paula Power and her conservative architect George Somerset about the merits of Gothic or Greek style anticipate the exchanges between Sue and Jude. When Jude proposes a visit to Wardour Castle, for example, Sue exclaims:

'Wardour is Gothic ruins—and I hate Gothic!'
'No. Quite otherwise. It is a classic building—Corinthian, I think; with a lot of pictures.'
'Ah—that will do. I like the sound of Corinthian. We'll go.' (*JO* 162.)

Though Sue Bridehead is a much more aggressive neo-pagan than Paula Power, and Jude's early commitment to medievalism is much narrower than Somerset's historicist eclecticism, nevertheless, as in *A Laodicean*, Hardy draws freely on the vocabulary of architecture to lend substance to his picture of Christminster. When, for example, Jude first enters the city at night, he is impressed by 'crocketed pinnacles and indented battlements', by 'porticoes, oriels, doorways of enriched and florid middle-age design.' (*JO* 92). The architecture of Christminster makes him think of

the worthies who had spent their youth within these reverend walls, and whose souls had haunted them in their maturer age. Some of them, by the accidents of his reading, loomed out in his fancy disproportionately large by comparison with the rest. The brushing of the wind against the angles, buttresses and door-jambs were as the passing of these only other inhabitants, the tappings of each ivy leaf on its neighbour were as the mutterings of their mournful souls. (*JO* 92.)

What is striking about a passage like this is that Jude's response to the architecture of Christminster is strictly speaking not visual at all. He does not enjoy the intrisic beauty of the buildings, the proportions, or the texture of the stone; instead, the architecture simply stimulates his romantic ideas. Under the cloak of darkness the fragments he is able to see are immediately assimilated into his private world, and call up the ghosts of his reading which 'loom out in his fancy'. Even by the light of day, moreover, he does not actually see the architecture of the city. Instead, he becomes the practical man 'feeling' the mouldings and observing the traceries simply in order to give an account of how long each took to produce or how much effort was required in their making. When he visits the mason's yard, his account of what he finds there resembles that of a student who has recently been studying Ruskin's chapter entitled 'The Nature of Gothic' in *The Stones of Venice*.[6]

He asked for the foreman, and looked round among the new traceries, mullions, transoms, shafts, pinnacles, and battlements standing on the bankers half worked, or waiting to be removed. They were marked by precision, mathematical straightness, smoothness, exactitude: there in the old walls were the broken lines of the original idea; jagged curves, disdain of precision, irregularity, disarray. (*JO* 98.)

By night, Christminster is a city populated by the dead worthies of Jude's imagination; by day, it is a place where a man can get work. He never enjoys it for its own sake; instead, 'the numberless architectural pages around him he read, naturally, less as an artist-critic of their forms than as an artizan and comrade of the dead handicraftsmen' (*JO* 97).

   Hardy is very careful to exclude Jude from the enjoyment of architectural forms which he sometimes shares with the reader. There are vivid glimpses of Shaston and of Melchester Cathedral which only the reader is permitted to 'see', and on one occasion the exclusion of Jude Fawley from this kind of sensuous awareness is quite explicit. Jude has just parted from Arabella after spending the night with her in Christminster. Waiting for the train to take him to Alfredston,

he strolled mechanically into the city as far as to the Fourways, where he stood as he had so often stood before, and surveyed Chief Street stretching ahead, with its college after college, in picturesqueness unrivalled except by such Continental vistas as the Street of Palaces in Genoa; the lines of the buildings being as distinct in the morning air as in an architectural drawing. (*JO* 223.)

Momentarily the reader is lulled into the belief that here at last Jude is permitted the solace of visual delight, the enjoyment of the fine outlines of the buildings against the clear morning sky. But the voice

---

   [6] In this Ruskin wrote that 'imperfection is in some sort essential to all that we know of life. . . . Neither architecture nor any other noble work of man can be good unless it be imperfect'. Ruskin, *Works* x. 203–4.

of the narrator dispels this suggestion. 'Jude', he says, 'was far from seeing or criticizing these things; they were hidden by an indescribable consciousness of Arabella's midnight contiguity, a sense of degradation at his revived experiences with her.' (*JO* 223). As in the episode of the walk outside Albrickham, in which the response of Sue and Jude to the visible world was inhibited by pressure of circumstances, Jude's inner turmoil obscures his sight, so that the beauty of the architecture of Christminster is permanently 'hidden' from his eyes. In the country walk, the surroundings of Sue and Jude were 'little in their consciousness' (*JO* 311); here in Christminster, Jude is blinded by his 'consciousness' of Arabella; and throughout the novel, circumstances persistently conspire to cloud the working of the eye.

Hardy's treatment of the architecture is characteristic of the way in which he manipulates visual language in *Jude the Obscure*. Jude's response to the buildings of Christminster—at one moment he idealizes them, at the next his attitude is simply utilitarian and practical— is part of a failure to reconcile the ideal and the real. The narrative is filled with unresolved conflicts generated by this problem. Jude's attachment to both his spiritual cousin and his fleshly wife, and his inability to compromise his ambitions in the face of impossible circumstances, are both aspects of a personality divided within itself. When we examine some of the other structures of the book—structures which include the visual patterning—we find similar divisions at work, and similar oppositions. The realm of the ideal is constantly being invaded by the real. From the moment that Jude's daydreaming is interrupted by the flying pig's pizzle, human ideals, high-minded principles, and romantic visions are for ever being challenged by demands of quite a different nature. The harsh, the ugly, the commonplace, and the brutal are always a threat to idealism, and Hardy seems to offer no possibility of a compromise or a reconciliation between the two.

Locally within the text, this opposition expresses itself in scenes and episodes in which tenderness and violence, the romantic and the pedestrian, occur together to create effects of considerable unease. Hardy's own contemporaries noticed the Zolaesque flavour of the book,[7] and we know from the numerous entries in Hardy's literary notes between 1887 and 1897 that he took a keen interest in the debate about realism in art which was being conducted in the French

---

[7] See, for example, the articles by Edmund Gosse, and R. Y. Tyrrell, in *Thomas Hardy: The Critical Heritage*, pp. 266 and 293.

press.[8] If we can judge by Hardy's essay 'The Science of Fiction',
written in 1891, he rejected the quasi-scientific basis of realism as 'an
artificiality distilled from the fruits of closest observation',[9] but he
welcomed the motives which had brought the new movement into
being. The word 'science', he said, was inappropriate for the art of
the story-teller, nor could it be used to describe the principles of selection, which must always be subjective and non-scientific. Nevertheless, there are episodes in *Jude the Obscure* which owe their inspiration
to contemporary views on realism in art. Jude's introduction to Arabella and the pig-sticking incident are perhaps the best known of
these, but there are many others in which Hardy employs the conventions of realism to create an atmosphere of harshness, despondency,
and gloom. As Hardy makes clear in his essay, the new techniques
were as selective and as carefully planned as the old ones. They dif-
fered only in what was selected—in those details which tended to en-
force the unromantic, the commonplace, or the vulgar aspects of life.
The way in which Hardy employs realist effects can be illustrated by
comparing two scenes, one from *Under the Greenwood Tree*, the other
from *Jude the Obscure*. Both involve two young lovers taking tea in an
inn. In *Under the Greenwood Tree* Dick and Fancy stop to refresh
themselves on their return journey following a stay in Budmouth.
This is the first time they have met outside Mellstock, and Fancy's
willingness to be seen in public with Dick has important sentimental
implications. '"You do know"', she says to Dick, '"that even if I
care very much for you I must remember that I have a difficult position to maintain. The vicar would not like me, as his schoolmistress,
to indulge in a *tête-à-tête* anywhere with anybody".' (*UGT* 130). The
outcome of this incident is that they become engaged, and no one's
sense of propriety is violated. In *Jude the Obscure* a similar event occurs
when Jude and Arabella take tea in an inn on *their* first public rendezvous. Arabella has none of Fancy's reservations about doing this.

Arabella said she would like some tea, and they entered an inn of an inferior
class, and gave their order. As it was not for beer they had a long time to wait.
. . . They sat and looked round the room, and at the picture of Samson and
Delilah which hung on the wall, and at the circular beer-stains on the table,
and at the spittoons underfoot filled with sawdust. The whole aspect of the
scene had that depressing effect on Jude which few places can produce like a
tap-room on a Sunday evening when the setting sun is slanting in . . . and the
unfortunate wayfarer finds himself with no other haven of rest. (*JO* 50–1.)

[8] See Ch. 8 above.   [9] *Personal Writings*, ed. Orel, p. 136.

Unlike the scene in *Under the Greenwood Tree*, this one abounds in visual details, each of which is superficially 'realist' and communicates a harsh and brutal tone to the episode—all perfectly in keeping with Arabella's sexual pragmatism. The sawdust, the beer stains, and the spittoons certainly have a 'depressing effect' on the overall picture, but it is characteristic of Hardy that one of those supposedly arbitrary details is redolent with symbolic meaning. Arabella's aggressive behaviour has an analogue in the picture within the picture—the illustration of Samson and Delilah—and it neatly anticipates that moment many years later when she forces Jude to remarry her. Having got Jude drunk in her father's house, 'Arabella ascended the stairs, softly opened the door of the first bedroom, and peeped in. Finding that her shorn Samson was asleep she entered to the bedside and stood regarding him.' (*JO* 457).

It is not difficult to identify the difference in tone between these two inn scenes; what is less clear is the exact source of Hardy's 'brutality'. It may well have derived from his reading of French literature—Flaubert, Zola, and Maupassant—but Hardy's dependence on a careful inventory of physical, visual details in both this scene and others, suggests a possible pictorial source.

In the latter part of the 1880s, French realist painting was enjoying a considerable vogue among younger British artists. This fashion for realism focused on the work of one man in particular—Bastien-Lepage. As early as 1878, Bastien-Lepage had sent a picture to the summer exhibition of the Royal Academy, and in subsequent years he painted a number of portraits of notable London figures, including the Prince of Wales (1880), the wife of Alma-Tadema, and Burne-Jones (1882).[10] His greatest impact on English art came in 1880, when seven of his portraits were shown at the Grosvenor Gallery, together with one of his peasant studies—*Les Foins* (1878). It was pictures like this last, rather than the portraits, which made such a strong impression on the English. He had a number of admirers amongst the Newlyn and Glasgow schools, including Fred Brown, Henry la Thangue, William Stott of Oldham, Edward Stott, and Henry Scott Tuke, each of whom tried to capture the direct and uncompromising treatment of rural life in their own work. Bastien-Lepage's principal English advocate, however, was George Clausen, whose view was based upon his admiration of the Frenchman's apparent objectivity:

[10] See Kenneth McConkey, 'The Bouguereau of the Naturalists: Bastien-Lepage and British Art', p. 372.

'All his personages', Clausen wrote, 'are placed before us in the most satisfying completeness, without the appearance of artifice, but as they live; and without comment, as far as is possible on the author's part'.[11]

Critical response was mixed. On the one hand it was claimed that Bastien-Lepage was 'not enough in love with beauty', and that he insisted 'too much on what is ugly in Nature';[12] on the other, he was praised in terms not unlike those in which Hardy praised realist writers. Theirs, Hardy said, 'was the exaggerated cry of an honest reaction from the false'.[13] Bastien-Lepage, it was said, helped to dispel 'the essential vapidity which under one form or another constitutes the "ideality" of the art that is always popular'.[14] Perhaps of greatest significance is the link which some critics detected between the techniques of Zola and the images of Bastien-Lepage. Wilfrid Meynell, for example, suggested that 'M. Bastien-Lepage's wild-eyed young peasants are as clearly "human documents" as the characters of Zola'. 'The attitude of these two artists', he added, 'is nearly identical'.[15]

Though Hardy makes no comment on either Bastien-Lepage or his English followers, there is no doubt that he had seen their work, and was perfectly familiar with their aims and methods. In 1891, for example, he saw pictures by la Thangue and Clausen at the Royal Academy (*EL* 308) which, said the *Art Journal*, are 'entirely based and built up on that [style] of the lamented Bastien-Lepage, the pathetic realist *par excellence* of the present generation'.[16] In the same year he paid one of his regular visits to the exhibition of the New English Art Club, which had long been the stronghold of modern realist painting. The painters of the Newlyn school were especially prominent. Theirs was a self-consciously anti-romantic, *plein air* style, which took as its subjects the everyday life of the West Country.[17] Market scenes were very popular; in these a virtue was made of the accurate delineation of the debris created by everyday life. In *Jude the Obscure* Hardy adopts

[11] Quoted in McConkey, p. 378.
[12] Wilfrid Meynell, *The Modern School of Art* iii. 31.
[13] *Personal Writings*, ed. Orel, p. 136.
[14] Meynell, *The Modern School of Art* iii. 31.
[15] Ibid., iii. 32.
[16] *Art Journal*, NS 29 (June 1890). p. 170.
[17] See Caroline Fox and Francis Greenacre, *Artists of the Newlyn School 1880–1890* (Newlyn: Newlyn Orion Galleries, 1979), and Alice Meynell, 'Newlyn', *Art Journal* NS 28 (Apr. 1889), pp. 97–102 and NS 28 (June 1889), pp. 137–42.

a very similar stance when Jude confesses to Sue about his early life with Arabella. The scene is set amongst the rubbish left by a recent market, and it is self-consciously anti-romantic in its tone.

The building by which they stood was the market-house; it was the only place available; and they entered, the market being over, and the stalls and areas empty. [Jude] would have preferred a more congenial spot, but, as usually happens, in place of a romantic field or solemn aisle for his tale, it was told while they walked up and down over a floor littered with rotten cabbage-leaves, and amid all the usual squalors of decayed vegetable matter and unsaleable refuse. (*JO* 198.)

But in *Jude the Obscure* the influence of contemporary realism does much more than merely provide the inspiration for one or two scenes, it also serves to establish one of the principal imaginative parameters of the novel. This influence can be detected mainly in the depiction of agrarian life, and this is also true of the paintings of Bastien-Lepage and George Clausen. In the paintings, the uncompromising harshness of country life is communicated in part through the choice of setting and in part through the treatment of light and colour. In works like Bastien-Lepage's *Saison d'Octobre* or *Poor Fauvette* (1881) (Plate 33) or George Clausen's *The Stonepickers* (1887) (Plate 34), not only is the setting featureless and dreary, but the colour range is very narrow. Both painters consciously avoided strong colour contrasts in favour of what were called 'relations'—a limited tonal range comprising mainly tertiary pigments. Walter Sickert reacted strongly against what seemed to him an unnecessarily spiritless manner of painting. 'What are the truths you have gained', he asked in connection with Bastien-Lepage's *Saison d'Octobre*, 'compared to the truths you have lost? To life and spirit, light and air?'[18] In Clausen's *The Stonepickers*, the foreground, the background, and the sky are brought into close contact with each other, almost losing their separate identities in the narrow range of whites and browns.

Even before Hardy wrote *Jude the Obscure*, there is evidence that he had experimented with the use of the pictorial conventions of this style. With the Turneresque visions of sunlight and colour left behind her in the valley of the Froom, Tess arrives at Flintcomb-Ash. Here the scene 'was almost sublime in its dreariness. There was not a tree within sight; there was not, at this season, a green pasture—nothing but fallow and turnips everywhere; in large fields divided by hedges

---

[18] André Theuriet, ed., *Jules Bastien-Lepage and his Art* (1892), p. 136.

plashed to unrelieved levels.' (*TD* 361). Not only does the setting strongly resemble those of Bastien-Lepage and his followers, the colouring also reflects their preoccupation with tonal relations.

The whole field was in colour a desolate drab; it was a complexion without features, as if a face, from chin to brow, should be only an expanse of skin. The sky wore, in another colour, the same likeness; a white vacuity of countenance with the lineaments gone. So these two upper and nether visages confronted each other all day long, the white face looking down on the brown face, and the brown face looking up at the white face. (*TD* 363–4.)

Anthropomorphism apart, the pictorialism in this scene is very strong. Two girls toiling in a colourless and monotonous field under an equally monotonous sky, where distance has all but been absorbed by the narrow tonal range, might, without incongruity, be the subject for a contemporary realist canvas entitled *The Swede-Cutters*.

In *Jude the Obscure* the scenes of rural hardship are concentrated in the early scenes at Marygreen, and most especially in the episode in which Jude is sent as a bird-scarer to a nearby field. In order to reach this, he 'pursued a path northward, till he came to a wide and lonely depression in the general level of the upland, which was sown as a corn-field. This vast concave was the scene of his labours . . . and he descended into the midst of it.' (*JO* 9–10). We know that the immediate inspiration for this episode was for Hardy a highly personal one. In 1892 he had been investigating his family records, and his researches had taken him to Great Fawley in Berkshire—the place where his grandmother, Mary Head, had been born. The visit was not a happy one, and it involved for Hardy the sense of a personality divided between past and present. He wrote in his diary:

October 1892. At Great Fawley, Berks. Entered a ploughed vale which might be called the Valley of Brown Melancholy. The silence is remarkable. . . . Though I am alive with the living I can only see the dead here, and am scarcely conscious of the happy children at play. (*LY* 13.)

Hardy's visit to Great Fawley was part of an attempt to identify his own origins, and, like his creator, Jude also feels cut off from his ancestors.

The brown surface of the field went right up towards the sky all round, where it was lost by degrees in the mist that shut out the actual verge and accentuated the solitude. The only marks on the uniformity of the scene were a rick of last year's produce standing in the midst of the arable, the rooks that rose at [Jude's] approach, and the path athwart the fallow by which he had come, trodden now by he hardly knew whom, though once by many of his own dead family. (*JO* 10.)

Once again, however, the scene bears a striking similarity to certain contemporary realist canvases. In Bastien-Lepage's *Poor Fauvette*, for example, a picture which, according to the *Art Journal* of 1896 'was probably better known in Britain than any other Bastien-Lepage painted',[19] a lonely child stands in the foreground of a dreary and sunless landscape, an emblem of vacancy and solitude. The low-keyed, muted colours, of which brown and olive-green predominate, the high horizon, the bare tree, and the single cow, all convey a sense of loneliness and alienation. Similarly, in Hardy's account of Jude's field, the high and unrelieved horizon-line shuts in the solitary figure, conveying a strong impression of bleak, but inescapable, dreariness. We have seen how the critics of this style of painting accused both Bastien-Lepage and his followers of overlooking the poetry of country life, and of concentrating exclusively on the harsh, the utilitarian, and the ugly. Jude responds to his own setting in a similar way. '"How ugly it is here!" he murmured', and his disgust is prompted by a sight which resembles the composition of a number of Bastien-Lepage's landscapes.

The fresh harrow-lines seemed to stretch like the channellings in a piece of new corduroy, lending a meanly utilitarian air to the expanse, taking away its gradations, and depriving it of all history beyond that of the few recent months. (*JO* 10.)

The utilitarian view of this scene, however, is only one way of perceiving it. As Hardy wrote in 1865, 'The poetry of a scene . . . does not lie in the scene at all' (*EL* 66), and to the eye attuned to the presence of the human mark on the land, the outward ugliness hides a deeper meaning; history is written everywhere on the landscape. Consequently, Jude's isolation is deepened, because he cannot see that

to every clod and stone there really attached associations enough and to spare—echoes of songs from ancient harvest-days, of spoken words, and of sturdy deeds. Every inch of ground had been the site, first or last, or energy, gaiety, horseplay, bickerings, weariness. (*JO* 10.)

This is not an appeal to a sentimental or nostalgic view of the land. It also involves an awareness of pain and suffering; it recognizes how

[19] *Art Journal*, NS 35 (1896), p. 200.

'under the hedge which divided the field from a distant plantation girls had given themselves to lovers who would not turn their heads to look at them by the next harvest.' (*JO* 10). But it also recognizes the continuity in human life, and how the ugliest and baldest scenes contain within them something of the poetry of that continuity. Jude's tragedy is that he has no access to this vision, and that he is no more responsive to it than the rooks that he has been sent to scare. 'This, neither Jude nor the rooks around him considered', since for them, Hardy adds, this was merely 'a lonely place, possessing, in the one view, only the quality of a work-ground, and in the other that of a granary good to feed in' (*JO* 10).

Lacking the creative perspective of his author, rootless, and unable to perceive the connection between himself and his fellow humans, Jude turns his back on the real world. He ignores its potential for transcendence, a potential which so many of Hardy's previous characters fully understood, and he seeks solace in a romantic vision. From the deep concave of the field with its mean and utilitarian air, he climbs upward—literally upward—on to the roof of the Brown House, from whence he has his first glimpse of the 'Celestial City'. The importance of this vision for Jude is that it appears so unlike the place in which he is forced to live and work. His aspirations are in part a reaction against his life at Marygreen, against the dull, the unimaginative, and the commonplace, and he endows the lights of Christminster which a romantic other-wordly power.

'The world', as Hardy wrote in *Tess of the d'Urbervilles*, 'is only a psychological phenomenon' (*TD* 108), and what Jude sees from the roof of the Brown House is a projection of his own needs and desires. The intimate connection between topography and psychology is one which frequently makes itself felt in Hardy's novels, and it has its roots in that crucial journey which Hardy made up the Rhine in 1876. It was just before he wrote *The Return of the Native* that he formulated the idea that modern man's true home lay in the wildernesses of the north. The south of Europe, with its 'myrtle-gardens' and its Alps suited man in his infancy, but it is desolate and drab landscapes which are in keeping with the modern mind, and in Hardy's view it is the role of the poet to discover beauty in the supposed ugliness of these scenes. His creation of Egdon Heath, the woods of Little Hintock, and the bleak landscapes of Flintcomb-Ash all grow out of the principle of 'a new kind of beauty, a negative beauty of tragic tone' (*TD* 397). None of them is conventionally beautiful; all have their melancholy side, and in each case Hardy stresses their affinity with the north rather than the south. The Arctic mallard makes its temporary home on Egdon Heath; the woods of Little Hintock are inhabited by Teutonic gods, and their legends remain alive amongst its branches; and Flintcomb-Ash is buffeted by winds from the North Pole. In *Jude the Obscure* Hardy takes up this theme once again. Marygreen and the surrounding land are superficially bleak and featureless; they, too, possess none of the conventional attractions of picturesque scenery, and they, too, face north. When Jude walks to the edge of the scarp slope of the downs, he has 'never before strayed so far north as this from the nestling hamlet in which he had been deposited by the carrier from a railway station southward, one dark evening some few months earlier' (*JO* 17). Like Flintcomb-Ash before it, Marygreen is situated on high chalkland which rises steeply out of the surrounding valleys. Flintcomb-Ash is a 'bracing calcerous region' (*TD* 457), whereas the Downs form a 'cold cretaceous upland' (*JO* 20), and both are exposed to the elements. Flintcomb-Ash, with its 'horizontal rain' and its frost and snow, seemed the coldest place in Wessex, but, according to Hardy, 'the coldest of all when a north or east wind is blowing is the crest of the down by the Brown House'— the spot from which Jude first saw Christminster (*JO* 472).

Perhaps most important is the contrast, expressed in visual terms, between these high spots and the land which they overlook. Above, all is featureless and colourless; below, the land is lush and the air full of moisture. In *Tess of the d'Urbervilles* these differences form the emblems of the stages in Tess's life. On her journey to Emminster,

she reached the edge of the vast escarpment below which stretched the loamy Vale of Blackmoor, now lying misty and still in the dawn. Instead of the colourless air of the uplands the atmosphere down there was a deep blue. . . . Here the landscape was whitey-brown; down there, as in Froom Valley, it was always green. (*TD* 378.)

Jude, too, makes his way to the edge of the escarpment, and when he looks over the countryside beneath, he is surprised by what he sees.

Till now he had had no suspicion that such a wide, flat, low-lying country lay so near at hand, under the very verge of his upland world. The whole northern semicircle between east and west, to a distance of forty or fifty miles, spread itself before him; a bluer moister atmosphere, evidently, than he breathed up here. (*JO* 17.)

Unlike Jude, however, Tess sees her view with the eyes of experience. She is one who has felt and suffered, and she has no illusions about what she sees.

It was in that vale that her sorrow had taken shape, and she did not love it as formerly. Beauty to her, as to all who have felt, lay not in the thing, but in the thing symbolized. (*TD* 378.)

Jude is not so wise, and has none of Tess's discrimination. His ascent to the roof of the Brown House is an attempt at escape. He is blind to the 'beauty in ugliness' of the commonplace, and seeks refuge in a vision or a 'mirage'.

Some way within the limits of the stretch of landscape, points of light like the topaz gleamed. The air increased in transparency with the lapse of minutes, till the topaz points showed themselves to be the vanes, windows, wet roof slates, and other shining spots upon the spires, domes, freestone-work, and varied outlines that were faintly revealed. It was Christminster, unquestionably; either directly seen, or miraged in the peculiar atmosphere. (*JO* 19.)

It is not difficult to see here a similarity between Jude's love of Christminster and Eustacia Vye's dreams of Paris or Budmouth, dreams which 'stood like gilded letters upon the dark tablet of surrounding Egdon.' (*RN* 78). Jude's attachment to a set of impossible ideals is more high-minded, and apparently more rational, than Eustacia Vye's thirst for the exotic, or Felice Charmond's love of Continental travel, but each of them represents the desire for escape, and their ideals are all rooted in false perspectives.

As is so often the case in Hardy's writing, visual perception and imaginative perception are closely allied. When Jude reaches Christminster, he fails to see either its external forms or its incipient deadness—he was 'far from seeing or criticizing these things' (*JO* 223)—and at Marygreen he is unable to see beyond the superficial dullness of the landscape. Unlike Clym or Thomasin Yeobright who perceive 'friendliness and geniality' written on the austere hills of Egdon Heath, unlike Giles Winterborne and Marty South whose 'clear gaze' permits them to read the hieroglyphs of nature, and unlike Tess even, who came to understand the symbolic meaning of Flintcomb-Ash, Jude, with his lack of visual imagination, fails to penetrate the outward forms of the land to which he is heir. Consequently, he becomes the slave of what Hardy called in *The Woodlanders* 'inner visions'; he is mastered by hopeless ideals, and as the story

progresses, both he and Sue, locked within their various predica-
ments, see less and less of the outer world. Their dilemma is summed
up in the peculiar child Little Father Time. This infant, says the narrator, is their 'nodal point' and their 'focus'; he is 'the expression in a
single term' of the older generation, and he is a child of darkness. 'On
that little shape had converged all the inauspiciousness and shadow
which had darkened the first union of Jude, and all the accidents,
mistakes, fears, errors, of the last' (*JO* 406), and Little Father Time
perceives even less of the external world than his parents. This
becomes very clear in the train journey to Marygreen which the child
makes. This is one of the last journeys in Hardy's novels, and it forms
an effective contrast with the very first—the journey of Cytherea
Graye and her brother Owen from Hockbridge to Budmouth. They,
too, travel by train, and from the carriage window they observe a
landscape filled with richness, variety, and colour. They see 'placid
flocks of sheep reclining under trees a little way off [which] appeared
of a pale blue colour. Clover fields were livid with the brightness of
the sun upon their deep red flowers'. (*DR* 18). Hardy makes a connection between the ability to respond visually to landscape and the
hopefulness of youth.

To see persons looking with children's eyes at any ordinary scenery is a proof
that they possess the charming faculty of drawing new sensations from an old
experience—a healthy sign, rare in these feverish days—the mark of an imperishable brightness of nature. (*DR* 18.)

In *Jude the Obscure* none of Hardy's characters exhibit that 'imperishable brightness of nature', least of all the most youthful—Little
Father Time. What was so vivid and alive for Owen and Cytherea is
for him a mere blank. As he travels to Marygreen, 'the houses, the
willows, the obscure fields beyond, were apparently regarded not as
brick residences, pollards, meadows; but as human dwellings in the
abstract, vegetation, and the wide dark world.' (*JO* 334).
    Again and again in the novels, Hardy equates the act of visual per-
ception, the active enjoyment of sensuous visible form, with vitality
and health. To see and respond to the beauty of nature is to comprehend one's place in the natural order; to be moved by natural forms
or by human comeliness is an index of consciousness—a measure of
being alive. In *Jude the Obscure* Hardy has moved into the twilight, into
a realm of uniformity and 'obscurity' in which the eye is denied its
power and has lost its function. If the present is gloomy, the future is

even darker. Little Father Time, the representative of the coming generation, has no visual link with the outer world; he sees not realities but abstractions. Such children, the doctor tells Sue and Jude at the end of the novel, 'are the outcome of new views of life. . . . They seem to see all its terrors before they are old enough to have staying power to resist them.' (*JO* 406).

34. George Clausen: *The Stonepickers*, 1887. Laing Art Gallery, Newcastle-upon-Tyne (107.6×79.2 cm)

33. Jules Bastien-Lepage: *Poor Fauvette*, 1881. Glasgow Art Gallery and Museum (162.5×125.5 cm)

35. John Everett Millais: *The North-West Passage*. 1874. Tate Gallery, Londo
(176×223.3 cm)

36. William Bradford: *The Steamer 'Panther' among the Icebergs and Field Ice in Melvil.
Bay and the Light of the Midnight Sun*. 1874. Royal Collection, Buckingham Palac
(46×76.2 cm)

Conclusion

'This world's no blot for us,
Nor blank—it means intensely and means good.'

The words which Browning put into the mouth of the painter Filippo
Lippi, as George Eliot realized when she reviewed *Men and Women*,
are not so much the sentiments of a Renaissance painter as those of
a mid-Victorian, and they derive as much from *Modern Painters* as
from any fourteenth-century theory of art. When *Men and Women* was
published in 1853, Hardy was only thirteen years old, and though he
was already busily painting from nature in and around his native
village of Bockhampton, it is likely that he discovered neither Browning's poetry nor Ruskin's *Modern Painters* until he went to London in
1862. By that time Ruskin had exercised a significant influence over a
whole generation of imaginative writers and painters. But both the
doctrine of expressiveness in art as Lippi states it and Ruskin's insistence on the moral power of observation in *Modern Painters* must
have confirmed for Hardy a set of attitudes to visualization which he
had begun to discover through his own painting and drawing.

Though Hardy was temperamentally very unlike Ruskin, his early
visual experience closely resembled that of the older man. In his
autobiography *Praeterita*, Ruskin recalls how we was deprived of many
of the normal childhood games, and how he depended almost exclusively on the pleasures of visual observation. He remembers how
'the carpet, and what patterns [he] could find in bed-covers, dresses,
or wall-papers . . . were [his] chief resources', and how, as a result,
his perceptions became sharpened and acute.[1] Likewise many of
Hardy's earliest memories were highly visual. He remembered the
light falling on a painted wall in the cottage at Bockhampton, and
how he used to wait with anticipation each evening for a repetition of
this experience as the sun set in the west (*EL* 19). The diaries and
notebooks of both writers show very clearly that their delight in
optical effects persisted into adult life: both continued to record
natural effects—wind, rain, cloud, and sunshine—and both responded
to the chance appearances of faces, figures, or scenes. Ruskin's observations are more precise and more scientific than those of Hardy,
which tend to be fanciful and whimsical, but both men developed the

---

[1] Ruskin, *Works* xxxv. 21.

life of the eye: they remained throughout their lives self-conscious spectators, each giving the impression of a man observing events from a distance. In 1888, for example, after recently enjoying the company of yet another aesthetic 'observer', Walter Pater, Hardy wrote:

If there is any way of getting a melancholy satisfaction out of life it lies in dying, so to speak, before one is out of the flesh; by which I mean putting on the manners of ghosts, wandering in their haunts, and taking their views of surrounding things. To think of life as passing away is a sadness; to think of it as past is at least tolerable. Hence even when I enter into a room to pay a simple morning call I have unconsciously the habit of regarding the scene as if I were a spectre not solid enough to influence my environment. (*EL* 275.)

The irreversible onward movement of life was a source of deep melancholy for Hardy, and many of his poems speak of the irretrievability of the past. In certain ways, however, art arrests this process— graphic art most of all—and a number of Hardy's poems conjure up the memory of Emma when he was drawing her in the early years of their courtship. Of course, the notion that the visual arts depend for their effect upon 'being' rather than 'becoming' is an ancient one, which received its most thoroughgoing theoretical expression in the writings of Lessing, and perhaps its most lyrical expression in Keats's 'Ode to a Grecian Urn'. It is also an idea which occurs prominently in the poetry of Dante Gabriel Rossetti, and his meditation on Giorgione's picture *The Fête Champêtre*, in which he described "Life touching lips with Immortality', helped inspire Pater's well-known view of Giorgione's work as a summation within a single instant of the continuum of life. Pater likened this to 'dramatic poetry', and said that 'it is part of the highest sort of dramatic poetry,

that it presents us with a kind of profoundly significant and animated instants, a mere gesture, a look, a smile, perhaps—some brief and wholly concrete moment—into which, however, all the motives, all the interests and effects of long history have condensed themselves, and which seem to absorb past and future in an intense consciousness of the present.[2]

In Hardy's novels the impression of life passing away is generated specifically by the narrative, for it is this which creates the chain of events whereby characters are driven irrevocably towards dissolution and decay. Set against the processes of 'becoming' are the moments

[2] Pater, *The Renaissance*, p. 118.

of 'being'—those numerous incidents where the narrative is interrupted by a tableau or set piece, or those points at which the story
comes to rest. 'It is', said Hardy in one of his notes,

the on-going—i.e. the 'becoming'—of the world that produces its sadness. If
the world stood still at a felicitous moment there would be no sadness in it.
The sun and the moon standing still on Ajalon was not a catastrophe for
Israel, but a type of Paradise. (*EL* 265.)

These moments of stasis are primarily the creation of Hardy's visual
imagination, and are the fruit of contemplative observation; they stem
directly from his temperamental love of careful watching, and are frequently structured on the pictorial model. Seen in this way, the
development of Hardy's style as a novelist can be interpreted as a
struggle between, on the one hand, the comfort and the solace of the
permanent or unchanging, and on the other, the destructive power of
'becoming'; between a sensuous delight in the significance of observed
phenomena and the dissolution brought about by the passage of time.
In this respect there is an affinity between *Desperate Remedies*, Hardy's
first novel, and *Jude the Obscure*, his last. In *Desperate Remedies*, the
'moments of vision', in which Hardy begins to reveal a deeper meaning underlying the significance of outer events, are swallowed up by a
complicated and fast-moving plot. In the second half of the novel he is
unable to sustain the contemplative mode which, at least in part, he
had established in the first half, and he is literally overtaken by the
events of his own narrative. In *Jude the Obscure* he employs a similar
device, but now he is master of all its implications. This time he
denies both reader and characters alike that sense of security and
well-being which is derived from active visual contemplation, and he
allows the processes of 'becoming' full rein. Polemical discussion and
argumentative dialogue are more prominent in this novel than in the
earlier ones, and the complex plot exemplifies what Hardy calls 'the
modern vice of unrest'. Its tortuous development generates a set of
events whose outcome is tragic.

Between these two books Hardy experimented with various means
of reconciling 'being' and 'becoming'. *Under the Greenwood Tree* is
simultaneously the most static and the most 'picturesque' of his
novels, and in spite of the changes which are seen to be taking place
within Mellstock society, it is the novel which most clearly projects a
feeling of permanence within rural life. In the novels which followed,
Hardy frequently invoked the aid of one or more of the central

characters to observe or watch over the unfolding narrative—characters who help to order or make sense of passing events. Gabriel Oak, Diggory Venn, Elizabeth-Jane, and Marty South all act as interpreters of the narrative by *seeing* events from within more clearly than the other protagonists. But it is the narrator himself whose eye is most penetrative and most agile, and it is the narrator who attributes most meaning to what he sees. In *Far from the Madding Crowd*, it is the eye of the narrator which is alive to the forms and colours of the scene in the great barn, and it is the mind of the narrator which interprets what that eye sees as an image of plenitude and social continuity. It is the eye of the narrator in *The Return of the Native* which creates the composite portraits of Eustacia Vye and Clym Yeobright, and which relates those portraits to others, ancient and modern, and it is also the eye of the narrator which, in the sunrise at Talbothays, perceives an archetype for the dawn of love itself.

Though by no means all the visionary moments in the novels are based upon specific pictorial sources, Hardy's tendency to attribute meaning to images derives substantially from the practice of the painter. Lloyd Fernando noticed this, and considered it to be one of Hardy's limitations. Eustacia Vye's portrait, he says,

> may be vivid, but the vividness is the static vividness of a painting. Hardy needs to have his figures hold a certain position, a pose, while he relates each of the elements of the scene to one another and to the whole preconceived scheme, as in a painting.[3]

What Fernando fails to explain is why Hardy does this, and what its effects are in the context of the narrative. The answer can be discovered partly in the writings of Ruskin, and most especially in his account of the 'imagination penetrative'. 'There is not the commonest subject', he says about Tintoretto, 'to which he will not attach a range of suggestiveness almost limitless';[4] according to Ruskin, the power of Tintoretto's imagination lies in 'reaching, by intuition and intensity of gaze . . . a more essential truth than is seen on the surface of things.[5] Hardy, whose explicit aim was to make the 'inner meaning . . . vividly visible' (*EL* 232), seems to have shared many of Ruskin's ideas about the expressive potential of visual forms; again and again he scans his verbally created 'pictures' and develops their

---

3 Lloyd Fernando, 'Thomas Hardy's Rhetoric of Painting', p. 68.
4 Ruskin, *Works*, iv. 250–1.
5 Ibid., iv. 284.

associative meanings 'by seeing into *the heart of a thing*' (*EL* 190; Hardy's emphasis).

The meanings which Hardy extracts from his strongly visualized moments vary from novel to novel, and in each book the visible essence takes a different form and has a different emphasis. In *The Return of the Native* he employs the features of the human face as the principal source of feeling and meaning; in *The Mayor of Casterbridge* he turns his attention to the symbolism of clothing in all its manifestations; and in *Tess of the d'Urbervilles* the pattern of light and darkness is possessed of an essence which finds visual expression within the text. It is in the earlier stories, however, that the distinction between 'being' and 'becoming' is most pronounced, and it is in these that moments of stasis are most clearly distinguished from the progressive forward movement of the narrative. In *Desperate Remedies* the suspended animation of the love-making scene at Budmouth Bay stands in sharp contrast to the frenzied activity of the murder mystery-story, and in *Far from the Madding Crowd* the magnificent episodes involving rural life act as a foil to the vicissitudes of Bathsheba Everdene's emotional development. As Hardy matured as a novelist, however, the simple alternatives of 'being' and 'becoming' seem to have become less and less effective. In *The Mayor of Casterbridge* the permanence of the material world, so carefully recorded by the eye of the narrator, begins to collapse so that what at first seems so firm, ancient, and substantial, turns out to be no more than a 'phantasmagoria', terribly vulnerable to changes of fame and fortune. In *The Woodlanders* this process is taken one stage further. Here, even the imagination of the narrator is conditioned by the forces of change, so that even the moments of stasis are permeated by a sense of struggle and conflict. In this novel the 'unfulfilled intention' makes itself felt everywhere and no comfort can be taken in either the permanence of nature or the continuity of the fabric of society.

The dialectical movement between stasis and development is not necessarily, as Fernando would have us believe, a flaw in Hardy's writing. It is, of course, a highly stylized device which makes no claims in the direction of realism. It employs the methods of a painter in a literary context, but like the work of the painter that Hardy most admired—J. M. W. Turner—it is not illusionist in its aims. In Turner's painting, said Hardy, 'the exact truth as to material fact ceases to be important' (*EL* 243), and in the finest passages of Hardy's writing, he is often concerned to direct the reader's attention away from the material circumstances of the narrative, and towards ideas or emotions which lie beyond or behind objective reality. Consequently, what Hardy said of Turner's work can also be said of his own, namely that 'art is the secret of how to produce by a false thing the effect of a true.' (*EL* 284).

Appendix: Hardy and the Arctic

Throughout *The Return of the Native* Hardy stresses the essential north-erness of Egdon Heath. Not only does he liken it to 'Thule'— the hyperborean Hades of classical mythology, he also describes it as 'Homer's Cimmerian land' (*RN* 60), a place inhabited by the ancient race of the Cimerii, a northern people who lived out their lives in mist and darkness. The bonfire on Rainbarrow, according to Hardy, is part of a long-standing tradition of 'festival fires to Thor and Woden', both northern gods, and in the final chapter of the book, the maypole is set up on the green, a fragment of 'Teutonic rites to divinities whose names are forgotten' (*RN* 459). In *The Return of the Native* and in many of the other novels, the 'south' is projected as a place of luxury and fantasy, standing in marked contrast to the har-sher realities of the north. In *A Laodicean* George Somerset's 'northern eyes are not prepared . . . for the impact of . . . images of warmth and colour as meet them southward', and for him the south of France is a place 'full of gaieties, sentiment, languor, seductiveness, and ready-made romance' (*L* 311). Similarly, the experiences on the 'romantic slopes' of Baden-Baden become for Fitzpiers and Felice Charmond in *The Woodlanders* 'a canvas for infinite fancies, idle dreams, luxurious melancholies, and pretty alluring assertions.' (*W* 233). Hardy may have borrowed the idea of some kind of moral superiority inhering in the northern way of life and under northern skies from Ruskin. In the famous chapter 'The Nature of Gothic' in *The Stones of Venice*, Ruskin identified northern Europe with the source of the Gothic style in architecture, a style which had grown out of a particular kind of human endurance and human endeavour foreign to those who lived in more temperate climates. Like Hardy, Ruskin stressed the 'con-trast in physical character which exists between Northern and Southern countries'.[1] and for both Ruskin and Hardy the south was the source of a greatness and grandeur which was now passed. Byzan-tine Venice in Ruskin's case, and the 'myrtle-gardens of the South of Europe' in Hardy's, may have been the cradle of civilization, but their moral qualities expressed in physical terms no longer met man's needs. Ruskin claimed to perceive a moral superiority in 'the strong spirit of men who may not gather redundant fruitage from the earth'

[1] Ruskin, *Works* x. 186.

in the north, men whose eyes are 'dimmed by moor mist, or blinded by the hail',[2] and he contrasted the 'terraced gardens, and flowers heavy with frankincense' in the south with the northern 'wall of ice, durable like iron [which] sets, death-like, its white teeth against us out of the polar twilight'.[3] Hardy also alludes to the Arctic in his novels—once in *The Return of the Native* and once in *Tess of the d'Urbervilles*—and on both occasions the allusions impart a bitter moral chill to the Wessex landscape. In *The Return of the Native* Diggory Venn is crossing Egdon Heath in order to find Eustacia Vye and to persuade her to give up Damon Wildeve. Suddenly he sees 'a wild mallard, just arrived from the home of the north wind'. This creature, Hardy says, 'brought within him an amplitude of Northern knowledge. Glacial catastrophes, snow-storm episodes, glittering auroral effects, Polaris in the zenith, Franklin underfoot—'the category of his commonplaces was wonderful.' (*RN* 100–1).

The hint of the Arctic north may owe its inspiration to Ruskin's example, but the detailed 'Northern knowledge' of the mallard almost certainly derives from quite a different source. The 1870s were an outstanding period of Arctic exploration in British history, and in 1876 (the same year in which Hardy was writing *The Return of the Native*), at least one anonymous writer tried to explain how 'in the frozen wastes and the snowy wildernesses lurks a powerful fascination, which proves almost irresistible to the adventurous spirit'. 'Whether,' he said,

the spell lies in the weird magnificence of the scenery, in the splendours of the heavens, in the mystery which still hovers over those far-off seas of ice and remote bays, or the excitement of a continual struggle with the forces of Nature, or whether all these influences are at work we cannot stop to enquire.

But he was certain that it was the north rather than the south which made the greatest claim on the imagination of modern man. 'It seems to us certain', he concluded, 'that the Arctic World has a romance and an attraction about it, which are far more powerful over the minds of men than the rich glowing lands of the Tropics'.[4] The immediate source of this excitement about the Arctic was a legendary journey undertaken in 1876 by George Nares and Clements Markham in their ship *The Alert*. They were exploring the west coast of Greenland, and in the course of their investigations they reached

2 Ibid., x. 188.
3 Ibid., x. 187.
4 Anon., *The Arctic World, Its Plants, Animals and Natural Phenomena*, p. 1.

the highest northern latitude ever attained by a sailing ship. But their journey coincided with a period of considerable interest in what was called 'The Unknown Region'. In the 1870s numerous books were published on the subject of Arctic exploration—some of them popular accounts, some of them technical and scientific[5]—and such was the general interest in the subject that Millais's famous picture *The North-West Passage* (Plate 35) was the most outstanding success of the 1874 Royal Academy exhibition. Representations of Arctic scenes were not unusual in the nineteenth century. One thinks of Gaspar David Friedrich's *Frozen Shipwreck* (1824), Frederick Church's *Icebergs* (1861), and, perhaps most famous of all, Landseer's *Man Proposes, God Disposes* of 1864 which may have been inspired by Charles Hall's book *Arctic Researches and Life Amongst the Esquimaux* of the same year. Landseer's picture shows polar bears contemplating the wreckage of some ill-fated expedition, and Hall himself had made great efforts to discover the remains of Sir John Franklin and his men who had perished in 1847. Since that time the British contribution to Arctic exploration had been relatively slight, and Millais's painting of 1874 represents a revival of British interest in the northern regions.[6] Hanging on the wall behind the two figures is a picture of an Arctic scene. This picture within a picture provides an illustration of another side of the current interest in the Arctic world, for not only did the British public wish to read stories about the rigours and privations of those who had visited Arctic regions, they also wished to see representations of icebergs, ice-flows, and glaciers. One artist in particular satisfied this wish. His name was William Bradford; the picture recorded in *The North-West Passage* may well be one of his, and Hardy may well have seen another work by Bradford at the Royal Academy.

Bradford was an American who owned a steam yacht called *The Panther*, and in 1869 he travelled to the coast of Greenland with the

---

[5] By 1873, Clements Markham's book *The Threshold of the Unknown Region* had become highly popular, and immediately after the voyage of Nares and Markham, the *Arctic World* (see n. 4) was reissued with a chapter dealing with that expedition. A collection of scientific papers entitled *Arctic Geography and Ethnology* was presented to members of the same expedition in 1875, and Markham wrote another book entitled *The Great Frozen Sea* (1878). Highly coloured accounts of the adventures on this expedition occur in *Recent Polar Voyages: A Record of Discovery and Adventure* (1876) and James Mason's *Ice World Adventures* (1876). Markham himself summed up the expeditions of this period in the 'Polar Regions' entry of *The Encyclopaedia Brittanica*, 9th edn 19 (1885), pp. 315–83.

[6] Landseer's painting was shown a second time, at the Royal Academy exhibition of 1874. See Richard Ormond, *Sir Edwin Landseer* p. 206.

intention of recording the strange colours and lights of the ice and sea.[7] A one-man show of his work in London in 1873 was a great success. It was, said the *Art Journal*, 'a glorious display of icy landscapes from the far north'[8] and its success lay in bringing before the public sights and scenes which were very different from the conventional landscapes of European painting. Bradford's pictures, said the same critic, show episodes 'abounding with colour which never entered the thought of painters who have not seen the places Mr Bradford has'. Such was the interest in scenes of the far north that Queen Victoria herself commissioned a picture from Bradford, and it is this picture which may have contributed to the appearance of the mallard on Egdon Heath.

At the end of May 1876, when Hardy was pondering *The Return of the Native* and preparing for his journey to Holland and the Rhine, he and his wife spent a fortnight in London visiting exhibitions and galleries.[9] The summer exhibition of the Royal Academy had recently opened, and Hardy, who always made a point of visiting the Academy, undoubtedly saw this show. It contained a number of pictures and sculptures which were important for *The Return of the Native*, including Woolner's bust of Tennyson, but one of them, shown 'by command of the Queen', was filled with evidence of the northern knowledge which Hardy ascribed to the mallard on Egdon Heath. It was Bradford's *The Steamer 'Panther' among the Icebergs and Field Ice in Melville Bay and the Light of the Midnight Sun* (Plate 36), which he had painted from the Arctic scenes witnessed in 1869.

Curiosity about the Arctic must have remained with Hardy, and over ten years later he introduced another 'Polar episode' into one of his novels. This one also involves Arctic birds which come to Wessex, though this time there are many of them, and their 'Northern knowledge' is even more detailed and specific. A snowstorm at Flintcomb-Ash in *Tess of the d'Urbervilles* is preceded by the appearance of 'strange birds from behind the North Pole' (*TD* 367). They are

gaunt spectral creatures with tragical eyes—eyes which had witnessed scenes of cataclysmal horror in inaccessible polar regions of a magnitude such as no human being had ever conceived, in curdling temperatures that no man could

[7] For an account of Bradford's journey, see anon., *Recent Polar Voyages: A Record of Discovery and Adventure*, (1876) pp. 319–83.
[8] *Art Journal*, NS 12 (1873), p. 255.
[9] *Letters* 1. 45.

endure; which had beheld the crash of icebergs and the slide of snow-hills by the shooting light of the Aurora; been half-blinded by the whirl of colossal storms and terraqueous distortions; and retained the expression of feature that such scenes had engendered. (*TD* 367.)

At the appearance of these birds the Wessex landscape is momentarily imbued with an Arctic chill; the polar winds bring with them cold and frost in the literal sense, but they also provide a reminder that Flintcomb-Ash, like Egdon Heath before it, and like the 'cold-cretaceous upland' (*JO* 20) of *Jude the Obscure* a little later, look to the savage places of the north rather than to the luxuriance of the south. In *Tess of the d'Urbervilles* Flintcomb-Ash is a place 'almost sublime in its dreariness' (*TD* 361), where agrarian labour becomes toil, the individual is made subject to the machine, and life, like the ground itself, is stony and barren. Lying to the south is the valley of the Froom, another land which can be glimpsed from the high windswept chalkland. But 'the south' in this novel also means 'the past', and Tess and Marian survive the wet and cold of the turnip fields by living 'in memories of green, sunny, romantic Talbothays' (*TD* 365).

When Hardy was writing *The Return of the Native*, his interest in the imaginative power of the Arctic was almost certainly stimulated by Britain's re-entry into the activity of exploration and the general excitement created by voyagers to the 'The Unknown Region'; in the late 1880s his impulse to introduce into a Wessex novel a 'blast . . . of icebergs, arctic seas, whales, and white bears' (*TD* 368) seems to have derived from one expedition and from the experiences of one man in particular. In the autumn of 1888 Fridtjof Nansen led the first expedition across the continent of Greenland. Many previous explorers had tried to penetrate the heart of the continent—including Nordenskjöld in 1883, and Peary in 1886. Both had attempted the trip from west to east, and both had failed. Nansen decided that it would be easier to travel from east to west; he was correct, and he brought back to civilization an account of scenes which 'no human being had ever conceived'. In June of 1889 he gave a talk to the Royal Geographical Society in London about his experiences in Greenland. In August, the month in which Hardy began to write *Tess of the d'Urbervilles*, Nansen's talk was published, and a number of his experiences reappear as the 'Northern knowledge' of the 'strange birds from behind the North Pole'.

Hardy mentions 'the curdling temperatures that no man could

endure', and Nansen said that 'the cold was considerable'. 'I am not . . . able', he added, 'to give an exact statement of the temperature, as our thermometers did not go low enough. I believe that on some nights it was between −45° and −50° Centigrade'.[10] Hardy mentions the way in which the birds had been 'half-blinded by the whirl of colossal storms', whereas Nansen told his audience about 'the intense snow-glare' where 'for six or seven weeks not a speck of black was to be seen anywhere'. 'Nothing', he added, 'could be more trying to the eyes'.[11] Nansen's account was filled with descriptions of 'the crash of icebergs and the slide of snow-hills' as he and his party made their way forward, inch by inch, over the intensely difficult terrain, but it was probably what Hardy calls 'the shooting light of the Aurora' that provided the most moving part of Nansen's talk. As he watched the extraordinary displays of the aurora borealis, he realized that he was witnessing scenes which had never before entered the eye of man. 'I shall never forget', he said,

the strange impressions, as from another world, we got in this solemn, silent nature, as we saw the lights spreading like a terrible fire over the whole sky, then gathering again in the zenith, as if swept together by a storm, always flitting, burning and scintillating, and then at once disappearing, leaving the monotonous snow-fields in darkness as they were before.[12]

Nansen was a privileged spectator of events to which most humans were denied access. It was as if, in Hardy's terms, he had glimpsed the future, and had seen something of the 'cataclysmal horror' which lay ahead in man's development. Nansen had voyaged across Greenland, and had returned to speak of his experiences, but the birds on Flintcomb-Ash lacked 'the traveller's ambition to tell'. They bore upon them, however, the mark of what they had seen, and were 'gaunt spectral creatures with tragical eyes'. In *Tess of the d'Urbervilles* the tragedy of Tess's life is offset to some degree by the fulfilment of her life in the valley of the Froom and her love in Talbothays; she is able to survive the cold of Flintcomb-Ash by living on her memories of the sunshine and fertility of an earlier existence. This is not so for the characters of *Jude the Obscure*, and most especially for the child of the future, Little Father Time.

[10] Nansen, 'Journey Across the Inland Ice of Greenland from East to West', *Proceedings of the Royal Geographical Society*, NS 11 (1889), p. 475. Nansen's journey was also reported in *The Times*, 25 May 1889, p. 8, and 26 June 1889, p. 15.

[11] Nansen, 'Journey', p. 484. [12] Nansen, 'Journey', p. 475.

Select Bibliography

Books

Abbot, Thomas K. *Sight and Touch: An Attempt to Disprove the Received (or Berkeleian) Theory of Vision.* 1864.

Anon. *Catalogue of Furniture and Paintings and Prints . . . from Max Gate.* Dorchester: H. Y. Duke. 1938.

—— *The International Exhibition, Official Catalogue of the Fine Art Department.* 1862.

Archer, William. *Real Conversations.* London: Heinemann, 1904.

Arnold, Matthew. *The Complete Prose Works,* ed. R. H. Super. 11 vols. Ann Arbor: Univ. of Michigan Press, 1960–77.

Bain, Alexander. *The Senses and the Intellect.* 1855. 3rd edn., 1868.

Bayley, John. *An Essay on Hardy.* Cambridge Univ. Press, 1978.

Beatty, C. J. P. Introduction to *Desperate Remedies* by Thomas Hardy. New Wessex Edition. London: Macmillan, 1975.

—— 'The Part Played by Architecture in the Life and Work of Thomas Hardy' (Unpubl. diss., Univ. of London, 1963).

—— *Thomas Hardy's Career in Architecture, 1856–1872.* Dorchester: Dorset Natural History and Archeological Society, 1978.

Björk, Lennart A. *The Literary Notebooks of Thomas Hardy.* 2 vols. London: Macmillan, 1985.

Brennecke, Ernest Jr. *The Life of Thomas Hardy.* New York: Greenberg, 1928.

Cain, T. Hall. *Recollections of Rossetti.* 1883.

Carlyle, Thomas. *Sartor Resartus.* 1831. In *Thomas Carlyle's Collected Works.* Library Edition, 30 vols. 1870.

Collins, Peter. *Changing Ideals in Modern Architecture.* London: Faber and Faber, 1965. 3rd edn, 1971.

Cox, J. S. and G. S., ed. *Thomas Hardy Yearbook.* St Peter Port, Guernsey: Toucan Press, 1970.

Cox, R. G., ed. *Thomas Hardy: The Critical Heritage.* London: Routledge, 1970.

Crowe, J. A. and Cavalcaselle, G. B. *A History of Painting in North Italy.* 2 vols. 1871.

Crowe, J. A., ed. [*Kugler's*] *Handbook of Painting: The German, Flemish and Dutch Schools.* 2 vols. 1874.

Darwin, Charles. *The Origin of Species.* 1859. Ed. Morse Peckham. Philadelphia: Univ. of Pennsylvania Press, 1959.

Davis, Martin. *National Gallery Pictures: the Early Italian Schools.* 2nd edn. London: National Gallery, 1961.

Donaldson, T. L. *Preliminary Discourse.* 1842.

Eliot, T. S. *After Strange Gods*. London: Faber and Faber, 1934.

Elliot, Ralph W. V. *Thomas Hardy's English*. Oxford: Basil Blackwell, 1984.

Emerson, Ralph Waldo. *The Compete Works*. Ed. J. E. Cabot. 12 vols. 1883–94.

Fergusson, James. *History of the Modern Styles of Architecture*. 1862.

Frith, W. P. *My Autobiography and Reminiscences*. 3 vols. 1887–88.

Gittings, Robert. *Young Thomas Hardy*. London: Heinemann, 1975.

—— *The Older Hardy*. London: Heinemann, 1978.

Grundy, Joan. *Hardy and the Sister Arts*. London: Macmillan, 1979.

Hagstrum, Jean. *The Sister Arts: The Tradition of Literary Pictorialism and English Poetry from Dryden to Gray*. Chicago: Univ. of Chicago Press, 1958.

Hamerton, Philip Gilbert. *Painting in France After the Decline of Classicism*. 1869.

Hamilton, Walter. *The Aesthetic Movement in England*. 1882.

Harrold, C. F., ed. Thomas Carlyle, *Sartor Resartus*. New York: Odyssey Press, 1937.

Heaton, Mary Margaret. *The History of the Life of Albrecht Dürer of Nürnberg*. 1870.

Helmholtz, H. L. F. von. *Popular Lectures on Scientific Subjects*. First Series, 1873. Second Series, 1881.

Holland, Clive. *Thomas Hardy, OM*. London: Jenkins, 1933.

Hynes, Samuel, ed. *The Complete Poetical Works of Thomas Hardy*. 3 Vols. Oxford: The Clarendon Press, 1982–85.

Jackson, Arlene M. *Illustration and the Novels of Thomas Hardy*. Totowa, NJ: Rowman and Littlefield, 1981.

Kaye, Barrington. *The Development of the Architectural Profession in Britain*. London: Allen and Unwin, 1960.

Keary, C. F. *Outlines of Primitive Belief*. 1882.

Kemp, Robert, ed. *What Do You Think of the International Exhibition? A Collection of the Best Descriptive Criticisms*. 1862.

Knight, Joseph. *Life of Dante Gabriel Rossetti*. 1887.

Kramer, Dale, ed. *Critical Approaches to the Fiction of Thomas Hardy*. London: Macmillan, 1979.

Layard, A. H., ed. *The Italian Schools of Painting Based on the Handbook of Kugler*. 2 vols. 1887. 4th edn, 1907.

Lewes, G. H. *The Study of Psychology: Its Object, Scope and Method*. 1879.

Lodge, David. Introduction to *The Woodlanders* by Thomas Hardy. New Wessex Edition. London: Macmillan, 1974.

Meynell, Wilfrid. *The Modern School of Art*. 3 vols. 1887–88.

Mill, John Stuart. *An Examination of Sir William Hamilton's Philosophy*. 1865. Ed. J. M. Robson. Toronto: Univ. of Toronto Press, 1979.

Miller, J. Hillis. *Fiction and Repetition*. Oxford: Basil Blackwell, 1982.

—— Introduction to *The Well-Beloved* by Thomas Hardy. New Wessex Edition. London: Macmillan, 1975.

—— *Thomas Hardy: Distance and Desire.* Cambridge, Mass: Harvard Univ. Press, 1970.

Millgate, Michael. *Thomas Hardy: A Biography.* Oxford Univ. Press, 1982.

Morison, James Cotter. *The Service of Man.* 1887.

Morris, William. *The Collected Works.* Ed. May Morris. 24 vols. London: Longmans, 1910–15.

Müller, Friedrich Max von. *Chips from a German Workshop.* 2nd edn. 4 vols. 1868–75.

[Murray, John, pub.]. *Handbook for Travellers in Holland and Belgium.* 19th edn., 1876.

Noakes, Aubrey. *William Frith: Extraordinary Victorian Painter.* London: Jupiter Books, 1978.

Orel, Harold, ed. *Thomas Hardy's Personal Writings.* London: Macmillan, 1967.

Ormond, Richard. *Sir Edwin Landseer.* London: Thames and Hudson, 1981.

Page, Norman. *Thomas Hardy.* London: Routledge, 1977.

Pater, Walter. *Imaginary Portraits.* 1887. Library Edition, 1901.

—— *Miscellaneous Studies.* 1895. 2nd edn. London: Macmillan, 1904.

—— *The Renaissance: Studies in Art and Poetry.* Ed. Donald L. Hill. Berkeley: Univ. of California Press, 1980.

Paulin, Tom. *Thomas Hardy: The Poetry of Perception.* London: Macmillan, 1975.

Paulson, Ronald. *Emblem and Expression: Meaning in English Art of the Eighteenth Century.* London: Thames and Hudson, 1975.

Pevsner, Nikolaus. *Some Architectural Writers of the Nineteenth Century.* Oxford: Clarendon Press, 1972.

Pinion, F. B. *A Hardy Companion.* London, Macmillan, 1968.

Pugin, Augustus Welby. *An Apology for the Revival of Christian Architecture in England.* 1843.

—— *Contrasts.* 1836. 2nd edn., 1841.

—— *The True Principles of Pointed or Christian Architecture.* 1841.

Redgrave, Richard. *A Catalogue of the British Fine Art Collections at South Kensington.* 1864.

Richards, Bernard A. 'The Use of the Visual Arts in the Nineteenth-Century Novel' (Unpubl. diss., Oxford, 1972).

Robertson, W. Graham. *Time Was.* London: Hamish Hamilton, 1931. 7th edn., 1945.

Rossetti, William Michael. *Dante Gabriel Rossetti as Designer and Writer.* 1889.

Ruskin, John. *The Works.* Ed. E. T. Cook and Alexander Wedderburn. 39 vols. London: George Allen, 1903–12.

Scott, William Bell. *Albert Dürer: His Life and Works.* 1869.

Sharp, William. *Dante Gabriel Rossetti: A Record and a Study.* 1882.

Spencer, Herbert. *Principles of Psychology.* 2nd edn. 2 vols. 1870.

Stanton, Phoebe. *Pugin*. London: Thames and Hudson, 1971.
Summerson, Sir John. *The Architectural Association 1854–1947*. London: Pléiade Books, 1947.
Symonds John Addington. *Essays Speculative and Suggestive*. 2 vols. 1890.
—— *Studies in the Greek Poets*. 1873.
Taylor, Richard H., ed. *Emma Hardy's Diaries*. Ashington: Carcanet New Press and Mid-Northumberland Arts Group, 1985.
——, ed. *The Personal Notebooks of Thomas Hardy*. London: Macmillan, 1978.
Vigar, Penelope. *The Novels of Thomas Hardy: Illusion and Reality*. London: Athlone Press, 1974.
Waterhouse, Ellis. *Sir Joshua Reynolds*. London: Routledge, 1941.
Weber, Carl J. *Hardy of Wessex. His Life and Literary Career*. New York: Columbia Univ. Press.
Witemeyer, Hugh. *George Eliot and the Visual Arts*. New Haven: Yale Univ. Press, 1979.
Wood, Christopher. *Victorian Panorama: Paintings of Victorian Life*. London: Faber and Faber, 1976.
Wornum, R. N. *The Abridged Catalogue of the Pictures in the National Gallery: Foreign Schools*. 1873.
—— *The Epochs of Painting*. 1864.

Articles.

Anon. 'Debased Hellenism and the New Renaissance', *Church Quarterly Review*, 10 (1880), 99–121.
—— 'Semper's Theory of Architectural Ornament', *The Builder*, 47 (1884), 244.
Bailey, J. O. 'Astrology? Stars, Sun and Moon as Symbols in Hardy's Works', *English Literature in Transition*, 14 (1971), 219–22.
Brunetière, Frédéric. 'Symbolistes et Decadens', *Revue des deux mondes*, 90 (1 Nov. 1886), 213–26.
Bullen, J. B. 'The Palace of Art: Sir Coutts Lindsay and the Grosvenor Gallery', *Apollo*, 102 (1975), 352–7.
—— 'Walter Pater's Interpretation of the Mona Lisa as a Symbol of Romanticism', in *The Romantic Heritage*, ed. K. Engelberg, Publications of the Department of English, 12, Copenhagen 1983, 139–52.
Burstein, Janet. 'Victorian Mythology and the Progress of the Intellect', *Victorian Studies*, 18 (1975), 309–24.
Carpenter, Richard C. 'Hardy and the Old Masters', *Boston University Studies in English*, 5 (1961), 18–28.
—— 'The Mirror and the Sword: Imagery in *Far From the Madding Crowd*', *Nineteenth Century Fiction*, 18 (1963–4), 331–45.
Connor, Steven. 'Myth as Multiplicity in Walter Pater's *Greek Studies* and "Denys L'Auxerrois"', *Review of English Studies*, NS 34 (1983), 28–42.

Cox, John G. 'John Power was Sir Samuel Morton Peto', *Dorset: The County Magazine*, issue 69 (n.d.), 15–17.

Davie, Donald. 'Hardy's Virgilian Purples', in *The Poet in the Imaginary Museum*, ed. Barry Alpert, Manchester: Carcanet Press, 1977, 221–35.

DeLaura, David J. 'The "Ache of Modernism" in Hardy's Later Novels', *English Literary History*, 34 (1967), 380–99.

Dorson, Richard M. 'The Eclipse of Solar Mythology', in *Myth: A Symposium*, ed. Thomas A. Sebeok, Bloomington: Indiana Univ. Press, 1965, 25–63.

Ettlinger, L. D. 'Science, Industry and Art: The Theories of Gottfried Semper', *Architectural Review*, 135 (1964), 57–61.

Fernando, Lloyd. 'Thomas Hardy's Rhetoric of Painting', *Review of English Literature*, 6 (Oct. 1965), 62–73.

Hardy, Evelyn. 'Thomas Hardy and Turner—'The Painter's Eye', *The London Magazine*, NS 15 (June–July, 1975), 17–27.

Harrison, J. S. 'Pater, Heine and the Old Gods of Greece', *PMLA*, 39 (1924), 655–86.

Harvey, Lawrence. 'Gottfried Semper', *The Architect*, 32 (1884), 244.

—— 'Semper's Theory of Evolution in Architectural Ornament', *Transactions of the Royal Institute of British Architects*, NS 1 (1885), 29–54.

Kissane, James. 'Victorian Mythology,' *Victorian Studies*, 6 (1962), 5–25.

Lewes, G. H. 'The Principles of Success in Literature,' *Fortnightly Review*, 1 (1865), 85–95, 185–96, 572–89.

Lodge, David. 'Thomas Hardy and Cinematographic Form', *Novel*, 7 (1973–4), 246–54.

McConkey, Kenneth. 'The Bouguereau of the Naturalists: Bastien-Lepage and British Art', *Art History*, 1 (1978), 371–82.

—— 'Rustic Naturalism in Britain', in *The European Realist Tradition*, ed. Gabriel P. Weisberg, Bloomington: Indiana Univ. Press, 1982, 215–28.

Müller, Friedrich Max von. 'Solar Myths', *The Nineteenth Century*, 18 (1885), 900–22.

Page, Norman. 'Hardy's Dutch Painting: *Under the Greenwood Tree*', *Thomas Hardy Yearbook*, 5 (1975), 39–42.

—— 'Hardy's Pictorial Art in The Mayor of Casterbridge', *Études Anglais*, 25 (1972), 486–92.

—— 'Visual Techniques in Hardy's *Desperate Remedies*', Ariel, 4 (Jan. 1973), 65–71.

Pater, Walter H. 'Romanticism', *Macmillan's Magazine*, 35 (Nov. 1876), 64–70.

Scott, James F. 'Thomas Hardy's Use of Gothic', *Nineteenth-Century Fiction*, 17 (1963), 363–80.

Sherman, H. T. 'Belgium's Eccentric Painter, Antoine Wiertz', *The International*, 5 (July 1910), 21–8.

Shuter, William. 'History as Palengenesis in Pater and Hegel', *PMLA*, 86 (1971), 411–21.

Smart, Alastair. 'Pictorial Imagery in the Novels of Thomas Hardy', *Review of English Studies*, NS 12 (1961), 262–80.

Stephen, Leslie, 'Belief and Conduct', *The Nineteenth Century*, 24 (1888), 372–89.

Tanner, Tony. 'Colour and Movement in Hardy's *Tess of the d'Urbervilles*', *Critical Quarterly*, 10 (Autumn 1968), 219–39.

Wedmore, Frederick. 'The Impressionists', *Fortnightly Review*, NS 33 (Jan. 1883), 75–82.

Wickens, G. Glen. 'Hardy and the Aesthetic Mythographers: The Myth of Demeter and Persephone in *Tess of the d'Urbervilles*', *University of Toronto Quarterly*, 53, no. 1 (Fall 1983), 85–106.

Wind, Edgar. 'Studies in Allegorical Portraiture—1: (i) In Defence of Composite Portraits,' *Journal of the Warburg Institute*, 1 (1937–8), 138–62.

Wittenberg, Judith Bryant. 'Early Hardy Novels and the Fictional Eye', *Novel*, 16 (1982–3), 151–64.

Index

Abbot, Thomas K. 80
Acland, Henry 207
Alison, Archibald 66
Allingham, Helen (neé Paterson) 27, 28, 62
Alma-Tadema, Lawrence 27, 95, 243
Alsloot, D. van 2
Antoinette, Marie 101
Apollo 207, 208; Angel Clare compared with 212–13; Hardy's purchase of a photograph of 26; myth of in *TD* 209–16
Archer, William 128
architecture: Carlyle on 162; Hardy's views on 128; in *JO* 239–40; in *MC* 159–64; modern 136 n.; in *PBE* 57; railway 134; treatment in the novels 121–2; *see also under names of architects*
Arctic: and the aesthetic of northerness 91, 259; appeal to modern mind 260; Hardy's interest in 259–64; in *RN* 259–62; in *TD* 262–3
Arnold, Matthew 131, 137, 175, 187, 210
Artemis 107, 217–18

Bagehot, Walter 80, 190 n.
Bailey, J. O. 212 n.
Bain, Alexander 85, 235; and perception theory 6, 67
Balder 210, 211, 220
Balzac 162 n.
Barnes, William 29
Bastien-Lepage, Jules 23, 29, 243–5, 247
Bayley, John 1
Baudry, Paul 19
Beatty, C. J. P. 38, 122 n., 162
Beaumont, Sir George 14

Beers, Jan van 10; London exhibition (1887) 24
Belgian art: contrasted with Italian 25
Belgium: Hardy's visit to (1876) 24–5
Bellini, Giovanni: *Agony in the Garden* 15; Hardy's art compared with 14; in National Gallery 21; pictures expressive of beauty in ugliness 29, 142–3; in Venice 27
Berkeley: and perception theory 66, 79–81
Berstein, Janet 210 n.
Björk, Lennart A. 152 n.
Blomfield, Arthur 16, 163
blushing 72
Boldini, Giovanni: *The Morning Walk* expressive of beauty in ugliness 94
Bonheur, Rosa 19, 39
Bonington, Richard Parkes 29, 30; compared with Turner 193; painting by, owned by Hardy 27, 193
Borgonone, Ambrogio 51
Bradford, William 261–2
Brandon, Raphael 127
Brennecke, Ernest Jr. 2
Breton, Jules 39
Brett, John 20
British Museum: *see* London
Britton, John 122
Brown, Fred 181, 243
Browne, Sir Thomas 88 n., 187 n.
Browning, Robert 191, 253
Brunetière, Frédérique 13; on symbolism 195
Brussels: Hardy's visit to (1876) 24
Bullen, J. B. 23 n., 47 n., 104 n.
Burlington Fine Arts Club: *see* London
Burne-Jones, Edward 27, 243
Byron 101 n., 191

Caird, Edward 179
Carlyle, Thomas 61 n., 70, 78, 117, 124, 139 n., 146, 151–5, 162, 166–70, 186; Hardy's view of *Sartor Resartus* 152; on portraiture 117; similarities to Gottfried Semper 164
Carpenter, Richard, C., 10 n.
Cavalcaselle, G. B. 142
Chambers, William 122
Christy, Henry 182
Church, Frederick 261
Cicero 66
Cimabue 21
Clausen, George 243–5
Clifford, William Kingdom 81 n.
Cole, Sir Henry 162
Collins, Peter 122, 123, 132, 133 n.
Collins, William 44
colour: absence of in *JO*, in *Adam Bede* 45, 238; expressiveness of in *DR* 33, 38–9; in *PBE* 56; words Hardy's use of 7–8
Colvin, Sir Sidney 229
Comte, Auguste: on sensations 79
Connor, Steven 213
Conrad, Joseph 5
Constable, John 20
Cook, Thomas (publisher) 24
Correggio, Antonio 56, 236
Courbet, Gustave 39, 49
Cousin, Victor 122
Cox, John G. 132 n.
Cressy, Edward 133
Crickmay, G. R. 127
Crivelli 10, 14, 29; in the National Gallery 21; pictures expressive of beauty in ugliness 142–3
Crowe, J. A. 99, 142

Dahl, Johan Christian 57
Danby, John 20
darkness: in Hardy's novels 12, 201, 235; in *FMC* 82–3; in *JO* 234–5; in *TD* 201–2; in *W* 191
Darwin, Charles 112, 175, 185, 188, 190; and 'the Unfulfilled Intention' 177–8

Daubigny, Charles 19, 39
Davie, Donald 38
Davis, Martin 21 n.
Degas, H.-G.-E. 181
Delacroix, Eugène 19
DeLaura, David J. 103
Demeter 217–18
Desperate Remedies 1, 4, 31–42; and Greuze 35; miniatures in 33; and modern French painting 19, 39; movement and stasis in 255, 277; pictorialism of 35; and statuary 34; sunsets in 4, 40–1, 89; use of colour in 35–8
Diana 107, 156
Donaldson, T. L. 122, 163 n.
doppelgänger 149–50.
Dorson, Richard M. 210 n.
Dowden, Earnest 223 n.
Dowdeswell's Gallery: *see* London
Duccio di Buoninsegna 26
du Maurier, George 27, 105
Duppa, Richard 23
Dürer, Albrecht 98, 99, 117; compared with Rembrandt 110; and expressive ugliness 100; as a northern artist 110
Dyce, William 20
Dyck, Sir Anthony van 107

Eastlake, Sir Charles Lock 20
ecphrasis 119–20
Edgcumbe, Robert Pierce 28
Egg, William Augustus 20, 167
Eliot, George 44, 51, 53, 106, 118, 253; and Dutch painting 7, 43
Eliot, T. S. 15, 30
Elliot, Ralph W.V. 6
Ellis, Havelock 234 n.
Emerson, Ralph Waldo 187–8
Ettlinger, L. D. 163

face(s): in *L* 119; obscured 78, 101, 102, 114; in *RN* 97, 98, 100–13, 115
Far From the Madding Crowd 5, 61–87; darkness in 82; and genre painting 29; Hardy's drawings

for 17, 61–2; modes of perception: (i) Bathsheba Everdene's 76–7, (ii) Boldwood's 73, 77–8, (iii) Gabriel Oak's 71–2, 75, 77, (iv) Frank Troy's 74, 76, 77; and moral judgement 75, 78, 82, 86–7; narrative perspectives in 63, 256; and pictorialism 64; and theories of perception 66–8, spies and watchers in 89; sunsets in 5, 85–6; and visual perception 68–78
Fergusson, James 134
Fichte 11; and Gottfried Semper 164 n.
Flaubert, Gustave 243
Florence: Hardy's visit to (1876) 26
Fox, Caroline 244 n.
framing device 33, 47–8
Franklin, Sir John 261
French Gallery: see London
Friedrich, Gaspar David 261
Frith, William Powell 20, 22, 27; his dislike of Turner's late painting 194
Fry, Roger 47 n.

Gérôme, Jean Léon 19, 29
Giorgione 136, 254
'Giotto' 21
Gittings, Robert 2
Gladstone, William Ewart 210
Gombrich, E. H. 3
Gosse, Edmund 241 n.
Gower, Lord Ronald 101 n.
Gray, Thomas 38
Greenacre, Francis 244
Greuze, Jean Baptiste 1, 21, 35, 57, 119, 157, 175
Grosvenor Galley: see London
Grundy, Joan 10, 29, 33, 45
Guays, Gabriel 29

Hagstrum, Jean 107
Hall, Charles 261
Hamerton, Philip Gilbert 49
Hand of Ethelberta, The 22, 89
Hardy [neé Gifford], Emma

Lavinia 23–4, 25, 38; enthusiasm for painting 17; her record of Continental journeys 26–7, 92–3; paintings at Max Gate 28
Hardy, Evelyn 43
Hardy, Thomas: architecture, views on 120, 127–8; architecture, training in 120, 126–7; and the Arctic 260–4; his own drawing: (i) 15–19, 61, 96, (ii) for FMC 61–2, (ii) technical 16, (iv) topographical 16, (v) 'Wessex Poems' vignettes for 18; essays: 'The Dorsetshire Labourer' 166, 'Profitable Reading of Fiction' 167–8, 'The Science of Fiction' 242; importance of impressions to 2, 3, 9, 56, 57, 190, 216–17; and Impressionism 3, 23, 181–2, 183, 185; knowledge of the visual arts 15–30; his journeys to: (i) France (1874) 23, (ii) Holland, Germany, and Belgium (1876) 24–5, 92, 93, 98, 193, 262, (iii) Italy (1887) 24, 25–7, 191; novels: see under separate titles; his ownership of pictures 26, 28–9, 193; poems: 'Beeny Cliff' 38, 'The Figure in the Scene' 17, 'Her Death and After' 18, 'Heredity' 228, 'In a Eweleaze near Wetherbury' 18, 'In a Wood' 188, 'To Outer Nature' 175, 'Why did I Sketch?' 17, 'Under the Waterfall' 17; repetition in the novels 228; Turner, his enthusiasm for 7, 14–15, 193–4, 197; visual metaphors for literary production 15–16, 142, 173, 217, 233, 256–7; on word-painting 2
Hegel, George Wilhelm Friedrich 177
Heidelberg: Hardy's journey to 92
Heine, Heinrich: his Gods in Exile 212–13
Helmholtz, Hermann von 6, 78, 82
Herkomer, Sir Hubert von 145, 167
Hillebrand, Karl 129, 136 n.

Hobbema, Meindert 43, 94
Holbein, Hans 119
Holland: Hardy's journey to 24, 92, 93, 262
Holland, Clive 2
Hopkins, Arthur 27
Horace 66
Hume, David 79–80
Hunt, William Holman 20, 86, 105, 167
Huxley, Thomas Henry 81, 112, 185, 216
Hynes, Samuel 18 n.

Ikler, A. Abbott 187
'Imagination Penetrative', The 65, 66, 75, 76, 256
impression(s): contrasted with word-painting 3; of J. S. Mill 9; as mental pictures 2, 185, 189; on the mind's eye 56, 57; Pater on 11, 79, 189; Shelley on 190; *TD* as 216–17
Impressionism 3, 8; contrasted with primitivism 183; Hardy's experience of 23, 29, 181–2; and the modern view 185; its significance for literature 182; Whistler and 182
Ingres, Jean Auguste Dominique 19
International Exhibition (1862): *see* London
Italian art: contrasted with Belgian art 25: *see also under names of artists*
Italy 25–7, 191, 192

Jacobus, Mary 175, 179, 188, 210
James, Henry 12, 118; Hardy's pictorialism contrasted with 7
Jansen, Cornelius 119, 136
Jude the Obscure 25, 120, 121, 231, 232, 234–52, 255, 264; architecture in 127, 134, 239–41; compared with *WB* 233; comparison with other novels 223, 235–6; darkness and 'obscurity' in 234–5, 251–2; drawing for at Shaftesbury 18; and railway travel

236–7; and realist painting 29, 243–7; sunset in 5; treatment of visual elements in 224, 234–6, 238; and Zola 241, 243
Juno 107, 225

Kant, Emmanuel 11, 82, 178, 189
Keary, C. F. 220 n.; on tree myths 174
Keats, John 254
Kemp, Robert 19 n.
Kerr, Robert 122, 133
Kissane, James 210 n.
Kneller, Sir Geoffrey 107, [called 'Sir Godfrey'] 119, 136
Knight, Joseph 230
Kugler, Franz Theodor 143 n.

Lafenestre, Georges 195
landscape: its significance to Hardy 27, 90–3; Turner's interpretation of 30, 192–9
Landseer, Edwin 39 n., 261
Lang, Andrew 210, 215 n.
Lange, Carl Georg 179
Laodicean, A 140, 141; and architecture 118–38; eclecticism in 122–3; *ecphrasis* in 118–19; engineering vs. architecture 133; and neo-paganism 130; and portraiture 7; and romanticism 132, 136, 137; and railway architecture 134; sunset(s) in 5, 41, 92, 124; techniques of parallelism in 126, 129, 136
la Thangue, Henry 243
Lawrence, Sir Thomas 119
Layard, Sir Henry 143
Leighton, Frederic, Lord 20, 95
Lely, Sir Peter 107, 119, 136
Lewes, George Henry 68, 80; on 'reasoned realism' 81; on verbal visualization 67
light: artificial 84, 86 n., 202–3; and blindness 83; contrast with darkness 12, 32, 37, 83, 84–5, 203; deceptive 84, 86 n.; emotive power of 34; and enlightenment

12, 83; physics of 77–8, power of in *TD* 198; of sun in *TD* 199–200; symbolism of in *TD* 199–204

Lindsay, Alexander, Lord (25th Earl of Crawford) 43

Lloyd, Fernando 10 n., 256, 257

Locke, John 10 n., 63, 66, 79

Lodge, David 63, 175

London:
  British Museum: 177, 130; Hardy reading in Library of 182; opening of Ethnology galleries (1886) 182–3
  Burlington Fine Arts Club 194, 229
  Dowdeswell's Gallery 181
  French Gallery 23
  Grosvenor Gallery 23, 95, 108, 243
  International Exhibition (1862) 19–20, 39, 106; Paxton's design for 133
  Marlborough House 162
  National Gallery 51, 184 n., 233; Bellini in 15, 142; Crivelli in 15, 142; Dutch art in 21, 43; Greuze in 35; Hardy's visits to 20; Hobbema in 94; Sebastiano del Piombo in 21
  National Portrait Gallery 57 n.
  New English Art Club 23, 181, 244
  Royal Academy: 22, 84, 261; Bastien-Lepage at 243; Moroni at 49; portraiture at 116; summer exhibition (1876) 113, 262; Reynolds at 23; Rossetti at 229; Turner at 23, 194
  Society of British Artists 181
  South Kensington Museum 21–2, 129

Louvre: *see* Paris

Luxembourg: *see* Paris

Lyle, Sir Charles 112

McConkey, Kenneth 39 n., 243 n.

Macmillan (publisher) 38

Mahaffy, J. P. 210 n.

Manet, Eduard, 39, 181

Mangiarelli, N. 95, 144

Mantegna, Andrea 142, 143

Markham, Clements 260, 261 n.

Mason, James 261 n.

Maupassant, Guy de 243

Max Gate 28 n., 126, 163; building of 141

Mayor of Casterbridge, The 4, 257; architecture in 159; and building of Max Gate 141; buildings of Casterbridge 161; clothing 147–9, 168, 257; conflict in 165–6; contrast with *W* 169–70, 171–2; furnishings 156; and Herkomer's *Hard Times* 145, 167, individual houses 159–61; interiors 158; pictorialism in 143–5, 167; sunsets in 41; tools 153–4

Meissonier, Ernest 19

Mengs, Raphael 21

Meredith, George 31

Meynall, Alice 244 n.

Meynall, Wilfrid 244

Michelangelo Buonarroti 26

Mill, John Stuart 4, 80, 81; Hardy's sight of 8–9; on perception theory 6, 67

Millais, John Everett 20, 261

Miller, J. Hillis 2, 12, 58, 68, 204, 223, 224 n., 231–2

Millet, Jean François 234

Millgate, Michael 139, 210 n., 223

Milton, John 175

Minerva 107, 225

Mirandola, Pico della 213

Moments of Vision 17

Mona Lisa, the 103, 107

Monet, Claude 181

Morison, James Cotter 216

Morley, John 9

Moroni, Giovanni Battista 6, 7, 21, 49, 57, 119

Morris, Jane 105

Morris, William 162

Moule, Henry 15, 28

Moule, Horace 19, 43; his poem 'Ave Caesar' 19 n.

Müller, Friedrich Max von 217, 221; on solar myth 209–12; on tree myths 174 n.
Mulready, William 22
Murray, John (publisher) 93
myth 2, 12, 105, 107; solar 204–9; *see also under names of deities*

Nansen, Fridtjof 263–4
Nares, George 200
National Gallery: *see* London
National Portrait Gallery: *see* London
Nesfield, William 162
New English Art Club: *see* London
Newman, John Henry 133
Noakes, Aubrey 22 n.
Nollekens, Joseph 57
Nordenskjöld, Nils Otto Gustav 263

obscurity: in *JO* 234–5
Oedipus 114
Oldham, William Stott of 243
Ormond, Richard 261

Page, Norman 2, 10, 29, 33, 35, 44 n., 45, 144
painting 13–30; advanced 183; as artifice 157; Belgian 24–5; Dutch 21, 28–9, 31, 43–4, 93–4 n., 94, 110; English 20, 44; French 19, 23–4, 39, 243; genre 17, 31, 44, 61, 99, 144; German 100; Hardy's own: *see* Hardy, Thomas; Italian 25–7, 43, 191, 233; miniature 33; Renaissance 99; 'Schools of Painting' notebook 21; Tuscan 157; *see also* Impressionism; London; portraiture; *and under names of painters*
Pair of Blue Eyes, A 17, 31, 53–60, 223–4; impressions in 3; parallelism in 54, 58–9; silhouettes in 54–5
Palgrave, Francis 23, 195
Paris: Hardy's visits to 23–4; studies pictures in the Louvre 24; pictures in the Luxembourg 24
Park, Richard Henry 27

Parsons, Alfred 27, 193
Pater, Walter Horatio 221; on Apollo 212–14; on the golden age 218–19; ideas on solipsism 179; 'impressions' in *The Renaissance* 11, 189; meeting with Hardy 11, 213; and the modern sensibility 130, 137; on sensations 79; on significance of moments 254; on symbolism of the *Mona Lisa* 103, 112
Paterson, Helen: *see* Allingham
Patmore, Coventry 59
Paulin, Tom 3, 11, 20
Paulson, Ronald 53 n., 66 n.
Paxton, William 133
Peary, Robert Edwin 263
Peckham, Morse 177 n.
Peel, Sir Robert 43
perception, theories of 6, 12, 66–8, 70–5, 76–82, 88, 90; Ruskin on accuracy of 13
Perugino, Pietro Vannucci 233
Peto, Samuel Morton 132 n.
Pevsner, Nikolaus 127 n., 133 n., 134 n., 162, 163 n.
Pheidias (*or* Phidias) 111
Philippoteaux, Henri 23 n.
Phillips, Claude 194 n., 197 n.
Philpot, J. H. 174
pictorialism 1–2, 5–10, 54, 69, 256–7; compared with George Eliot's 45–7; in *FMC* 69–70; framing 33, 47–8, 64; Gittings, Page and Miller on 2 n., 35; in *JO* 243–8; in *MC* 142–6; in *PBE* 56–7; in *TD* 198; in *UGT* 49–50, 53, 64–5, 144
Pinion, F. B. 11
Poems of Past and Present 3
Poor Man and the Lady, The 31
portraiture 7, 71, 116, 119; Carlyle on 117; composite in *RN* 107–8; Hardy's interest in 57; sculptural 112–13
Proctor, Richard 178
Proust, Marcel 58, 59, 223–4
Pugin, Augustus Welby 122, 124,

132, 135, 136, 161; views on
gothic architecture different from
Hardy's 126; and *Contrasts* 125;
on railway architecture 134 n.

Quincy, Quatremère de 23

railways: architecture 134; Ruskin's
dislike for 135; travel by 251
Raphael 7, 21, 56, 136
Rawlinson, W. G. 194
Redgrave, Richard 44
Rembrandt Harmensz van Rijn 6,
7, 109–10, 110–11, 117
Reni, Guido 58
Return of the Native, The 5, 88–117;
and anthropomorphism 97–8;
Arctic in 260; copy given to
Woolner 113; and *ecphrasis* 119–
20; faces in 114–17, 257; Hardy's
drawings for 18; pictorialism in
101; and portraiture 96–114, 116;
sunset in 5, 89
Revett, Nicholas 122
Reynolds, Sir Joshua 20, 28 n.,
106, 116–17, 119
Rickman, Thomas 122
Robertson, Graham 105
Romanticism: of Bathsheba Ever-
dene 70; of Eustacia Vye 104,
108; in *JO* 248; in *L* 132, 137; of
modern utilitarianism 136; *Mona
Lisa* as symbol of 104; of Paula
Power 121; in *RN* 137
Rome: Hardy's visit to 26
Romney, George 136
Rosa, Salvator 136
Rossetti, Dante Gabriel 105, 107,
117, 229–31, 245
Rossetti, William Michael 113, 230
Rousseau, Théodore 19, 39
Royal Academy of Arts: *see* London
Rubens, Peter Paul 56, 225
Ruskin, John 4, 36, 68, 124–5, 161,
191, 192, 221, 240, 241 n., 253,
265, 259–60; on accuracy of per-
ception 13; dislike of Dutch art
43; dislike of railways 135, 237;

on Greek myths 207, 218; Hardy
reading in 23, 194; and the
'imagination penetrative' 11, 65–
6; on morality and perception
75–8; on Tintoretto 63–4; and
Turner 11, 194, 206 n., 207, 220;
verbal visualization 6

Sallaert, Anthony 2
Sappho 101
Schalken, Godfried 28
Schiller, J. C. F. von 187 n.
Schlegel, F. von 191 n.
Scott, Sir George Gilbert 112, 127
Scott, William Bell 98
sculpture 27, 34, 102, 109, 116,
223; Hardy's possession of 26
Sebastiano del Piombo 114, 233
Semper, Gottfried 146, 168: ideas
on decoration and ornament
162–4
Sharp, William 230
Sheepshanks, John 22
Shelley, Percy Bysshe 11, 80, 189,
191, 233, 226
Sherman, H. T. 24 n.
Shuter, W. 213 n.
Siddons, Sarah 101
silhouette: in *UGT* 50–1; in *PBE*
54–5
Simcox, F. G. 112 n.
Smart, Alastair 10, 39 n., 114
Smith, Roger T. 127
Society for the Protection of Ancient
Buildings 128, 162
South Kensington Museum: *see*
London
Spencer, Herbert 112, 175, 177,
185, 210; on primitive tribes
173–4; on visual perception 67
Steer, Philip Wilson 181
Stephen, Leslie 61 n., 117 n., 216
Stephens, F. G. 113 n., 230
Stewart, Dugald 66
Stonehenge 219–21
Stott, Edward 181
Street, George Edmund 122, 127
sunset(s) 4–5, 40–1, 85, 89, 92

Swinburne, Algernon Charles 121
Symonds, John Addington 31 n.,
    32, 209, 219 n.

Taine, Hippolyte 168
Tanner, Tony 12, 43, 204
Taylor, Richard H. 21, 26 n.
Teniers, David, the younger 43
Tennyson, Alfred Lord 105; his
    bust by Woolner 113
Tess of the d'Urbervilles 2, 4, 10, 11,
    12, 191–222, and the Arctic 260;
    an impression not an argument 4,
    216; and Belgian art 25; colour
    red in 204; Druidical symbols in
    219–20; and Italian art 191;
    landscape in 192–3; pictorial
    references in 2; and solar myth
    204–9; sunset(s) in 5, 124;
    treatment of light in 192, 199–
    204; and Turner 7, 197–9,
    220–1
Thackeray, W. M. 162
Théuriet, André 245
Thomson, Rosamund 27, 193
Thornton, Alfred 181 n.
Thornycroft, Hamo 27
Tinsley (publisher) 38
Tintoretto, Jacopo Robusti, il 63,
    64, 65, 136, 256
Titian 135, 156, 233
Troyen, Constant 19, 39
Trumpet Major, The 18
Tuke, Henry Scott 243
Turner, Joseph Mallord William 2,
    191, 221; compared with Bon-
    ington 193, 199; depiction of
    Stonehenge 220; at the 1862
    International Exhibition 20; late
    work 29, 193–4; in the National
    Gallery 21; and realism in art
    14–15, 257–8; and solar myth
    206, 207; treatment of light 192,
    197–9
Two on a Tower 139
Tylor, E. B. 174 n., 175, 189
Tyndale, Walter 28
Tyrrell, R. Y. 241

Under the Greenwood Tree 31, 42–53;
    colour in 52; pictorialism of 46–7,
    64, 144; silhouettes in 54–5;
    stasis of 255
'Unfulfilled Intention', the 177

Vandyck, Sir Anthony 136
Venice: Hardy's visit to 27
Vernon, Robert 21
Versailles: Hardy's visit to 23
Victoria, Queen 262
Vigar, Penelope 12, 149, 150
Violette-le-Duc, Eugène: Hardy's
    knowledge of 134
'visible essence(s)' 103, 173, 257
visual perception: psychology of 66–8

Wagner, Richard 90
Waterhouse, Ellis 107
Watts, George Frederick 20, 27
Webb, Philip 162
Webster, Thomas 22, 44, 46, 145
Wedmore, Frederick 181
Well-Beloved, The 223–33; and
    heredity 226; treatment of shape
    in 225; treatment of time in 227–
    8; two endings of 231–2
Wessex Poems 3 n., Hardy's vignettes
    for 18–19
Whistler 27, 181–2
Whitman, Walt 234
Wickens, G. Glen 221 n.
Wiertz, Antoine 10, 24
Wilde, Oscar 118
Wilkie, David 22, 43, 44
Wind, Edgar 107–8
Witemeyer, Hugh 5, 44, 45, 51,
    68, 106 n.
Wittenberg, Judith B. 3
Wood, Christopher 145
Woodlanders, The 88, 169–90;
    characterization in 180; elegiac
    mood of 175; and Hardy's views
    on the novel 172; and Impres-
    sionism 3, 8, 181, 185; narrative
    perspective in 171–2, 257;
    physical appearances in 169; and
    primitivism 183–5; sunset in 5

Woolf, Virginia 12
Woolner, Thomas 20, 27, 112, 113, 117, 193, 262
Wordsworth, William 14, 65
Wornum, R. N., 94 n., 143

Wouvermans (or Wouwerman), Philips de 6, 184

Zola, Émile 191 n., 196, 243, 244